face2face

Intermediate Teacher's Book

Chris Redston, Lindsay Warwick,
Anna Young & Theresa Clementson
with Gillie Cunningham

Tests by Anthea Bazin

CAMBRIDGE
UNIVERSITY PRESS

CAMBRIDGE UNIVERSITY PRESS

Cambridge, New York, Melbourne, Madrid, Cape Town,
Singapore, São Paulo, Delhi, Mexico City

Cambridge University Press
The Edinburgh Building, Cambridge CB2 8RU, UK

www.cambridge.org
Information on this title: www.cambridge.org/9780521676854

First published 2006
6th Printing 2012

Printed in the United Kingdom at the University Press, Cambridge

A catalogue record for this publication is available from the British Library

ISBN 978-0-521-67685-4 Teacher's Book
ISBN 978-0-521-60336-2 Student's Book with CD-ROM/Audio CD
ISBN 978-0-521-67684-7 Workbook with Key
ISBN 978-0-521-60340-9 Class Audio CDs
ISBN 978-0-521-60344-7 Class Audio Cassettes
ISBN 978-0-521-61398-9 Network CD-ROM
ISBN 978-0-521-69167-3 Intermediate and Upper Intermediate DVD
ISBN 978-8-483-23369-6 Student's Book with CD-ROM/Audio CD, Spanish Edition
ISBN 978-3-12-539743-9 Student's Book with CD-ROM/Audio CD, Klett Edition

Teacher's Book Contents

Welcome to face2face!

Teaching Notes

Photocopiable Materials Ph

Class Activities

Vocabulary Plus

Study Skills

Progress Tests

Welcome to face2face!

face2face

face2face is a general English course for adults and young adults who want to learn to communicate quickly and effectively in today's world.

face2face is based on the communicative approach and it combines the best in current methodology with special new features designed to make learning and teaching easier.

The face2face syllabus integrates the learning of new language with skills development and places equal emphasis on vocabulary and grammar.

face2face uses a guided discovery approach to learning, first allowing students to check what they know, then helping them to work out the rules for themselves through carefully structured examples and concept questions.

All new language is included in the interactive *Language Summaries* in the back of the face2face Student's Book and is regularly recycled and reviewed.

There is a strong focus on listening and speaking throughout face2face.

Innovative *Help with Listening* sections help students to understand natural spoken English in context and there are numerous opportunities for communicative, personalised speaking practice in face2face. The *Real World* lessons in each unit focus on the functional and situational language students need for day-to-day life.

The face2face Student's Book provides approximately 80 hours of core teaching material, which can be extended to 120 hours with the photocopiable resources and extra ideas in this Teacher's Book. Each self-contained double-page lesson is easily teachable off the page with minimal preparation.

The vocabulary selection in face2face has been informed by the *Cambridge International Corpus* and the *Cambridge Learner Corpus*.

face2face is fully compatible with the *Common European Framework of Reference for Languages* (CEF) and gives students regular opportunities to evaluate their progress. face2face Intermediate completes B1 and starts B2 (see p13).

face2face Intermediate Components

Student's Book with free CD-ROM/Audio CD

The Student's Book provides 48 double-page lessons in 12 thematically linked units, each with 4 lessons of 2 pages. Each lesson takes approximately 90 minutes.

The free CD-ROM/Audio CD is an invaluable resource for students, with over 200 exercises in all language areas, plus video, recording and playback capability, a fully searchable *Grammar Reference* section and *Word List*, all the sounds in English, customisable *My Activities* and *My Test* sections, and *Progress* sections where students evaluate their own progress. Help students to get the most out of the CD-ROM/Audio CD by giving them the photocopiable instructions on p10–p12.

Class Audio Cassettes and Class Audio CDs

The three Class Audio Cassettes and three Class Audio CDs contain all the listening material for the Student's Book, including conversations, drills, songs and the listening sections of the *Progress Tests* for units 6 and 12.

Workbook

The Workbook provides further practice of all language presented in the Student's Book. It also includes a 24-page *Reading and Writing Portfolio* based on the *Common European Framework of Reference for Languages*, which can be used either for homework or for extra work in class.

Teacher's Book

This Teacher's Book includes *Teaching Tips*, *Teaching Notes* and photocopiable materials: 35 *Class Activities*, 12 *Vocabulary Plus* and 4 *Study Skills* worksheets, and 12 *Progress Tests*.

Network CD-ROM

The Network CD-ROM is a network version of the CD-ROM material from the Student's Book CD-ROM/Audio CD for use in school computer laboratories by up to 30 users.

Intermediate and Upper Intermediate DVD

Available in 2007, the Intermediate and Upper Intermediate DVD contains all the video sequences from the Intermediate and Upper Intermediate Student's Book CD-ROMs. The User Guide accompanying the DVD gives ideas for exploiting the video material in class.

Website

Visit the face2face website www.cambridge.org/elt/face2face for downloadable activities, sample materials and more information about how face2face covers the language areas specified by the CEF.

The face2face Approach

Listening

A typical listening practice activity checks understanding of gist and then asks questions about specific details. The innovative *Help with Listening* sections take students a step further by focusing on the underlying reasons why listening to English can be so problematic. Activities in these sections:

- focus on the stress system in English and how this relates to the main information in a text.
- examine features of connected speech.
- raise awareness of features of informal spoken English.
- focus on different native English speakers' accents.
- highlight how intonation conveys mood and feelings.
- encourage students to make the link between the written and the spoken word by asking them to work with the *Recording Scripts* while they listen.

For *Teaching Tips* on Listening, see p18.

Speaking

All the lessons in **face2face** Intermediate and the *Class Activities* photocopiables provide students with numerous speaking opportunities. Many of these activities focus on accuracy, while the fluency activities help students to gain confidence, take risks and try out what they have learned. For fluency activities to be truly 'fluent', however, students often need time to formulate their ideas before they speak. This preparation is incorporated into the *Get ready … Get it right!* activities at the end of each A and B lesson.

For *Teaching Tips* on Speaking, see p18.

Reading and Writing

In the **face2face** Intermediate Student's Book, reading texts from a wide variety of genres are used both to present new language and to provide reading practice. Reading sub-skills, such as skimming and scanning, are also extensively practised. In addition there are a number of writing activities, which consolidate the language input of the lesson.

For classes that require more practice of reading and writing skills, there is the 24-page *Reading and Writing Portfolio* in the **face2face** Intermediate Workbook. This section contains 12 double-page stand-alone lessons, one for each unit of the Student's Book, which are designed for students to do at home or in class. The topics and content of these lessons are based closely on the CEF reading and writing competences for levels B1 and B2. At the end of this section there is a list of 'can do' statements that allows students to track their progress.

Vocabulary

face2face Intermediate recognises the importance of vocabulary in successful communication. There is lexical input in almost every lesson, all of which is consolidated for student reference in the interactive *Language Summaries* in the back of the Student's Book. The areas of vocabulary include:

- lexical fields (*concerned, annoyed, scared, glad*, etc.)
- collocations (*work overtime, meet deadlines*, etc.)
- sentence stems (*Whatever you do …, Make sure you …*, etc.)
- fixed and semi-fixed phrases (*Oh, how awful!*, etc.)

When students meet a new vocabulary area, they are often asked to tick the words they know before doing a matching exercise or checking in the *Language Summaries*. This is usually followed by communicative practice of the new vocabulary. In addition, each unit in **face2face** Intermediate includes at least one *Help with Vocabulary* section, designed to guide students towards a better understanding of the lexical systems of English. Students study contextualised examples and answer guided discovery questions before checking in the *Language Summaries*.

For longer courses and/or more able students, this Teacher's Book also contains one *Vocabulary Plus* worksheet for each unit. These worksheets introduce and practise new vocabulary that is **not** included in the Student's Book.

For *Teaching Tips* on Vocabulary, see p18.

Grammar

Grammar is a central strand in the **face2face** Intermediate syllabus and new grammar structures are always introduced in context in a listening or a reading text. We believe students are more likely to understand and remember new language if they have actively tried to work out the rules for themselves. Therefore in the *Help with Grammar* sections students work out the meaning and form of the structure for themselves before checking in the *Language Summaries*. All new grammar forms are practised in regular recorded pronunciation drills and communicative speaking activities, and consolidated through written practice.

For *Teaching Tips* on Grammar, see p19.

Functional and Situational Language

face2face Intermediate places great emphasis on the functional and situational language students need to use immediately in their daily lives. Each unit has a double-page *Real World* lesson that introduces and practises this language in a variety of situations. Typical functions and situations include:

- functions: showing concern, giving warnings and advice.
- situations: at the doctor's, on the phone.

Pronunciation

Pronunciation is integrated throughout **face2face** Intermediate. Drills for every new grammar structure and all new *Real World* language are included on the Class Audio Cassettes/CDs and indicated in the Student's Book and Teacher's Book by the icon **P**. These drills focus on sentence stress, weak forms, intonation and other phonological features.

For *Teaching Tips* on Pronunciation, see p19.

Reviewing and Recycling

We believe that regular reviewing and recycling of language are essential and language is recycled in every lesson. Opportunities for review are also provided in the *Quick Review* sections at the beginning of every lesson, the comprehensive *Review* sections at the end of each unit, and the 12 photocopiable *Progress Tests* in this Teacher's Book.

For *Teaching Tips* on Reviewing and Recycling, see p20.

The Student's Book

Lessons A and B in each unit introduce and practise new vocabulary and grammar in realistic contexts.

Menu boxes list the language taught and reviewed in each lesson.

Help with Grammar sections encourage students to work out the rules of form and use for themselves before checking their answers in the interactive *Language Summary* for the unit.

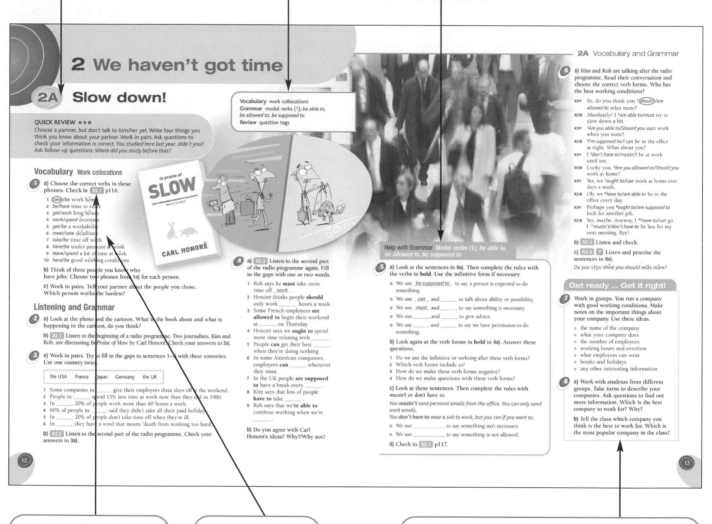

Students can learn and check the meaning of new vocabulary in the interactive *Language Summary* for the unit in the back of the Student's Book.

There are practice activities immediately after the presentation of vocabulary to help consolidate the new language.

Get ready ... Get it right! sections are structured communicative speaking tasks that focus on both accuracy and fluency. The *Get ready ...* stage provides the opportunity for students to plan the language and content of what they are going to say before *Getting it right!* when they do the communicative stage of the activity.

Reduced sample pages from **face2face** Intermediate Student's Book

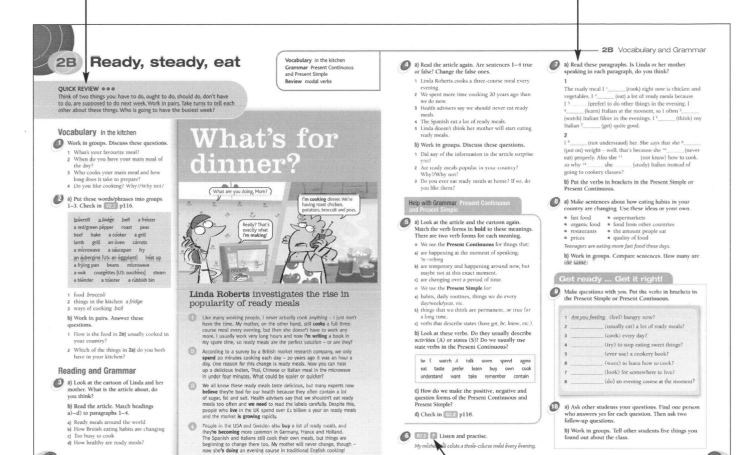

Quick Reviews at the beginning of each lesson recycle previously learned language and get the class off to a lively, student-centred start.

Controlled practice exercises check students have understood the meaning and form of new language.

New grammar structures are always presented in context in a listening or a reading text.

The integrated pronunciation syllabus includes drills for all new grammar structures.

Lesson C *Vocabulary and Skills* lessons develop students' range of receptive skills by providing opportunities to work with different types of semi-authentic text, then exploring and developing areas of lexical grammar.

Help with Vocabulary sections encourage students to work out the rules of form and use of new vocabulary themselves before checking in the interactive *Language Summary* for the unit.

2C It's a nightmare

VOCABULARY AND SKILLS

QUICK REVIEW ● ● ●
Make a list of six items of food. Work in pairs. Take turns to describe the food and say how you can cook it. Your partner guesses what it is: *A It's a type of vegetable and it's round. You can fry it, boil it or roast it. B Is it a potato?*

Vocabulary and Listening

1 Tick the words/phrases you know. Then check new words/phrases in V2.3 p116.

have a dream   fall asleep   wake up
get (back) to sleep   snore   be fast asleep
be wide awake   have insomnia   not sleep a wink
have nightmares   be a light/heavy sleeper   take a nap
doze off   have a lie-in   talk in your sleep

2 a) Choose six words/phrases from 1 that are connected to you, or people you know.

b) Work in groups. Take turns to talk about the words/phrases you chose. Ask follow-up questions if possible.

3 a) Work in pairs. Look at these sentences about sleep. Choose the correct words/phrases.

1 Tiredness causes *more/less* than 50% of all road accidents in the USA.
2 *10%/30%* of people in the UK have problems getting to sleep or staying asleep.
3 Nowadays people are sleeping *half an hour/one and a half hours* less than they did 100 years ago.
4 Teenagers need *more/less* sleep than adults.
5 We use *less/the same amount* of energy when we're asleep compared to when we're resting.
6 A thirty-minute nap at work can improve people's performance for an *hour/a few hours*.

b) R2.6 Listen to a TV interview with a sleep scientist. Check your answers to 3a).

c) Listen again. Answer these questions.

1 How many British people have serious insomnia?
2 How were sleeping habits different 100 years ago?
3 Who needs the least amount of sleep?
4 What do our brains do when we're asleep?
5 What is a siesta salon?

Help with Listening   Weak forms (1)

● In sentences we say many small words with a schwa /ə/ sound. These are called weak forms.

4 a) R2.7 Listen to the strong and weak forms of these words. Do we usually say these words in their strong or weak forms?

	strong	weak		strong	weak
do	/duː/	/də/	of	/ɒv/	/əv/
you	/juː/	/jə/	and	/ænd/	/ən/
at	/æt/	/ət/	to	/tuː/	/tə/
for	/fɔː/	/fə/	can	/kæn/	/kən/

b) Match the words in 4a) to these parts of speech.

1 auxiliary   do   3 preposition
2 pronoun   4 connecting word

c) Look at these sentences from the beginning of the interview. Which words do we hear as weak forms?

Do people you know have problems sleeping at night? Or maybe you just can't get to sleep yourself. For many people, insomnia is a way of life and not being able to get to sleep isn't just annoying – it can also be very dangerous.

d) R2.6 Listen and check. Are weak forms ever stressed?

e) Look at R2.6, p143. Listen to the interview again. Notice the weak forms and sentence stress.

Reading and Vocabulary

5 a) Work in groups. Tell other students what you do when you can't get to sleep. Which is the most unusual method of getting to sleep?

b) Read the article. Why does Emma have insomnia? What has she tried to do to get a good night's sleep?

6 a) Read the article again. Answer these questions.

1 How much sleep did Emma get last night?
2 What happens on a typical night?
3 Why is her job very tiring?
4 Why does she have money problems?
5 Which cures for insomnia hasn't she tried? Why not?

b) Work in pairs. What advice would you give Emma?

I just can't sleep!

Emma talks about how her stressful life has made getting a good night's sleep impossible.

Last night I was fast asleep by 11 p.m., but I woke up again at 1 a.m. Even though I was exhausted when I went to bed, I was suddenly wide awake and it was impossible to get back to sleep again. So I just lay there watching the clock change from three to four to five without sleeping a wink – it was very frustrating. Finally, I got up at 6.15 and went off to work feeling terrible. That's a typical night for me. I've had insomnia for so long I'm amazed that anyone else actually sleeps through the night. And when this goes on for too many nights I feel really shattered.

I'm a sales manager, and I work really long hours and have to do a lot of travelling. I worry about work all the time, which makes it incredibly difficult to get to sleep. Sometimes I get home from work extremely late and when I go to bed everything is still going round my head. Money's also a huge worry for me. I borrowed a lot when I was a student and I still owe £15,000. I only get a full night's sleep once a month – but when I do I feel absolutely fantastic the next day.

I've tried nearly everything to cure my insomnia – herbal teas, yoga, meditation – you name it, I've tried it. I've also started going to the gym three times a week, but it hasn't made any difference. I have a fairly healthy diet and I don't smoke or drink coffee. I haven't tried hypnosis because it's very expensive and that would just add to my money worries. I don't want to start taking sleeping pills because I'm terrified of becoming addicted to them. Although I know it's an awful way to live, I've learned to accept that insomnia is part of my life.

Adapted from the Evening Standard 3/12/02

2C Vocabulary and Skills

Help with Vocabulary Gradable and strong adjectives; adverbs

7 a) Complete the table with the strong adjectives in **pink** in the article.

gradable adjectives	strong adjectives
tired	*exhausted* , _____
bad	_____ , _____
good	_____
big	_____
difficult	_____
frightened	_____
surprised	_____

b) Match the gradable adjectives in A to the strong adjectives in B.

A	B
tasty small cold	filthy furious delicious
hot beautiful big	delighted fascinated
interested angry	gorgeous boiling tiny
happy dirty	enormous freezing

tasty → delicious

c) Look at the adverbs in **blue** in the article. Which of these adverbs do we use with: gradable adjectives (G), strong adjectives (S)? Which adverb do we use with both types of adjective?

very G really incredibly extremely absolutely fairly

d) What other strong adjectives do you know that mean 'very good'?

e) Check in V2.4 p117.

8 a) Fill in the gaps with an adverb from 7c). Use different adverbs where possible. Then complete the sentences for you.

1 I'm usually _____ exhausted after …
2 It's _____ difficult for me to …
3 The last time I felt _____ awful was …
4 I'm _____ interested in …
5 I've got a/an _____ gorgeous …
6 The last place I went to that was _____ cold was …

b) Work in pairs. Take turns to say your sentences.

9 a) Work in groups. Write a sleep survey. Write at least six questions. Use words/phrases from 1 or your own ideas.
How many hours do you usually sleep a night?

b) Ask other students in the class. Write the answers.

c) Work in your groups. Compare answers.

d) Tell the class what you found out about other students.

Sidebar (top middle):

Vocabulary sleep; gradable and strong adjectives; adverbs
Skills Listening: A sleep scientist; Reading: I just can't sleep!
Help with Listening weak forms (1)
Review Present Simple and Present Continuous

16

17

Help with Listening sections focus on the areas that make spoken English so difficult to understand and teach students how to listen more effectively.

Students are often encouraged to refer to the *Recording Scripts* in the back of the Student's Book to help develop their ability in both listening and pronunciation.

Lesson D *Real World* lessons focus on the functional/situational language students need for day-to-day life.

The *Pair and Group Work* section in the back of the Student's Book provides numerous communicative speaking practice activities.

The *Review* sections at the end of every D lesson provide revision of key language from the unit. These activities can be done in class or for homework and will help students prepare for the *Progress Test* for the unit.

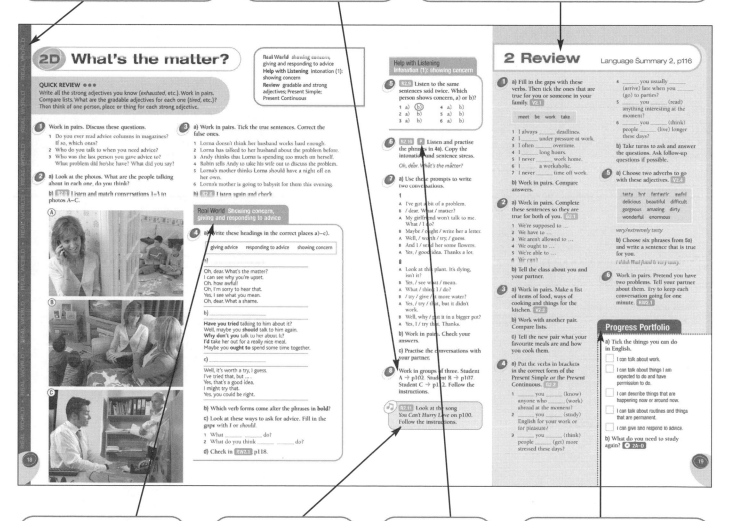

Real World sections help students to analyse the functional and situational language for themselves before checking in the interactive *Language Summary* for the unit.

The *Songs* section on Student's Book p100-p101 contains fun activities based on popular songs appropriate for Intermediate students.

The integrated pronunciation syllabus includes drills for all new *Real World* language.

Based on the requirements of the *Common European Framework of Reference for Languages* (see p13), the *Progress Portfolios* allow students to monitor their own language development by checking what they can remember from the unit. Students are then directed to the CD-ROM for further practice of areas they are unsure about.

Reduced sample pages from **face2face** Intermediate Student's Book

The CD-ROM/Audio CD: Instructions

- Use the CD-ROM/Audio CD in your computer to practise language from the Student's Book and to review language at the end of each lesson.

- Use the CD-ROM/Audio CD in CD players at home or in your car. You can listen to and repeat the day-to-day language from the *Real World* lessons (lesson D in each unit).

Look at the *Language Summary* reference for the *Grammar* and *Real World* language you have learned in the lessons. You can also add your own notes.

Read, listen and record yourselves saying any word or phrase from the Student's Book.

Learn the phonemic symbols and practise saying the sounds.

Check your progress.

Make your own *Tests* from over 600 questions.

Practise the language from the Student's Book in over 200 different activities.

Read and listen again to the main recordings from the Student's Book.

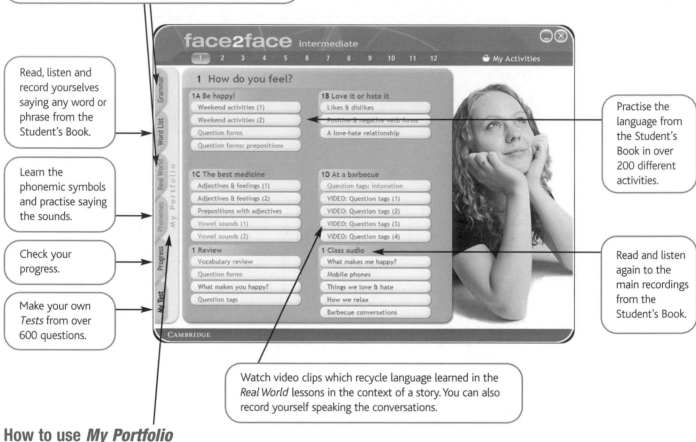

Watch video clips which recycle language learned in the *Real World* lessons in the context of a story. You can also record yourself speaking the conversations.

How to use *My Portfolio*

Grammar

Click on the *Grammar* tab to open the *Grammar* screen. It gives all the information from the *Language Summaries* in the Student's Book so you don't need to have the Student's Book to hand when you are working.

Click on the name of a grammar area to find the information you need.

When you are working on an activity, you can click on *Grammar* to get help.

You can write your own grammar notes.

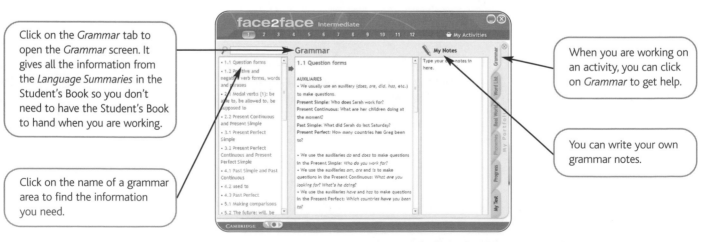

Two screen grabs from **face2face** Intermediate CD-ROM/Audio CD

face2face Intermediate Photocopiable

Phonemes

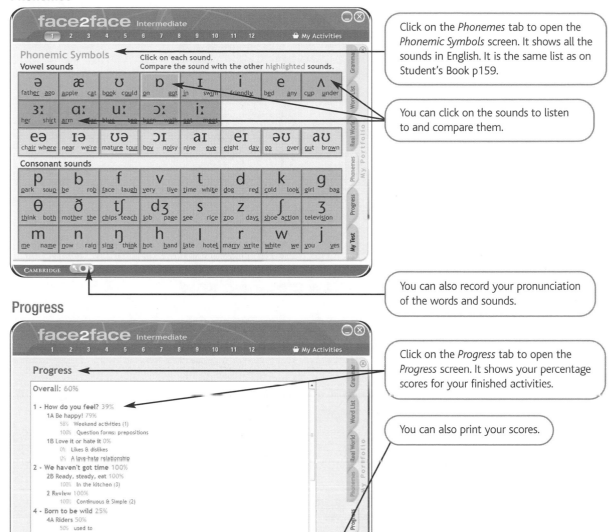

Click on the *Phonemes* tab to open the *Phonemic Symbols* screen. It shows all the sounds in English. It is the same list as on Student's Book p159.

You can click on the sounds to listen to and compare them.

You can also record your pronunciation of the words and sounds.

Progress

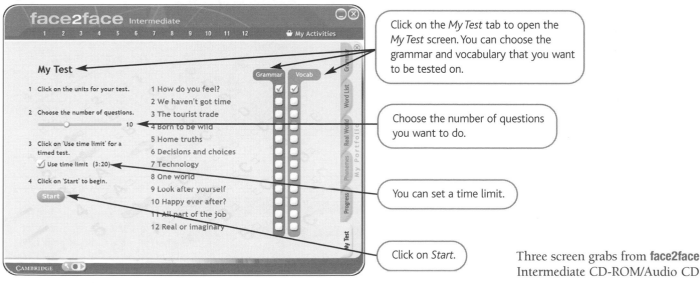

Click on the *Progress* tab to open the *Progress* screen. It shows your percentage scores for your finished activities.

You can also print your scores.

My Test

Click on the *My Test* tab to open the *My Test* screen. You can choose the grammar and vocabulary that you want to be tested on.

Choose the number of questions you want to do.

You can set a time limit.

Click on *Start*.

Three screen grabs from **face2face** Intermediate CD-ROM/Audio CD

The CD-ROM/Audio CD

How to practise new language

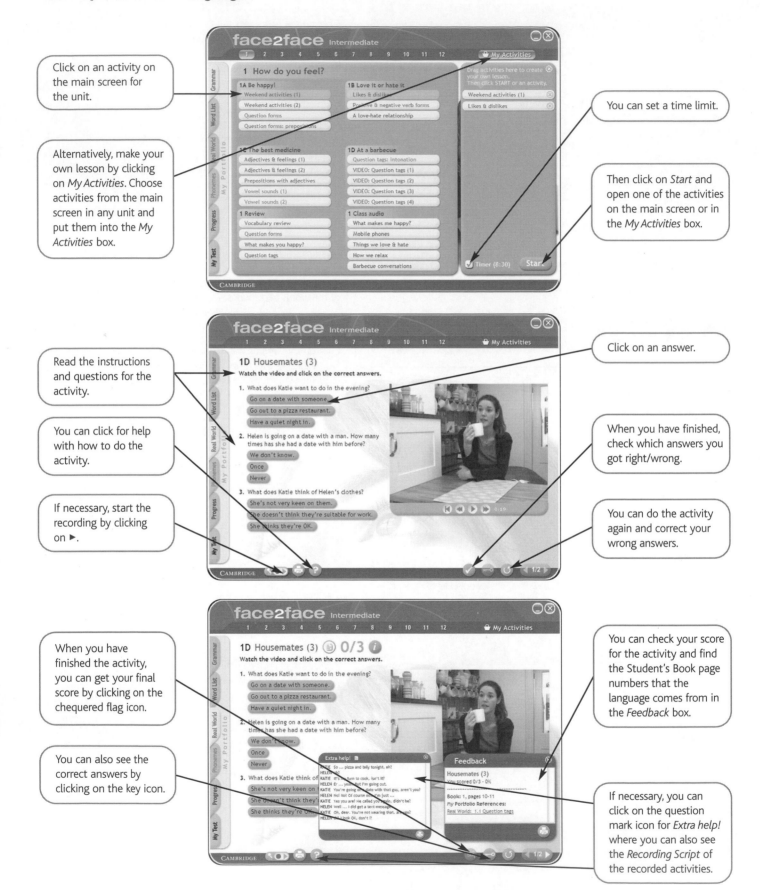

Click on an activity on the main screen for the unit.

Alternatively, make your own lesson by clicking on *My Activities*. Choose activities from the main screen in any unit and put them into the *My Activities* box.

You can set a time limit.

Then click on *Start* and open one of the activities on the main screen or in the *My Activities* box.

Read the instructions and questions for the activity.

You can click for help with how to do the activity.

If necessary, start the recording by clicking on ▶.

Click on an answer.

When you have finished, check which answers you got right/wrong.

You can do the activity again and correct your wrong answers.

When you have finished the activity, you can get your final score by clicking on the chequered flag icon.

You can also see the correct answers by clicking on the key icon.

You can check your score for the activity and find the Student's Book page numbers that the language comes from in the *Feedback* box.

If necessary, you can click on the question mark icon for *Extra help!* where you can also see the *Recording Script* of the recorded activities.

Three screen grabs from **face2face** Intermediate CD-ROM/Audio CD

The Common European Framework (CEF)

What is the Common European Framework? (CEF)

Since the early 1970s, a series of Council of Europe initiatives has developed a description of the language knowledge and skills that people need to live, work and survive in any European country. *Waystage 1990*[1], *Threshold 1990*[2] and *Vantage*[3] detail the knowledge and skills required at different levels of ability.

In 2001, the contents of these documents were further developed into sets of 'can do' statements or 'competences' and officially launched as the *Common European Framework of Reference for Languages: Learning, teaching, assessment* (CEF)[4]. A related document, *The European Language Portfolio*, encourages learners to assess their progress by matching their competence against the 'can do' statements.

The **face2face** series has been developed to include comprehensive coverage of the requirements of the CEF. The table above right shows how **face2face** relates to the CEF and the examinations which can be taken at each level through University of Cambridge ESOL Examinations (Cambridge ESOL), which is a member of ALTE (The Association of Language Testers in Europe).

face2face Student's Book	CEF level	Related examinations	Council of Europe document
Elementary	A1		*Breakthrough*
Elementary	A2	KET Key English Test	*Waystage*
Pre-intermediate	B1	PET Preliminary English Test	*Threshold*
Intermediate	B1	PET Preliminary English Test	*Threshold*
Upper Intermediate	B2	FCE First Certificate in English	*Vantage*

In the spirit of *The European Language Portfolio* developed from the CEF, **face2face** provides a *Progress Portfolio* at the end of every Student's Book unit. Students are encouraged to assess their ability to use the language they have learned so far and to review any aspects by using the CD-ROM/Audio CD. In the Workbook there is a 24-page *Reading and Writing Portfolio* section linked to the CEF and a comprehensive list of 'can do' statements in the *Reading and Writing Progress Portfolio*, which allows students to track their own progress.

face2face Intermediate and CEF levels B1 and B2

The table on the right describes the general degree of skill required at B1 of the CEF. Details of the language knowledge required for B1 are listed in *Threshold 1990*. The 'can do' statements for B1 are listed in the *Common European Framework of Reference for Languages: Learning, teaching, assessment*.

face2face Intermediate completes level B1, which students started in **face2face** Pre-intermediate. The Listening, Reading, Speaking and Writing tables on p14–p17 show where the required competences for level B1 are covered in **face2face** Intermediate.

face2face Intermediate also takes students into level B2, which students will complete in **face2face** Upper-intermediate. The 'can do' statements from B2 that are covered in **face2face** Intermediate are indicated on p14–17 by an asterisk (*).

More information about how **face2face** Intermediate covers the grammatical, lexical and other areas specified by *Threshold 1990* and *Vantage 1990* can be found on our website www.cambridge.org/elt/face2face.

UNDERSTANDING	Listening	I can understand the main points of clear standard speech on familiar matters regularly encountered in work, school, leisure, etc. I can understand the main point of many radio or TV programmes on current affairs or topics of personal or professional interest when the delivery is relatively slow and clear.
UNDERSTANDING	Reading	I can understand texts that consist mainly of high frequency everyday or job-related language. I can understand the description of events, feelings and wishes in personal letters.
SPEAKING	Spoken Interaction	I can deal with most situations likely to arise whilst travelling in an area where the language is spoken. I can enter unprepared into conversation on topics that are familiar, of personal interest or pertinent to everyday life (e.g. family, hobbies, work, travel and current events).
SPEAKING	Spoken Production	I can connect phrases in a simple way in order to describe experiences and events, my dreams, hopes and ambitions. I can briefly give reasons and explanations for opinions and plans. I can narrate a story or relate the plot of a book or film and describe my reactions.
WRITING	Writing	I can write simple connected texts on topics which are familiar or of personal interest. I can write personal letters describing experiences and impressions.

[1] *Waystage 1990* J A van Ek and J L M Trim, Council of Europe, Cambridge University Press
[2] *Threshold 1990* J A van Ek and J L M Trim, Council of Europe, Cambridge University Press
[3] *Vantage* J A van Ek and J L M Trim, Council of Europe, Cambridge University Press
[4] *Common European Framework of Reference for Languages: Learning, teaching, assessment* (2001) Council of Europe Modern Languages Division, Strasbourg, Cambridge University Press

The CEF

Listening

A language user at level B1 and B2* can:	1	2	3
follow clearly articulated speech in everyday conversation	This interactive competence is practised		
follow the main points of a clearly articulated discussion between native speakers	1C 1D	2D	3C 3D
understand a short narrative and form hypotheses about what will happen next			
understand the main points of recorded materials on familiar subjects	1A 1B	2A 2C	3A 3C
catch the main points in TV and radio programmes on familiar topics			3C
follow in outline straightforward short talks on familiar topics			
follow films in which the visuals and action carry much of the storyline	This competence is practised throughout		
understand TV and radio programmes, and identify the speaker's mood and tone*			
use a variety of strategies to achieve comprehension, including listening for main points; checking comprehension by using contextual clues*			

Reading

A language user at level B1 and B2* can:	1	2	3
understand the main points in short newspaper articles	1A 1C WB1C	2B 2C WB2C	3B WB3C 3C
distinguish fact from comment in columns or interviews in newspapers and magazines	1B		3C
skim short texts to find relevant facts and information		WBP2	3C
understand information in everyday material such as brochures and letters		WBP2	
understand simple messages			WBP3
understand standard letters			WBP3
understand descriptions of events, feelings and wishes	WBP1	2C	3C
guess the meaning of single unknown words from their context			
understand straightforward instructions			
identify the main conclusions in clearly signalled argumentative texts			
understand in a narrative the motives for the characters' actions and their consequences for the development of the plot*			
understand articles on current problems in which the writers express specific attitudes and points of view*			

* refers to descriptors for B2
1A = **face2face** Intermediate Student's Book unit 1 lesson A

WB1A = **face2face** Intermediate Workbook unit 1 lesson A
WBP1 = **face2face** Intermediate Workbook Reading and Writing Portfolio 1

4	5	6	7	8	9	10	11	12
throughout the course, in particular in the *Get ready ... Get it right!* sections.								
4B 4D	5A 5B 5D	6A 6C 6D	7D	8B 8D	9D	10A 10B 10D	11A 11B 11D	12A
4C							11C	
4A 4C	5C		7B	8C	9B 9C	10C		12B
4C				8C	9C	10C		
			7C					
the course on the interactive CD-ROM/Audio CD.								
						10C	11C	12C
						10A 10B 10C	11C 11D	12B 12C

4	5	6	7	8	9	10	11	12
4A 4C WB4C	5B 5C	6B 6C WB6C	WB7C	8A 8C	9A 9C WB9C	10C	WB11C	12C
		6B WBP6		WBP8				
4C WB4C	5A 5C WB5C WBP5		7C	8A 8C	WB9C WBP9	10C	WB11C	WB12C
	5A		7A		WBP9			
	WBP5		7C	8A 8C	9A	10C WBP10	WBP11	WB12C WBP12
4C WB4C						10C		
			WBP7					
WBP4		WBP6						
				8C	9C	10C WB10C WBP10	11C WBP11	WB12C WBP12
				WBP8 8A	9A			

The CEF

Speaking

A language user at level B1 and B2*can:	1	2	3
enter unprepared into conversations on familiar topics		2B 2D	3B 3C
start, maintain and close a simple face-to-face conversation on familiar topics	1A 1B 1D	2B 2D	3A
deal with most situations likely to arise when travelling			3A 3D
express and respond to feelings (surprise, happiness, sadness, interest, etc.)	1A 1B	2C 2D	
make his/her opinions/reactions clear as regards finding solutions to problems, etc.	1C	2D	3D
agree and disagree politely			
express beliefs, views and opinions in discussing topics of interest	1A 1B 1C	2A 2C	3C 3D
use a prepared questionnaire and make spontaneous follow-up questions	1A 1D	2B	3A 3B
narrate a story			
give detailed accounts of experiences, describing feelings and reactions	1C		3B 3C
describe dreams, hopes and ambitions			
explain and give reasons for his/her plans, intentions and actions			
paraphrase short written passages orally in a simple fashion			
give straightforward descriptions on a variety of familiar subjects		2A	
ask someone to clarify or elaborate what he/she has just said			
use a simple word with a similar meaning when he/she can't think of the exact word			
help a discussion along on familiar ground, confirming comprehension, etc.*			
speculate about causes, consequences, hypothetical situations*			
initiate, maintain and end discourse naturally with effective turn-taking*			

Writing

A language user at level B1 and B2* can:	1	2	3
write simple connected texts on a range of topics, express personal views/opinions			
link a series of discrete items into a connected linear sequence of points		2C	
narrate a story			
write a description of an event -- real or imagined	WBP1		
write accounts of experiences, describe feelings and reactions			
write very brief reports to a standard conventionalised format			
write notes conveying simple information		WBP2	
write personal letters describing experiences, feelings and events in some detail	WBP1		
convey information/ideas on abstract and concrete topics, ask about/explain problems			WBP3
express feelings such as grief, happiness, interest, regret and sympathy in a letter	WBP1		
describe the plot of a film or a book or give an account of a concert			
reply in written form to adverts and ask for more information			
convey short simple factual information to friends/colleagues or ask for information			WBP3
describe how to do something, giving detailed instructions			
write detailed descriptions on a range of familiar subjects			
write about events/real or fictional experiences in a detailed and easily readable way*			
make a note of 'favourite mistakes' and consciously monitor his/her work for them*			

* refers to descriptors for B2

1A = **face2face** Intermediate Student's Book unit 1 lesson A

WBP1 = **face2face** Intermediate Workbook Reading and Writing Portfolio 1

4	5	6	7	8	9	10	11	12
4C 4D		6B 6D	7C	8C	9A 9B 9C	10C 10D	11C 11D	12C
4A 4B 4D	5A	6A 6B 6D	7A 7B	8B	9A 9B	10C 10D	11B	12A 12C
	5D		7D	8D	9D			
	5B	6A 6D	7C	8D	9D		11D	
4D		6D		8B		10A 10D		
4D	5A	6B 6C 6D	7B	8A 8B	9A	10A 10B 10C	11B 11C	12A
4A	5C	6A	7B			10A 10C		
4C				8C	9C			12B
4A	5B			8C	9C 9D	10A		12B
			7B					12A
	5B	6A 6D	7C		9D	10A		12A
	5C	6A						
4B	5A 5D		7A		9A	10B	11A	12C
							11D	
	5D							
		6D						
			7B	8D		10B		12A 12B
		6D		8D		10D		12A

4	5	6	7	8	9	10	11	12
4C WBP4	5C WBP5	WBP6		WBP8			WBP11	WBP12
WBP4	5C	6B WBP6	WBP7				11C	
4C						WBP10	11C WBP11	WBP12
4C	WBP5						11C WBP11	WBP12
						WBP10	WBP11	WBP12
	5C	WBP6						
			WBP7				11D	
	WBP5			WBP8				
			WBP7					
WBP4								
					WBP9			
	WBP5							
			WBP7					
						WBP10	WBP11	
							11C WBP11	WBP12
								WBP12

Teaching Tips

Listening

- Make full use of the *Help with Listening* sections in the Student's Book, which are designed to help students understand natural spoken English and develop their ability to anticipate and understand what is being said.

- Before asking students to listen to a recording, establish the context, the characters and what information you want them to listen for.

- Give students time to read the comprehension questions in the Student's Book. Deal with any problems or new language in these questions before playing a recording.

- Be sensitive to the difficulties that students might be having and play a recording several times if necessary.

- If you use a cassette recorder in class, don't forget to set the counter to zero each time.

- When you play a recording for a second or third time, you can ask students to read the *Recording Scripts* at the back of the Student's Book while they listen. This helps them to 'tune in' to spoken English and connect what they hear with what they read.

- When students need to listen and write their answers, you can stop the recording after each answer in second and subsequent listenings to give them time to write.

- Use the activities for the *Songs* on Student's Book p100–p101 at the points suggested in the course.

- Encourage students to listen again to the classroom recordings on their CD-ROM/Audio CD on their computer at home. Note that students can only listen to these classroom recordings on a computer, not on a CD player.

Speaking

Pair and Group Work

- Make full use of all the communicative speaking activities in the Student's Book, particularly the *Get ready … Get it right!* sections.

- Help students with the language they need to do speaking tasks by drawing their attention to the 'transactional language' in the speech bubbles. If necessary, drill this language with the class before they do the speaking activity in their pairs or groups.

- Try to ensure that students work with a number of different partners during a class. If it is difficult for students to swap places in class, you can ask them to work with students in front or behind them as well as on either side of them.

- It is often useful to provide a model of the tasks you expect students to do. For example, before asking students to talk about their family in pairs, you can talk about your family with the whole class to give students a model of what they are expected to do.

- Remember that students often find speaking activities much easier if they are personalised, as they don't need to think of ideas as well as language.

- Go around the class and monitor students while they are speaking in their pairs or groups. At this stage you can provide extra language or ideas and correct any language or pronunciation which is impeding communication.

- Avoid becoming too involved in speaking activities yourself unless you see students have misunderstood your instructions or you are asked for help. As soon as you join a group, students often stop talking to each other and talk to you instead.

- When giving feedback on speaking, remember to praise good communication as well as good English, and focus on the result of the task as well as the language used.

Correction

- When you hear a mistake, it is often useful to correct it immediately and ask the student to say the word or phrase again in the correct form. This is particularly effective if the mistake relates to the language you have been working on in the lesson.

- Alternatively, when you point out a mistake to a student you can encourage him/her to correct it himself/herself before giving him/her the correct version.

- Another approach to correction during a freer speaking activity is to note down any mistakes you hear, but not correct them immediately. At the end of the activity write the mistakes on the board. Students can then work in pairs and correct the mistakes. Alternatively, you can discuss the mistakes with the whole class.

Vocabulary

- Give students time to work through the exercises in the *Help with Vocabulary* sections on their own or in pairs rather than doing this with the whole class. This gives students the opportunity to try to work out the rules themselves before checking in the *Language Summaries*. You can then check students have understood the main points with the whole class.

- Point out the stress marks (*) on all new words and phrases in the vocabulary boxes in the lessons and the *Language Summaries*. These show the main stress only on words and phrases.

- When you write a new vocabulary item on the board, make sure students know the stress and part of speech. Students then copy new vocabulary into their notebooks.

- Make sure students are aware of collocations in English (for example *make an appointment, do the housework, go to exhibitions, work shifts*) by pointing them out when they occur and encouraging students to record them as one phrase in their notebooks.

- Encourage students to notice patterns in new vocabulary, for example *lose/keep/be/get in touch with someone*.

- Review and recycle vocabulary at every opportunity in class, using the *Reviews*, the *Language Summaries*, the *Classroom Activities and Games* and the *Class Activities*.

- Use the photocopiable *Vocabulary Plus* worksheets to introduce and practise extra vocabulary which is not included in the Student's Book. They can be used for self-study in class or as homework, or as the basis of a classroom lesson. There is one *Vocabulary Plus* worksheet for each unit in the Student's Book.

- Use the photocopiable *Study Skills* worksheets to help students understand other aspects of vocabulary, such as collocations.

Grammar

- Give students time to work through the exercises in the *Help with Grammar* sections on their own or in pairs. This gives students the opportunity to try to work out the grammar rules themselves before checking their answers in the *Language Summaries*. You can then check students have understood the main points with the whole class, as shown in the *Teaching Notes* for each lesson.

- Teach your students useful grammatical terms (for example past participle, etc.) when the opportunity arises. This helps students become more independent and allows them to use grammar reference books more effectively.

- Use different colour pens for different parts of speech when writing sentences on the board (for example Present Perfect Continuous questions). This helps students see patterns in grammar structures.

- If you know the students' first language, highlight grammatical differences between their language and English. This raises their awareness of potential problems if they try to translate. It is also useful to highlight grammatical similarities to show students when a structure in English is the same as in their own language.

- After teaching a grammatical item, use reading and listening texts as reinforcement by asking students to find examples of that grammatical item in the text. This helps students to see the language in a realistic context.

Pronunciation

- Make full use of the pronunciation drills on the Class Audio CDs/Class Audio Cassettes. These drills are marked with the pronunciation icon **P** in the Student's Book and give standard British native-speaker models of the language being taught.

- Point out the stress marks on all new vocabulary in the vocabulary boxes in the lessons and the *Language Summaries*. Note that only the main stress in each new word or phrase is shown. For example in the phrase *go for a walk*, the main stress on *walk* is shown, but the secondary stress on *go* is not. We feel this is the most effective way of encouraging students to stress words and phrases correctly.

- Also point out the example sentences in the Student's Book before using the pronunciation drills. Note that in the examples of sentences in *Grammar* or *Real World* drills, all stresses in the sentences are shown.

- When using the recordings of these drills, there are usually sufficient pauses for students to repeat chorally without stopping the recording. Alternatively, you can pause the recording and ask each student to repeat individually before continuing.

- For variety, model and drill the sentences yourself instead of using the recordings.

- Point out the stress, linking and weak forms marked in some of the *Recording Scripts* (Student's Book p142).

- Encourage students to listen to the audio component of the CD-ROM/Audio CD on their CD player. This contains *Real World* drills from each lesson D in the Student's Book.

Helping students with sounds

- Consider teaching your students the phonemic symbols (Student's Book p159). This allows students to look up the pronunciation of words in a dictionary and record difficult pronunciation in their notebooks. It is often easier to take a 'little and often' approach to teaching these symbols, rather than trying to teach them all in one lesson.

- Encourage students to use the phonemes section of the CD-ROM/Audio CD at home. This will help them to learn the symbols and allow them to practise the sounds.

- Highlight the phonemic transcriptions in the *Language Summaries*. Note that transcriptions are given only for vocabulary that is particularly problematic.

- Write the phonemic transcription for difficult words on the board and ask students to work out the pronunciation.

- For sounds students often have problems with (for example /θ/) you can demonstrate the shape of the mouth and the position of the tongue in front of the class (or draw this on the board). Often students can't say these sounds simply because they don't know the mouth position required.

- Draw students' attention to the English sounds which are the same in their own language(s) as well as highlighting the ones that are different.

Helping students with stress and intonation

- Drill all new words, phrases and sentences, and pay particular attention to words that sound different from how they are spelt.

- When you write words or sentences on the board, mark the stress in the correct place or ask the students to tell you which syllables or words are stressed.

- When you model sentences yourself, it may be helpful to over-emphasise the stress pattern to help students hear the stress. You can also 'beat' the stress with your hand or fist.

- Emphasise that intonation is an important part of meaning in English and often shows how we feel. For example a falling intonation on the word *please* can sound very impolite to a native English speaker.

- Show the intonation pattern of model sentences by drawing arrows on the board or making hand gestures.

- Hum the sentences you are focusing on. It is sometimes easier for students to hear the stress or intonation pattern when there are no words.

Drilling

- Make sure students know the meaning of new language before drilling this with the class.

- When you model a phrase or sentence, make sure that you speak at normal speed with natural stress and contractions. Repeat the target language two or three times before asking the whole class to repeat after you in a 'choral drill'.

- After choral drilling it is usually helpful to do some individual drilling. Start with the strongest students and drill around the class in random order.

- As the aim of drilling is accuracy, you should correct students when they make a mistake. However, avoid making the students feel uncomfortable and don't spend too long with one student.

- Praise students for good/comprehensible pronunciation and acknowledge weak students' improvement, even if their pronunciation is not perfect.

- Use 'mumble' drills. Ask students to say the phrase or sentence to themselves initially, then increase the volume each time until they are speaking at a normal volume. Shy students often appreciate the chance to say things quietly until they feel more confident.

Reviewing and Recycling

- Use the *Quick Reviews* at the beginning of each lesson. They are easy to set up and should take no more than five to ten minutes. They are a good way of getting the class to speak immediately as well as reviewing what students learned in previous lessons.

- Exploit the *Review* sections at the end of each unit. They can be done in class when students have finished the unit, or set for homework. Note that the *Review* exercises are organised in lesson order, so individual exercises can be used as quick fillers at the beginning or end of a lesson (see the Extra practice and homework boxes in the *Teaching Notes*).

- After a mid-lesson break, ask students to write down in one minute all the words they can remember from the first part of the lesson. These quick *What have we just learned?* activities are very important for helping students to transfer information from their short-term memory to their long-term memory.

- Start a class vocabulary box. You or the students write each new vocabulary item on a separate card and put the cards in the box. The cards can be used for various revision activities, for example Know, Might Know, Don't Know (see p21).

- Encourage students to use the **face2face** CD-ROM/Audio CD to review each lesson at home. Also encourage students to review new language by reading the *Language Summary* for the lesson.

- Set homework after every class. The **face2face** Intermediate Workbook has a section for each lesson in the Student's Book, which reviews all the key language taught in that lesson.

Teaching Intermediate Classes

Although most students at Intermediate level have reached a reasonable level of communicative competence, they often tend to be rather inaccurate, particularly in spontaneous conversation. Another problem with Intermediate classes is that students often don't feel that they are making progress quickly enough. This 'Intermediate plateau' can sometimes be rather demotivating for students. If this is the case for your class, try some of the following suggestions:

- Give students time to prepare what they are going to say, as in the *Get ready … Get it right!* sections of the Student's Book. This allows students to work out what language they are going to use before they do the communicative stage of the activity, which will help them retain the accuracy that has been built up during the lesson.

- Use every opportunity for correction during the class and praise students who use new language correctly.

- Focus particularly on 'fossilised errors' which have become part of the students' lexis or grammar (for example, leaving off the *-s* with *he/she/it* forms of the Present Simple).

- Encourage students to make a list of their own typical mistakes, or collect typical mistakes for the class yourself. You can collect together the 'top ten' mistakes of the class and make a poster of these for the classroom.

- Record or video your students during communicative activities, then use the recordings for error correction later in the class or in the next class.

- Encourage students to broaden their vocabulary whenever possible, for example by using *brilliant* or *amazing* instead of *very good*. Students at this level often like to stay in their linguistic 'comfort zone' and often need to be persuaded to use more advanced language.

- Increase the amount of speaking practice by using the *Class Activities* (p118) whenever possible.

- Use the *Review* section in the Student's Book and the *Progress Tests* in the Teacher's Book (p195). Keep a record of students' scores on the *Progress Tests* for end-of-term reports.

- Use the *Vocabulary Plus* worksheets (p173) to give classes extra input of new lexical items.

- Ask students to tick the things they can do in the *Progress Portfolios* at the end of each unit to help give them a sense of progress.

- Plan which students are going to work together in pair and group work. Mix stronger students with weaker ones when they can give help, for example in a vocabulary matching activity. On other occasions, for example in freer speaking activities, it is often a good idea to place stronger students in the same group. Weaker students may feel more confident speaking with other students at their own level.

- Have ideas for extra activities to give early finishers something to do while the slower students are still working, for example an exercise from a *Review* section or the Workbook, or a *Vocabulary Plus* worksheet.

- Set weaker students extra homework from the Workbook or the CD-ROM/Audio CD to help them catch up with areas of language that the rest of the class is confident with.

Classroom Activities and Games

These *Classroom Activities and Games* can be used to practise a variety of different language areas in class. The *Teaching Notes* suggest when they can be used alongside the lessons in the Student's Book.

Hot Seats

This whole-class activity reviews vocabulary taught during the course through a lively, enjoyable team game.

- Place two chairs or 'hot seats' at the front of the class facing the students, one on each side of the room.

- Divide the class into two teams. Ask one confident student from each team to come and sit in the hot seats.

- Write a word/phrase that you want to review on the board. Alternatively, prepare cards before the class with the words/phrases written on them and hold one card up behind the two students. The students in the hot seats are not allowed to turn round and see the word/phrase.

- Each team tries to convey the meaning of the word/phrase in any way they can (definition, mime, synonym, etc.) without saying or spelling the word/phrase.

- The first student in the hot seats who says the correct word/phrase gets a point for his/her team. Note down each team's points on the board.

- After the students in the hot seats have tried to guess a few words/phrases, ask them to change places with two other students, one from each team. Continue the activity with several different students in the hot seats.

- The team with the most points in the time available wins.

Know, Might Know, Don't Know

This activity helps you to find out what vocabulary students already know. It is a good activity for mixed level classes, as stronger students can teach weaker students vocabulary that they don't know.

- Before the lesson, write a worksheet containing 15–20 words or phrases you want to teach or review.

- Photocopy one worksheet for each student.

- In class, give each student a copy of the worksheet. Tell students to divide the words into three groups: *Know* (I know this word/phrase and can give an example or definition), *Might Know* (I think I know this word/phrase but I'm not sure) and *Don't Know* (I don't know this word/phrase).

- Students work in pairs or groups and compare their answers. If one student knows a word, he/she should teach it to his/her partner or the other members of the group. Alternatively, students can move around the room and talk to various students.

- When they have finished, students say which word/phrases they still don't know. Encourage other groups to give definitions to help them, or give the meanings and examples yourself.

- Allow time for students to record any new vocabulary in their notebooks.

Dialogue Build

This activity focuses on grammatical accuracy as well as giving students confidence in speaking.

- Before the lesson, prepare a 6–8 line conversation based on language the students should know. Find a magazine picture of each person in the conversation (or draw two people on the board).

- In class, set the context, for example on the telephone. Put the two speakers' pictures on either side of the board.

- Draw a speech bubble from the person who speaks first and insert a prompt, for example *What/matter?* Elicit the target sentence, for example *What's the matter?* Model and drill the target language with the whole class and then individually. Don't write the sentence on the board at this stage.

- Draw a reply speech bubble from the other person and insert a prompt, for example *just/have/accident.* Elicit the target sentence, for example *I've just had an accident.* and continue as above, establishing one line each time until the conversation is complete.

- Students practise the conversation in pairs. They then change roles and practise the conversation again.

- Re-elicit the whole conversation, writing each line on the board by the appropriate prompt. Give students time to copy the conversation into their notebooks.

Running Dictation

This activity involves all four skills (reading, writing, speaking and listening) and is a good way to inject some energy into a class.

- Before the lesson, choose a short text. This text can be used to introduce a topic in a lesson, provide a context for new language, revise a language area already covered or simply provide extra reading practice.

- Photocopy one copy of the text for each student.

- In class, divide students into pairs, one reporter and one secretary. Secretaries sit near the back of the class with pen and paper.

- Put one copy of the text on the board. With larger classes, you can put other copies on the wall at the front of the class.

- When you say *Go*, the reporters go to the board, remember as much as they can of the text, then run back to their partners, who must write down the exact words they hear. When a reporter has told his/her secretary all he/she can remember, he/she goes back to the board and repeats the process.

- In the middle of the activity, clap your hands and tell students to change roles.

- The first pair to complete the text wins. Continue the activity until most or all of the students have finished.

- Give a copy of the text to each student. Students then check their version of the text against the original.

Classroom Activities and Games

Words Connected to Me

This activity practises vocabulary in a personalised way and provides a springboard to freer speaking practice.

- Ask students to draw a two-column table on a piece of paper with the headings *Words connected to me* and *Words not connected to me*.

- Dictate a set of words/phrases that you have taught in a recent lesson. If a word/phrase (for example *have insomnia*) is connected to them in some way, they write the phrase in the *Words connected to me* column. If not, they write the phrase in the other column.

- Point out that the word/phrase can be connected to them in any way they like, for example it could relate to the students' lives now or in the past, people in their family, something they want to do in the future, etc.

- Students compare their lists in groups and discuss why they have written all the words/phrases in the *Words connected to me* column.

Grammar Auction

This is a fun grammar revision activity which involves the whole class.

- Before the class, prepare a worksheet with 10–12 sentences on it, based on the grammar areas you have covered with your class. Some of the sentences should be correct English and some should contain mistakes.

- Photocopy one worksheet for each student.

- In the lesson, divide the class into teams of four or five. Give one worksheet to each student. Students discuss in their groups which sentences are correct and which are incorrect. Students should speak quietly so that other teams can't hear them.

- Check that they know what an auction is and how to buy something. Tell the class each group has £20,000 to spend. Act as the auctioneer and sell the sentences one at a time.

- Students try to buy the correct sentences. They can also use tactics to persuade other teams to buy the incorrect ones, for example bidding for incorrect sentences to put doubt into the minds of the other students.

- When a group buys a sentence, they mark that sentence on their worksheet. Students must stop bidding when they have no more money.

- When all the sentences have been sold, check which are correct with the class. The team with the most correct sentences wins. In the case of a tie, the team with the most money left wins.

- At the end of the auction, students work in their groups and correct the incorrect sentences. Check answers with the class.

Pyramid Discussion

This activity encourages students to exchange ideas and opinions in a fun, student-centred way.

- Set a context (for example tell students they are going on a two-week jungle survival trip and that they need to decide what to take with them).

- Give each student a list of 10–15 items or write them on the board.

- Students work on their own and choose the five most useful items to take with them. Students should also think of a reason for choosing each one.

- Each student then shows their list of five items to a partner. Together they must agree on only five items from both their lists.

- Students work in groups of four and repeat the previous stage so that they end up with a new list of only five items. If you have a big class, you can then put students into groups of eight, and so on.

- Finally, bring the whole class together for students to share their ideas and try to agree on the best five items.

Consequences

This activity gives students freer practice of collaborative writing. It allows them to be creative while practising language taught in the lesson (for example narrative verb forms or connecting words).

- Give each student a clean piece of paper to write on (or ask each of them to take one page from their notebooks).

- Give students a series of instructions about what to write (for example a woman's name, a man's name, where and how they met, what they were doing when they met, what they said to each other, what they did next, when they saw each other again, what happened in the end). Check that students are writing full sentences.

- After each student has written their answer to each instruction, they fold their paper just enough to hide what they have written and pass it on to the student on their left.

- When students have finished the story, they fold the paper one more time and pass it to the person on their left. This student opens it and reads it. Ask students to read out any funny or interesting examples to the class.

- Display the stories around the class for everyone to read. Students decide which one is the best and why.

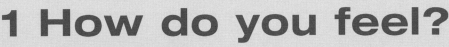

1A Be happy!

> **Vocabulary** weekend activities
> **Grammar** question forms
> **Help with Listening** questions with *you*

QUICK REVIEW ●●●

• Quick Reviews begin each lesson in a fun, student-centred way. They are short activities which review previously taught language and are designed to last about five or ten minutes. For more information on Reviewing and Recycling, see p20.

This activity gives students the opportunity to meet each other. Students move around the room and talk to five other students, or to five students sitting near them. At the end of the activity, ask students to tell the class two things they found out about two people.

Vocabulary Weekend activities

 a) Ask students to tell the class one or two things they did last weekend that they enjoyed. Then ask students to do the matching exercise on their own or in pairs.

Students check their answers in Language Summary 1 **V1.1** SB (Student's Book) p114. Note that in **face2face** Intermediate only the meanings of **new** words/phrases are shown in the Language Summaries. These words/phrases are highlighted by an asterisk (*) and the meanings are given in a dictionary box 📖 . Also point out that only the **main** stress (●) in phrases is shown in vocabulary boxes and Language Summaries.

Check answers with the class. Highlight the difference between *do some exercise* (running, etc.) and *do an exercise*.

Point out that we also use *chat* to mean 'talk to someone in a friendly and informal way': *He's chatting with friends*.

Model and drill the phrases. Highlight the pronunciation of *tidy* /ˈtaɪdi/ and *exhibition* /ˌeksɪˈbɪʃən/. Point out the stress on *lie-in*.

> go clubbing; have a lie-in; meet up with friends; do some gardening; have a quiet night in; tidy up the house/the flat; do some exercise; go to exhibitions; chat to people online; have people round for dinner; go for a walk/a run

b) Students do the exercise on their own by referring back to the phrases in **1a)**. Students should also think of other things they do at the weekend and how often they do them.

c) Use the speech bubbles to remind students of the phrase *Yes, so do I.* to agree with a positive statement. Also remind them of the phrases *No, neither do I.* and *No, nor do I.* to agree with a negative statement.

Students do the activity in pairs. Encourage them to ask follow-up questions if possible.

Ask students to tell the class two things their partner does at the weekend.

Reading

 a) Focus students on the article. Pre-teach *research*. Avoid discussing what makes students happy at this stage, as they are asked to do this in **10** and **11**.

Students read the beginning of the article and find out how scientists made their list. Check the answer with the class.

> Scientists reviewed hundreds of research studies from around the world.

b) Focus students on the ten reasons for happiness. Pre-teach *genes* /dʒiːnz/ and *religion* /rɪˈlɪdʒən/. Drill these words with the class.

Students do the exercise on their own.

c) Students compare lists in pairs and explain their order.

> ── **EXTRA IDEA** ──
> • 🖉 Ask the class to vote for what they think is the most important reason for happiness and write it on the board. Continue to ask for votes until you have a class list of ten reasons in order on the board. Students can then compare the class list to the list in the article after they have done **3**.

3 Ask students to turn to SB p113.

a) Students read the rest of the article and compare the list with their own from **2b)**.

Find out which student's list is the closest to the article.

b) Students discuss the questions in groups. Ask students to share interesting ideas and opinions with the class.

Listening and Grammar

 a) Focus students on the photos of Sarah, Greg and Jenny on SB p5. 🖉 Ask the class what they think makes each person happy and write their ideas on the board.

b) **R1.1** Play the recording (SB p142). Students listen and write two things that make each person happy.

Check answers with the class and compare them with the students' ideas on the board from **4a)**.

> SARAH watching her children when they're sleeping; going to museums and art galleries
> GREG travelling and visiting new places; gardening
> JENNY having a lie-in; dancing/going clubbing

c) Give students time to read questions 1–9, then play the recording again. Students listen and answer the questions, then check answers in pairs. Check answers with the class.

> 2 They're watching TV. 3 She went to an exhibition.
> 4 About 20. 5 South America. 6 Every weekend (when he's in the UK). 7 Yes, she does. 8 Toast and coffee. 9 Doing some exercise.

— EXTRA IDEA —
- If students find the recording difficult, ask them to look at R1.1, SB p142. Play the recording again. Students listen, read and check their answers.

Help with Grammar Question forms

- Help with Grammar boxes help students to examine examples of language and discover the rules of meaning, form and use for themselves. Students should usually do the exercises on their own or in pairs, then check their answers in the Language Summaries. You can then check the main points with the class as necessary. For more information on the **face2face** approach to Grammar, see p5.

5 a)–f) Focus students on the questions in **4c)**. Students do the exercises on their own or in pairs, then check their answers in **G1.1** SB p115.

✎ While students are working, draw the table from **5b)** on the board so that you are ready to check their answers. Check answers with the class.

- **a)** **Present Perfect Simple** question 4; **Past Simple** question 3; **Present Continuous** question 2
- **b)** Focus students on the table on the board. Elicit which words in questions 2–4 from **4c)** go in each column and complete the table (see the table in **G1.1** SB p115).
- Highlight the typical word order in questions: question word + auxiliary + subject + verb + … .
- **c)** We use the auxiliaries *do* and *does* to make questions in the Present Simple; *have* and *has* in the Present Perfect Simple; *did* in the Past Simple; *am*, *is* and *are* in the Present Continuous.
- Students will study all of these verb forms again in **face2face** Intermediate, so don't go into detail here.
- **d)** 1 In question 8 in **4c)**, the question word *What* is the object (*she* is the subject). In question 9, *What* is the subject. 2 Because we don't use auxiliaries *do* or *does* with Present Simple subject questions.
- Use question 9 to point out that the word order in subject questions is the same as positive sentences.
- Also point out that we don't use the auxiliary *did* in Past Simple subject questions: *Who lived here?*
- **e)** Questions 1 and 4 have prepositions at the end.
- Point out that we don't usually put prepositions at the beginning of questions: *What are you talking about?* not ~~*About what are you talking?*~~ Remind students that questions with prepositions at the end are very common.

6 Focus students on the example and tell students they have to fill in the gaps with the correct auxiliary, or no auxiliary (for subject questions). Use the example to teach *Whereabouts* (in which part of a town/city/country).

Students do the exercise on their own, then check in pairs. Check answers with the class. Point out that questions 4, 6 and 9 are subject questions and don't have an auxiliary.

> 2 have 3 do 4 – 5 are 6 – 7 Did 8 have 9 – 10 did

Help with Listening Questions with *you*

- Help with Listening boxes are designed to help students understand natural spoken English. They often focus on phonological aspects of spoken English which make listening problematic for students. For more information on the **face2face** approach to Listening, see p5. This Help with listening section focuses on how we say auxiliaries and *you* in questions.

7 a) Students work in pairs and discuss how we usually say *do you*, *have you*, *are you* and *did you* in the questions in **6**. Encourage students to say questions to each other at normal speed and notice how they say the auxiliary + *you*.

b) R1.2 Play the recording (SB p142). Students listen and notice how we say *do you* /dʒə/, *have you* /həvjə/, *are you* /əjə/ and *did you* /dɪdʒə/.

Use the questions to teach students the schwa /ə/. Point out that this is the most common sound in spoken English. Note that students study the schwa and weak forms in more detail in lessons 2C and 7C.

8 a) R1.2 P Play the recording again and ask students to repeat. Check their pronunciation of the auxiliary + *you*.

b) Students do the exercise in pairs.

c) Ask students to tell the class three things they found out about their partner.

9 Put students into pairs, student A and student B. Student As turn to SB p102 and student Bs turn to SB p107.

a) Focus students on the example and highlight the prepositions at the end of the question.

Students then work on their own and make questions with the words. While they are working, monitor and check their questions for accuracy.

> **Student A** 2 Who do you usually go on holiday with?
> 3 What do you like spending your money on? 4 Which radio station do you normally listen to? 5 What do you and your friends argue about?
>
> **Student B** 2 What do you and your friends like talking about? 3 Which countries do you want to go to?
> 4 Who do you usually go to the cinema with? 5 Which town or city does your best friend come from?

b) Students work with their partner and take turns to ask and answer their questions. Encourage students to pronounce the auxiliary + *you* correctly and to ask follow-up questions.

Get ready … Get it right!

- There is a Get ready … Get it right! activity at the end of every A and B lesson. The Get ready … stage helps students to collect their ideas and prepare the language they need to complete the task. The Get it right! stage gives students the opportunity to use the language they have learned in the lesson in a communicative (and often personalised) context. These two-stage activities help students to become more fluent without losing the accuracy they have built up during the controlled practice stages of the lesson. For more on the **face2face** approach to Speaking, see p5.

10 a) Focus students on the examples. Students do the exercise on their own.

b) Put students into pairs and ask them to swap lists. Focus students on the example questions. Students write one question about each thing on their partner's list.

11 a) Students work in pairs and take turns to ask and answer their questions. Encourage students to ask follow-up questions about topics they are interested in.

b) Finally, ask students to tell the class some of the things that make their partner happy.

EXTRA PRACTICE AND HOMEWORK

Ph **Class Activity** 1A Our free time p132 (Instructions p118)
1 Review Exercises 1 and 2 SB p11
CD-ROM Lesson 1A
Workbook Lesson 1A p5

1B Love it or hate it

QUICK REVIEW ●●●

This activity reviews question forms. Put students into pairs, but don't let them talk to each other yet. Students write five questions to ask their partner. They then work in pairs and take turns to ask and answer their questions. Encourage students to continue the conversations if possible. Ask students to share interesting answers with the class.

Vocabulary likes and dislikes
Grammar positive and negative verb forms, words and phrases
Help with Listening sentence stress (1)
Review question forms

Vocabulary Likes and dislikes

1 Focus students on meanings a)–c). Students do the exercise on their own or in pairs before checking in **V1.2** SB p114. Check answers with the class (see **V1.2** SB p114).

Check students understand that *I can't stand …* and *I can't bear …* mean the same as *I really hate*, and that *I don't mind …* means 'it's not a problem for me'.

Highlight the prepositions in the phrases *interested in* and *keen on*, and check students understand that *great, brilliant* and *wonderful* all mean 'very good'.

You can point out that the phrases *… really get(s) on my nerves* and *… drive(s) me crazy* are informal.

Also highlight that we can use pronouns, nouns or verb+*ing* with the phrases for likes and dislikes: *I enjoy it. I can't stand football. Waiting in queues drives me crazy.*

Model and drill the phrases, using *it* to complete each phrase (*I really love it, I really hate it*, etc.). Highlight the pronunciation of *nerves* /nɜːvz/ and *bear* /beə/. Point out that only the main stress (•) in phrases is shown in vocabulary boxes and Language Summaries.

2 a) Check students understand the six phrases and highlight the verb+*ing* form at the beginning of each phrase. Students do the exercise on their own.

b) Students compare sentences in pairs, giving reasons why they feel like this. Ask each pair to tell the class one or two things they felt the same about.

Students list other things they like and don't like in **11**, so avoid personalising the activity further at this stage.

Reading and Grammar

3 Students discuss the questions in groups.

Elicit good things and bad things about mobile phones and write them on the board in two lists.

4 a) Focus students on the article and the photos of Amy and Jeremy. Ask students who they think likes mobile phones (Amy) and who hates them (Jeremy).

R1.3 Play the recording. Students listen and read the article. Ask students to say which things on their lists, or the list on the board, that Amy and Jeremy talked about.

b) Students read the article again and answer the questions. They check answers in pairs. Check answers with the class.

1F 2F 3T 4F 5F

c) Ask the class who they agree with, Amy or Jeremy. Encourage students to give reasons for their answers.

EXTRA IDEA

- Teach vocabulary related to mobile phones: *text someone; send/get a text; a ring tone*, etc.

5 **a)–e)** Students do the exercises on their own or in pairs, then check their answers in **G1.2** SB p115.

- **a) Present Simple 5** I don't have **7** we meet up
  Present Continuous 4 I'm trying **6** I'm not feeling
  Present Perfect Simple 2 I haven't taken **3** that's
  happened **Past Simple 1** I didn't get **8** we went out

- Use the examples to point out that we make: Present
  Simple negatives with *don't/doesn't* + infinitive;
  Present Continuous negatives with *'m not/aren't/isn't*
  + *verb+ing*; Present Perfect Simple negatives with
  haven't/hasn't + past participle; Past Simple negatives
  with *didn't* + infinitive.

- Note that these verb forms are dealt with in more
  detail in later units of **face2face** Intermediate.

- **b)** We usually make *I think …* negative, not the main
  verb: *I don't think I could live without one.* not ~~I think I
  couldn't live without one.~~

- **c)** We can use *no* to make negatives with *there is/there
  are*: *There's no signal.* = *There isn't a signal. There are no
  taxis.* = *There aren't any taxis.*

- Remind students that we can also use *no* to make
  negatives with *have got/has got*: *I've got no money.*
  = *I haven't got any money.*

- **d)** always – never; usually – hardly ever; everyone –
  no one; all – none; both – neither

- Point out that we can say *don't always/usually/often*,
  but not ~~don't sometimes/hardly ever/never~~.

- Remind students that we can say *no one* or *nobody*.
  Nothing and *nowhere* also have a negative meaning.

- Also point out that we don't usually use double
  negatives. We say *I didn't talk to anyone.* not ~~I didn't
  talk to no one.~~

- Highlight that we use plural verb forms with *both*
  (*both of my brothers have got mobiles*) and singular
  verb forms with *neither* (*neither of them ever
  switches their phone off*).

 6 Focus students on the example before asking them
to do the exercise on their own. Point out that there can
sometimes be more than one possible answer. Students
check answers in pairs.

 7 **R1.4** **P** Play the recording (SB p142). Students listen and
check. Ask students if they have any alternative answers
they would like to check.
Play the recording again and ask students to repeat.

2 No one in my family has a mobile. **3** Miranda hasn't
sent me a text. **3** I don't think I'll buy a new phone.
4 There's no message for you./There isn't a message for
you. **5** None of my friends have got mobiles. **6** Neither
of my sisters likes texting.

 8 **a)** Students do the exercise on their own. Tell students
they can write true and false sentences about anything,
not just mobile phones. Encourage them to use the verb
forms and other words/phrases from **5** in their sentences.

b) Put students into pairs. Students take turns to tell each
other their sentences and guess which are false.

Listening

 9 **a)** Pre-teach *customer service phone lines* (you call these
when you have a problem with a product or a service).
Use the photos on SB p6 to remind students who Amy
and Jeremy are.
R1.5 Play the recording (SB p142). Students listen and
decide who is talking about topics 1–4 and whether they
love them or hate them. Check answers with the class.

1 cooking (Jeremy loves it) **2** football on TV
(Amy hates it) **3** flying (Amy loves it) **4** customer
service phone lines (Jeremy hates them)

b) Play the recording again. Students listen and find two
reasons why Amy and Jeremy love or hate each topic.
Check answers with the class.

Jeremy loves cooking because it helps him to stop
thinking about work; he loves going to the local fruit
and vegetable market; it's very satisfying to see friends
enjoying the food he has prepared. **Amy hates football
on TV because** it's on almost every evening; her
husband watches it all the time; he always thinks it's
more important than what she wants to watch; it's
boring. **Amy loves flying because** it's much safer than
driving; she loves sitting back and watching the clouds
go by; she can stay up and watch films all night; the
food. **Jeremy hates customer service phone lines
because** you have to listen to terrible music while you're
waiting; you have to wait a long time; when you finally
speak to someone it's usually the wrong department.

- This Help with Listening section introduces students
  to sentence stress and highlights that we stress the
  important words in spoken English.

10 **a)** **R1.5** Focus students on the examples before playing
the beginning of the recording again. Students listen and
notice the stressed words.

b) Students turn to R1.5, SB p142. Play the first half of
the recording again. Students listen and notice the
sentence stress. Note that students are asked to work out
what parts of speech are usually stressed in lesson 1C.

 11 Focus students on the phrases for likes and dislikes in **1**.
Remind them that we can use these phrases with *verb+ing*
forms or nouns. Students do the exercise on their own.

a) Students move around the room saying their sentences, or say their sentences to people sitting near them. They must find one student in the class who agrees with each of their sentences. Encourage students to ask follow-up questions where possible, as shown in the speech bubbles. While students are working, monitor and help with any problems.

b) Finally, ask students to tell the class two things they have in common with other students.

EXTRA PRACTICE AND HOMEWORK

Ph **Study Skills** 1 Independent learning p191
(Instructions p189)

Ph **Class Activity** 1B Celebrity match p133
(Instructions p118)

1 Review Exercises 3 and 4 SB p11

CD-ROM Lesson 1B

Workbook Lesson 1B p6

 # The best medicine

QUICK REVIEW ●●●

This activity reviews phrases for likes and dislikes. Students do the first part of the activity on their own. Put students into pairs. Students take turns to tell each other about the people on their list. Ask students to share interesting ideas with the class.

Vocabulary adjectives to describe feelings; prepositions with adjectives
Skills Listening: How we relax; Reading: Laugh? I feel better already!
Help with Listening sentence stress (2)
Review free time activities; likes and dislikes

Listening

1 a) Focus students on the phrases in the box. Teach the new phrases *have a massage* and *meditate*. Point out the difference in pronunciation between *massage* /ˈmæsɑːʒ/ and *message* /ˈmesɪdʒ/ and check students can pronounce *yoga* /ˈjəʊɡə/ correctly. Drill the new phrases with the class. Students do the exercise on their own.

b) Students compare answers in pairs. Ask students to share anything they have in common with their partners with the class.

2 a) Remind students of Jeremy from lesson 1B. If necessary, ask them to look at his picture on SB p6. Tell students that he and his wife, Anne, have invited two friends, Mike and Sally, round for dinner. Ask students who they think did the cooking (Jeremy, because he loves cooking).

R1.6 Play the recording (SB p142). Students listen and write down what each person does to relax. Students check answers in pairs. 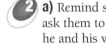 Check answers with the class and write them on the board.

> **Mike** does yoga. **Anne** goes to a health club. **Sally** paints watercolours. **Jeremy** sits in front of the TV.

b) Play the recording again. Students listen and write down how often the four people do the things that help them relax. Check answers with the class.

> MIKE Every morning when he gets up.
> ANNE Two or three times a month.
> SALLY Every Sunday.
> JEREMY Six nights a week.

Help with Listening Sentence stress (2)

- This Help with Listening section develops students' understanding of sentence stress by focusing on what types of words are usually stressed or unstressed.

3 a) R1.6 Focus students on the examples, then play the recording again. Students listen, read and notice the sentence stress.

b) Check students know the parts of speech in the box. Students do the exercise on their own or in pairs. Check answers with the class. Point out that we always stress names (*Jeremy*, etc.), and we don't usually stress the verb *be*, even when it is the main verb.

> **main verbs** (*was*), *had, know,* (*were*), (*'m*), *enjoyed, want.* Usually stressed (except *be*).
> **adjectives** *wonderful, good, glad.* Usually stressed.
> **positive auxiliaries** *do.* Usually unstressed.
> **negative auxiliaries** *haven't, didn't.* Usually stressed.
> **nouns** *meal, months, cook, coffee.* Usually stressed.
> **pronouns** *I, you, it.* Usually unstressed.

--- EXTRA IDEA ---

- If your students don't know the words for parts of speech in English, write this sentence on the board: *My brother has bought a new car, but his wife doesn't like it.* Ask students to match the underlined words to the parts of speech in **3b)**. Check answers with the class.

> main verb *like*; adjective *new*; positive auxiliary *has*; negative auxiliary *doesn't*; noun *brother*; pronoun *it*

c) Students turn to R1.6, SB p142. Play the recording again. Students listen and notice the sentence stress.

Students work on their own or in pairs and find two more examples of the stressed parts of speech in **3b)** in the recording. Check answers with the class.

> **main verbs** *love*, *relax*, etc.
> **adjectives** *nice*, *busy*, etc.
> **negative auxiliaries** *don't*, *doesn't*, etc.
> **nouns** *milk*, *sugar*, etc.

Vocabulary and Reading

4 a) Students work on their own or in pairs and tick the words they know, then check in **V1.3** SB p114.

Check students understand the meaning of any new words. Point out that many of the adjectives end in *-ed* as they describe how people feel.

Model and drill the words. Highlight the *-ed* endings of *relaxed* /rɪˈlækst/, *embarrassed* /ɪmˈbærəst/, *confused* /kənˈfjuːzd/ and *concerned* /kənˈsɜːnd/. Point out that the *-ed* ending of *frustrated* /frʌˈstreɪtɪd/ is pronounced /ɪd/ because of the final /t/ sound. Also point out that *pleased*, *stressed*, *scared* and *shocked* are one-syllable words.

b) Students check answers in pairs. Check with the class.

> nervous; embarrassed; annoyed; fed up; disappointed; stressed; upset; scared; confused; shocked; frustrated; concerned

5 a) Students do the exercise on their own. You can ask them to make notes at this stage.

b) Focus students on the example, then put students into pairs. Students take turns to tell each other about the adjectives. Ask students to share interesting ideas with the class.

6 a) Focus students on the photo on SB p9. Ask the class where they people are and what they think they're doing.

Discuss interesting answers with the class, but don't tell them whether their ideas are correct or not yet.

b) Be prepared with definitions, examples, etc. to pre-teach the vocabulary in the box, or bring in a set of dictionaries for students to check the meaning themselves.

Note that the aim of these boxes is to highlight which words you need to pre-teach to help students understand the text that follows. The vocabulary in these boxes is not in the Language Summaries.

Tell students that *reduce* is a verb and that *fake* can be an adjective, a verb or a noun.

c) Students do the exercise on their own. Early finishers can check answers in pairs. Check answers with the class.

> 1c) 2e) 3b) 4d) 5a)

d) Students do the exercise on their own. Use the example to highlight that they can write one or two words only in the gaps before they begin.

Students check answers in pairs. Check answers with the class.

> 2 more (often) 3 over 1,300 4 healthy/relaxed 5 good
> 6 enjoyed/liked

e) Ask the students if they would like to go to a Laughter Club. Encourage students to give reasons for their answers.

Help with Vocabulary

Prepositions with adjectives

- Help with Vocabulary boxes help students to explore and understand how vocabulary works, often focusing on aspects of lexical grammar. Students should usually do the exercises on their own or in pairs, then check their answers in the Language Summaries. Check the main points with the class as necessary. For more information on the **face2face** approach to Vocabulary, see p5.

7 a)–c) Students do the exercises on their own or in pairs, then check their answers in **V1.4** SB p114. Check answers with the class.

- **a)** happy with; interested in; nervous about; keen on; worried about; surprised by; upset about; fed up with; pleased with
- **b)** bored **with** (by); frightened **of** (by); annoyed **at** (with, by); bad **at**; satisfied **with** (by); embarrassed **by** (about); concerned **about** (by); angry **about** (at) something; angry **with** (at) someone
- Point out that the prepositions in **bold** are the most common. Other prepositions we can use with these adjectives are in brackets. You could suggest that students only use the most common prepositions.
- Also highlight that after a preposition we use a noun, a pronoun or verb+ing: *I'm not very keen on the idea. They're bored with it. He's worried about being late.*

┌─ **EXTRA IDEA** ─────────────

- Students work in pairs and take turns to test each other on the adjective-preposition collocations. One student says an adjective, for example *good*, and his/her partner says the whole collocation, for example *good at*.

8 a) Students do the exercise on their own. Make sure students write the adjectives and the names of the people.

b) If possible, put students in pairs with someone they haven't worked with in this lesson. Students take turns to tell their partner about the people on their list. While they are working, monitor and correct any mistakes you hear.

a) Organise the class into groups of three or four. Focus the students on the prompts and tell the class that each group is going to create a Happiness Club.

Point out to students that they can include anything in their clubs that they like, but everything they choose must create a feeling of happiness.

Tell students that they must all make notes on their Happiness Club, as they will each have to describe it to other students.

While they are working, move around the room and help students with language and ideas. Allow students about ten minutes for this stage.

b) Reorganise the class so that students from different groups are working together. Students take turns to describe their Happiness Club.

Finally, ask each group to tell the class which club they thought was the best, and why.

EXTRA PRACTICE AND HOMEWORK

Ph **Vocabulary Plus** 1 *-ed/-ing* adjectives p177 (Instructions p173)

1 Review Exercise 5 SB p11

CD-ROM Lesson 1C

Workbook Lesson 1C p8

 At a barbecue

QUICK REVIEW ●●●
This activity reviews adjectives and prepositions. Students do the activity in pairs. Encourage students to use *Me too.*, *So am I.* and *Oh, I'm not.* in response to their partner's sentences. Ask students to share interesting answers with the class.

Real World question tags
Review auxiliaries; short answers; adjectives and prepositions

Real World Question tags

 a) Focus students on the picture and ask students where the people are (at a barbecue).

Ask students if they ever go to barbecues. If so, ask a few students to describe the last barbecues they went to.

b) Focus students on the phrases in the box and tell them that these are called 'question tags'.

Students do the exercise on their own.

Don't check answers at this stage.

c) Students do the exercise on their own, then check answers in pairs.

d) R1.7 Play the recording (SB p142). Students listen and check. Check answers with the class.

A You work with Dave, don't you? Yes, I do.
B Kate went to Bristol University, didn't she? Yes, she did.
C You haven't been to China, have you? No, I haven't.
D Jack's vegetarian, isn't he? No, he isn't, actually.

 Tell students they are going to listen to the next part of conversations A–D. Give them time to read answers 1–4.

R1.8 Play the recording (SB p142). Students listen and choose the correct answers.

Check answers with the class.

1 email address
2 wants to go
3 has
4 doesn't eat

 a)–d) Students do the exercises on their own or in pairs, then check their answers in RW1.1 SB p115. Check answers with the class.

- **a)** We usually use questions with question tags (*isn't he?*; *aren't you?*, etc.) to check information that we think is correct.

- **b)** We usually use the auxiliary in question tags: *You work with Dave, don't you?*
- We only use pronouns in question tags: *Kate went to Bristol University, didn't she?*
- If the main part of the question is positive, the question tag is usually negative: *Jack's vegetarian, isn't he?*
- If the main part of the question is negative, the question tag is usually positive: *You haven't been to China, have you?*
- If the main part of the question is in the Present Simple or Past Simple, we use *don't/doesn't* or *didn't* in the question tag: *Jim lives in the USA, doesn't he? You lived in Australia, didn't you?*
- Also point out that we say *aren't I?*, not ~~*amn't I?*~~: *I'm late, aren't I?* and that we use commas before question tags.

- **c)** 1 Yes, I do.; Yes, she did.; No, I haven't. 2 No, he isn't, actually. 3 When the information isn't correct, we often use *actually* after the short answer to sound more polite, then give more information: A *Jack's vegetarian, isn't he?* B *No, he isn't, actually. He just doesn't eat red meat.*
- Point out that we often use short answers (*Yes, she did.*, etc.) to reply to questions with question tags.

a) Play the recording. Students listen and decide if the intonation on the question tag goes up or down (it goes down).

Note that intonation on question tags can also go up when we are asking a question we don't know the answer to. However, 'down' intonation is the most common pattern and therefore the most useful for students to learn.

b) P Play the recording again. Students listen and repeat. Check they are copying the intonation of the question tags correctly.

5 **a)** Students do the exercise on their own, then check answers in pairs.

b) Students do the exercise on their own or in pairs. Don't check answers with the class at this stage.

c) R1.10 Play the recording (SB p143). Students listen and check their answers. Check answers with the class.

> 1 didn't she? 2 doesn't she? (Conversation B)
> 3 aren't you? 4 has he? (Conversation A)
> 5 don't you? 6 haven't you? (Conversation D)
> 7 didn't he? 8 is he? (Conversation C)

d) Play the recording again. Students listen and tick the information in **5a)** that is correct. Check answers with the class.

> The information in 1, 3, 4, 5, 6 and 7 is correct.
> The information in 2 and 8 isn't correct.

6 **a)** Focus students on the examples, then ask students to do the exercise on their own.

While they are working, monitor and check their questions for accuracy. Encourage students to think of follow-up questions. If students aren't able to move around the room, they should only write questions about the students that are sitting near them.

> ── EXTRA IDEA ──
> • ✍ If students need help with ideas for questions, write these prompts on the board before they do **6a)**: *live, work, family, free time, things he/she loves/hates, how he/she relaxes, countries visited,* etc.

b) Students move around the room and ask their questions with question tags. If this isn't possible, students ask questions to people sitting near them. Encourage students to respond with a short answer. If the information is correct, students then ask their follow-up questions.

c) Students do the activity in pairs. Finally, ask students to tell the class one or two things that they have found out.

> ── EXTRA PRACTICE AND HOMEWORK ──
> Ph **Class Activity** 1D Make it snappy! p135 (Instructions p119)
> **1 Review** SB p11
> **CD-ROM** Lesson 1D
> **Workbook** Lesson 1D p9
> **Workbook** Reading and Writing Portfolio 1 p64
> **Progress Test 1** p200

1 Review

- The Review section reviews the key language taught in the unit. It includes communicative and personalised speaking stages as well as controlled grammar, vocabulary and writing practice.
- This section is designed to be used in class after students have finished lesson D, but individual exercises can be used as 'fillers' if you have a few minutes left at the end of a lesson. The Extra practice and homework boxes list which exercises are relevant to each lesson.
- The icons refer to the relevant sections in the Language Summary. Students can refer to these if they need help when doing the exercises.
- For more information on the **face2face** approach to Reviewing and Recycling, see p5.

> **1a)** 2 go 3 tidy up 4 go to 5 visit 6 chat 7 have 8 meet up
> **2a)** 1 do 2 – 3 Did 4 are 5 have 6 does 7 have 8 Are
> **4a)** 1 Everyone I know watches TV. 2 I don't think I'll go out tonight. 3 I usually eat fish. 4 None of my friends like football. 5 I have two sisters and neither of them likes their job. 6 I never get up early at the weekend.
> **5a)** 1 on 2 about 3 in 4 about 5 at 6 by 7 of 8 with

Progress Portfolio

- Progress Portfolio boxes encourage students to reflect on what they have learned and help them decide which areas they need to study again.
- Note that the *I can …* statements reflect communicative competences as set out in the *Common European Framework of Reference for Languages* (CEF) for levels B1 and B2. For more information on the CEF, see p13.

a) Students work through the list of *I can …* statements on their own and tick the things they feel they can do. They can refer to Language Summary 1 if they wish.

Students can also work in pairs or groups and compare which statements they have ticked.

b) Students work on their own or in pairs/groups and decide which areas they need to study again. Encourage students to use the CD-ROM/Audio CD, lessons 1A–D to help them improve in these areas. For more information on the CD-ROM/Audio CD, see p10. There is also further practice on all key language taught in the Student's Book in the **face2face** Intermediate Workbook.

2 We haven't got time

Student's Book p12–p19

2A Slow down!

This activity reviews questions with question tags. Put students into pairs, but don't let them talk to each other yet. Ask students to write four things they think they know about their partner. Students then work with their partner and take turns to ask questions with question tags to check the information they wrote is correct. At the end of the activity, ask students to share interesting ideas with the class.

Vocabulary work collocations
Grammar modal verbs (1); *be able to, be allowed to, be supposed to*
Review question tags

Vocabulary Work collocations

1 a) Students do the exercise on their own or in pairs, then check in **V2.1** SB p116. Check answers with the class.

Check students understand the new words in the dictionary box in the Language Summary.

Model and drill the phrases. Check students can hear the difference between *work* /wɜːk/ and *walk* /wɔːk/, and also highlight the pronunciation of *pressure* /ˈpreʃə/. Note that only the main stress in phrases is shown in vocabulary boxes and the Language Summaries.

> 2 have time to relax 3 work long hours 4 work overtime 5 be a workaholic 6 meet deadlines
> 7 take time off work 8 be under pressure at work
> 9 spend a lot of time at work 10 have good working conditions

b) Students do the exercise on their own.

c) Students do the exercise in pairs. Encourage students to say more about each person if possible (their relationship to the person, their jobs, where they work, etc.).

Each pair decides which of the people they talked about works the hardest. Ask students to tell the class about this person.

> **── EXTRA IDEA ●●●**
> • Students work in pairs and take turns to test each other on the collocations. One student says a word/phrase, for example *work home*, and his/her partner says the whole collocation, for example *take work home*.

Listening and Grammar

2 a) Focus students on the photo and the cartoon, and use the title of the book to pre-teach *praise* /preɪz/ (when you say positive things about someone or something).

Discuss with the class what they think the book is about and what is happening in the cartoon. Don't tell the class the answers to these questions yet.

b) Tell students they are going to listen to a radio programme where two journalists, Kim and Rob, are discussing Carl Honoré's book *In Praise of Slow*.

R2.1 Play the recording (SB p143). Students listen and check their answers to the questions in **2a)**. Check answers with the class.

In Praise of Slow tells us that we are living too fast and should all slow down. The cartoon on SB p12 shows one of the members of the group in Austria called The Society for the Deceleration of Time, which tries to stop people hurrying. If members of the society think a person is walking too fast without a good reason, that person has to walk behind a puppet tortoise for 50 metres.

3 a) Students do the exercise in pairs. Remind students that they must use one country twice.

b) **R2.2** Play the recording of the second part of the radio programme (SB p143). Students listen and check their answers to **3a)**.

Check answers with the class.

> 1 France
> 2 Germany
> 3 the UK
> 4 the UK
> 5 the USA
> 6 Japan

4 a) **R2.2** Give students time to read sentences 1–9, then play the recording again. Students listen and fill in the gaps with one or two words.

Students check answers in pairs. Check answers with the class.

> 2 thirty-five
> 3 3 p.m.
> 4 our families
> 5 ideas
> 6 sleep
> 7 four
> 8 work home
> 9 travelling

b) Students discuss Carl Honoré's ideas in groups or with the whole class. You can begin by asking students if they think they need to slow down or not, giving reasons for their answers.

Help with Grammar Modal verbs (1); *be able to, be allowed to, be supposed to*

5 **a–d)** Students do the exercises on their own or in pairs, then check their answers in **G2.1** SB p117. Check answers with the class.

- **a)** We use *be supposed to* to say a person is expected to do something: *In the UK people are supposed to have a break every four hours.*
- We use *can* and *be able to* to talk about ability or possibility: *People can get their best ideas when they're doing nothing. We're able to continue working when we're travelling.*
- We use *must* and *have to* to say something is necessary: *I really must take more time off work. Lots of people have to take work home.*
- We use *should* and *ought to* to give advice: *No one should work more than 35 hours a week. We ought to spend more time relaxing with our families.*
- We use *be allowed to* and *can* to say we have permission to do something: *Some French employees are allowed to begin their weekend at 3 p.m. on Thursday. In some American companies, employees can sleep whenever they want.*
- Highlight that *can, must, have to, should* and *ought to* are modal verbs.
- You can teach the students how to say *ought to* /ˈɔːtə/ at this stage.

- **b)** 1 We use the infinitive (*he must take,* etc.). 2 *be allowed to, ought to, to be supposed to, have to, be able to.* 3 and 4 See the table and bullet points in **G2.1** SB p117.

- **c)** We use *don't have to* to say something isn't necessary: *You don't have to wear a suit to work, but you can if you want to.*
- We use *mustn't* to say something is not allowed: *You mustn't send personal emails from the office. You can only send work emails.*
- Remind students that *must* and *have to* are very similar in meaning in their positive forms.
- Check students understand all the **TIPS!** in **G2.1** SB p117.

6 **a)** Remind students of Kim and Rob from the radio programme. Ask what jobs they do (they're journalists). Students do the exercise on their own, then check answers in pairs.

b) **R2.3** Play the recording. Students listen and check their answers. Check answers with the class. Ask the class who has the best working conditions (Kim).

> 2 must 3 Are you able to 4 I'm supposed to
> 5 don't have to 6 Are you allowed to 7 can
> 8 have to 9 ought to 10 have to 11 mustn't

c) **R2.4** **P** Play the recording, pausing after each sentence. Students listen and repeat. Check students pronounce *do you* /dʒə/, *have to* /ˈhæftə/, *ought to* /ˈɔːtə/ and *mustn't* /ˈmʌsnt/ correctly.

Get ready … Get it right!

7 Put students into groups of three or four. Tell each group that they run a company with good working conditions.

Each group makes notes on the ideas listed. Tell students that they must all make notes on their company, as they will each have to describe it to other students.

While students are working, monitor and help with ideas and language. Make sure students use the language from **5** in their discussions.

> **EXTRA IDEA**
> - If you think your students will have problems thinking of ideas, you can allocate each group a company, for example a fast food restaurant, a website design company, an organic café, a clothes shop, a travel agent's, a language school, a small hotel, etc.

8 **a)** Reorganise the class so that students from different groups are working together. Students take turns to describe their companies. Encourage students to ask questions to find out more information about each company.

Each group then decides which is the best company to work for.

b) Each group tells the class which company they think is the best to work for, giving reasons for their answers. Finally, ask the class to vote for the most popular company in the class.

> **EXTRA IDEA**
> - Ask each group to write a profile of their company, using the language from the lesson. Students can then read all the groups' profiles and decide which company they think is the best to work for.

> **EXTRA PRACTICE AND HOMEWORK**
> **Ph** **Class Activity** 2A World rules p136 (Instructions p119)
> **2 Review** Exercises 1 and 2 SB p19
> **CD-ROM** Lesson 2A
> **Workbook** Lesson 2A p10

2B Ready, steady, eat

Vocabulary in the kitchen
Grammar Present Continuous and Present Simple
Review modal verbs

QUICK REVIEW ●●●

This activity reviews modal verbs and *be supposed to*. Students do the first part of the activity on their own. Put students into pairs. Students tell their partners about the things they have to do, ought to do, etc. next week and then decide who is going to have the busiest week. Ask students to share interesting ideas with the class.

Vocabulary In the kitchen

1 Check students understand *main meal* (your biggest meal of the day). Students discuss the questions in groups. Ask each group to tell the class about some of the things they discussed.

2 **a)** Focus students on groups 1–3 below the vocabulary box and check they understand the examples.

Students do the exercise on their own or in pairs, then check their answers in **V2.2** SB p116. Check answers with the class.

Point out that *broccoli* is an uncountable noun and that *beans* can also refer to green beans, which are long and thin. Highlight that we can say *a microwave* or *a microwave oven*.

Also check students understand the difference between *roast* and *bake*, both of which you do in an oven, and point out that *roast* can also be an adjective (*roast chicken*, etc.). You can also teach students that you *stir fry* food in a wok.

Model and drill the words. Highlight the pronunciation of *broccoli* /'brɒkəli/, *lamb* /læm/, *oven* /'ʌvən/, *aubergine* /'əʊbəʒiːn/, *courgettes* /kɔː'ʒets/ and *zucchinis* /zuːkiːnɪz/.

---

1 a red/green pepper, peas, beef, lamb, carrots, an aubergine [US: an eggplant] beans, courgettes [US: zucchinis] **2** a freezer, a cooker, a grill, an oven, a microwave, a saucepan, a frying pan, a wok, a blender, a toaster, a rubbish bin **3** roast, bake, grill, fry, heat up, microwave, steam

---

EXTRA IDEAS

- Do this as a Know, Might Know, Don't Know activity (p21).
- To review this vocabulary after a break or at the beginning of the next class, organise the team activity Hot Seats (p21).

---

b) Students do the exercise in pairs. Ask students to share any interesting or unusual answers with the class.

Reading and Grammar

3 **a)** Focus students on the cartoon of Linda (the writer of the article) and her mother. Ask students to guess what the article is about. Use the cartoon to teach *ready meals*.

b) Students do the exercise on their own. You can set a time limit of two minutes to encourage students to read for gist.

Check answers with the class.

1c)
2b)
3d)
4a)

---

4 **a)** Students do the exercise on their own. Check answers with the class.

1F (She never cooks anything.)
2T
3F (Health advisers say that we shouldn't eat ready meals too often.)
4F (The Spanish still cook their own meals).
5T

---

b) Students discuss the questions in groups. Ask each group to share interesting answers with the class.

Help with Grammar
Present Continuous and Present Simple

5 **a)–d)** Focus students on the verb forms in **bold** in the article and the cartoon.

Students do the exercises on their own or in pairs, then check answers in SB p118. Check answers with the class.

- **a) Present Continuous a)** 'm making **b)** 'm writing; 's doing **c)** is growing; 're becoming
- **Present Simple a)** cooks; spend **b)** live; buy **c)** believe; need
- Point out that we often use *still* with the Present Simple and Present Continuous to mean something that started in the past and continues to the present: *My mother **still** cooks a full three-course meal every evening. I'm still waiting to hear about the job.*

- **b) Activities** *talk, spend, eat, learn, buy, cook, take.* **States** *seem, agree, taste, prefer, own, understand, want, remember, contain.* We don't usually use state verbs in the Present Continuous (or other continuous verb forms).
- Focus students on the table of common state verbs in **G2.2** SB p118. Check the meaning of any new words. Encourage students to learn the verbs in the table.

- Point out that we often use *can* with verbs that describe the senses to talk about what is happening now: *I can hear a noise outside. I can't see anything.*
- Also highlight that some verbs can be both activity verbs and state verbs: *I'm having dinner at the moment* (activity). *They have two dogs* (state). *What are you thinking about?* (activity). *I think football is boring* (state).

- **c) Present Continuous** We make positive and negative sentences with: subject + *be* + (*not*) + verb+*ing*. We make questions with: (question word) + *am/are/is* + subject + verb+*ing*.
- **Present Simple** For *I/you/we/they*, the positive is the same as the infinitive. For *he/she/it*, we add *-s* or *-es* to the infinitive: *he lives*; *she goes*; *it works*. We make the Present Simple negative with: subject + *don't/doesn't* + infinitive. We make Present Simple questions with: (question word) + *do/does* + subject + infinitive.

6 R2.5 **P** Play the recording (SB p143). Students listen and practise. Check students are copying the sentence stress correctly.

7 a) Give students one minute to read paragraphs 1 and 2. Students decide who is speaking in each paragraph. Check answers with the class.

> 1 Linda 2 her mother

b) Students do the exercise on their own, then check answers in pairs. Encourage students to say why they chose the Present Simple or Present Continuous in each case. Check answers with the class.

> 1 'm/am cooking 2 eat 3 prefer 4 'm/am learning 5 watch
> 6 think 7 's/is getting 8 don't understand 9 's/is putting
> 10 never eats 11 doesn't know 12 is .... studying

8 a) Pre-teach *organic food* (food grown or produced without chemical fertilisers or pesticides). Students do the exercise on their own.

b) Put students into groups of three or four. Students compare sentences to find out how many are the same. Encourage students to discuss any differences. Ask students to share interesting ideas with the class.

Get ready … Get it right!

9 Students do the exercise on their own. Check answers with the class.

> 2 Do you usually eat 3 Do you cook 4 Are you trying
> 5 Do you ever use 6 Do you want 7 Are you looking
> 8 Are you doing

10 a) Students move around the room and ask other students their questions, or ask as many people as they can sitting near them. When they find a student who answers *yes*, they write the person's name next to the question.
Students then ask two follow–up questions to find out more information. Students should try and find a different person who answers *yes* for each question.

b) Students do the activity in groups. Finally, ask each group to share one or two interesting things they found out about other students with the class.

EXTRA PRACTICE AND HOMEWORK

Ph **Vocabulary Plus** 2 Food and drink p178 (Instructions p173)
Ph **Class Activity** 2B Opening night p137 (Instructions p119)
2 Review Exercises 3 and 4 SB p19
CD-ROM Lesson 2B
Workbook Lesson 2B p11

2C It's a nightmare

QUICK REVIEW ●●●

This activity reviews food and ways of cooking. Students work on their own and make a list of six food items. Focus students on the examples, then put students into pairs. Students take turns to describe their food items and the ways of cooking. Their partner guesses what the food items are.

Vocabulary and Listening

1 Students work on their own and tick the words/phrases they know, then check any new words/phrases in V2.3 SB p116.

Vocabulary sleep; gradable and strong adjectives; adverbs
Skills Listening: A sleep scientist; Reading: I just can't sleep!
Help with Listening weak forms (1)
Review Present Simple and Present Continuous

Check any new words with the class. Point out that *dream* can be a noun and a verb. Compare *sleep*, which can also be a noun or verb, with the adjective *asleep*. Highlight the collocations *be fast asleep*, *be wide awake* and *be a light/ heavy sleeper*. Also tell students that we can *wake up* or *wake someone up*: *Can you wake me up at eight?*
Model and drill the words/phrases.

2 a) Students do the exercise on their own.

b) Students do the activity in groups, asking follow-up questions where appropriate. Ask each group to tell the class one or two interesting things they have found out.

— EXTRA IDEA —
• Do **2** as a Words Connected to Me activity (p22).

3 a) Focus students on the cartoons and ask which man has sleep problems (the man in the first cartoon). Use the cartoons to teach *an alarm clock* and *go off*: *My alarm clock goes off at half past seven every morning.*

Students do the exercise in pairs. Don't check answers at this stage.

b) R2.6 Tell students they are going to listen to an interview with a sleep scientist. Play the recording (SB p144). Students listen and check their answers to **3a)**. Students check their answers in the same pairs. Check answers with the class.

> 1 more 2 30% 3 one and a half hours 4 more
> 5 the same amount of 6 a few hours

c) Give students time to read questions 1–5, then play the recording again. Students listen and answer the questions before checking answers in pairs.

Check answers with the class. Ask students if they were surprised by any of the information in the interview.

> 1 10%. 2 People went to sleep when it got dark and got up when it got light. 3 Older people. 4 They organise information they've collected during the day. 5 A place where you can go for a quick nap during the day.

Help with Listening Weak forms (1)

• This Help with Listening section focuses on common weak forms and highlights the relationship between weak forms and sentence stress.

4 a) Focus students on the introductory bullet point and remind students of the schwa /ə/ sound.

R2.7 Play the recording. Students listen and notice the difference between the strong and weak forms of these words. Ask students if we usually say these words in their strong or weak forms (their weak forms). Also highlight the schwa sound in the weak forms.

You can point out that we usually use these words in their strong forms when they are at the end of a sentence or question: *Yes, I do* /duː/. *What are you looking for* /fɔː/? *I don't think I can* /kæn/, etc.

b) Students do the activity on their own before checking answers in pairs. Check answers with the class.

> 1 can 2 you 3 at; for; of; to 4 and

c) Focus students on the sentences from the beginning of the interview. Students work on their own or in pairs and circle the words they think they will hear as weak forms. Highlight the examples before they begin.

While students are working, write the sentences on the board.

d) R2.6 Play the beginning of the recording again. Students listen and check their answers. Elicit students' answers and circle the weak forms on the board. Ask students if weak forms are ever stressed (they aren't).

> (Do) people (you) know have problems sleeping (at) night? Or maybe (you) just can't get (to) sleep yourself. (For) many people, insomnia is a way (of) life (and) not being able (to) get (to) sleep isn't just annoying – it (can) also be very dangerous.

e) Students turn to R2.6, SB p144. Play the whole recording again. Students listen and notice the weak forms and sentence stress.

— EXTRA IDEA —
• Before they do **4e)**, ask students to decide which words in the sentences on the board are stressed. Students can check their answers in R2.6, SB p144.

Reading and Vocabulary

5 a) Students do the activity in groups. Ask each group to tell the class their most unusual method of getting to sleep.

b) Focus students on the article and photo on SB p17. Ask students what Emma's problem is (she has insomnia). Pre-teach *hypnosis* /hɪpˈnəʊsɪs/, *sleeping pills* and *become addicted to something*, and check students remember *meditation*.

Students read the article and answer the questions. Check answers with the class.

> She has insomnia because she worries about work all the time. To try and get a good night's sleep she has tried herbal teas, yoga, meditation and going to the gym.

6 a) Students do the exercise on their own, then check answers in pairs. Check answers with the class.

> 1 Two hours (from 11 p.m. to 1 a.m.) 2 She sleeps for a short time, then wakes up and can't get back to sleep. 3 She works really long hours and has to do a lot of travelling. 4 She borrowed a lot of money when she was a student and still owes £15,000. 4 Hypnosis, because it's very expensive; sleeping pills, because she is terrified of becoming addicted to them.

b) Students discuss their advice for Emma in pairs. Remind students of the ways of giving advice from lesson 2A, *She should ...* and *She ought to ...*, before they begin.

Ask students to share some of their advice for Emma with the class.

Help with Vocabulary Gradable and strong adjectives; adverbs

 7 **a)–e)** Students do the exercises on their own or in pairs, then check their answers in **V2.4** SB p117.

Check answers with the class.

Alternatively, students can do each exercise in turn and check answers with you after each exercise.

- **a)** tired → shattered; bad → terrible, awful; good → fantastic; big → huge; difficult → impossible; frightened → terrified; surprised → amazed
- Check students understand that strong adjectives already include the idea of *very*, for example *exhausted* means *very tired*.
- Model and drill the words, paying particular attention to the pronunciation of *exhausted* /ɪgˈzɔːstɪd/, *awful* /ˈɔːfəl/ and *huge* /hjuːdʒ/.

- **b)** small → tiny; cold → freezing; hot → boiling; beautiful → gorgeous; big → enormous; interested → fascinated; angry → furious; happy → delighted; dirty → filthy
- Model and drill the words, paying particular attention to the pronunciation of *delicious* /dɪˈlɪʃəs/, *tiny* /taɪniː/, *gorgeous* /ˈgɔːdʒəs/, *furious* /ˈfjʊəriəs/ and *filthy* /ˈfɪlθiː/.
- Point out that *huge* and *enormous* both mean 'very big'.

- **c)** We use *very*, *incredibly*, *extremely* and *fairly* with gradable adjectives. We use *absolutely* with strong adjectives. We use *really* with both types of adjective.
- Point out that *incredibly* and *extremely* are stronger than *very*. *Fairly* and *rather* are less strong than *very*.
- Remind students that we can also use *quite* with gradable adjectives: *It was quite good*.

- **d)** These strong adjectives all mean 'very good': *amazing*, *brilliant*, *excellent*, *fabulous*, *fantastic*, *incredible*, *marvellous*, *superb*, *terrific*, *wonderful*.
- Drill these words with the class, highlighting the stress.
- Also point out the difference between *terrible* (very bad), *terrified* (very frightened) and *terrific* (very good).

--- EXTRA IDEA ---
- Students work in pairs and take turns to test each other on the gradable and strong adjectives. One student says the gradable adjective, for example *small*, and his/her partner says the strong adjective, for example *tiny*.

 8 **a)** Students do the exercise on their own. Encourage students to use different adverbs from **7c)** in each sentence if possible. While they are working, monitor and check their sentences for accuracy.

b) Put students into new pairs. Students take turns to say their sentences. Encourage students to ask questions about each sentence if possible.

Ask students to share interesting sentences with the class.

9 **a)** Put students into groups of four and give each group a letter (A, B, etc.). Each group writes questions for a sleep survey, as in the example. Encourage students to use the words/phrases in **1** in their questions. Each group should write at least six questions.

Make sure all the students write the questions as they will be working separately in **9b)**.

While students are working, monitor and check their questions for accuracy.

--- EXTRA IDEA ---
- ✎ Write the following prompts on the board to help students think of questions for their sleep surveys: *How often do you ... ?*; *What time do/did you ... ?*; *When did you last ... ?*; *Do you usually/ever ... ?*; *Are you a ... ?*; *Is it easy/difficult for you to ... ?*; *Does anyone in your family ... ?*

b) Reorganise the class so that students are sitting with students from other groups. Students take turns to ask and answer their questions. Make sure all the students write the answers.

Alternatively, students can move around the room and ask each other questions. Students should check if the other person has answered his/her group's sleep survey by saying the letter of his/her group before asking their questions.

c) Students work in the same groups as in **9a)**. Students compare their answers and produce a set of results for their survey.

d) Finally, ask students to tell the class some of the things they found out about other students.

--- EXTRA IDEA ---
- For homework, students write a report about their class based on the results of their sleep survey. These reports can be displayed around the room for other students to read.

--- EXTRA PRACTICE AND HOMEWORK ---
Ph **Class Activity** 2C The absolutely amazing game! p139 (Instructions p120)
2 Review Exercise 5 SB p19
CD-ROM Lesson 2C
Workbook Lesson 2C p13

2D What's the matter?

Real World showing concern, giving and responding to advice
Help with Listening intonation (1): showing concern
Review gradable and strong adjectives; Present Simple; Present Continuous

QUICK REVIEW ●●●
This activity reviews gradable and strong adjectives. Students work on their own and write all the strong adjectives they know. Set a time limit of two minutes. Students compare lists in pairs, then decide what the gradable adjective is for each strong adjective on their lists. Students think of one person, place or thing for each strong adjective. Ask each pair to share one or two of their ideas with the class.

1 Check students understand *advice column* (part of a magazine where someone gives advice to people who write in). Also remind students that *advice* is an uncountable noun: we say *some advice* not ~~an advice~~.

You can also teach students that when we want to say 'one advice', we say *a piece of advice*: *Let me give you a piece of advice.*

Students discuss the questions in pairs. Ask students to share interesting answers with the class.

2 a) Focus students on photos A–C. Discuss what students think the people are talking about in each photo with the class. Don't tell students if they are right or wrong at this stage.

b) R2.8 Tell students they are going to hear three conversations. Play the recording (SB p144). Students listen and match conversations 1–3 to photos A–C. Check answers with the class.

You can ask who is in each picture (A: Lorna; B: Lorna and her friend, Diane; C: Andy and his colleague, Robin).

> 1B 2C 3A

3 a) Students do the exercise in pairs. Don't check the answers yet.

b) R2.8 Play the recording again. Students listen and check their answers to **3a)**. Students can then check answers with their partner. Check answers with the class.

> 1F (She thinks her husband works too hard.) 2T 3F (He thinks she is spending too much on things for the house and their children.) 4T 5F (She thinks Lorna and Andy both need a night off.) 6T

Real World Showing concern, giving and responding to advice

4 a)–d) Check students understand *showing concern* (you show concern when you are worried about someone or something). Students do the exercises on their own, then check their answers in RW2.1 SB p118. Check answers with the class.

- **a)** a) showing concern b) giving advice
  c) responding to advice
- Check students understand when to use *What a shame* (when something bad has happened and we want to be sympathetic). Teach *What a pity* as an alternative.
- Point out that *I'd take her out ... = I would take her out ... .*

- **b)** After *Have you tried ...* we use verb+*ing*: *Have you tried **talking** to him about it?*
- After *should ...* , *Why don't you ...* , *I'd* (= I would) ... and *ought to ...* we use the infinitive: *Well, maybe you should **talk** to him again.*

- **c)** 1 What **should I** do? 2 What do you think **I should** do?
- Point out that we use these sentences to ask for advice and highlight the word order of *should* and *I* in each sentence.
- Note that students study indirect questions with *do you think* in lesson 7D.

EXTRA IDEA
- R2.8 Ask students to turn to R2.8, SB p144. Play the recording again. Students listen, read and underline all the phrases for showing concern, giving and responding to advice.

Help with Listening
Intonation (1): showing concern

- This Help with Listening section focuses on the natural intonation patterns we use when we show concern.

5 R2.9 Play the recording (SB p144). Students listen and circle the sentence which shows concern. Play the recording again if necessary. Check answers with the class.

Use the examples on the recording to point out that we often use a large voice range when we are showing concern. If our voices are flat, people might think we're bored.

> 2a) 3b) 4b) 5a) 6a)

6 R2.10 P Play the recording. Students listen and repeat. Check they are copying the polite intonation and sentence stress correctly. Students can look at the phrases in RW2.1 SB p118 while they practise.

7 **a)** Student do the exercise on their own.

b) Students check their answers in pairs. Check answers with the class.

> 1
> A I've got a bit of a problem.
> B **Oh**, dear. What's **the** matter?
> A My girlfriend won't talk to me. What **should** I do?
> B Maybe **you** ought **to** write her a letter.
> A Well, **it's** worth **a** try, I guess.
> B And I**'d** send her some flowers.
> A Yes, **that's a** good idea. Thanks a lot.
>
> 2
> A Look at this plant. It's dying, isn't it?
> B Yes, I see what **you** mean.
> A What **do you** think I **should** do?
> B **Have you tried giving** it more water?
> A Yes, **I've tried** that, but it didn't work.
> B Well, why **don't you** put it in a bigger pot?
> A Yes, I **might** try that. Thanks.

c) Students practise the conversations in pairs. Encourage students to memorise the conversations and then practise them without looking at their books.

Ask a few pairs to practise the conversations for the whole class.

> — EXTRA IDEA —
> • Do this activity as a Dialogue Build (p21).

 8 Put students into groups of three, student A, student B and student C. Student As turn to SB p102, student Bs turn to SB p107 and student Cs turn to p112. If you have one or two extra students, ask them to work in pairs with student Bs.

a) Students do the exercise on their own.

b) Focus students on the speech bubbles to show how to start the conversation. Students work in their groups and take turns to explain their problems. Their partners show concern and give advice. Students decide which piece of advice is the best.

While they are working, monitor and correct any mistakes you hear. Encourage students to use natural intonation when showing concern.

c) Finally, students tell the class the best piece of advice they received for each problem.

 Ask students to turn to p100 and look at *You Can't Hurry Love*. This song was first recorded by the American group The Supremes in 1966. The song was also recorded by Phil Collins in 1982.

 1 **a)** Students do the activity on their own. If you think your students will have difficulty with this, make a list of ten famous love songs and ask students to decide which they like, which they don't like and why.

b) Students compare songs in groups, then decide which they think is the best and worst song. Compare answers with the class. You can ask the class to vote on the best (and worst!) love song.

 2 **a)** R2.11 Give students time to read the song, then play the recording. Students listen and choose the correct words/phrases. Play the recording again if necessary.

b) Students check answers in pairs. Play the recording again, pausing after each line for students to check answers. Check answers with the class.

> 2 need 3 can't 4 have to 5 easy 6 game 7 have to
> 8 long 9 must 10 find 11 thing 12 almost 13 can
> 14 break 15 bear 16 call 17 go on 18 words 19 wait
> 20 long 21 waiting 22 talk 23 arms 24 waiting

 3 Remind students what *rhyme* means. Students do the exercise in pairs. Check answers with the class.

> **Possible answers** on/gone; take/break; alone/own; waiting/anticipating; night/tight

> — EXTRA PRACTICE AND HOMEWORK —
> **2 Review** SB p19
> **CD-ROM** Lesson 2D
> **Workbook** Lesson 2D p14
> **Workbook** Reading and Writing Portfolio 2 p66
> **Progress Test 2** p202

2 Review

See p30 for ideas on how to use this section.

> **1a)** 1 meet 2 'm/am 3 work 4 work 5 take 6 'm/am
> 7 take
>
> **4a)** 1 Do ... know; 's/is working 2 Are ... studying
> 3 Do ... think; are getting 4 Do ... arrive; go
> 5 Are ... reading 6 Do ... think; live/are living

Progress Portfolio

See p30 for ideas on how to use this section.

3 The tourist trade

3A Your holiday, my job

QUICK REVIEW ●●●

This activity reviews ways of giving advice. Students write three problems on their own. Put students into pairs. Students take turns to tell their partners the problems and give advice. Encourage students to show concern when hearing about their partner's problems. You can ask students to share one or two problems with the class.

Vocabulary Phrasal verbs (1): travel

 a) Check students remember *souvenirs* /suːvən'ɪəz/. Students do the exercise in pairs. Encourage students to guess the meaning of all the phrasal verbs in **bold** before they check in V3.1 SB p119.

Check students understand the meaning of the phrasal verbs by asking questions using each verb, for example *What's the best way to get around this city?*, etc.

Point out that we can also say *check in* and *check out* to mean *check into/out of a hotel*. Highlight that we say *get back home*, not ~~get (back) to/from home~~ and that we often use a verb+ing form after *look forward to*: *I'm looking forward to seeing you*. Note that the grammar of phrasal verbs is taught in lesson 10C. We suggest you don't begin teaching the position of objects in phrasal verbs at this stage.

Model and drill the phrasal verbs. Note that only the main stress in words/phrases is shown in vocabulary boxes and the Language Summaries.

b) Use the speech bubbles to remind students of short answers and follow-up questions. Students do the activity in new pairs. Ask students to share interesting information with the class.

Listening and Grammar

 a) Focus students on the photos. Use Sam's photo to teach *rainforest guide*. Check students know Costa Rica is a country in Central America and Cornwall is a county in the UK that is very popular with tourists. Ask students which of these jobs they would prefer to do and why. Pre-teach *idiot* and *guy* (informal for *man*).

R3.1 Give students time to read questions 1 and 2, then play the recording (SB p144). Students listen and answer the questions. Check answers with the class.

1 Sam likes his job, but Marcia doesn't. 2 Sam has to deal with some very difficult people and has to put up with some idiots. Marcia thinks managing a hotel is quite stressful and doesn't like people complaining all the time. She can't stand it when people steal things. Also either she or her husband has to be at the hotel and it's very hard to get a holiday together.

Vocabulary phrasal verbs (1): travel
Grammar Present Perfect Simple: experience, unfinished past and recent events
Help with Listening Present Perfect Simple or Past Simple
Review Past Simple

b) Students do the exercise in pairs.

c) Play the recording again. Students listen and check their answers. Check answers with the class.

> **SAM** 1e) 2a) 3d) 4g)
> **MARCIA** 5c) 6f) 7h) 8b)

EXTRA IDEA

- R3.1 Students turn to R3.1 on SB p144. Play the recording again. Students listen and underline all the phrasal verbs.

Help with Grammar Present Perfect Simple

 a)–f) Students do the exercises on their own or in pairs, then check their answers in G3.1 SB p120. Check answers with the class.

Alternatively, students can do each exercise in turn and check answers with you after each one.

- **a)** We use the Present Perfect Simple to talk about experiences in our life up to now, but we don't say when they happened. To give more information about an experience we use the Past Simple, as shown in sentences a) and b) in **2b)**.
- We use the Past Simple to say when something happened, as shown in sentences c) and d).
- We use the Present Perfect Simple for something that started in the past and continues in the present, as shown in sentences e) and f).
- We use the Present Perfect Simple for something that happened a short time ago, but we don't say exactly when, as shown in sentences g) and h).
- **b)** We make the Present Perfect Simple positive and negative with:
  I/you/we/they + *'ve* (= have)/*haven't* + past participle
  he/she/it + *'s* (= has)/*hasn't* + past participle.
- We make Present Perfect Simple questions with: (question word) + *have/has* + subject + past participle: *How long have I/you/we/they lived here? Has he/she/it been there before?*
- **c)** We use *for* with a period of time (how long): *I've lived in this country for three years.*

- We use *since* with a point in time (when something started): *My husband and I have had this place since 2001.*
- *Go* has two past participles, *been* and *gone*. We use *been* to mean 'go and come back': *I've just been to San Isidro to pick up a guest* (he's back at the place he started from now). We use *gone* to mean 'go, but not come back yet': *My husband's gone to see some friends off* (he's not back yet).
- Point out that we don't use *during* with the Present Perfect Simple: *I've been here for six months.* not ~~I've been here during six months.~~

- **d)** We can use these words/phrases with the Present Perfect Simple: *never, ever, recently, lately, before, this week, just, yet, already.*
- We must use the Past Simple with phrases that say a definite time (*ago, in 1997, last week, at 10 o'clock*, etc.).
- Point out that we often use the Present Perfect Simple with *just* to say something happened a short time ago: *I've just been to San Isidro.*
- For more information on these adverbs and time phrases, see **G3.1** SB p120.

- **e)** We use the Present Perfect Simple after *this is the first time, this is the second time*, etc., not the Present Simple: *This is the first time we've been here.* not ~~This is the first time we are here.~~
- Point out that we also use the Present Perfect Simple with *this morning, afternoon*, etc. if it is still that time of day and that we use the Present Perfect Simple with *this week/month/year.*

4 **R3.2** **P** Play the recording (SB p145). Students listen and practise. Encourage students to copy the sentence stress and the contractions (*I've, We've*, etc.). Play the recording again if necessary.

Help with Listening Present Perfect Simple or Past Simple

- This Help with Listening section focuses on how we say the Present Perfect Simple and the Past Simple, and helps students to hear the difference between these two verb forms.

5 **a)** **R3.3** Play the recording. Students listen and notice the difference between the pairs of phrases. Highlight the extra sound of the auxiliary (*'ve* and *'s*) in each Present Perfect Simple phrase.

b) **R3.4** Play the recording (SB p145). Students listen and decide if the verbs are in the Present Perfect Simple or the Past Simple. Play the recording again, pausing after each sentence to check students' answers.

> 1 Past Simple 2 Present Perfect Simple
> 3 Present Perfect Simple 4 Past Simple
> 5 Present Perfect Simple 6 Past Simple

6 **a)** Focus students on the photo of Kara and Brian and their restaurant. Tell students they are British, but they run a restaurant in Greece.

Students do the exercise on their own.

b) Students compare answers in pairs and discuss why they have chosen each answer.

c) **R3.5** Play the recording. Students listen and check. Play the recording again if necessary, pausing where appropriate to check answers with the class.

> **2** decided (we know when this happened) **3** 've/have lived (started in the past and continues in the present) **4** 've/have just opened (happened a short time ago) **5** 've/have been (experience) **6** was (we know when this happened) **7** haven't had (started in the past and continues in the present) **8** 've/have visited (it is still the same year) **9** 's/has just gone (happened a short time ago)

7 Put students into pairs, student A and student B. Student As turn to SB p102 and student Bs turn to SB p107.

a) Focus students on the example and highlight that all the questions have *you* as the subject. Students do the exercise on their own.

If necessary, check the verb forms only (not the questions) with the class.

> **Student A** **2** Have you spoken **3** Did you rent **4** Have you decided **5** have you known **6** Did you go away **7** Have you … had **8** you've studied
>
> **Student B** **2** Have you seen **3** Have you been on **4** Did you do **5** have you had **6** Did you get **7** Have you looked **8** you've studied

b) Students work with their partner and take turns to ask and answer the questions. Student A asks the first question. Encourage students to ask follow-up questions if possible.

While students are working, monitor and correct any mistakes you hear.

Ask students to share any interesting or surprising answers with the class.

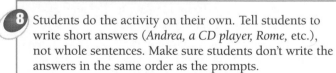

Get ready … Get it right!

8 Students do the activity on their own. Tell students to write short answers (*Andrea, a CD player, Rome*, etc.), not whole sentences. Make sure students don't write the answers in the same order as the prompts.

9 **a)** Students work in pairs and swap papers. Students take turns to ask questions about the information on their partner's papers (*Have you know Andrea for most of your life? Did you get a CD player for your last birthday? Have you been to Rome this year?*, etc.).

Encourage students to ask follow-up questions and continue each conversation for 30 seconds.

b) Finally, ask students to tell the class two interesting things they found out about their partner.

 EXTRA IDEA

- To demonstrate the Get ready … Get it right! activity, write your own answers to the prompts in **8** on the board. Before doing **9a)**, elicit questions from students for each of the prompts you wrote on the board.

EXTRA PRACTICE AND HOMEWORK

3 Review Exercises 1 and 2 SB p27
CD-ROM Lesson 3A
Workbook Lesson 3A p15

3B Lonely Planet

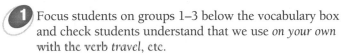

QUICK REVIEW ●●●

This activity reviews Present Perfect Simple questions with *Have you ever … ?*. Students do the activity in pairs.
 If you think your students will have trouble thinking of questions, write these prompts on the board: *go, do, eat, try, meet, study, see, visit, play, win*. Ask students to share interesting answers with the class.

Vocabulary phrases with *travel*, *get* and *go on*
Grammar Present Perfect Continuous and Present Perfect Simple
Review state and activity verbs; *for* and *since*

b) Students tick the sentences in **2a)** that are true for them.

c) Students compare sentences in pairs. Encourage students to ask follow-up questions if possible.

Vocabulary Phrases with *travel*, *get* and *go on*

1 Focus students on groups 1–3 below the vocabulary box and check students understand that we use *on your own* with the verb *travel*, etc.

Students do the activity in pairs, then check their answers in V3.2 SB p119. Check answers with the class (see V3.2 SB p119).

Check students understand all the new phrases with *travel*, *get* and *go on*. Point out that *a journey* refers to travelling in one direction (for example, from London to Paris), while *a trip* includes the return journey (you go to Paris and then come back to London).

Check students remember that *travel* is usually a verb. When we want to use a noun, we usually use *a trip* or *a journey*: *How was your trip/journey?*

Point out that we *get into/out of* a car or a taxi, and *get on/off* public transport (buses, planes, trains, boats, etc.) and bikes/motorbikes. Highlight that we say *get a taxi home* not ~~get a taxi to home~~. Also check students understand *by* in *get here by 10.30* (= 10.30 or earlier).

Model and drill the phrases. Pay particular attention to the pronunciation of *tour* /tɔː/, *journey* /ˈdʒɜːni/, *cruise* /kruːz/, *separately* /ˈseprətli/ and *package* /ˈpækɪdʒ/. Point out the stress on *indepèndently*.

2 a) Students do the exercise on their own. Remind students to use the correct form of the verb in each sentence. Check answers with the class.

2 get 3 went on 4 've/have … been on 5 get
6 going on/to go on 7 travel

Reading and Grammar

3 Check students understand *guidebook*, *advantages* /ədˈvɑːntɪdʒɪz/ and *disadvantages* /ˌdɪsədˈvɑːntɪdʒɪz/. Drill these words with the class.

Students discuss the questions in groups. Ask students to share their ideas with the class.

4 a) Focus students on the photos. Ask students who they think Tony and Maureen Wheeler are (the people who started the company, Lonely Planet). Ask the class if anyone has ever used a Lonely Planet guidebook. If so, ask them to tell the class what they thought of it.

b) Pre-teach *publish*, *park bench*, *van* and *best-seller*.
Students do the exercise on their own. Check answers with the class.

A3 B1 C2 D4

c) Students do the exercise on their own. Early finishers can check their answers in pairs. Check answers with the class.
Ask students what they think is the most interesting or surprising thing in the article.

1 English, Spanish, Italian and French.
2 Because everyone they met asked them about their journey from England to Australia.
3 In a Singapore hotel room.
4 Over a million copies.
5 Over 650 guidebooks.
6 It also has a website and a television company.

Help with Grammar Present Perfect Continuous and Present Perfect Simple

 5 a)–f) Students do the exercises on their own or in pairs, then check their answers in **G3.2** SB p121. Check answers with the class.

Alternatively, students can do each exercise in turn and check answers with you after each one.

- **a)** We usually use the **Present Perfect Continuous** to talk about an **activity** that started in the past and continues in the present: *Their company, Lonely Planet, has been publishing guidebooks for 30 years.* Check students understand this use by focusing on sentence 1 and asking: *When did Lonely Planet start publishing travel guides?* (30 years ago.) *Do they still publish them now?* (Yes, they do.)
- We usually use the **Present Perfect Simple** to talk about a **state** that started in the past and continues in the present: *They've been married since 1972.*
- Check students understand the three **TIPS!** below the timelines in **G3.2** SB p121.
- Point out that we often use *for* and *since* with the Present Perfect Continuous: *They've been watching TV for three hours. I've been trying to call you since lunchtime.*

- **b)** We make the positive form of the Present Perfect Continuous with: *I/you/we/they* + *'ve* (= *have*) + *been* + verb+*ing* and *he/she/it* + *'s* (= *has*) + *been* + verb+*ing*.
- We make the negative form of the Present Perfect Continuous with: *I/you/we/they* + *haven't* + *been* + verb+*ing* and *he/she/it* + *hasn't* + *been* + verb+*ing*.

- **c)** We usually use the Present Perfect Continuous to say how long an activity has been happening: *The company has also been running a website for several years.*
- We usually use the Present Perfect Simple to say how many things are finished: *Lonely Planet has published over 650 guidebooks since the company began.*
- Check students understand the two **TIPS!** below the *How long* and *How many* rules in **G3.2** SB p121.

- **d)** We make Present Perfect Continuous questions with: *How long* + *have/has* + subject + *been* + verb+*ing* … .

- **e)** We make Present Perfect Simple questions with: *How many* (+ noun) + *have/has* + subject + past participle … .

6 a) Go through the example with the class. Students do the exercise on their own.

b) Students check their answers in pairs, giving reasons why they chose each verb form. Don't check answers with the class at this stage.

c) **R3.6** Play the recording (SB p145). Students listen and check their answers.

Check answers with the class. Ask students to say why they chose each verb form.

> **2** have … been travelling (activity) **3** 's/has been writing (activity); since **4** 's/has written (number of things finished) **5** haven't been playing (activity); for **6** 've/have known (state); since **7** has … been (state) **8** haven't had (state); for

P Play the recording again. Students listen and practise. Check they copy the sentence stress and the weak forms of *been* /bɪn/, *for* /fə/, *have* /əv/ and *has* /əz/. Play the recording again if necessary.

You can also ask students to turn to R3.6, SB p145. They can then follow the sentence stress and weak forms as they listen and practise.

 7 Put students into two groups, group A and group B. Students in group A turn to SB p102 and students in group B turn to SB p107. Check they are all looking at the correct exercise.

a) Focus students on the photo. Check students know where Mount Kilimanjaro is (in Kenya).

Students work on their own and read about Polly's job.

b) Students work with a partner from the same group and make questions with *How long … ?* or *How many … ?* to complete the text. Focus students on the example before they start.

While students are working, monitor and check their questions for accuracy.

> **Student A 2** How long has she/Polly been living in Africa? **3** How many different places has she visited so far? **4** How long have they been walking? **5** How many elephants has she seen (so far)? **6** How many times has he/Polly's guide/Shola climbed Kilimanjaro this year?
>
> **Student B b)** How long has she/Polly been travelling around Kenya? **c)** How long has she wanted to climb Mount Kilimanjaro/this mountain? **d)** How many kilometres have they travelled today? **e)** How long has Polly's guide/Shola been doing this job? **f)** How long has Polly/she known him/Shola?

c) Reorganise the class so that each student from group A is sitting with a student from group B. Students are not allowed to look at each other's text.

Students take turns to ask and answer their questions. Student A asks the first question. Students fill in the gaps in the text.

Encourage students to give natural short answers at this stage (*For four years. Three.*, etc.).

d) Students compare texts and check their answers. Check answers with the class if necessary.

8 a) Focus the students on the prompts. Draw your own timeline on the board and write a few years or dates when some of these things happened on the line. Alternatively, focus students on the timeline in the Student's Book.

Students work on their own and draw their own timeline. They write a year, month or date on the line for each prompt.

While they are working, monitor and check they are doing the activity correctly.

b) Focus students on the timeline on the board (or in the Student's Book) again. Elicit sentences for each year, month or date on the timeline using the Present Perfect Continuous or the Present Perfect Simple: *I've known Kathy since 1997; I've been living in my flat since 2003/ for ... years. I've had this job since March.*, etc.

Students work on their own and plan what they are going to say about their timeline, using the Present Perfect Continuous or the Present Perfect Simple with *for* or *since*.

9 a) Put students into pairs. Students take turns to tell their partner about their timeline using the language they have prepared in **8b)**. Encourage students to ask follow-up questions when they want more information.

b) Reorganise the class so that students are working in new pairs. Students tell their new partner five things they remember about the person they talked to in **9a)**. Finally, ask students to share any unusual information.

— EXTRA IDEA —
- For homework, ask students to visit the Lonely Planet website and read what it says about their country, town or city.

— EXTRA PRACTICE AND HOMEWORK —

Ph Class Activity 3B The world's greatest traveller p140 (Instructions p120)
3 Review Exercises 3 and 4 SB p27
CD-ROM Lesson 3B
Workbook Lesson 3B p16

3C Call that a holiday?

This activity reviews questions in the Present Perfect Simple and Present Perfect Continuous with *How long ...?*. Elicit the question for the first prompt (*How long have you been coming to this school?*) before organising the class into groups of four. Students do the activity in their groups. Ask each group to share their answers with the class.

Vocabulary word formation (1): suffixes for adjectives and nouns
Skills Listening: Call that a holiday?; Reading: Holiday reviews
Help with Listening linking (1): consonant-vowel links
Review Present Perfect Simple and Present Perfect Continuous; Past Simple

Listening

1 Students discuss the questions in pairs. Ask each pair to share any interesting answers with the class.

2 Focus students on the TOP TV article. Ask students what the name of the programme is (*Call that a holiday?*) and when it is on (Tuesday at 6.45 p.m.).
Pre-teach *organic farm, cosmetic surgery* and *safari*.
Students read about the programme and answer the questions. Students check answers in pairs. Check answers with the class. Discuss question 3 with the class.

> 1 holidays with a difference 2 four 3 Students' answers

3 a) Tell students they are going to listen to part of the TV programme *Call that a holiday?*. Ask students the name of the presenter of the programme (Judith Gardner).

R3.7 Play the recording (SB p145). Students listen and answer the questions. Check answers with the class.

Alan is going on the South African cosmetic surgery and safari holiday. He chose this because he wants a facelift/thinks he needs to do something about his face. **Emily** is going to work on an organic farm in Australia. She chose this because she's bored with going on package holidays every year, wants a different kind of holiday and is interested in organic farming.

b) Give students time to read questions 1–8, then play the recording again. Students listen, tick the true sentences and correct the false ones.

c) Students check answers in pairs. Check answers with the class.

> 1T 2F He's been working in advertising for **more than thirty** years. 3F He's going on a safari **after** the operation. 4T 5T 6F She's flying to Australia **tomorrow morning**. 7F 8T

Help with Listening Linking (1): consonant-vowel links

- This Help with Listening section focuses on consonant-vowel linking and shows students that we often link words together in natural spoken English.

4 a) **R3.7** Play the beginning of the recording again. Students listen and notice the consonant-vowel links that are marked on the example sentences.

Use these examples to show that we usually link words that end in a consonant sound with words that start with a vowel sound.

b) Ask students to turn to R3.7, SB p145. Play the whole recording again. Students listen, read and notice the linking.

Reading and Vocabulary

5 Tell students that Alan and Emily have now been to South Africa and Australia, and they have written reviews of their holidays for the TV programme's website.

Divide the class into two groups, group A and group B. Ask students in group A to cover Emily's review and students in group B to cover Alan's review.

Students in group A read about Alan's holiday and answer questions 1–6. Students in group B read about Emily's holiday and answer the same questions.

Early finishers can check their answers with a student from the same group. Students shouldn't read the other review at this stage.

6 a) Reorganise the class so that each student from group A is working with a student from group B.

Students take turns to ask and answer the questions in **5**. Don't check the answers at this stage.

b) **R3.8** Play the recording. Students listen and read the two reviews, checking their partner's answers to the questions in **5** as they do so.

If necessary, check answers with the class.

ALAN 1 Three weeks. 2 The medical centre had a swimming pool. The jungle guest house was extremely comfortable. 3 First week: he had his operation. Second week: he relaxed by the pool. Third week: he went on safari. 4 The safari. 5 Spending five days inside after his operation. 6 Yes, he would.
EMILY 1 Two weeks. 2 She stayed in a fairly basic farmhouse, which was OK. 3 She worked five hours a day, six days a week and spent all her spare time at the beach. 4 The people she met and eating organic food every day. 5 Doing what the couple who ran the farm asked her to do because she wasn't very strong. 6 Yes, she would.

Help with Vocabulary Word formation (1): suffixes for nouns and adjectives

7 a)–c) Ask students to do exercises a)–c) on their own or in pairs. While they are working, draw the table from **7b)** on the board so that you are ready to check their answers. Make each line of the table big enough for three words. Check answers with the class.

- **a) adjectives/nouns** patient/ patien<u>ce</u>; kind/ kind<u>ness</u>; popular/popular<u>ity</u>
- **nouns/adjectives** danger/danger<u>ous</u>; comfort/comfort<u>able</u>; nature/natur<u>al</u>; health/health<u>y</u>
- **b)** Check answers with the class by pointing to each space in the table on the board and eliciting the correct word (see the table in **V3.3** SB p120).
- Drill the words with the class. Point out the different stress in *pópular* and *populárity*. Highlight that *comfortable* is three syllables, not four.
- Point out that we can often tell whether a word is a noun or an adjective by looking at the suffix. Also highlight that both nouns and adjectives can end in *-y* (*difficulty, healthy,* etc.).
- **c)** *Difficult, kind, popular, danger, comfort* and *health* only add the suffix. *Patient → patience* and *nature → natural* have extra changes in spelling. Use these examples to show that we sometimes have to change the spelling if the word ends in *-t* or *-e*.

d)–f) Students do the exercises on their own or in pairs, then check their answers in **V3.3** SB p120. Check answers with the class.

- **d)** Check answers by asking students where each of the words in **7d)** goes in the table on the board (see the table in **V3.3** SB p120).
- Be prepared to teach the meanings of any words students might not know (for example *modesty*). Point out that we describe places with lots of tourists as *touristy*, not ~~touristic~~.
- **e)** Elicit the matching nouns and adjectives for the words in **7d)** and write them in the table on the board (see the table in **V3.3** SB p120).
- Drill the words with the class. Highlight the pronunciation of *knowledge* /ˈnɒlɪdʒ/ and *knowledgeable* /ˈnɒlɪdʒəbəl/, and the different stress in *póssible/possibílity* and *áctive/actívity*.
- Point out that words ending in *-y* (*lazy → laziness,* etc.) often change their spelling.

8 Put students into pairs. Students take turns to test each other on the nouns and adjectives in **7**, as shown in the speech bubbles.

9 a) Put students into new pairs. Students make a list of five things that they think make a good holiday (a nice beach, a quiet hotel, etc.).

b) Reorganise the class so that students are working together in groups of four.

Students compare lists and decide on the five best things from both lists.

c) Either put the class in larger groups or finish the discussion with the whole class. Students agree on the five best things that make a good holiday.

Ask students to choose the best thing from their final list.

EXTRA IDEA

• For homework, students write a description of the last holiday they had. Collect the descriptions next class and display them around the room.

EXTRA PRACTICE AND HOMEWORK

Ph **Class Activity** 3C Suffix dominoes p141 (Instructions p120)
3 Review Exercise 5 SB p27
CD-ROM Lesson 3C
Workbook Lesson 3C p18

 # 3D A trip to India

Real World asking for and making recommendations
Review travel vocabulary

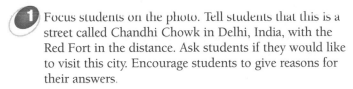

QUICK REVIEW ●●●

This activity reviews suffixes for nouns and adjectives. Put students into pairs. Student As write six adjectives that they can remember from lesson 3C (*patient, kind,* etc.). Student Bs write six nouns they can remember from the same lesson (*comfort, sadness,* etc.). Students work with their partner and take turns to say their words. Their partner should give the corresponding noun or adjective, as in the example.

1 Focus students on the photo. Tell students that this is a street called Chandhi Chowk in Delhi, India, with the Red Fort in the distance. Ask students if they would like to visit this city. Encourage students to give reasons for their answers.

EXTRA IDEAS

• Before focusing on the photo of Delhi, ask students to list the top three cities in the world they would like to visit. Students work in groups and compare cities, giving reasons for their choices. Students can then share some of their ideas with the class.

• Alternatively, start the class by asking students to work in pairs and write down six things they know about India. Ask students to share their ideas with the class.

---

2 a) Tell students that Michael is going to Delhi and is asking his friend Ellen for recommendations.

R3.9 Give students time to read the topics, then play the recording (SB p145). Students listen and tick the topics Michael and Ellen talk about.

Check answers by asking the class which two topics Michael and Ellen don't talk about (the best time to visit; changing money).

b) Point out the Red Fort in the photo. Ask students if they know which Indian city the Taj Mahal is in (Agra). Tell students that Connaught /ˈkɒnɔːt/ Place is an important commercial and shopping centre in Delhi. Also pre-teach *rickshaw*.

Give students time to read sentences 1–6, then play the recording again. Students listen, tick the correct sentences and change the incorrect ones.

Students check answers in pairs. Check answers with the class.

1T **2F** It's better to travel to other cities by **train**.
3F He **shouldn't** visit the museums in Delhi. **4T**
5T **6F** There **are lots of really good restaurants** in Connaught Place.

Real World Asking for and making recommendations

 3 a)–c) Students do the exercises on their own or in pairs, then check answers in **RW3.1** SB p121. Check answers with the class.

• **a)** 2 best 3 visiting 4 about 5 tips 6 best 7 recommend 8 definitely 9 worth 10 must 11 bother 12 worth 13 Don't 14 wouldn't 15 know 16 sounds 17 useful 18 heard

• **b)** 1 After *It's (well/not) worth …* we use verb+ing: *That's well worth seeing.* 2 After *Don't bother …* we use verb+ing: *Don't bother going to the museums.* 3 After *I'd/I wouldn't …* we use the infinitive: *I'd recommend the trains.*

4 **R3.10** **P** Play the recording. Students listen and practise. Encourage students to copy the sentence stress correctly. Play the recording again if necessary.

5 **a)** Students work in pairs and write conversations from the prompts. Check the conversations with the class.

> **1**
>
> A **Do you** know **any** good places to eat?
> B You **should** definitely go **to** Henry's in the centre.
> A What **about** places near the hotel?
> B **I'd** recommend the Rose restaurant.
> A Thanks, **that's really** useful.
>
> **2**
>
> A Where's **the** best place **to** stay?
> B It's probably best **to** stay in the Station Hotel.
> A **Have you** got **any** other tips?
> B I **wouldn't** carry too much money at night.
> A **That's** good **to** know.
>
> **3**
>
> A What **are the** best places **to** visit?
> B **You really** must go to the City Art Gallery. It's amazing.
> A **Is** there anything **else** worth **seeing**? What about the museums?
> B Well, I **wouldn't** bother **going to** the National Museum. It isn't worth **visiting**.
> A Yes, **I've** heard **that** before.

b) Student practise the conversations with their partners. Encourage students to memorise the conversations and practise them without looking at the Student's Book.

Ask each pair to role-play one conversation for the class.

6 **a)** Put students into new pairs. If possible, put students from different countries in the same pairs. Students choose a town, city or country that they know well, but their partner doesn't know and hasn't been to.

b) Students work on their own and think of the recommendations they can give to their partner about the places they have chosen. They can make recommendations based on the topics in **2a)** or their own ideas. Encourage students to make notes (*time to visit: Sept to Dec; see: museums, opera house; not see: art gallery,* etc.) but not write complete sentences.

c) Students work in pairs with their partner from **6a)**. Ask students to imagine they are going to visit their partner's town, city or country. Students take turns to ask for and give recommendations about each place.

d) Each pair decides which is the most interesting of the two places they talked about.

Finally, ask students to tell the class about the place they thought was the most interesting.

─ EXTRA IDEA ─

• If all your students are from the same town, city or country, put students into pairs and ask them to think of recommendations they would make to someone visiting this place. Students can compare their ideas in groups of four, or with the whole class.

─ EXTRA PRACTICE AND HOMEWORK ─

Ph **Vocabulary Plus** 3 Travelling by car p179 (Instructions p173)

Ph **Class Activity** 3D Memory maze p142 (Instructions p121)

3 Review SB p27

CD-ROM Lesson 3D

Workbook Lesson 3D p19

Workbook Reading and Writing Portfolio 3 p68

Progress Test 3 p204

3 Review

See p30 for ideas on how to use this section.

1 2b) 3e) 4a) 5d) 6j) 7h) 8f) 9i) 10g)

2 A Have you ever visited the USA?
B Yes, I've been there several times. I've just got back from Boston, actually.
A What was it like?
B Fantastic! I had a great time. Have you been anywhere recently?
A Yes, we went to our holiday home in France last week.
B How long have you had that?
A We've had it since the kids were tiny. It belonged to my parents before us, so it's been the family holiday home for a long time.
B Did you go there when you were a child?
A Yes. Then my father wanted to sell it so I bought it.

3a) travel economy class; travel on your own; get on/off a plane, get a taxi; go on a guided tour, go on a package holiday

4a) 2 ✓ 3 How many CDs have you bought recently? 4 How long have you been coming to this school? 5 ✓ 6 How long have you known the teacher?

5a) Nouns: health, tourist, patience, nature, danger. Adjectives: difficult, kind, comfortable, popular.

5b) nouns to adjectives: health → healthy, tourist → touristy, patience → patient, nature → natural, danger → dangerous. Adjectives to nouns: difficult → difficulty, kind → kindness, comfortable → comfort, popular → popularity.

Progress Portfolio

See p30 for ideas on how to use this section.

4 Born to be wild

Student's Book p28–p35

4A Riders

Vocabulary music collocations
Grammar Past Simple and Past Continuous; *used to*
Review Present Perfect Simple

QUICK REVIEW ●●●

This activity reviews ways of asking for and giving recommendations. Students work on their own and think of two holiday places they have been to. Put students into pairs. Students take turns to ask for and give recommendations about their places. Students can start each conversation by asking: *Have you ever been to ... ?* Ask each pair to tell the class what the most interesting place they discussed was.

Vocabulary Music collocations

1 Students do the exercise on their own or in pairs, then check their answers in **V4.1** SB p122.

Check answers with the class. Point out that *a gig* is an informal word for any kind of concert except a classical concert. Highlight that we can also use *tour* as a verb (*My favourite band are touring at the moment.*) and that we use *live* to talk about TV programmes or events we can see at the same time as they are happening (*The World Cup Final is shown live in over 160 countries.*). You can also teach *a venue* /'venjuː/ to talk about a place where bands or singers play concerts. *There are lots of great venues in London.*

Model and drill the phrases. Pay particular attention to the pronunciation of *tour* /tʊə/ and *live* /laɪv/. Note that only the main stress in words/phrases is shown in vocabulary boxes and the Language Summaries.

> appear on TV; release a new album/CD; go to a concert/a gig/a festival; have a hit single; be/go on tour; have an album/a CD in the charts; see someone play live, be/go onstage

2 a) Students do the exercise on their own. Ask students to think of at least two phrases from **1** that they can use to talk about each band, musician or singer they have chosen. Point out that we can say *a band* or *a group*.

b) Students do the activity in pairs. Encourage students to ask questions about the bands, musicians or singers their partner has chosen if possible.

Students share their ideas with the class. Note that students talk about concerts they have been to in **10**, so don't go into too much detail about specific concerts here.

― EXTRA IDEA ―

- Use mime to teach students some vocabulary for musical instruments, for example *guitar, drums, bass guitar, violin, piano,* etc. Ask students what the words for the people who play these instruments are (*a guitarist, a drummer, a bass guitarist, a violinist, a pianist,* etc.).

Reading and Grammar

3 **a)** Focus students on the photos. Students work in pairs and discuss what they know about the people or bands in the photos. Check students' ideas with the class.

> Jennifer Lopez is an American singer and actress. Elton John is a British singer, songwriter and musician. Luciano Pavarotti is an Italian opera singer. Prince is an American signer, songwriter and musician. The Rolling Stones are a British rock band. Foreigner were an American rock band. Britney Spears is an American pop singer.

b) Focus students on the article and ask them to read the first paragraph only. Check students understand *promoter* (a person who organises rock tours and concerts) and *riders* (requests for things that musicians want which are written in their contract with the promoter). Pre-teach *snooker table, dressing room, clear plastic* and *pie*.

Students read the rest of the article and fill in the gaps with the names of the people or bands in the photos. Early finishers can check answers in pairs. Don't check answers at this stage.

c) **R4.1** Play the recording. Students listen, read and check their answers to **3b)**. Check answers with the class. Ask students which rider in the article they thought was the most surprising.

> 1 Elton John 2 The Rolling Stones 3 Jennifer Lopez
> 4 Britney Spears 5 Prince 6 Luciano Pavarotti
> 7 Foreigner

Help with Grammar Past Simple and Past Continuous

4 **a)–d)** Students do the exercises on their own or in pairs, then check their answers in **G4.1** SB p123. Check answers with the class.

- **a) Past Simple a)** went **b)** said **c)** wanted
  Past Continuous a) were touring **b)** were having
- We can also use the Past Continuous when the longer action is interrupted: *While we were having a picnic, it started to rain* (so we stopped having the picnic).

- We can also use the Past Continuous to talk about an activity in progress at a point of time in the past: *At four o'clock I was driving home* (I started driving home before four o'clock and continued driving after four o'clock).
- Also point out that we don't usually use the Past Continuous with state verbs: *I loved my old car.* not *I was loving my old car.*
- Remind students that we can use *when* or *while* with the Past Continuous: *He called me when/while I was waiting for the train.* We don't usually use *while* with the Past Simple: *While he called me, I was waiting for a train.*

- **b)** 1 was staying 2 asked 3 staying in the hotel 4 Yes, he did.
- If necessary, draw the timeline in **G4.1** SB p123 on the board and use this to highlight the relationship between the Past Continuous (the longer action) and the Past Simple (the shorter action).

- **c)** We make the Past Simple positive of regular verbs by adding *-ed* or *-d* to the infinitive: *work → worked, live → lived*, etc. Remind students that there are no rules for irregular verbs and point out that there's an Irregular Verb List on SB p159.
- We make the Past Simple negative with: subject + *didn't* + infinitive. We make Past Simple questions with: (question word) + *did* + subject + infinitive.
- We make the Past Continuous positive and negative with: subject + *was/were* + (*not*) + verb+*ing*. We make Past Continuous questions with: (question word) + *was/were* + subject + verb+*ing*.

---

5 **R4.2** **P** Play the recording (SB p145). Students listen and practise. Encourage students to copy the rhythm and sentence stress. Play the recording again if necessary.

6 **a)** Focus students on the photo of Van Halen and ask students what they know about the band. (Van Halen is an American heavy rock band who have been together since the 1970s.)

If necessary, pre-teach *bowl, technician, equipment* and *damage* /ˈdæmɪdʒ/.

Students read the text and find out why the rider was important. Check answers with the class.

> Van Halen put the M&M rider in their contract because they wanted to check if the promoters read the contract properly.

b) Students do the exercise on their own.

c) Students check their answers in pairs. Check answers with the class.

> 2 included 3 found 4 were getting 5 happened 6 were doing 7 were putting 8 crashed 9 cost 10 forgot

---

Help with Grammar *used to*

7 **a)–c)** Students do the exercises on their own or in pairs, then check their answers in **G4.2** SB p124. Check answers with the class.

- **a)** Sentences a) and b). **2** We can use *used to* in sentence b) because it's a repeated action in the past: *He always used to say what size sofa he wanted.* We can't use *used to* in sentence c) because the sentence talks about one action in the past. **3** The infinitive.
- Point out that we can only use *used to* to talk about the past. When we want to talk about habits or repeated actions in the present, we use *usually* + Present Simple: *I used to work at the weekend* (but I don't work at the weekend now). *I usually work at the weekend* (I work at the weekend now).
- Remind students that we can also use the Past Simple to talk about a repeated action or habit in the past, as shown in **4a)**.

- **b)** We make positive and negative sentences with *used to* with: subject + *used to/didn't use to* + infinitive. We make questions with *used to* with: (question word) + *did* + subject + *use to* + infinitive.
- Point out that *used to* is the same for all subjects.
- Remind students that the short answers to *yes/no* questions with *used to* are: *Yes, I did./No, I didn't.; Yes, he did./No, he didn't.*, etc.
- Also point out the spelling of *use to* in negatives and questions, and that in the negative we can use *didn't use to* or *never used to*.

---

8 **R4.3** **P** Play the recording (SB p146). Students listen and practise. Check they are saying *used to* /ˈjuːstə/ correctly. Play the recording again if necessary.

9 **a)** Students do the exercise on their own. Tell students to use a form of *used to* in their questions if possible.

Check questions with the class. Point out that we use *used to* (without *did*) in question 1 because it is a subject question.

Note that all the questions would also be correct in the Past Simple.

> 1 Who used to be your best friend when you were 12? 2 When did you first meet him or her? 3 Did you use to like the same music? 4 Did you use to go to gigs together? 5 Did you use to play the same sports? 6 Did you use to like the same TV programmes? 7 When did you last see him or her?

b) Give students a minute or two to think of their answers to the questions in **9a)**.

Put students into pairs. Students take turns to ask and answer the questions. Encourage students to ask follow-up questions if possible.

Ask students to share interesting information with the class.

Get ready … Get it right!

 Ask students to look at SB p112. Check they are looking at the correct exercise.

a) Pre-teach *orchestra* /ˈɔːkɪstrə/ and *audience* /ˈɔːdiəns/. Give students time to think of a concert they have been to that they really enjoyed.

Students work on their own and make notes on the concert based on the prompts.

Make sure students write notes, not complete sentences.

While students are working, monitor and help with language and ideas.

b) Put students into groups of three or four. Students take turns to talk about their concert. Encourage other students to ask questions to find out more information, as shown in the speech bubbles.

c) Each group decides which concert was the best. Finally, ask each group to tell the class about the concert.

EXTRA PRACTICE AND HOMEWORK

Ph **Class Activity** 4A Celebrity engagement p143 (Instructions p121)
4 Review Exercises 1, 2 and 3 SB p35
CD-ROM Lesson 4A
Workbook Lesson 4A p20

4B Adventurers

QUICK REVIEW ●●●

This activity reviews the Past Continuous. Students work on their own and write three true and three false sentences. Put students into pairs and ask them to swap sentences. Students ask questions about each sentence to try and find out which ones are false. Ask students to share a few of their true sentences with the class.

Vocabulary character adjectives
Grammar Past Perfect
Help with Listening Past Perfect or Past Simple
Review Past Simple

Vocabulary Character adjectives

1 a) Students do the activity on their own or in pairs, then check the meanings of any new words in **V4.2** SB p122.

Check that students understand the difference between *sensible* and *sensitive* by asking: *What does a sensible person do the day before an exam?* (revise, go to bed early, etc.). Ask students which two adjectives have a negative meaning (*stubborn* and *mean*). Model and drill the words. Highlight the pronunciation of *sensible* /ˈsensɪbl/, *determined* /dɪˈtɜːmɪnd/, *stubborn* /ˈstʌbən/, *ambitious* /æmˈbɪʃəs/ and *responsible* /rɪˈspɒnsəbl/, and the stress on *independent* and *organised*.

b) Students do the exercise on their own. Encourage students to choose at least two adjectives for each person.

c) Students work in pairs and take turns to tell their partner about the people they thought of in **1b)**. Encourage students to ask questions about each person.

At the end of the activity, students decide which of the people they talked about is the most interesting. Ask a few pairs to tell the class about the person they chose.

Reading and Grammar

2 a) Check students know where the *English Channel* is (between England and France) and that they understand *North Pole* and *South Pole*. Also pre-teach *reach a place*. Students work in new pairs and try to complete the table.

b) Students check their answers on SB p141. Find out how many pairs got all the answers right.

Who were the first people to …	fly a plane across the English Channel?	reach both the North and the South Poles?	travel in space?
men	Louis Bleriot	Sir Ranulph Fiennes and Charles Burton	Yuri Gagarin
dates	1909	1979 and 1982	1961
women	Harriet Quimby	Ann Daniels and Caroline Hamilton	Valentina Tereshkova
dates	1912	2000 and 2002	1963

c) Ask students to match the women in the table to photos A–C. Check answers with the class.

A Harriet Quimby B Valentina Tereshkova
C Ann Daniels and Caroline Hamilton

3 a) Tell students that they are going to listen to two TV producers, Beth and Luke, talking about a new TV series that Beth is going to make.

R4.4 Give students time to read questions 1–3, then play the recording (SB p146). Students listen and answer the questions. Check answers with the class.

1 Famous women in history. 2 Harriet Quimby
3 Because the day she flew across the English Channel was the same day the story of the *Titanic* was on the front page of every newspaper in the world.

b) Pre-teach *a licence, land* (a plane) and *sink (sank, sunk)*. Give students time to read questions 1–6, then play the recording again. Students listen, answer the questions and then check answers in pairs. Check answers with the class.

> 1 She saw a newspaper article about men and women adventurers. 2 She became the first woman to get a pilot's licence in the USA. 3 In April 1912. 4 The weather was really bad. 5 No, she didn't. 6 She died two months later in June 1912 in a flying accident in the USA.

Help with Grammar Past Perfect

4 **a)–e)** Students do the exercises on their own or in pairs, then check their answers in **G4.3** SB 124. Check answers with the class.

> - **a)** 1 'd seen; had changed 2 decided; got up 3 'd seen; had changed
>
> - **b)** When there is more than one action in the past, we often use the Past Perfect for the action that happened first. The Past Perfect is often referred to as 'past-in-the-past'.
> - Also highlight that if the order of past events is clear, we don't usually use the Past Perfect: *We had dinner, watched TV and then went to bed.*
> - Similarly, we don't always use the Past Perfect with *before* and *after* because the order of events is clear: *David went home after the meeting (had) finished.*
>
> - **c)** In the first sentence, I turned on the TV, then the programme started almost immediately. In the second sentence, first the programme started, then I turned on the TV.
>
> - **d)** We make the Past Perfect positive with: subject + *had/'d* + past participle. We make the Past Perfect negative with: subject + *hadn't* + past participle.
> - Highlight that we usually use *'d* after pronouns (*I'd seen, she'd arrived,* etc.) and *had* after names and nouns (*Harriet had flown, the boat had sunk,* etc.).
> - Tell students that the Past Perfect is the same for all subjects, and that the short answers to Past Perfect *yes/no* questions are: *Yes, I had./No, I hadn't,* etc.
> - You can also point out that we make Past Perfect questions with: (question word) + *had* + subject + past participle (*What had he done before you met him?*), but these questions are not very common.
> - Check students understand all the **TIPS!** in **G4.3** SB p124.

5 **a)** **R4.4** Ask students to look at R4.4, SB p146. Play the recording again. Students listen and underline all the examples of the Past Perfect they can find.

b) Students check their answers in pairs. Check answers with the class.

> I'd seen; I'd learned; I hadn't heard; they'd achieved; She'd only had; the weather had changed; the *Titanic* had sunk

6 **R4.5** **P** Play the recording (SB p146). Students listen and practise. Encourage students to copy the sentence stress. Also highlight the contractions *I'd* and the weak form of *had /əd/* in *the weather had changed* and *the Titanic had sunk*.

7 **a)** Go through the example with the class. Students do the exercise on their own.

b) Students check answers in pairs. Check answers with the class.

> 2 had finished; got 3 invited; 'd/had already arranged 4 got; had forgotten 5 asked; 'd/had already booked 6 saw; was; hadn't seen

Help with Listening Past Perfect or Past Simple

> - This Help with Listening section highlights how we say the Past Perfect and helps students to hear the difference between the Past Perfect and the Past Simple.

8 **a)** **R4.6** Play the recording. Students listen and notice the difference between the Past Perfect and the Past Simple. Play the recording again, highlighting the contacted form *'d* in *I'd, He'd* and *They'd*, and the weak form *had /əd/* in *Nick had worked there.*

b) **R4.7** Play the recording (SB p146). Students listen to six pairs of sentences and decide which verb form they hear first. Play the recording again, pausing after each sentence to check students' answers.

> 1 Past Simple 2 Past Perfect 3 Past Simple 4 Past Perfect 5 Past Simple 6 Past Perfect

9 **a)** Focus students on photo C again and ask what the two women were the first to do (reach the North and South Poles).

Students read the text about their journey to the North Pole and answer the question. Note that the aim of this exercise is for students to get a general idea of the content of the text. They shouldn't fill in any gaps at this stage.

> Pom Oliver didn't reach the North Pole because her feet became so painful she couldn't continue.

b) Students do the exercise on their own. Early finishers can check answers in pairs.

c) **R4.8** Play the recording. Students listen and check their answers. Play the recording again, pausing after each sentence to check answers with the class.

> 2 were 3 'd/had already walked 4 left 5 'd/had trained 6 'd/had put on 7 set off 8 started 9 got 10 had become 11 arrived 12 'd/had walked 13 received 14 had ever walked

10 Put students into two groups, group A and group B. Students in group A turn to SB p103 and students in group B turn to SB p108. Check they are all looking at the correct exercise.

a) Students work in pairs with someone from the same group. Students put the verbs in brackets into the correct verb form.

While students are working, monitor and correct any mistakes. Early finishers can check their answers with another pair from the same group.

> **Student A** 1 was; 'd/had written 2 had been; shot 3 broke up; had recorded 4 had already played; was 5 died; 'd/had won
>
> **Student B** 1 stopped; had walked 2 had won; was 3 had written; died 4 retired; 'd/had scored 5 died; had sold

b) Reorganise the class so that a pair from group A is sitting with a pair from group B. Students are not allowed to look at each other's worksheets.

Pairs take turns to read out the sentences from **a)**. The other pair guesses the correct answer. Point out that the correct answers are in **bold**.

c) Students work out which pair got more answers right. Finally, ask each group to tell the class which pair got more answers right and find our how many pairs got all five answers correct.

EXTRA PRACTICE AND HOMEWORK

 Vocabulary Plus 4 Compound adjectives for character p180 (Instructions p174)

4 Review Exercises 4 and 5 SB p35

CD-ROM Lesson 4B

Workbook Lesson 4B p21

4C Natural medicines

QUICK REVIEW ●●●
This activity reviews the Past Perfect. Students work on their own and make a list of things they had done, or had learned to do, by the time they were 5, 10 and 15 years old. Put students into pairs. Students share their ideas and find out how many of the things they had done, or had learned to do, are the same. Ask students to share these ideas with the class, as in the example.

Vocabulary guessing meaning from context
Skills Reading: Natures little helpers; Listening: Life in the jungle
Help with Listening linking (2): /w/, /j/ and /r/ sounds
Review Past Simple; Past Continuous; Past Perfect

Reading and Vocabulary

1 Students discuss the questions in groups. Ask students to share interesting ideas with the class. Encourage students to give reasons why they think natural medicines are/ aren't as good as normal medicines.

2 a) Focus students on the article and pictures A–F. Note that foxgloves, lavender and willow trees are all common in the UK.
Check students understand health problems 1–6 and pre-teach *pain, burns* and *fever* if necessary.
Students read the article and match the pictures to the health problems.

b) Students check their answers in pairs. Check answers with the class.

> 1E 2F 3D 4A 5B 6C

c) Students do the exercise, then check answers in pairs. Check answers with the class.

> 1 Quinine came from a tree in **South America**.
> 2 Dr Withering heard about foxglove from a **local woman**. 3 Cleopatra used to put aloe vera on her **skin/body**. 4 If you have a **stomach** problem, try taking garlic.

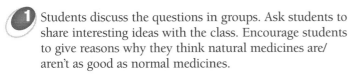

3 a)–b) Discuss the importance of being able to guess meaning from context with the class. Point out that you can sometimes guess the meaning of a word by deciding which part of speech it is, understanding the rest of the sentence and the general meaning of the story, or by recognising a similar word in your language or another language you know.

Remind students to be careful of words/phrases that are 'false friends' in their language when guessing meaning from context. For example *sensible* in Spanish means *sensitive* and *fast* in German means *almost*, not *quickly*.

Focus the students on the words in pink in the article. Students do exercises a) and b) on their own or in pairs, then check their answers in **V4.3** SB p122. Check answers with the class.

- **a)–b)** 1 noun, a) 2 noun, a) 3 verb, b) 4 noun (plural), b) 5 verb a) 6 noun, b) 7 adjective, a)
- Point out that the singular of *leaves* is *a leaf*, and that *battle* and *scar* are also verbs.

c)–d) Put students into pairs and focus them on the words in blue in the article. Students decide what parts of speech the words are and guess what the words mean from the context.

Students check their answers in **V4.3** SB p123. Check the meanings of the words with the class.

- **c)** See **V4.3** SB p123 for definitions of the words in blue in the article.
- Point out that *cure* and *beat* are also nouns.

Listening

4 a) Focus the students on the map and the photos. Check students know what part of the world Borneo is in (Southeast Asia). Note that Borneo is an island and is shared by three countries: Malaysia, Singapore and Brunei.

Ask students what they think the connection between the map and the photos is, and to guess the name of the plant (a banana tree). Don't tell them the answers at this stage.

b) Tell students they are going to listen to the beginning of an interview with Monica and Kaz.

R4.9 Give students time to read questions 1–3, then play the recording (SB p146). Students listen and answer the questions. Check answers with the class.

1 Because Monica was studying how the Pa'Dalih people grow rice. 2 Molly was about 18 months old. 3 She was badly burned./A teapot full of boiling water fell on her.

5 a) Students discuss the questions in pairs.

Elicit students' ideas for answers to questions 1 and 2 on the board in two columns. Don't tell them the answers at this stage.

b) **R4.10** Play the recording (SB p146). Students listen and check their answers to the questions in **5a)**.

Focus students on the answers on the board and ask if any of them were correct. Play the recording again if necessary.

1 They took off Molly's clothes and then they took her to a doctor in the next village. 2 They put sap from the flowers from the banana trees on Molly's burns.

6 a) Students work in the same pairs and read the summary. Students find five mistakes and correct them. Early finishers can check their ideas with another pair.

b) **R4.10** Play the recording again. Students listen and check their answers. Check answers with the class.

… burns on her **body** … sap from banana **flowers** … the nearest doctor **20** miles away … they **didn't take** Molly to hospital … The Pa'Dalih people **thought** …

7 a) Pre-teach *treatment* and *recover*. Students work in the same pairs and guess the answers to questions 1–3.

b) **R4.11** Play the recording (SB p146). Students listen and check. Check answers with the class.

Ask students if they think Monica and Kaz did the right thing, giving reasons for their answers.

1 They put sap from banana flowers on Monica every two hours. 2 For about ten days. 3 Yes, she did.

Help with Listening Linking (2): /w/, /j/ and /r/ sounds

- This Help with Listening section introduces extra linking sounds that we often use to link words together in natural spoken English.

8 a) Go through the introductory bullet point with the class. Point out that we use the extra sounds /w/, /j/ and /r/ to link words that end with a vowel sound with words that begin with a vowel sound. Focus students on the table to show which sounds at the end of a word produce each linking sound.

Note that students don't need to learn this table, but they can look at the Phonemic Symbols on SB p159 to check the sounds if necessary.

R4.12 Play the recording. Students listen and read the sentences from the interview and notice the linking sounds.

Play the recording again, pausing after each sentence to highlight the three linking sounds in each sentence.

Note that in British English the final /r/ sound in words is not usually pronounced, unless it is followed by a vowel sound, as in the third example sentence. In American English the final /r/ sound is usually pronounced in all cases. Note that students study British and American accents in lesson 9C.

b) **R4.11** Ask students to turn to R4.11, SB p146. Play the recording again. Students listen and notice the linking sounds.

Note that students study linking again in lesson 8C.

9 a) Give students a minute or two to think of an interesting story about when they were children, using the ideas in the box or their own ideas.

b) Students work on their own and make notes about their story.

While they are working, monitor and help students with vocabulary.

c) Students work in pairs and take turns to tell their stories. Students can ask questions at any point to clarify anything they don't understand or to find out more information. While they are working, monitor and help students with language problems.

> **EXTRA IDEA**
> * Students can make up a story using Consequences (p22).

10 a) Students work on their own and write their story. You can set a time limit of 15 minutes.

b) Ask students to pass their stories around the class for other students to read. If possible, allow each student time to read at least three of the other stories. Alternatively, display students' stories around the classroom and then ask them to read all the stories.

Finally, ask students to say which story they like the most, giving reasons for their answers.

> **EXTRA IDEAS**
> * Students do (or finish) **10a)** for homework, then do **10b)** next class.
> * Instead of asking students to read each other's stories in **10b)**, students can take turns to read out their stories to the class.

> **EXTRA PRACTICE AND HOMEWORK**
> **Ph Class Activity** 4C Rainforest adventure p144 (Instructions p121)
> **CD-ROM** Lesson 4C
> **Workbook** Lesson 4C p23

4D It's just a game!

Real World softening opinions and making generalisations
Vocabulary adjectives to describe behaviour
Review character adjectives

QUICK REVIEW ●●●
This activity reviews adjectives to describe people's character. Students make a list of these words on their own. Set a time limit of three minutes. Students compare their lists in pairs. Find out which pair has the most words and write them on the board. Ask if other pairs have any different words and add them to the list. Students then use the adjectives from their lists or the list on the board to describe people in their family.

1 Pre-teach *support a football team*, *football match* and *fight*. Students discuss the questions in groups. Ask students to share interesting ideas with the class.

2 a) Students do the exercise on their own or in pairs, then check new words in **V4.4** SB p123.

Check any problematic meanings with the class by asking what a violent, arrogant, etc. person would do or say in certain situations. Highlight that *spoilt* is usually used for children. Also tell students that we often use *offensive* to talk about what people say: *I thought what he said was very offensive*. Point out that all these adjectives describe people's *behaviour* and ask students what the verb is for the noun (*behave* /bɪ'heɪv/).

Model and drill the words, focusing on stress. Pay particular attention to the pronunciation of *violent* /'vaɪələnt/ and *enthusiastic* /ɪn,θjuːzɪ'æstɪk/.

b) Students answer the questions in pairs. Check answers with the class.

> **1 Negative meaning** violent; arrogant; rude; noisy; loud; selfish; aggressive; stupid; lazy; spoilt; offensive; bad-tempered **Positive meaning** polite; hard-working; loyal; enthusiastic; considerate; patient; helpful; well-behaved **2** Students' answers

3 a) Tell students they are going to listen to a conversation between Ewan /'juːwən/ and Michelle about football fans.
R4.13 Give students time to read sentences 1–5, then play the recording (SB p147). Students listen and circle the correct words/phrases in each sentence. Students can check answers in pairs. Check answers with the class.

> 1 night
> 2 most
> 3 most
> 4 some of the things
> 5 doesn't change

b) Focus students on the vocabulary box in **2a)**, then play the recording again. Students listen and tick the adjectives they hear. Check answers with the class.

> stupid; rude; noisy; loud; aggressive; violent; loyal; enthusiastic; spoilt; offensive

Real World Softening opinions and making generalisations

4 a)–d) Focus students on the introductory bullet point. Check students understand what we mean by *softening opinions* and *making generalisations*.

Students do the exercises on their own or in pairs, then check answers in **RW4.1** SB p124.

Check answers with the class.

- **a)** 2d) 3e) 4f) 5b) 6a)
- Point out that the phrases in **bold** are ways to soften opinions and make generalisations. These phrases can be quantifiers (*Some of them, not very, most, a bit*), adverbs (*quite, rather*), fixed phrases (*at times, Generally speaking, On the whole*) or verbs (*can, tend to*).
- Check students understand the meaning of *tend to* (= usually behave in a particular way).
- Point out that we often use *a lot of* with *rather*: *They tend to make rather a lot of noise.*

- **b)** After *tend to* we use the infinitive: *He tends to be a bit aggressive.*
- *Rather, quite, not very* and *a bit* usually come before an adjective: *They can get quite/rather/a bit noisy at times.*
- We often put *generally speaking* and *on the whole* at the beginning of a sentence: *Generally speaking/ On the whole, most football fans aren't violent at all.* Also highlight that we use a comma after these phrases.
- Also point out that we usually put *at times* at the end of a sentence: *Some of them can be quite rude at times.*

- **c)** 1 They're not very intelligent. 2 A positive adjective.
- Check students understand that we often use '*not very* + positive adjective' to criticise someone or something politely: *He wasn't very polite. (= He was rude.)*

5 R4.14 **P** Play the recording. Students listen and practise. Check students are copying the sentence stress correctly. Play the recording again if necessary.

You can ask students to turn to RW4.1 SB p124 and follow the sentence stress while they listen and repeat.

6 a) Tell students that sentences 1–7 are all about children. Students do the exercise on their own. Early finishers can check their answers in pairs. Check answers with the class.

2 They tend to be a bit spoilt. 3 They can be quite rude to their teachers at times. 4 Some of them aren't very healthy. 5 On the whole, they tend to watch quite a lot of TV. 6 Generally speaking, they're not very patient. 7 Some of them can be rather selfish.

b) Students work in pairs and discuss whether they agree with their sentences. Encourage students to give reasons. Ask students to share any interesting differences of opinion with the class.

— EXTRA IDEA —

- Before doing **6b)**, review ways to agree and disagree with the class. Write these ways of agreeing and disagreeing on the board: *Yes, definitely. Yes, I tend to agree (with that). Yes, I think that's right. I'm not sure about that. Maybe, but … . I'm not sure I agree with that. For one thing, … .* Drill the phrases.

7 a) Students work on their own and think of reasons why they tend to agree or disagree with these sentences.

b) Students discuss the sentences in **7a)** in groups. Encourage students to use the language from **4a)** in their conversations. Students should try to continue each conversation for at least 30 seconds.

Finally, ask students to share any interesting opinions with the class.

— EXTRA PRACTICE AND HOMEWORK —

Ph **Study Skills** 2 Using dictionaries for pronunciation p192 (Instructions p189)

Ph **Class Activity** 4D Adjective crossword p145 (Instructions p122)

4 Review SB p35

CD-ROM Lesson 4D

Workbook Lesson 4D p24

Workbook Reading and Writing Portfolio 4 p70

Progress Test 4 p206

4 Review

See p30 for ideas on how to use this section.

1a) 1 released 2 had 3 appeared 4 seen 5 are 6 did

2 1 was 2 was running 3 fell 4 didn't know 5 was wearing 6 kept 7 died 8 was running 9 saw 10 jumped 11 pulled

3a) 2 I used to get into trouble a lot. 3 I used to smoke. 4 I used to do a lot of sports. 5 I used to spend a lot of time playing computer games.
We can't use *used to* in sentences 1, 6 and 7.

3b) 2 Did you use to get into trouble a lot? 3 Did you use to smoke? 4 Did you use to do a lot of sports? 5 Did you use to spend a lot of time playing computer games?

5 2 wasn't; 'd/had already had 3 realised; 'd/had left 4 'd/had read (*or* read); went 5 got; had gone 6 bought; had already read

6 Possible answers 2 Teenage boys tend to be a bit aggressive. 3 Most of the cafés near here aren't very good. 4 On the whole, the winters in this country aren't very nice. 5 Golf can be a bit boring at times. 6 Generally speaking, public transport in my country isn't very reliable.

Progress Portfolio

See p30 for ideas on how to use this section.

5A Moving house

Vocabulary homes
Grammar making comparisons: comparatives, superlatives, *much, a bit, (not) as … as, different from*, etc.
Review adjectives to describe character and behaviour

Vocabulary Homes

1 Focus students on groups 1–3 below the vocabulary box. Check they understand *location* and go through the examples with the class.

Students work in pairs and put the rest of words/phrases into groups 1–3. Students can then check their answers and the meaning of any new words in **V5.1** SB p125. Check answers with the class (see **V5.1** SB p125).

Check students understand the difference between the types of home. Point out that *a cottage* is usually in the country, and that we say *a three-storey house* but we live on *the first floor*, not ~~the first storey~~.

Tell students that in the UK *the suburbs* of a town/city often have a lot of detached houses and are usually quite expensive places to live. Point out that British people often say *part of town* to mean *neighbourhood*: *Which part of town are you living in now?*

Check students understand the difference between *a basement* (where people can live) and *a cellar* (where you put things).

Model and drill the words/phrases. Pay particular attention to the pronunciation of *terraced* /ˈterɪst/, *detached* /dɪˈtætʃt/, *cottage* /ˈkɒtɪdʒ/, *garage* /ˈgærɑːʒ/, *suburbs* /ˈsʌbɜːbz/, *cellar* /ˈselə/, *rough* /rʌf/, *neighbourhood* /ˈneɪbəhʊd/ and *en-suite* /ɒnˈswiːt/.

Note that only the main stress in words/phrases is shown in vocabulary boxes and the Language Summaries.

2 **a)** Students do the exercise on their own. Focus students on the examples before they begin.

b) Students compare their lists in pairs. Students choose the five most important things from both lists.

c) Put the students in groups of four or six, or conclude the activity with the whole class. Students agree on a final list of five things in their groups or with the whole class.

If you have done this stage in groups, ask each group to tell the class their top five things.

Avoid discussing students' own homes at this stage, as they do this in **9** and **10**.

Reading, Listening and Grammar

3 **a)** Focus students on the advertisement. Tell students that the places are in Manchester, in the north of England.

Pre-teach the new vocabulary in the advertisement: *luxury, overlooking* and *spacious* /ˈspeɪʃəs/.

Give students a minute or two to read the advertisement and look at the photos. Students work in groups or with the whole class and discuss which house or flat they like best, giving reasons for their answers.

b) Tell students that Ian and Liz are looking for a new place to live, and have just been to look at the three places in the advertisement. They are now back home discussing what they thought of them.

R5.1 Play the recording (SB p147). Students listen and decide which place Ian and Liz both like. Check the answer with the class (they both like the flat in Salford).

4 **a)** Students do the exercise in pairs. Tell students not to worry about the words/phrases in colour at this stage.

b) **R5.1** Play the recording again. Students listen and check their answers to **4a)**. Check answers with the class.

Ask students which house/flat they would prefer to live in now, giving reasons for their answers.

1B 2B 3C 4C 5C 6A 7A 8C 9B 10A

5 **a)–d)** Students do the exercises in pairs, then check answers in **G5.1** SB p126. Check answers with the class.

- **a) 1** bigger; noisier; smaller; more spacious; further; less expensive **2** least expensive; oldest; most amazing; worst **3** We use *-er* and *-est* to make comparatives and superlatives of one-syllable adjectives (*old → older, oldest*, etc.), and 2-syllable adjectives ending in *-y* (*noisy → noisier, noisiest*, etc.). **4** We use *more* and *most* to make comparatives and superlatives of other 2-syllable adjectives (*spacious → more spacious, most spacious*, etc.), and long adjectives (*amazing → more amazing, most amazing*, etc.). **5** The irregular adjectives are *bad → worse, worst* and *far → further, furthest*. **6** The opposite of *more* is *less*. The opposite of *most* is *least*.

- Use sentences 2, 4 and 10 in **4a)** to show that we use *than* after a comparative when we are comparing two things in the same sentence.
- Use sentence 3 in **4a)** to highlight the common structure *one of the* + superlative.
- Check students remember the spelling rules in the **TIPS!** in **G5.1** SB p126.
- Point out that we can also say *far → farther, farthest* and that *good* is also irregular (*good → better, best*).
- Remind students that we use *the*, possessive *'s* or a possessive adjective before a superlative: *It had the most amazing view. He's Peter's best friend. This is their biggest room.* '*the* + superlative' is the most common form.
- Also point out that we can use *more* or *most* with nouns: *It's got more rooms than the last house.*

- **b)** We use *much*, *far* or *a lot* before a comparative to say there's a big difference. We use *slightly* /'slaɪtli/, *a little* or *a bit* before a comparative to say there's a small difference.
- Point out the difference between *far* as an adjective (*I live far away from here*) and *far* to say there is a big difference (*It's far bigger than I thought*).

- **c) 1 a)** the same ... as; as ... as **b)** similar to **c)** not as ... as; different from **2** With *(not) as ... as* we use the adjective, not its comparative form.
- Point out that we can say *different from* or *different to*. *Different from* is more common.

6 **R5.2** **P** Focus students on the examples. Play the first two sentences of the recording. Point out we usually say *than* /ðən/ and *as* /əz/ in their weak forms in comparative sentences.

Play the whole recording (SB p147). Students listen and practise, copying the sentence stress and weak forms.

7 Focus students on the advertisement again and ask students which is the detached house (C), which is the terraced house (B) and which is the flat (A).

Students do the exercise on their own. Remind students to use *the* where necessary with superlatives. Students check answers in pairs. Check answers with the class.

> 2 more attractive 3 the furthest/farthest 4 fewer
> 5 the most beautiful 6 larger 7 brighter
> 8 the most modern 9 the most fashionable

8 **a)** Focus students on the example and point out that they must use the word in brackets when rewriting the sentences.

Students do the exercise on their own, then check answers in pairs. Check answers with the class.

> 2 She's not as ambitious as me. 3 She looks different from me./I look different from her. 4 She's a bit less stubborn than me. 5 She's more organised than me.
> 6 She's as old as me./I'm as old as her. 7 My taste in music is similar to hers./Her taste in music is similar to mine.

b) Give students a few moments to choose a woman/girl they know well (for example a friend or a family member). Students look at the sentences in **8a)** and their rewritten versions, and choose sentences from each pair that are true for them and the woman/girl they have chosen.

c) Students work in pairs and take turns to tell their partner about the woman/girl, using the sentences they have chosen. Students should first tell their partner how they know the woman/girl before saying their sentences.

Encourage students to ask follow-up questions if possible.

Ask a few students to tell the class about the woman/girl they have chosen.

─ EXTRA IDEA ─
- Ask students to repeat **8b)** and **8c)** by talking about a man/boy they know well with a different partner.

Get ready ... Get it right!

9 Give students a minute or two to choose two houses/flats that their friends or family live in. They should choose places that they know well.

Focus students on the prompts and the examples, then allow students to do the exercise on their own.

Encourage students to use language from **5** that is new to them, not just simple comparatives and superlatives.

While students are working, monitor and correct any mistakes you see.

10 **a)** Put students into different pairs from **8c)**. Students take turns to tell their partners about the two houses/flats they chose and their own home.

Encourage students to ask follow-up questions and give more information where possible.

While students are working, monitor and correct any mistakes you hear.

b) Each pair decides which they think is the best home of the ones they have discussed and why.

Finally, ask students to tell the class which of the homes they discussed they think is the best, giving reasons for their answers.

─ EXTRA PRACTICE AND HOMEWORK ─
Ph **Class Activity** 5A House hunting p146 (Instructions p122)
5 Review Exercises 1 and 2 SB p43
CD-ROM Lesson 5A
Workbook Lesson 5A p25

Vocabulary phrasal verbs (2)
Grammar the future: *will*, *be going to*, Present Continuous
Help with Listening the future
Review making comparisons

Vocabulary Phrasal verbs (2)

1 a) Be prepared with definitions, examples, etc. to pre-teach the vocabulary in the box, or bring in dictionaries for students to check the meanings themselves.

Point out that *get rid of* and *keep* are opposites, and that we use *stuff* to refer to things in general and *junk* to talk about things we think are useless. Point out that *stuff* and *junk* are both uncountable nouns, and are informal.

Model and drill the words. Pay particular attention to the pronunciation of *drawer* /drɔː/ and *cupboard* /ˈkʌbəd/.

b) Focus students on the title of the article and ask them what they think the article is about.

Students read the article, tick the true sentences and correct the false ones. Students check answers in pairs. Check answers with the class.

> 1T 2F You need **at least two hours** for each room.
> 3T 4F You put things you **can't decide about** in a junk drawer. 5T

c) Students discuss what they think of the advice in the article in groups or with the whole class. Find out how many students think they need to do this in their home and ask them what kind of things they need to throw out.

2 Focus students on the phrasal verbs in **bold** in the article. Students work in pairs and guess the meanings of these verbs. Students check their answers in **V5.2** SB p125. Check answers with the class (see **V5.2** SB p125).

Point out that *throw away* and *throw out* are synonyms, and that we can *tidy up* (*I've been tidying up this morning*) or *tidy something up* (*I've tidied up the study*). Model and drill the phrasal verbs. Note that the grammar of phrasal verbs is taught in lesson 10C. We suggest you don't begin teaching the rules governing the position of objects in phrasal verbs at this stage of the course.

3 Put students into pairs, student A and student B. Student As turn to SB p103 and student Bs turn to SB p108.

a) Students do the exercise on their own.

If necessary, check the answers with the class. Only check the words they need to fill in the gaps, so that the other group doesn't hear the questions they are about to be asked.

> **Student A** 1 out 2 up 3 away 4 out 5 away 6 through; away/out 7 away/out   **Student B** 1 away 2 out 3 up 4 away/out 5 out 6 through 7 out

b) Students work with their partner, take turns to ask and answer their questions, and then decide who is tidier.

Listening and Grammar

4 a) Focus students on the picture and ask students who Ian and Liz are (the married couple who were looking for a new house in lesson 5A). Ask students what they are doing (deciding what to keep and what to throw away) and why they are doing this (because they are going to move house).

b) Students work in pairs and discuss what is in each pile. Check answers with the class.

> 1 a lamp; a TV; some old records; two pillows; some old photos 2 some magazines; some letters; a microwave (oven); a frying pan; some women's shoes 3 some books; a CD player; a box of children's toys; a picture

c) Students do the exercise on their own or in pairs. You can ask students what they think Ian and Liz are going to do with each pile, but don't tell them the answers yet.

d) **R5.3** Play the recording (SB p147). Students listen and check their answers to **4c)**. Check answers with the class.

> They're going to give away pile 3, throw away pile 2 and keep pile 1.

5 a) Check students know the words for things a)–e): c) = *a tennis racket*. Students do the exercise in the same pairs.

b) Play the recording again. Students listen and check their answers to **5a)**. Check answers with the class.

> 1e) 2d) 3b) 4a) 5c)

Help with Grammar The future

6 a)–d) Students do the exercises on their own or in pairs, then check their answers in **G5.2** SB p127. Check answers with the class.

> • **a) a)** We use *will* when we decide to do something at the time of speaking: *OK, I'll throw those away.*

- b) We use *be going to* when we already have a plan or an intention to do something: *I'm going to sort out the rest of them at the weekend.*
- c) We use **the Present Continuous** when we have an arrangement with another person: *She's picking them up tomorrow evening after work.*
- Point out that the arrangement doesn't have to be in the 'near future'. The important thing is how certain we are about them: *We're flying to Rio in May* (we've decided on the dates and booked the flights).
- b) d) We use *be going to* for a prediction that is based on present evidence (we predict the future because of something we can see in the present): *It's going to break the first time he uses it!*
- e) We use *will* for a prediction that is not based on present evidence: *But you'll never listen to them again.*
- c) We make the positive and negative forms of *will* with: subject + *'ll* (= *will*)/*won't* + infinitive. We make questions with *will* with: (question word) + *will* + subject + infinitive.
- Highlight that we often use *Do you think … ?* to make questions with *will*: *Do you think you'll use this again?*
- We make the positive and negative forms of *be going to* with: subject + *am/are/is* + *(not)* + *going to* + infinitive. We make questions with: subject + *am/are/is* + *(not)* + subject + *going to* + infinitive.
- For how to make the positive, negative and question forms of the Present Continuous, see G2.2.
- Check students understand the **TIPS!** in **G5.2** SB p127.

─ EXTRA IDEA ─

- **R5.3** Ask students to turn to R5.3, SB p147. Play the recording again. Students listen and underline all the future verb forms they hear. Check answers with the class.

Help with Listening The future

- This Help with Listening section helps students to hear the difference between future verb forms and highlights the two different ways we say *going to*.

7 **a)** **R5.4** Play the recording (SB p147). Students listen and write the sentences they hear. Point out that students will hear each sentence twice. Play the recording again. Pause to check students' answers for each sentence. ✍ As you check, elicit the sentences and write them on the board. Highlight the contractions *I'll* and *he'll* in sentences 4 and 5, and the weak forms of *are you* /əjə/ in sentence 6.

1 I'm going to finish the report tonight. 2 Look, it's going to rain soon. 3 I'm meeting her after school. 4 I'll call you at about six. 5 I think he'll find another job. 6 What are you doing tonight?

b) Play sentence 1 and 2 again and ask students how each person says *going to*. Point out that in the first sentence the speaker says /ˈɡəʊɪŋtə/ and in the second the speaker says /ɡənə/. Tell students that both ways are correct.

c) Focus students on the sentences from **7a)** on the board. Students do the exercise on their own, then check answers in pairs. Check answers with the class.

1b) 2d) 3c) 4a) 5e) 6c)

8 **R5.5** **P** Play the recording. Students listen and practise. Check they copy the pronunciation of *going to*, the contractions and the weak forms correctly.

9 **a)** Focus students on the picture again and ask students what Ian and Liz are doing (sorting things out). Students do the exercise on their own.

They're going to give away the guitar. They're going to throw away the dress. They're going to keep the running shoes and the mirror.

b) Students do the exercise on their own, then check answers in pairs.

c) **R5.6** Play the recording (SB p147). Students listen and check their answers. Check answers with the class.

1 it's going to fit 2 I'll throw 3 He's coming 4 I'll put 5 I'm going to start 6 It'll look 7 we're meeting 8 I'll finish When Ian leaves, Liz throws out the records, the running shoes and the tennis racket, and keeps her old letters.

10 **a)** Students do the exercise on their own.

b) Students work in groups and take turns to compare their lists. Each group then decides who is going to have the busiest or the most interesting four weeks.

Get ready … Get it right!

11 Students do the exercise on their own. Make sure each student writes a list of eight things.

12 **a)** Students move around the room and try to sell or give away the things on their lists to other students.

Point out that they all have £50 to spend, but remind them that they can also give items away if they choose. Tell students to try and get rid of as many items as possible. Point out the use of *will* in the example conversation in the speech bubbles before they start.

b) Students work in groups and tell each other what they have sold and given away. Finally, ask each group to tell the class who made the most money and who got rid of all the items on their list.

─ EXTRA PRACTICE AND HOMEWORK ─

Ph **Class Activity** 5B Look into the future p147 (Instructions p122)
5 Review Exercises 3 and 4 SB p43
CD-ROM Lesson 5B
Workbook Lesson 5B p26

5C Flatpack world

Vocabulary verb patterns (1)
Skills Reading: A furniture empire; Listening: Shopping at IKEA
Help with Listening fillers and false starts
Review Past Simple and Past Continuous

QUICK REVIEW ●●●

This activity reviews *be going to* for future plans. Focus students on the examples. Students do the activity in pairs. Ask each pair to share interesting ideas with the class.

Reading and Vocabulary

 a) Focus students on the photos on SB p40. Point out that *IKEA* is pronounced /aɪˈkiːə/ and use the photos to teach *flatpack furniture* (furniture that the customers build themselves). Students answer the questions in pairs.
Ask students to share their answers with the class.

b) Students do the exercise on their own. You can set a time limit of three minutes to encourage students to read for gist. Check answers with the class.

> 4a) 1b) 2c) 3d)

 a) Students read the article again to find out what it says about the numbers and people a)–i).

b) Students work in pairs and take turns to tell each other about the words and numbers in **2a)**. Before putting students into pairs ask them to cover the article. This will encourage students to summarise the information in their own words. Students may refer to the article if they need to.
Check answers with the class.

> a) IKEA opened its first store in 1943. b) IKEA has over 365 million customers worldwide. c) IKEA's customers spend over £8 billion a year. d) Gillis Lundgren invented flatpack furniture. e) Russell Crowe attacked some flatpack furniture with a knife because he couldn't put it together. f) There are over 200 IKEA stores in over 30 countries. g) 6,000 people were waiting outside a new IKEA store in London when it opened for business at midnight. h) The new London store was only open for 40 minutes that night. i) The new store sold all 500 sofas that were on special offer.

c) Discuss students' ideas with the class. Ask if they would like to shop at IKEA. Elicit reasons for their answers.

Help with Vocabulary Verb patterns (1)

 a) Remind students that when we use two verbs together, the form of the second verb usually depends on the first verb.
Focus the students on the table. Ask students to find the five verbs in the left-hand column of the table (*keep, need, would, pay* and *make*) in the article and underline the verb form that follows. Use these to check students understand the five verb forms in the right-hand column.

Students work on their own and put the other verbs in **bold** in the article in the correct place in the table. Tell students there are two more verbs in **bold** for each verb pattern. Remind students to write the infinitive form.
While students are working, copy the table on the board so that you are ready to check their answers. Check answers with the class.

- **a)** Focus students on the table on the board. Elicit which verbs in **bold** go in each row and fill in the table (see the verbs in **bold** in the table in V5.3 SB p126).
- Tell students that in this context *keep = continue*, and that *let someone do something = allow someone to do something*.

b)–c) Students do the exercise in pairs. Point out that some verbs can go in more than one place.
Students check answers in V5.3 SB p126.
Check answers with the class.

- **b)** Focus students on the table on the board. Elicit which verbs go in each row and complete the table (see the table in V5.3 SB p126).
- Point out that some verbs (shown in blue in V5.3) have more than one verb pattern. Both verb patterns have the same meaning.
- Also highlight that we usually say *like/love/hate* + verb+ing in British English (*I like watching sport on TV.*) and *like/love/hate* + infinitive with *to* in American English (*I live to watch sport on TV.*).

 a) Students do the exercise on their own.
Early finishers can check in pairs. Check answers with the class.

> 2 to buy 3 to get 4 to buy
> 5 helping/to help; choose/to choose
> 6 buy 7 wear 8 going/to go; do

b) Students work in pairs and take turns to ask and answer the questions.
Encourage students to ask follow-up questions if possible.
Ask students to share interesting things they have found out about their partner with the class.

Listening

5 a) Focus students on the photo of Gillian and Sue. Ask students where the two women are (outside an IKEA store).

R5.7 Play the recording (SB p147). Students listen and answer the questions.

Check answers with the class.

> Gillian doesn't like shopping at IKEA, but Sue does. They agree that things are very cheap there.

b) Give students time to read the bullet points, then play the recording again. Students listen and make notes on each of the topics.

Students check answers in pairs. Check answers with the class.

> **GILLIAN**
> • She loves the things they sell. They're good quality and well designed.
> • She'd prefer to have more personal service. She can never find anyone to help her.
> • On Saturdays the queues are enormous.
> • Putting the furniture together drives her crazy. There are always bits missing, which is very frustrating.
>
> **SUE**
> • There aren't many shop assistants. She doesn't like shop assistants who ask you if you want help all the time.
> • She always seems to buy things she didn't plan to buy, like candles, glasses and plants.
> • She furnished an empty flat in Paris with things she bought during one trip to IKEA.
> • She was able to put the furniture together quite easily.

Help with Listening Fillers and false starts

• This Help with Listening section focuses on ways we give ourselves time to think when we are speaking.

6 a) Focus students on the introductory bullet and highlight the examples of fillers and false starts.

Students do the exercise on their own, then check in pairs. Check answers with the class.

Point out that fillers have no meaning and we use them to give us 'thinking time' when we're deciding what to say next.

Note that students often confuse fillers such as *like, kind of, sort of*, etc. with other uses of these words: *What is he like?*, *What kind of place is it?*, *What sort of music do you like?*, etc.

> **1 fillers** er, er, let me think **2 fillers** I mean, well, like; **false start** Everything's … **3 fillers** you know, um, kind of; **false start** You can never … **4 fillers** You see, um, sort of; **false start** I haven't …

b) R5.7 Ask students to turn to R5.7, SB p147.

Play Gillian's section of the recording and ask students to listen and notice all the fillers and false starts. (The fillers and false starts are underlined in the recording script.)

Then play Sue's section of the recording. Students listen and underline all the fillers and false starts.

Check answers with the class by playing Sue's section of the recording again and pausing after each sentence to elicit students' answers.

> <u>Er</u>, <u>well</u>, IKEA's more like a supermarket than a department store. <u>I mean</u> at IKEA you get your trolley or, <u>um</u>, your big blue bag and away you go. <u>You see</u>, <u>there isn't</u> … there aren't many assistants so no one's <u>like</u> asking you if you want any help all the time. I hate that, I just <u>kind of</u> want people to let me walk around on my own. But <u>I</u>, <u>um</u>, … I always seem to buy lots of little things, candles and, <u>er</u>, glasses and plants, <u>you know</u>, stuff that I didn't actually plan to buy. But you can furnish an entire house in a day, in fact we did, <u>er</u> … when we lived in Paris. <u>Well</u>, it wasn't a house actually. <u>We got</u>, <u>um</u>, we rented an unfurnished flat and there was nothing in it, obviously. So, <u>um</u>, we went to IKEA and bought loads of things and <u>you know</u>, just took them home in the back of the car. <u>We were</u>, <u>um</u>, … we were able to put all the furniture together quite easily, and by the evening, we had a furnished flat. And everything was <u>like</u> really cheap. <u>I mean</u>, what more do you want from a store?

7 a) Tell students that they are going to make a shopping survey for the class. Focus students on question 1 and point out the three possible answers.

Students work in pairs and write three possible answers for questions 2–5.

Each pair then writes two more questions of their own, each with three possible answers.

While students are working, monitor and check they are doing the activity correctly.

Also check students' own questions for accuracy.

b) Students move around the room and interview five other students.

Students should interview the five students on their own, not in their pairs. Remind students to make notes on their answers.

If your students aren't able to move around the room, ask one student in each pair to swap places with someone else in a different area of the classroom. They can then interview five students that are sitting near them.

While students are working, monitor and correct any mistakes you hear.

c) Students work with their partner from **7a)**. Students compare their results and work out the number of a), b) and c) answers they have for each question in their survey.

Ask each pair to tell the class the two most interesting things they found out.

 8 a) Students work in the same pairs and write a short report on the results of their survey.

EXTRA IDEA
- Write these phrases on the board to help students with their report: *Most people … ; Almost everyone … ; Six out of ten students … ; Hardly anyone in the class … ; No one in the class … ; About half the class … .*

b) Students swap reports with other students. Students read the reports and decide if they agree with them or not. Finally, ask students to tell the class if they agree with their classmates' reports, giving reasons for their answers.

EXTRA PRACTICE AND HOMEWORK
- Ph **Vocabulary Plus** 5 Shopping p181 (Instructions p174)
- Ph **Class Activity** 5C Who said what? p148 (Instructions p123)
- **5 Review** Exercise 5 SB p43
- **CD-ROM** Lesson 5C
- **Workbook** Lesson 5C p28

5D Is this what you mean?

Vocabulary materials
Real World explaining what you need
Review verb patterns

QUICK REVIEW ●●●

This activity reviews verb patterns. Students write five sentences about themselves, using the prompts. If they need to check any verb patterns, they can look at V5.3 SB p126. Put students into pairs. Students take turns to say their sentences and ask follow-up questions. Ask students to share any interesting information with the class.

 1 a) Students work on their own and tick the words they know. Students then do the exercise in V5.4 SB p126. Check answers with the class. Model and drill the words.

V5.4 2e) 3g) 4a) 5l) 6d) 7i) 8j) 9b) 10k) 11h) 12f)

b) Students do the exercise in pairs. While they are working, monitor and help with any vocabulary. Also make sure that they are writing the things in random order, not in the order of the vocabulary box in **1a)**.

c) Students swap papers with another pair and write the correct materials next to the things on the paper.

d) Students check their answers to **1c)** with the pair who wrote the list.

2 a) Focus students on the photo of Lars and ask students who he's talking to (a shop assistant). Tell students that Lars needs to buy some things for his new house.

R5.8 Play the recording (SB p148). Students listen to four conversations that Lars has with different shop assistants and tick the things in photos A-G that he buys.

Check answers with the class by asking students to tell you the letter for each picture only. Don't tell them the words for the things he bought at this stage.

Lars buys items E, B, G and C.

b) Students do the exercise in pairs.

c) Play the recording again. Students listen and check that they have identified the things Lars bought correctly. Check answers with the class.

Model and drill the new vocabulary, focusing on stress.

E = a corkscrew; B = stain remover; G = drawing pins; C = a charger

Real World Explaining what you need

 3 a)–c) Students do the exercises on their own or in pairs, then check their answers in RW5.1 SB p127. Check answers with the class.

- **a)** a) saying you don't know the name of something
  b) describing what something is used for
  c) describing what something looks like
  d) checking something is the right thing
- **b)** We often use *stuff* to talk about uncountable nouns we don't know the name of: *It's stuff for getting marks off your clothes.*
- After *It's a thing for …* and *It's stuff for …* we use verb+ing: *It's a thing for opening bottles of wine.*
- After *You use it/them …* we use the infinitive with to: *You use them to put posters up on the wall.*
- Also remind students that we also use *stuff* to talk about things in general, as in lesson 5B: *Is your home full of stuff that you never use?*
- Point out that we often say *Excuse me?* to get people's attention in shops.

 4 R5.9 P Play the recording. Students listen and practise. Check students copy the sentence stress correctly.

a) Pre-teach *mend*, *hole* and *perfume*. Students do the exercise on their own.

b) Students check answers in pairs. Check answers with the class.

Drill *needles*, *kettle* /ˈketəl/ and *air freshener*.

> **1**
> L I'm **looking for** something **to mend** my clothes.
> SA **Do you** mean cotton? This stuff?
> L No, they're **made of** metal. They've got **a hole/holes** in the end.
> SA Oh, **you** mean needles.
>
> **2**
> L It's **a** thing for **boiling** water. **I'm** sorry, **I don't** know **the** word **for** it.
> SA **Do you** mean one **of** these?
> L Yes, that's it. What's **it** called **in** English?
> SA A kettle.
>
> **3**
> L It's stuff **for making** things smell nice. **I've forgotten** what **it's** called.
> SA **Do you** mean perfume? Like this?
> L No, you use **it** when **you** want **to** make **the** house smell better.
> SA Oh, **you** mean air freshener.
>
> needles = A; a kettle = F; air freshener = D

c) Students practise the conversations in **5a)** with their partner. Encourage students to memorise the conversations.

Ask a few pairs to role-play the conversations for the class.

┌─ **EXTRA IDEA** ─────────────
│ • Do these conversations using a Dialogue Build (p21).
└─────────────────────────────

 Put students into new pairs, student A and student B. Student As turn to SB p104 and student Bs turn to SB p109.

a) Focus students on the pictures. Tell students that they want to buy these things, but don't know the English words for them. Students work on their own and decide how they can explain them to a shop assistant. Encourage students to make notes on what they're going to say. Tell them not to write the whole conversation.

b) Students work with their partners. Student A is the customer and student B is the shop assistant.

Student A buys the things in **a)** from his/her partner's shop, using the language he/she has prepared. When student B understands what student A is describing, he/she tells him/her the English word. Student A writes the word in the correct place in his/her book. Students are not allowed to look at their partner's book. Note that the shop assistants have four things in their shop that the customers don't want to buy.

c) Students swap roles, so that student A is the shop assistant and student B is the customer.

d) Students work in pairs and check their answers.

Ask how many students bought all four things they wanted.

Finally, model and drill the new words and the words for the other things in the shops that students didn't buy.

♪ Ask students to turn to SB p100 and look at *Our House*. This song was written and recorded by the English band Madness in 1982.

1 Students discuss the questions in groups. Ask students to share interesting childhood memories with the class.

2 **a)** R5.10 Students read the song. Play the recording. Students listen and put the lines of the song in order.

b) Students check answers in pairs.
Play the song again. Pause to check students' answers.

> 2e) 3d) 4f) 5c) 6a) 7i) 8h) 9l) 10g) 11k) 12j) 13q)
> 14n) 15r) 16p) 17m) 18o) 19t) 20s) 21v) 22u)

3 Students do the activity in pairs.
Ask students to share interesting things they found out.

┌─ **EXTRA PRACTICE AND HOMEWORK** ─────────
│ **5 Review** SB p43
│ **CD-ROM** Lesson 5D
│ **Workbook** Lesson 5D p29
│ **Workbook** Reading and Writing Portfolio 5 p72
│ **Progress Test 5** p208
└──

5 Review

See p30 for ideas on how to use this section.

2a) fewer, fewest; brighter, brightest; more amazing, most amazing; older, oldest; worse, worst; busier, busiest; more confident, most confident; more organised, most organised; cheaper, cheapest; easier, easiest; more spacious, most spacious; further/farther, furthest/farthest

3a) 2 tidy/clear 3 throw/give 4 put 5 clear; throw/give 6 give 7 go

5a) 1 to look/looking 2 to look 3 showing 4 borrow 5 borrowing 6 to buy

Progress Portfolio

See p30 for ideas on how to use this section.

6A   Make up your mind

Vocabulary *make* and *do*
Grammar first conditional and future time clauses
Review question forms

QUICK REVIEW ●●●
This activity reviews materials and ways of describing things. Students work on their own and write a list of six things in their house. Put students into pairs. Students take turns to describe the things and guess what their partner's things are, as in the example. Students must not say the word for the thing itself.

Vocabulary *make* and *do*

 a) Students do the exercise on their own or in pairs. Students check their answers in V6.1 SB p128.
Check answers with the class (see V6.1 SB p128).
Point out these patterns:
- We often use *make* for 'food' words: *make lunch*, etc.
- We often use *do* for 'study' words: *do homework*, etc.
- We usually use *do* for jobs connected with the house: *do the cleaning*, etc.

Highlight that we use *do* with *nothing, something* and *anything*: *I'm not doing anything this weekend.* Check students understand the difference between *do exercise* (go for a run, etc.) and *do an exercise* (in the Workbook, etc.). Point out that we say *do the washing-up* in British English and *do the dishes* in American English, and that *make a decision* and *make up your mind* are synonyms. Highlight that we use *make an appointment* with a doctor, etc., not with friends. We usually use *arrange to meet* with friends: *I've arranged to meet a friend after work.*

Model and drill the phrases with *make* and *do*. Note that only the main stress in words/phrases is shown in vocabulary boxes and the Language Summaries.

b) Students work in pairs and take turn to test each other on the phrases in **1a)**, as shown in the speech bubbles.

 a) Students do the exercise on their own. Check answers with the class.

> 2 done 3 making 4 does 5 doing 6 make 7 doing
> 8 made 9 do 10 make

b) Focus students on the example questions. Students work on their own and make *yes/no* questions for the other sentences in **2a)**. Check answers with the class.

> Are you good at making people laugh?
> Do you usually do the washing-up every day?
> Do you like doing nothing at the weekend?
> Do you usually have to make dinner for other people?
> Are you doing another course at the moment?
> Have you made some new friends this year?
> Are you going to do some shopping after class?
> Do you often have to make excuses for being late?

c) Students move around the room and ask other students their questions, or ask as many people as they can sitting near them. When they find a student who answers *yes*, they write the person's name next to the question. Students then ask one or two follow-up questions to find out more information. Students should try and find a different person who answers *yes* for each question.
Ask students to tell the class a few things they found out about their classmates.

Listening and Grammar

 a) Students discuss the questions in groups. Ask students to share interesting ideas with the class.

b) Focus students on the photos and tell the class that Kate and Steve are sister and brother. Give students time to read questions 1–3.
Divide the class into pairs, student A and student B. Tell student As to answer the questions about Kate and student Bs to answer the questions about Steve.
R6.1 Play the recording (SB p148). Students listen and answer the questions about Kate or Steve.

c) Students work in their pairs and tell their partner their answers. Students then discuss what they think Kate and Steve should do.
Check answers with the class. Ask students what their advice is for Kate and Steve.

> **KATE**
> 1 No, she doesn't. 2 She has to decide if she should go back to work as a French teacher, or go to university to do Business Studies. 3 She advises Steve to work part-time and write on his days off.
> **STEVE**
> 1 Yes, he does. He's a doctor. 2 He's trying to decide if he should leave his job and become a writer.
> 3 He advises Kate to ask their parents to lend her some money, and also to do what will make her happiest.

 a) Students do the exercise in the same pairs. Don't check answers with the class at this stage.

b) R6.1 Play the recording again. Students listen and check their answers to **4a)**. Check answers with the class.

> 1 Kate 2 Steve 3 Steve 4 Kate 5 Kate 6 Kate 7 Steve
> 8 Steve 9 Kate

Help with Grammar First conditional and future time clauses

5 **a)–d)** Students do the exercises on their own or in pairs, then check their answers in `G6.1` SB p129. Check answers with the class.

- **a)** The main clause is *I'll be exhausted after a year*. The *if* clause is *If I start teaching again*.

- **b)** a) First conditional sentences talk about the result of a possible event or situation in the future.
- **b)** The *if* clause talks about things that are possible, but not certain (maybe I will start teaching again). The main clause says what we think the result will be in this situation (I'm sure I will be exhausted after a year).
- **c)** We make the first conditional with: *if* + Present Simple, *will/won't* + infinitive.
- **d)** The *if* clause can be first or second in the sentence.
- **e)** We often use *might* to mean 'will perhaps'.
- Point out that when the *if* clause is first in the sentence, we use a comma after this clause: *If I see him, I'll ask him to call you*. When the main clause is first in the sentence, we don't use a comma: *I'll ask him to call you if I see him*.

- **c)** a) We often use *unless* to mean 'if not' in first conditional sentences. b) But if I don't do it now, I'll be too old.

6 **a)–b)** Students do **6a)** on their own or in pairs, then check their answers in `G6.2` SB p129. Check answers with the class.

- **a)** a) These sentences with *before, as soon as, after, until* and *when* also talk about the future.
- **b)** In these sentences we use *will/won't* + infinitive in the main clause: *I'll believe it when I see it!*
- **c)** We use the **Present Simple** in the clauses beginning with *before, as soon as, after, until* and *when*: *I won't tell them until I decide what to do*.
- Point out that we use *when* to say we are certain that something will happen: *I'll tell Sally when I see her* (I'm certain I will see Sally). *I'll tell Sally if I see her* (maybe I will see Sally).
- We use *as soon as* to say that something will happen immediately after something else: *As soon as I make up my mind, I'll let you know*.
- As with first conditional sentences, the future time clause with *before, when*, etc. can come first or second in the sentence.

7 `R6.2` `P` Play the recording (SB p148). Students listen and practise. Check students copy the contraction *I'll* /ˈaɪəl/ and the sentence stress correctly.

You can also ask students to turn to R6.2, SB p148. They can then follow the sentence stress as they listen and practise.

8 Focus students on the example. Students do the exercise on their own, then check answers in pairs. Check answers with the class.

2 I'll come out tonight unless I have to work. **3** He might call you if he gets home in time. **4** I'll have to move house if I don't find a job soon. **5** Unless Tony arrives soon, we'll go without him. **6** I might go away this weekend if my friends don't come to visit.

9 Students do the exercise on their own before checking in pairs. Check answers with the class.

2 'll make; do **3** 'll do **4** do; I'll do **5** make **6** 'll do **7** make; do **8** 'll make **9** 'll do; make

— EXTRA IDEA —

- Before doing **9**, ask students to close their books. Then give students two minutes to write down all the phrases with *make* and *do* that they can remember. Students can check their answers in pairs or groups.

10 **a)** Students complete the sentences for themselves.

b) Students work in pairs and take turns to say their sentences. Encourage students to ask follow-up questions. Students tick any of their sentences that are the same.

Pairs tell the class any sentences that are the same.

Get ready … Get it right!

11 Put students into groups of three, student A, student B and student C. Student As turn to SB p103, student Bs turn to SB p108 and student Cs turn to SB p112.

a) Tell students they have a problem. Students read about their problem and think of three ways they can deal with it. They decide what will happen if they choose each of the options. Focus students on the example.

b) Students work with the other members of their group. Students take turns to tell the group about their problem (in their own words, if possible), and their three options. Students discuss what will happen if they choose each option. Other students can suggest other options.

Encourage students to use first conditionals and sentences with future time clauses in their conversations.

c) Students decide what to do to solve their problems. The rest of the group decides if they think the solution is the correct one or not.

Finally, ask students to tell the class how they are planning to solve their problems.

— EXTRA PRACTICE AND HOMEWORK —

`Ph` **Class Activity** 6A Men and women p149 (Instructions p123)
6 Review Exercises 1 and 2 SB p51
CD-ROM Lesson 6A
Workbook Lesson 6A p30

QUICK REVIEW ●●●
This activity reviews expressions with *make* and *do*. Give students a minute or two to write their six phrases with *make* and *do* that are connected to their lives, or the lives of people they know. Students work in pairs and take turns to tell their partner why they chose these phrases, as in the example. Students ask one or two follow-up questions for each phrase. Ask students to share ideas with the class.

Vocabulary reflexive pronouns
Grammar zero conditional; conditionals with imperatives and modal verbs; *in case*
Help with Listening zero or first conditional
Review *made*, *do* and *let*; first conditional; *used to*

Reading and Grammar

 Focus students on the title of the lesson and pre-teach *protective*. Ask students whether either of the two photos reminds them of their own childhood.

Check students understand the difference between things that parents make children do (things that children don't want to do) and things that parents let them do (things children want to do).

Students discuss the questions in groups. Ask each group to share interesting ideas with the class. If you have students with children, ask them how their children spend their free time and how they feel about their children's choice of activities.

> **EXTRA IDEA**
>
> * To review *make* and *let* in more detail, write these ideas on the board before doing **1:** 1 *go to bed early* 2 *go to bed late* 3 *tidy your room* 4 *play computer games* 5 *watch as much TV as you want* 6 *wash your hands before meals* 7 *sleep at a friend's house* 8 *do jobs around the house* 9 *eat all your vegetables* 10 *put posters up in your room*. Ask students to decide which things parents make children do (1, 3, 6, 8, 9) and which things parents let children do (2, 4, 5, 7, 10). Students can then use these phrases as a basis for discussion in **1**.

 a) Be prepared with definitions, examples, etc. to pre-teach the vocabulary in the box, or bring in dictionaries for students to check the meanings themselves.

Note that the aim of these boxes is to highlight which words you need to pre-teach to help students understand the text that follows. The vocabulary in these boxes is not in the Language Summaries in the Student's Book.

b) Focus students on the article. Students read the article and choose a sentence that describes the article best. You can set a time limit of two minutes to encourage students to read for gist.

Check the answer with the class (sentence 2).

Students do the exercise on their own, then check answers in pairs. Check answers with the class.

Ask students for their opinion on the content of the article. Ask students to give reasons for their answers.

1F We used to worry about our children **less** than we do now. 2F Most British parents **don't let** their children walk to school. 3T 4F Life is **safer** for children now than it used to be. 5T

Help with Grammar Zero conditional; conditionals with imperatives and modal verbs; *in case*

 a)–d) Students do the exercises on their own or in pairs, then check their answers in **G6.3** SB p129. Check answers with the class.

* **a)** Zero conditionals talk about things that are always true. *If you have children, you worry about them all the time.*
* In zero conditionals both verbs are in the Present Simple: *If children stay indoors all the time, they become unfit.*
* Point out that *if* and *when* have the same meaning in zero conditionals: *If/When I'm worried, I don't sleep very well.*
* Focus students on the 'Zero or first conditional' section in **G6.3** SB p129 to clarify the difference between these two conditional forms.

* **b)** a) sentences 3 and 4 b) sentence 5 c) the Present Simple
* Use the example sentences in the article to highlight that we can use modal verbs (*should, can,* etc.) and imperatives (*give, don't tell,* etc.) in the main clause of conditionals. As with first conditionals, we use the Present Simple in the *if* clause in these types of conditionals.
* Point out that we can use other modal verbs (*must, have to, might,* etc.) in these types of conditionals: *If you don't understand, you must tell me immediately.*

* **c)** We use *in case* to say that we are prepared for something that might happen.
* *In case* and *if* have different meanings.
* To highlight the difference between *in case* and *if*, write on the board: **A** *I'll buy some water in case I get thirsty.* **B** *I'll buy some water if I get thirsty.* Person A is definitely going to buy some water, so that he/she is prepared for a time in the future when he/she might get thirsty. Person B might buy some water, but only if he/she gets thirsty in the future.

5 R6.3 P Play the recording (SB p148). Students listen and practise. Check students copy the sentence stress correctly. Play the recording again if necessary.

You can ask students to turn to R6.3, SB p148 and to follow the sentence stress as they listen and practise.

6 a) Pre-teach *urgently* /'ɜːdʒəntli/ and check students remember *thirsty* /'θɜːsti/. Students do the exercise on their own before checking in pairs. Check answers with the class.

> 1 if; don't get 2 have; in case; get 3 If; need; call
> 4 should start; in case; lose 5 can't work; if; is playing

b) Students do the exercise on their own.

c) Students work in pairs and find out how many sentences they have both ticked.

Ask students to share these sentences with the class.

Help with Listening Zero or first conditional

- This Help with Listening section helps students to hear the difference between zero conditionals and first conditionals.

7 a) Focus students on the example sentences and ask students which is a zero conditional (the first sentence) and which is a first conditional (the second sentence). R6.4 Play the recording. Students listen and notice the difference between the sentences. Highlight the contracted form *they'll* in the first conditional sentence.

b) R6.5 Play the recording (SB p148).

Students listen and write the sentences they hear. Play the recording again if necessary.

Students check answers in pairs and decide which are zero conditionals and which are first conditionals.

Play the recording again, pausing after each sentence. ✎ Elicit each sentence and write it on the board. Ask students if each sentence is a zero conditional or a first conditional.

> 1 If I don't know where my children are, I worry a lot. (zero) 2 If they don't do more exercise, they'll get fat. (first) 3 We'll pick up the kids if we have time. (first) 4 If it's a nice day, I take them to the park. (zero) 5 If they can't sleep, I'll read them a story. (first) 6 They play computer games all day if they can. (zero)

Help with Vocabulary Reflexive pronouns

8 a)–c) Focus students on sentences 1–3 from the article and tell the class that *themselves* is called a reflexive pronoun.

Students do the exercises on their own or in pairs, then check their answers in V6.2 SB p128. Check answers with the class.

- **a)** In sentence 1, *They* and *themselves* are the same people.
- In sentence 2, *by themselves* means *alone*.
- In sentence 3, *themselves* emphasises that children do this instead of someone else.

- **b)** *myself, yourself, himself, herself, itself, ourselves, yourselves, themselves*. Model and drill these words with the class. Point out that the stress is always on the second syllable.
- If appropriate, point out that some verbs that are reflexive in other languages aren't reflexive in English, for example *meet, relax* and *feel*.
- Highlight that we usually say *have a wash/shave*, not *wash/shave myself*, and *get dressed* not ~~dress myself~~.
- Also highlight that we often use reflexive pronouns with the verb *enjoy*: *I really enjoyed myself last night*.
- Teach students that we can say *on my own, on your own*, etc. instead of *by myself, by yourself*, etc: *I enjoy living by myself/on my own*.
- Use the pictures in V6.2 SB p128 to highlight the difference between *themselves* and *each other*.

9 Students do the exercise on their own before checking answers in pairs. Check answers with the class.

> 2 himself 3 ourselves 4 herself 5 myself 6 themselves
> 7 myself

— EXTRA IDEA —
- Students think of three things they like doing by themselves and three things they don't, for example *I (don't) like going to the cinema by myself*. Students compare sentences in groups.

Get ready ... Get it right!

10 Focus students on the examples. Students work in pairs and write their top ten tips for parents. Students should make sentences using zero conditionals, conditionals with modal verbs and imperatives, and *in case*.

11 a) Students work in groups of four with another pair. Students take turns to tell each other their tips. Then the group decides on the best ten tips.

b) Either organise the class into larger groups, or conclude the activity with the whole class. Students decide which they think are the best ten tips. If students have done this stage in groups, ask each group to tell the class their top ten tips.

Finally, ask students to choose the best tip for parents.

— EXTRA PRACTICE AND HOMEWORK —
6 Review Exercises 3 and 4 SB p51
CD-ROM Lesson 6B
Workbook Lesson 6B p31

6C Touch wood

QUICK REVIEW ●●●
This activity reviews zero conditionals. Students work on their own and think about what they usually do in these situations. Put students into groups of three or four. Students take turns to tell each other their ideas, as in the example. Ask each group to share interesting ideas with the class.

Vocabulary synonyms
Skills Listening: The history of superstitions; Reading: Learn to be lucky
Help with Listening sentence stress (3)
Review conditionals, adjectives

Ask students which reason for a superstition they found most interesting or surprising.

1 the Romans 2 babies 3 trees 4 medicine 5 left

Vocabulary and Listening

1 **a)** Tell the class that the lesson is about luck and superstition. Focus students on photos A–H. Students do the exercise on their own or in pairs. Check answers with the class. Note that these words are not in Language Summary 6.
Model and drill the words/phrases.

A a black cat B salt C a shooting star D a ladder
E wood F a mirror G an umbrella H a lucky charm

b) Pre-teach *make a wish* and *spill*.
Focus students on the common British superstitions 1–7. Students do the exercise on their own, then check answers in pairs. Check answers with the class.

2 a ladder, an umbrella 3 a mirror 4 a lucky charm
5 a shooting star 6 wood 7 salt

2 Students discuss the questions in groups. Include students from different countries in each group if possible.
Ask students to share interesting ideas and superstitions with the class. Find out which is the most popular superstition.

3 **a)** Be prepared with definitions, examples, etc. to pre-teach the vocabulary in the box, or bring in dictionaries for students to check the meanings themselves.
Model and drill the words/phrases with the class, focusing on stress.

b) Tell students that they are going to listen to two friends, Edward and Charlotte, talking about superstitions.
R6.6 Focus students on sentences 1–7 in **1b)**, then play the recording (SB p149). Students listen and tick the superstitions that Edward and Charlotte talk about. Check answers with the class.

Edward and Charlotte talk about: **1** (black cats); **3** (breaking mirrors); **4** (lucky charms/a rabbit's foot); **6** (touching wood); **7** (spilling salt)

c) Give students time to read sentences 1–5 before playing the recording again. Students listen and complete the sentences. Students check answers in pairs. Check answers with the class.

Help with Listening Sentence stress (3)

• This Help with Listening section reviews and extends students' understanding of sentence stress, which they studied in lessons 1B and 1C.

4 **a)** Students do the exercise on their own. Check answers with the class. If necessary, check that students know all the parts of speech by eliciting a few examples of each one.

We usually stress nouns, verbs, adjectives and negative auxiliaries.
We don't usually stress pronouns, prepositions, connecting words and positive auxiliaries.

b) Focus students on the beginning of the conversation between Edward and Charlotte. Students work in pairs and decide which words are stressed. Early finishers can check their answers with another pair.
While students are working, copy the beginning of the conversation onto the board ready for checking.

c) R6.6 Play the recording again. Students listen to the beginning of the conversation and check their answers.
Check answers with the class by playing each sentence, then pausing and eliciting which words are stressed. Mark the stressed words on the board.
Ask students if question words (*Why*, etc.) and adverbs (*very, absolutely*, etc.) are usually stressed (they are).

EDWARD	Charlotte, are you very superstitious?
CHARLOTTE	No, not really. Why do you ask?
EDWARD	I'm reading this absolutely fascinating book about the history of superstitions. Did you know that in the UK, people think that seeing a black cat is good luck, but in nearly every other country it's bad luck? Don't you think that's strange?

d) Ask students to turn to R6.6, SB p149. Play the rest of the recording. Students listen and notice the sentence stress.

Reading and Vocabulary

 5 a) Student discuss the questions in groups. Ask each group to tell the class about things they have won and their reasons why they think people are or aren't born lucky.

b) Be prepared with definitions, examples, etc. to pre-teach the vocabulary in the box, or bring in dictionaries for students to check the meanings themselves. You can also teach *a pessimist* as the opposite of *an optimist*, and point out that *volunteer* is also a verb.

Model and drill the words with the class.

 6 a) Focus students on the article. Students read the article and choose the correct answers. Check answers with the class.

> **1** studies luck **2** doesn't think **3** can

b) Students read the article again and answer the questions. Early finishers can check answers in pairs. Check answers with the class.

Ask students if they agree with Dr Wiseman's ideas, giving reasons for their answers.

> **1** No, she didn't. **2** For ten years. **3** Yes, they do.
> **4** To teach unlucky people to be lucky. **5** 80% (320).

Help with Vocabulary Synonyms

 7 a) Tell students that we often use synonyms (words that mean the same, or almost the same) when we are speaking or writing so that we don't repeat words.

Focus students on the words in pink in the article. Check students know the meanings of all the words. Be prepared to teach any of these words if necessary.

b) Focus students on the words in blue in the article. Students work on their own and match them to the synonyms in the table. Remind students to write the infinitive forms of the verbs.

✎ While students are working, copy the table onto the board ready for checking. Check answers with the class.

Model and drill the words. Pay particular attention to the pronunciation of *fortunate* /ˈfɔːtənət/. Point out that the stress on *contént* is on the second syllable, not the first.

> satisfied → content; lucky → fortunate; behave → act;
> notice → spot; by chance → accidentally; attitude →
> approach; sure → certain; deal with → cope with;
> show → reveal

c)–d) Students do the exercise on their own or in pairs, then check answers in V6.3 SB p128. Note that most of these words/phrases have appeared earlier in the Student's Book.

Check answers with the class. Model and drill the words/phrases, focusing on sentence stress.

Note that *try* + infinitive with *to* means 'attempt to do' or 'make an effort to do': *I'm trying to get a job with a TV company.* *Try* + verb+*ing* means 'do something as an experiment to see if it works': *Have you tried talking to him about it?* This meaning was introduced in lesson 2D.

> frightened → scared; make a decision → make up your
> mind; try to do → have a go at doing; talk to someone
> → chat to someone; nice → pleasant; enormous → huge;
> pleased → glad; wonderful → brilliant; terrible → awful

8 Students do the exercise in pairs. One student says a word, for example *choose*, and his/her partner says the synonym, for example *pick*. You can ask the student who is being tested to close his/her book.

9 Put students into two groups, group A and group B. Students in group A turn to SB p103 and students in group B turn to SB p108.

a) Students work in pairs with someone from the same group and write the synonyms for the words in **bold**. Students can check words in V6.3 SB p128.

If necessary, check answers with the class. Only check the synonyms, so that the other group doesn't hear the questions they are about to be asked.

> **Group A 2** satisfied **3** make up your mind **4** chat to
> **5** scared **6** lucky
> **Group B 2** by chance **3** attitude **4** concerned
> **5** coping with **6** had a go at doing

b) Students work in pairs with someone from the other group. Students take turns to ask and answer their questions. Make sure students say the questions with the synonym they have just written, as well as all three possible answers. Students circle the answers that their partner chooses.

c) Students work out their partner's score on their own.

d) Students tell their partner his/her score before looking at SB p141 to find out what their score means. Students then decide who is luckier.

Ask students to tell the class their scores to find out who is the luckiest student in the class!

Finally, ask students if they think the summary of how lucky they are is correct or not, giving reasons for their answers.

> ┌─ **EXTRA PRACTICE AND HOMEWORK** ─
> **Ph** **Vocabulary Plus** 6 Antonyms p182
> (Instructions p174)
> **Ph** **Class Activity** 6C Synonyms bingo p150
> (Instructions p123)
> **6 Review** Exercise 5 SB p51
> **CD-ROM** Lesson 6C
> **Workbook** Lesson 6C p33

6D What's your opinion?

QUICK REVIEW ●●●

This activity reviews synonyms. Students work on their own and write all the pairs of synonyms they know, as in the example. Students work in pairs and take turns to say one of their words/phrases. Their partner guesses the synonym.

1 Students discuss the questions in groups.

Ask students to share any interesting experiences of music festivals with the class. Also check students' answers to questions 2–4.

2 a) Focus students on the picture and tell students that the people are at a local village meeting in the UK.

Go through the bullet points with the class and teach *chairperson, local resident* and *farmer*.

Students work on their own or in pairs and match the people listed in the bullet points to the people in the picture. Don't check answers at this stage.

b) R6.7 Play the recording (SB p149). Students listen to the beginning of the meeting and check their answers to **2a)**.

Check answers with the class. Also ask students what the meeting is about.

> Sarah Clark: the chairperson
> Sergeant Jim Matthews: a police officer
> Terry Gibson: the festival organiser
> Felicity Richards: a local resident
> Paul Davidson: a local farmer
>
> The meeting is about an application for a music festival on Mr Davidson's farm.

3 a) R6.8 Play the recording (SB p149). Students listen to the next part of the meeting and find out who is for and who is against the festival. Check answers with the class.

> For the festival: Terry Gibson, Paul Davidson.
> Against the festival: Sergeant Jim Matthews, Felicity Richards.
> Neither for nor against the festival: Sarah Clark.

b) Give students time to read sentences 1–6, then play the recording again. Students listen, tick the true sentences and correct the false ones. Students check answers in pairs. Check answers with the class.

> 1T 2F There will be **30,000** people at the festival. 3T 4F Most people going to the festival **won't** pass through the village because it's over four miles away. 5F The live music will stop at **midnight**. 6F Sergeant Matthews is most worried about the **traffic**.

EXTRA IDEA
● Students decide if sentences 1–6 are true or false before they listen again to check their answers.

c) Students work in groups of three or four and discuss whether Sarah Clark should give permission for the festival. Encourage students to give reasons for their answers.

Ask each group to tell the class if they think the festival should go ahead or not, giving reasons for their answers. You can then have a class vote on whether to allow the festival to go ahead.

Real World Discussion language

4 a)–b) Students do **4a)** on their own or in pairs, then check their answers in RW6.1 SB p129. Check answers with the class.

> ● 2 opinion 3 think 4 true 5 absolutely 6 with
>   7 not 8 sure 9 agree 10 interrupt 11 say 12 point
>   13 ahead 14 course 15 just 16 making
> ● Point out that we often use *I'm not sure about that.* as a polite way of disagreeing.

EXTRA IDEA
● R6.8 Ask students to look at R6.8, SB p149. Play the recording again. Students listen and underline all the discussion language from **4a)** that they hear.

5 R6.9 P Play the recording (SB p149). Students listen and practise. Check students copy the sentence stress and polite intonation correctly. Play the recording again if necessary.

You can also ask students to turn to R6.9, SB p149. They can then follow the sentence stress as they listen and practise.

6 a) Students work on their own and think of reasons why they agree or disagree with sentences 1–6. Encourage students to make brief notes on their ideas.

b) Put students into groups of four. Students discuss each topic for at least a minute. Encourage students to use the phrases from **4a)** in their discussions. Focus students on the language in the speech bubbles before they start.

While they are working, monitor and help students with appropriate language.

When they have finished, ask each group which topic generated the most discussion and what the different points of view were.

> **EXTRA IDEAS**
>
> - To encourage students to use a wide range of discussion language, tell them to tick each phrase in **4a)** on SB p50 when they use it. Students should try to use all the phrases in their discussions.
>
> - To avoid students interrupting each other too often, tell the class that each student can only interrupt twice during the whole activity.

7 Put students into four groups. Students in group A turn to SB p104, students in group B turn to SB p109, students in group C turn to SB p112 and students in group D turn to SB p113. Check they are all looking at the correct exercise.

Include an equal number of students in each group. If you have extra students, put them in groups A, B and C.

a) Give students a minute or two to read the information and check they understand the situation. Note that money from the National Lottery in the UK is often spent on community projects.

Students work in pairs with a student from the same group. If you have extra students, have some groups of three. Students follow the instructions.

While they are working, monitor and help students with language and ideas. Allow about 5 or 10 minutes for this stage.

b) Give students a few moments to read their instructions. Check that student Ds understand how to run their meetings and remind them that they are in control of who speaks during the meeting.

Reorganise the class into groups of four, with a student from groups A, B, C and D in each group. If you have extra students, have some groups of five or six. Ask student Ds to start the meeting.

While students are discussing their ideas, monitor and help with language as necessary.

Allow at least 10 or 15 minutes for this stage of the activity. Warn students when time is running out so that they have time to vote on which idea they want to choose.

c) Finally, ask each chairperson to tell the class which idea their group chose, giving reasons for their decision.

> **EXTRA IDEA**
>
> - While students are working, note down any mistakes and examples of good language you hear. ✎ Write them on the board. After discussing the outcome of the meetings, focus students on the language on the board and invite them to correct the mistakes in pairs or with the whole class. Also highlight the examples of good language that you heard.

> **EXTRA PRACTICE AND HOMEWORK**
>
> **Ph** **Class Activity** 6D Round the board p151 (Instructions p124)
> **6 Review** SB p51
> **CD-ROM** Lesson 6D
> **Workbook** Lesson 6D p34
> **Workbook** Reading and Writing Portfolio 6 p74
> **Progress Test 6** p210

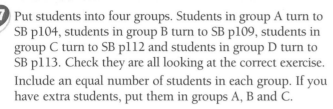

6 Review

See p30 for ideas on how to use this section.

1a) 1 make 2 do 3 did 4 make 5 makes 6 doing 7 done

2a) 1 gets; 'll tell 2 'll phone; go 3 won't go; feel 4 finish; I'll 5 'll wait; get

3 1 In sentence a), I might take the car, but only if it rains in the future. In sentence b) I'm definitely going to take the car because I think it might rain later. 2 Sentence a) talks about something that is always true. Sentence b) talks about one specific time in the future. 3 Both sentences have the same meaning. 4 In sentence a), maybe I will help if you can't do it. In sentence b), I will definitely help if you can't do it.

4 1 themselves 2 herself 3 myself 4 yourself 5 ourselves 6 himself

5 1 fortunate 2 approach 3 sure 4 dealing with 5 picked 6 satisfied

Progress Portfolio

See p30 for ideas on how to use this section.

7 Technology

7A Save, copy, delete

Vocabulary computers
Grammar ability: *be able to, manage, have no idea how, be good at*, etc.
Review discussion language; question forms

QUICK REVIEW ●●●

This activity reviews discussion language. Give students a minute or two to decide if they agree or disagree with sentences a)–c). Put students into groups of three or four. Students discuss the sentences in groups, using the discussion language from lesson 6D where appropriate. You can write the language from **RW6.1** SB p129 on the board before they begin. Briefly ask groups whether they agreed or disagreed with the sentences, giving reasons for their answers.

Vocabulary Computers

1 **a)** Students tick the words they know, then do the matching exercise in **V7.1** SB p130. Check answers with the class.

Check students understand the difference between *a monitor* and *a screen*, and that you use *a memory stick* to store information and take it from one computer to another.

Model and drill the words. Note that only the main stress in words/phrases is shown in vocabulary boxes and the Language Summaries.

> **V7.1** 1d) 2h) 3a) 4c) 5f) 6b) 7e) 8g)

b) Students discuss the questions in groups. Ask students to share interesting information with the class. You can also find out how many students have got a computer at home.

2 **a)** Students do the exercise in pairs, then check any new words in **bold** in **V7.2** SB p130. Check answers with the class.

Tell students that the opposite of *log on* is *log off*, and that we can also say *log in/log out*: *You have to log on/in before you can go online*.

Point out that we can say *the Net* or *the Web* instead of *the Internet*: *I found a cheap flight on the Net*.

Highlight that we say *broadband* in British English and *ADSL* in American English.

You can also teach students that we usually *sign in* to a website: *Enter your email address and password to sign in*.

Model and drill any new words with the class.

> **2** close **3** reply to **4** make **5** log on **6** click on **7** go; download **8** have; search

b) Students do the exercise in new pairs. Ask students to tell the class a few things they have both done in the last seven days.

Reading and Grammar

3 **a)** Focus students on the questionnaire. Teach the phrase *computer literate* (have a good knowledge about computers).

Students answer the questions on their own. Tell students not to worry about the phrases in **bold** at this stage.

b) Students compare their answers to the questionnaire in pairs to find out how many are the same.

c) Ask students to turn to SB p141. Students check their answers and then read what their score means.

Students share their scores with the class. Ask students if they agree with the questionnaire's assessment.

Help with Grammar Ability

4 **a)–e)** Students do the exercises on their own or in pairs, then check answers in **G7.1** SB p131. Check answers with the class.

- **a)** Things you can do now: *manage, 'm quite good at; can; find this quite easy; know how; 'm able to*. Things you can't do now: *'m … useless at; haven't got a clue how; have no idea how; find it difficult, 'm no good at*. Ability in the past: *was able to; could*.
- We can also use the other phrases to talk about ability in the past: *I managed to do this*, etc.
- **b)** 1 Yes, he/she did. 2 It was difficult.
- **c)** 2 verb+*ing* 3 infinitive 4–8 infinitive with *to*
- Point out that we can also use *find something easy/difficult* without 'infinitive with *to*': *I find using a computer really difficult*.
- Highlight that we can also use a noun or a pronoun after *be good at, be useless at*, etc.: *Mark's really useless at football, but Chris is brilliant at it*.
- **d)** We can also use: *be brilliant/great/excellent/not bad at* to say people are good at something and *be hopeless/bad/terrible/awful/rubbish at* to say people are bad at something.
- Point out that is often more polite to say: *I'm not bad at something* when we're very good at it.

71

5 R7.1 P Play the recording (SB p149). Students listen and practise. Check students copy the sentence stress and the weak forms of *to* /tə/ and *at* /ət/.

6 **a)** Give students one minute to read the text and find out what Bill does now. Check the answer with the class (he teaches retired people basic computer skills).

b) Students do the exercise on their own, then check answers in pairs. Don't check the answers with the class at this stage.

c) R7.2 Play the recording. Students listen and check their answers. Check answers with the class.

> 2 to save 3 type 4 to go 5 send 6 search 7 to create
> 8 working 9 to sort out

— EXTRA IDEA —
- Ask students to think about the computer skills their parents and grandparents have. Students can swap information in pairs or groups.

7 **a)** Pre-teach *fix* (= repair). You can also teach *touch-type* (type without looking at the keyboard).

Students work on their own and write sentences for each of the prompts, as in the example. Encourage students to use a different phrase from **4c)** for each idea.

b) Students compare sentences in pairs to find out what they can do that their partner can't. Ask students to share this information with the class.

Get ready … Get it right!

8 Students do the exercise on their own. Students should write sentences about their abilities in general, not about computers. Encourage them to use phrases from **4c)** and point out that some of their sentences can be about the past.

While students are working, monitor and correct any mistakes you see.

— EXTRA IDEA —
- If you think your students might have problems thinking of ideas in **8**, write some prompts on the board, for example *musical instruments, machines in the home, mobile phones, mornings, cooking, cars, languages, saving money, abilities as a child, choosing presents for people, doing exams, jobs around the house, singing, dancing, sports.*

9 **a)** Put students into pairs. Students take turns to say one of their sentences from **8**. Their partner can ask two questions only about each sentence before guessing if it is true or false. The student who gets most guesses right wins.

b) Ask students who got the most guesses right in each pair.

Finally, students tell the class two things that their partner can or can't do.

Ask students to tell the class about any interesting or unusual abilities they found out.

— EXTRA PRACTICE AND HOMEWORK —

Ph **Study Skills** 3 Developing reading skills p193 (Instructions p190)

Ph **Class Activity** 7A Guess my name p153 (Instructions p125)

7 Review Exercises 1 and 2 SB p59

CD-ROM Lesson 7A

Workbook Lesson 7A p35

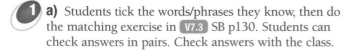

7B Want it, need it!

QUICK REVIEW ●●●
This activity reviews computer vocabulary. Students work on their own and write two things that you can save, click on, etc. Put students into pairs to compare answers. Students then discuss which of these things they have done this week.

Vocabulary electrical equipment
Grammar second conditional
Help with Listening first or second conditional
Review first conditional

Tell students that we sometimes use brand names to talk about hand-held computers (Palm®, BlackBerry®, etc.) and other types of digital music players (an iPod®, etc.).

Point out that we can say *a GPS* (global positioning system) or *sat nav* (satellite navigation). They are often installed in cars and tell us where we are and how to get to places. Also point out that we can say *a hands-free phone* or *a hands-free set*.

Vocabulary Electrical equipment

1 **a)** Students tick the words/phrases they know, then do the matching exercise in V7.3 SB p130. Students can check answers in pairs. Check answers with the class.

Explain that we use *central heating* to talk about the heating system in a house, flat or building: *Has your house got central heating?* You can teach students that the machine that heats the water is called *a boiler*, which sends hot water through the *pipes* to the *radiators* in each room.

Similarly, we use *air conditioning* to talk about the cooling system in a house, flat or building: *Our office has got air conditioning.* An individual machine is called *an air conditioner* or *an air conditioning unit.*

Model and drill the words/phrases, focusing on stress. Pay particular attention to the pronunciation of *straighteners* /ˈstreɪtənəz/.

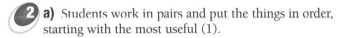

V7.3 1d) 2f) 3h) 4e) 5l) 6c) 7k) 8a) 9j) 10g) 11b) 12i)

b) Students do the exercise on their own.

c) Students compare answers in groups. Ask each group which things all the students in the group have or want.

2 a) Students work in pairs and put the things in order, starting with the most useful (1).

b) Students compare answers with another pair, giving reasons for their choices.

Ask each pair to tell the class what they think the top three most useful things are. Encourage students to explain why they chose these things.

Listening and Grammar

3 a) Focus students on the people in the photos and tell students that they are going to listen to them talk about things from **1a)**. Students guess which of the things in **1a)** the three people talk about.

b) R7.3 Play the recording (SB p150). Students listen and check their answers. Check answers with the class.

Don talks about air conditioning. Holly talks about hair straighteners. Kathy talks about a GPS.

c) Pre-teach *clown*. Students do the exercise on their own or in pairs.

d) Play the recording again. Students listen and check their answers to **3c)**. Check answers with the class and ask if the people have the things they talk about.

1 Holly 2 Kathy 3 Don 4 Kathy 5 Don 6 Holly
Don and Holly have the things they talk about, but Kathy doesn't.

Help with Grammar Second conditional

4 a)–e) Students do the exercises on their own or in pairs, then check their answers in G7.2 SB p131. Check answers with the class.

- **a)** We use the second conditional to talk about imaginary situations. We often use it to talk about the opposite of what is true or real: *If my car had a GPS, life would be so much easier* (but my car doesn't have a GPS).
- The second conditional talks about the present or the future.
- The *if* clause can be first or second in the sentence.

- **b)** 1 the second sentence 2 the first sentence

- **c)** We make the second conditional with: *if +* subject + Past Simple, subject + *'d (= would)/ wouldn't* + infinitive.
- Point out that we can say *If I/he/she/it was ...* or *If I/he/she/it were ...* in the second conditional: *If I was/were rich, I'd buy a big house.*
- Tell students that we can use *could +* infinitive in the main clause of the second conditional to talk about ability: *If I had a lot of money, I could buy a new car* (= I would be able to buy a new car).
- Highlight that we can also use *might +* infinitive in the main clause of second conditionals to mean 'would perhaps': *If I bought a GPS, I might not get lost all the time.*

- **d)** 1 What would you do if you didn't have one? 2 If you didn't have one, would you get lost?
- Use sentences 1 and 2 to highlight that we often make questions in the second conditional with *What would you do ... ?* and that this phrase can come at the beginning or the end of the sentence.
- Also highlight that we can make *yes/no* questions in the second conditional: *If you didn't have one, would you get lost?*
- The short answers to second conditional *yes/no* questions are *Yes, I would.* and *No, I wouldn't.* We can also say *Yes, I might.*

5 R7.4 P Play the recording (SB p150). Students listen and practise. Encourage students to copy the rhythm and sentence stress correctly.

You can also ask students to turn to R7.4, SB p150. They can then follow the sentence stress as they listen and practise.

6 a) Students do the exercise on their own. Tell students that they can complete the sentences in any way they like. Check the answers to the verb forms only with the class.

1 won; 'd go 2 didn't live; 'd like 3 could; 'd choose 4 was/were; 'd like 5 lived; 'd miss 6 could; 'd talk

b) Put students into pairs. Students take turns to say their sentences from **6a)**. Encourage students to continue the conversation if possible, as shown in the speech bubbles.

Ask students to share interesting sentences with the class.

7 Put students into pairs, student A and student B. Student As turn to SB p105 and student Bs turn to SB p110.

a) Check students remember *a karaoke* /ˌkærɪ'əʊkiː/ *bar* and *a personal diary* (a diary in which you write your personal thoughts, feelings and experiences).

Students fill in the gaps in the questions on their own. If necessary, check the answers with the class. Only check the words they need to fill in the gaps, so that the other group doesn't hear the questions they are about to be asked.

> **Student A 1** would … do; became **2** didn't study; would … like **3** had to; would … sing **4** would … be; lived **5** could; would … choose
>
> **Student B a)** weren't; would … be **b)** would … do; found **c)** had to; would … take **d)** would … change; became **e)** found; would … do

b) Focus students on the speech bubbles and use them to highlight that we don't usually repeat the *if* clause when answering questions in the second conditional.

Students work with their partner and take turns to ask their questions. Encourage students to continue the conversation if possible. While they are working, monitor and correct any mistakes you hear.

Ask students to share interesting answers with the class.

Help with Listening First or second conditional

- This Help with Listening section helps students to hear the difference between first and second conditionals.

8 a) Focus students on the example sentences and ask which is a first conditional (the first sentence) and which is a second conditional (the second sentence).

R7.5 Play the recording. Students listen and notice the difference between the verb forms. Play the recording again, highlighting the difference between *have* and *had*, and the contractions *I'll* and *I'd*.

b) **R7.6** Play the recording (SB p150). Students listen to the six pairs of sentences and decide whether they hear the first conditional or the second conditional first. Play the recording again if necessary. Check answers with the class.

> **1** first conditional
> **2** second conditional
> **3** second conditional
> **4** first conditional
> **5** second conditional
> **6** first conditional

EXTRA IDEA

- Play the recording again and ask students to write the sentences. Students can check their answers in pairs or in R7.6, SB p150.
---

9 a) Remind students who Don and Kathy are by focusing on their photos.

Students do the exercise on their own, then check their answers in pairs.

Don't check answers at this stage.

b) **R7.7** Play the recording. Students listen and check their answers.

Check answers with the class.

You can ask students to explain why the speaker uses the first or the second conditional in each case.

> **1** I'd **2** didn't **3** see **4** I'll **5** wouldn't **6** knew **7** didn't **8** I'd **9** write **10** I'll

Get ready … Get it right!

10 a) Students do the exercise on their own. Encourage them to write the six things in random order, not in two groups of three. Students can use words/phrases from **1a)** or their own ideas.

b) Students think how their lives would be different with or without the things they wrote in **10a)**, using second conditionals.

Focus students on the examples and then ask students to write at least one sentence about each thing.

While students are working, monitor and correct any mistakes you see.

11 a) Students work in pairs and swap papers. Students ask questions about the things on their partner's paper, as shown in the speech bubbles. Students should include the reasons why their lives would be different from **10b)** in their conversations.

While students are working, monitor and help with any language problems.

b) Finally, students tell the class two things that they have found out about their partner.

EXTRA IDEA

- Demonstrate **10** by writing some things you have and haven't got on the board in random order and think of reasons why your life would be different with or without these things. Before students do **11**, they ask you questions about the things you have written on the board.

EXTRA PRACTICE AND HOMEWORK

Ph **Vocabulary Plus** 7 Machines p183 (Instructions p175)

Ph **Class Activity** 7B The conditional game p154 (Instructions p125)

7 Review Exercises 3 and 4 SB p59

CD-ROM Lesson 7B

Workbook Lesson 7B p36

7C Virus alert!

Vocabulary use of articles: *a*, *an*, *the*, no article
Skills Listening: Computer viruses; Reading: Virus writers
Help with Listening weak forms (2)
Review second conditional; computers

Listening

1 Check students understand *a computer virus*. Model and drill *virus* /ˈvaɪrəs/ with the class. Students discuss the questions in groups.

Ask students to tell the class about any experiences they have had with computer viruses.

2 a) Be prepared with definitions, examples, etc. to pre-teach the vocabulary in the box, or bring in dictionaries for students to check the meanings themselves.

Note that the aim of these boxes is to highlight which words you need to pre-teach in order to help students understand the text that follows. The vocabulary in these boxes isn't in the Language Summaries.

b) Tell students they are going to listen to the beginning of a lecture about computer viruses.

Give students time to read the information in boxes A and B. R7.8 Play the recording (SB p150). Students listen and match the names in A to the facts in B. Students can check answers in pairs. Check answers with the class.

> 1b) 2f) 3a) 4d) 5e) 6c)

> ── EXTRA IDEA ──
> • Students can try and match the names in A to the facts in B before they listen. They can then listen to the recording and check their answers.

c) Give students time to read questions 1–6 before playing the recording again. Students check answers in pairs. Check answers with the class. Ask students if they have ever heard of the viruses mentioned in the recording.

> 1 They travel from computer to computer in the same way as flu viruses travel from person to person. 2 So that they could find out how many people were stealing their software. 3 No, it wasn't. 4 In his bedroom. 5 Because it could infect any computer online. 6 Your passwords and credit card details.

Help with Listening Weak forms (2)

• This Help with Listening section reviews and extends students' knowledge of weak forms, which they first studied in lesson 2C.

3 a) Focus students on the introductory bullet point and check students remember what a weak form is. Point out that many weak forms contain the schwa /ə/ sound.

Students work in pairs and decide how we say the strong and weak forms of the words in the box. If students are having difficulty, you can refer them back to **4a)**, SB p16.

Check answers with the class.

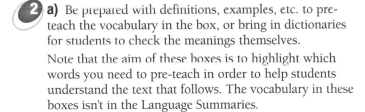

	strong	weak		strong	weak
do	/duː/	/də/	of	/ɒv/	/əv/
you	/juː/	/jə/	and	/ænd/	/ən/
at	/æt/	/ət/	to	/tuː/	/tə/
for	/fɔː/	/fə/	can	/kæn/	/kən/

> ── EXTRA IDEA ──
> • R2.7 Check answers to **3a)** by asking students to look back at **4a)**, SB p16 and playing the recording.

b) R7.9 Focus students on the tables, then play the recording. Students listen and notice the difference between the strong and the weak forms of the words. Highlight the schwa in the weak forms.

c) Focus students on the sentences from the beginning of the lecture and on the two circled examples of weak forms. Students work on their own or in pairs and circle the words they think they will hear as weak forms.

While students are working, copy the sentences onto the board ready for checking.

d) Ask students which words they think they will hear as weak forms and circle these words on the board.

R7.8 Play the recording again. Students listen and check their answers. Check the text on the board and make any changes necessary. Play the recording again if necessary.

Ask students if weak forms are ever stressed (they aren't).

> These days, computer viruses (are) /ə/ part (of) /əv/ everyday life. But (as) /əz/ early (as) /əz/ 1940, a man called John von Neumann predicted (that) /ðət/ computer programmes would be able (to) /tə/ make copies (of) /əv/ themselves — (and) /ənd/ he (was) /wəz/ right. This ability (has) /həz/ meant (that) /ðət/ people (have) /həv/ been able (to) /tə/ create viruses which (can) /kən/ travel (from) /frəm/ computer (to) /tə/ computer.

- Ask students to predict which words in the sentences on the board are stressed. ✏ Elicit their answers and mark the stress on the board. Students can check their answers when they look at R7.8, SB p150 in **3e**).

e) Ask students to turn to R7.8, SB p150. Play the recording again. Students listen and notice the sentence stress and weak forms. Note that only the weak forms that students have studied so far in the course are marked in the recording scripts.

Reading and Vocabulary

4 Divide the class into two groups, group A and group B. Ask students from group A to read the text about David L Smith on SB p57. Ask students from group B to read the text about Onel de Guzman on the same page. Tell students to cover the text they aren't going to read.

Students read their text and answer questions 1–6. Early finishers can check answers with someone from the same group.

5 a) Reorganise the class so that a student from group A is working with a student from group B. Students take turns to ask and answer the questions from **4**.

b) **R7.10** Ask students to uncover the text that they haven't read yet. Play the recording. Students read and listen to both articles, and check that their partner's answers are correct. If necessary, check answers with the class.

Ask students which facts from the articles they think are the most surprising.

David L Smith 1 The USA. 2 The Melissa virus. 3 David L Smith named it after a dancer he knew while he was living in Miami, Florida. 4 As soon as it infected a computer, it forwarded itself to the first 50 email addresses in the computer's address book. 5 More than $80 million in North America alone. 6 Yes, he was sent to prison for 20 months.

Onel de Guzman 1 The Philippines. 2 The Love Bug virus. 3 Because the virus came as an email attachment which said "I love you". 4 When people opened the attachment, it sent itself to everyone in their address book. 5 Over $10 billion. 6 No, because at that time there were no laws in the Philippines for computer crime.

Help with Vocabulary Use of articles: a, an, the, no article

6 a–b) Students do the exercise on their own or in pairs, then check their answers in **V7.4** SB p130.
Check answers with the class.

- **a)** b) a dancer c) a computer d) the computer e) the Melissa virus f) the USA g) the worst h) Miami i) email systems j) prison
- Point out that we use *the* with public places (*school, hospital, university, college, prison, church*, etc.) when we talk about the building. Compare these two sentences: *His mother's in hospital* (she's ill: we are thinking of hospital as a general idea). *He's gone to the hospital to visit his mother* (to the building: we're thinking of a specific hospital).
- Remind students that we use *the* in some fixed phrases: *in the morning/afternoon, at the weekend, go to the cinema/the theatre/the bank/the shops, the news*, etc.

7 a) Focus students on the words/phrases in **bold** in the article about Onel de Guzman. Students work on their own or in pairs and match them to the rules a)–j) in **6a**). Point out that there is one word/phrase for each rule.

b) Students compare answers in pairs, giving reasons for their choices. Check answers with the class.

the Philippines f); the most famous g); university j); an email attachment c); the attachment d); an unopened file a); the world e); businesses i); Asia h)

8 Put students into pairs, student A and student B. Student As turn to SB p105 and student Bs turn to SB p110. Check they are all looking at the correct exercise.

a) Students fill in the gaps on their own. While they are working, monitor and correct any mistakes you see.

If necessary, check answers with the class. Only check the gaps, so that the other group doesn't hear the questions they are about to be asked.

Student A 1 a 2 a; the 3 the; the 4 the; – 5 –; – 6 – 7 an; a
Student B 1 a b) an; a; the c) – d) –; the e) the; the f) –; – g) a; an; a

b) Students work with their partner and take turns to ask and answer their questions. Encourage students to ask follow-up questions if possible.
Ask students to share interesting answers with the class.

9 a) Put students into groups of three or four. If you have students of similar ages, backgrounds or nationalities, or with similar hobbies and interests, put them in the same group.

Tell the class that each group is going to start its own website. Give students a few moments to read the ideas in the box. Check they understand *a fan site* (a website set up by fans of a particular film star, etc. where they can discuss the star's latest film, swap news stories, etc.).

Students work in groups and decide what their website is going to be about. They can choose from the topics in the box or use their own ideas.

b) Pre-teach *home page* (the first page you see when you go to the website).

Students work in their groups and discuss what is going to be on their website. They can use the ideas from the prompts or their own. Make sure that each student makes notes on the decisions the group makes about their website, as they will have to describe the website to other students in a different group. While students are working, monitor and help with language and ideas.

 a) Reorganise the class so that students from different groups are working together. Students take turns to describe their websites.

When all the students in the group have described their websites, they decide which they think is the best.

b) Students from each group tell the class which website is the best, giving reasons for their choice. Finally, ask students to choose which is the best website in the class.

─ **EXTRA PRACTICE AND HOMEWORK** ─
Ph **Class Activity** 7C Article auction p155 (Instructions p125)
CD-ROM Lesson 7C
Workbook Lesson 7C p38

 ## 7D What's the password?

─────

Real World indirect and direct questions
Help with Listening intonation (2): being polite
Review computers; verb forms

QUICK REVIEW ●●●
This activity reviews computer collocations. Students work on their own and make their lists. Set a time limit of three minutes. Students work in pairs and compare lists to find out who has the most words. Students then decide which words on both lists they can use together, as in the example. Ask students to share some of their collocations with the class.

Real World Indirect and direct questions

1 **a)** Focus students on the photos. Discuss with the class where the people are and what problems they might have.

b) Tell students they are going to listen to Carol talking to people at work and then to her husband, Ben, later the same day (as shown in the photos).

R7.11 Give students time to read sentences a)–h), then play the recording (SB p150). Students listen, tick the true sentences and correct the false ones. Students check answers in pairs. Check answers with the class.

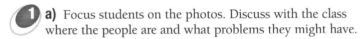
a)T b)F They have changed **the email system** in the office. c)T d)F He will be back around 3 p.m. e)F He's gone to **the cinema**. f)T g)T h)F She **forgot to call/didn't call him** earlier in the day.

2 **a)** **R7.11** Give students time to read questions a)–j). Play the recording again. Students listen and put the questions in the order they hear them.

b) Students compare answers in pairs. Check answers with the class.

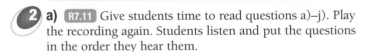
Conversation 1 1b) 2e) 3d) 4c) 5a)
Conversation 2 1h) 2f) 3j) 4g) 5i)

3 **a)–d)** Tell students that questions a)–e) in **2a)** are called indirect questions and questions f)–j) are called direct questions. Students do the exercises on their own or in pairs, then check in **RW7.1** SB p131.

🖊 While students are working, draw the table from **RW7.1** SB p131 on the board ready to check their answers. Check answers with the class.

- **a)** In more formal situations we often use indirect questions because they sound more polite. For example *Could you tell me whether he'll be back soon?* sounds more polite than *Will he be back soon?*

- **b)** Focus students on the table on the board and ask them which part of questions a)–d) in **2a)** goes in each column. Write students' answers in the table (see **RW7.1** SB p131).

- Use the table to highlight the phrases we use to introduce indirect questions: *Could you tell me ... ?; Do you know ... ?; Have you got any idea ... ?; Can you tell me ... ?*.

- We use *if* or *whether* in indirect questions when there isn't a question word.
- In indirect questions, *if* and *whether* are the same: *Do you know if/whether we asked Alex Ross to come?*
- We don't use *if* or *whether* with *Do you think … ?*: *Do you think he's changed his password?* not ~~Do you think if/whether he's changed his password?~~
- **c)** In indirect questions, the main verb is in the positive form. We say: *Do you know if we asked Alex Ross to come?* not ~~Do you know if did we ask Alex to come?~~
- Focus students on the other phrases in pink in questions a)–e) in **2a)** to show that we use the positive verb form, not the question form.

Help with Listening
Intonation (2): being polite

- This Help with Listening section introduces students to polite intonation patterns for asking indirect questions.

 Focus students on the introductory bullet point. Highlight the importance of using polite intonation when asking indirect questions. Many students have problems achieving the required voice movement, so it is worth stressing that if their voices are flat, they often sound rude or impatient to native English speakers.

R7.12 Play the recording (SB p151). Students listen and decide which sentences sound polite. Check answers with the class by playing the recording again and pausing after each pair of sentences to elicit students' answers. Point out that in the polite versions the speaker's voices start at a higher pitch and move up and down more.

2a) 3a) 4b) 5b)

 R7.13 P Play the recording (SB p151). Students listen and practise. Check students copy the polite intonation and sentence stress. Play the recording again if necessary.

 Students do the exercise on their own, then check answers in pairs. Check answers with the class.

1 Do you know how this ticket machine works?
2 Have you any idea what Jim wants for his birthday?
3 Can you tell me whether this is room D? 4 Do you think Ruth will be at the meeting? 5 Could you tell me how often the trains run?

7 **a)** Check students understand *give someone a tip*. Students do the exercise on their own, then check answers in pairs. Check answers with the class.

1 Do you know if/whether there's a bookshop near here?
2 Could you tell me how I get to the station? 3 Do you think I should give taxi drivers a tip? 4 Have you any idea what time the banks close? 5 Can you tell me where the nearest post office is?

b) Students do the exercise on their own. While students are working, monitor and check their questions are correct.

c) Put students into pairs. Students take turns to ask their questions from **7a)** and **7b)**. Students should answer with the correct information if they know it. Encourage students to continue the conversation if appropriate and to thank the person for their help at the end. While they are working, monitor and correct any mistakes that you hear. Finally, ask a few pairs to role-play their conversations for the class.

┌─ **EXTRA PRACTICE AND HOMEWORK** ─────
7 Review SB p59
CD-ROM Lesson 7D
Workbook Lesson 7D p39
Workbook Reading and Writing Portfolio 7 p76
Progress Test 7 p212
└──────────────────────────────────

7 Review

See p30 for ideas on how to use this section.

1a) 1 delete 2 forward 3 click on 4 search for 5 download 6 go
3a) 2 hand-held computer 2 hair dryer 3 webcam 4 central heating 5 air conditioning 6 hands-free phone 7 MP3 player 8 dishwasher
4a) 1 If I could find him, I'd tell him. 2 Carla would help you if she had time. 3 If he lived with us, we'd look after him. 4 If you didn't like the flat, we'd move.
4b) 2 a) first conditional b) second conditional 3 a) first conditional b) second conditional 4 a) second conditional b) first conditional

5a) 2 Can/Could you tell me what time it is? 3 Do you know if this bus goes to Acton? 4 Have you any idea where Pete has gone? 4 Do you think we should leave now? 6 Can you tell me what Sally's home phone number is? 7 Do you think he has changed his email address?

Progress Portfolio

- See p30 for ideas on how to use this section.

8A Changing weather

Vocabulary weather
Grammar the passive
Review indirect questions; verb forms

QUICK REVIEW ●●●

This activity reviews indirect questions. Students do the first part of the activity on their own. If students are having problems thinking of ideas, write the following prompts on the board: *time open/close, weekends, name of teacher/director of studies, teachers' room/computer room/library, how many levels, exam courses, number of students, nearest café*. Put students into pairs. Students take turns to ask and answer their questions. Ask students to ask you any questions that their partner didn't know the answer to.

Vocabulary Weather

1 a) Point out that all the words in the box talk about bad weather conditions. Students work in pairs and tick the words they know. Don't help students with words they don't know at this stage.

b) Students continue working in pairs and put the words in order, starting with the coldest.

c) Ask students to check any new words in **1a)** and their answers to **1b)** in V8.1 SB p132. Check answers with the class (see V8.1 SB p132).

Tell students that the adjective for *storm* is *stormy* and the adjective for *fog* is *foggy*.

Highlight that *thunder, lightning* and *fog* are uncountable nouns, and that we say *thunder and lightning* not ~~lightning and thunder~~.

Point out that *humid* is an adjective (the noun is *humidity*), and that *flood* can be a noun and a verb. You can also tell students that *heat wave* is sometimes written as one word (*heatwave*).

Also point out that *boiling* and *freezing* are strong adjectives, so we can say *absolutely boiling/freezing*, but not ~~very boiling/freezing~~.

Model and drill the words. Pay particular attention to the pronunciation of *humid* /ˈhjuːmɪd/, *flood* /flʌd/ and *tornado* /tɔːˈneɪdəʊ/. Note that only the main stress in words/phrases is shown in vocabulary boxes and the Language Summaries.

— EXTRA IDEA —
* Begin the lesson with a discussion of any stories about bad weather that have been in the news recently.

2 Students discuss the questions in groups. If possible, include students of different nationalities in the same group. Ask students to share interesting answers with the class.

Reading and Grammar

 3 a) Be prepared with definitions, examples, etc. to pre-teach the vocabulary in the box, or bring in dictionaries for students to check the meanings themselves.

Note that the aim of these boxes is to highlight which words you need to pre-teach in order to help students understand the text that follows. The vocabulary in these boxes is not in the Language Summaries.

Model and drill the words/phrases. Pay particular attention to the pronunciation of *atmosphere* /ˈætməsfɪə/ and *climate* /ˈklaɪmət/.

— EXTRA IDEA —
* Put the students into pairs, student A and student B. Student A checks the meaning of the first row of words in the box, and student B checks the meaning of the words in the second row. Students work in pairs and teach their partner the words. Check students have understood all the words before continuing.

b) Focus students on the web page of FAQs (Frequently Asked Questions) about global warming and climate change. Students read the web page quickly and match questions a)–d) to paragraphs 1–4. Set a time limit of two minutes to encourage students to read for gist.

Check answers with the class.

1c) 2a) 3d) 4b)

 4 a) Students do the exercise on their own, then check answers in pairs. Remind students that they can only fill in each gap with one word.

Check answers with the class.

1 colder
2 climate/weather
3 hot
4 rising
5 energy/electricity

b) Students discuss the questions in groups. Ask students to share their ideas with the class.

Note that students discuss their attitudes to global warming and climate change in **9**, so don't let this discussion go on too long.

Help with Grammar The passive

5 **a)–e)** Students do the exercises on their own or in pairs, then check their answers in **G8.1** SB p133.

 While students are working, draw the table from **5c)** on the board so that you are ready to check their answers. Check answers with the class.

- **a)** The subject of the active sentence is *A huge hurricane*. The subject of the passive sentence is *New Orleans*. The object of the active sentence is *New Orleans*.

- **b)** The **object** of the active sentence becomes the **subject** of the passive sentence.
- We often use the **passive** when we are more interested in what happens to someone or something than in who or what does the action.
- In passive sentences we can use '*by* + the agent' to say who or what does the action: *New Orleans was hit by a huge hurricane*.
- Point out that we only use '*by* + the agent' when it is important or unusual information. We don't use it when the agent is clear from the context: *Twelve people were arrested by the police*.
- Also highlight that we often use the passive when we don't know who or what the agent is: *A lot has been written about what governments and businesses should do*.

- **c)** We make the passive with: subject + *be* + past participle.
- Focus students on the table on the board. Elicit which words from the phrases in **bold** in the article go in each column and complete the table (see the table in **G8.1** SB p133).
- Point out that we can also use other modal verbs (*could, must, should, might*, etc.) in passive verb forms: *Many people could be made homeless. These pills must be taken four times a day.*

- **d)** We make negative passive sentences by making the verb form of *be* negative: *it isn't held, they aren't being kept, it hasn't been caused, it wasn't hit*, etc.

6 **R8.1** **P** Play the recording (SB p151). Students listen and practise. Check they copy the sentence stress correctly. Play the recording again if necessary.

7 **a)** Students read the text about Roy Sullivan and find out what happened to him. Note that students don't choose the correct answers at this stage.

Check the answer with the class (he was hit by lightning seven times in his lifetime).

b) Pre-teach *park ranger* /ˈreɪndʒə/, *toenail*, *eyebrow* and *lightning strike*.

Students do the exercise on their own. Early finishers can check answers in pairs.

c) **R8.2** Play the recording. Students listen and check their answers. Check answers with the class.

> **1** is hit **2** will be hit **3** spend **4** was hit **5** lost
> **6** happened **7** was taken

8 **a)** Focus students on the photo. Ask students which city it is (Venice, in Italy) and what problems the city has (it is often flooded).

b) Students do the exercise on their own before checking their answers in pairs. Check answers with the class.

> **2** will be flooded/is going to be flooded **3** has already been collected **4** have now been repaired/are now being repaired **5** be found **6** be saved **7** isn't done
> **8** will be lost/are going to be lost

Get ready … Get it right!

9 Put students into two groups, group A and group B. Students in group A turn to SB p106 and students in group B turn to SB p111.

a) Check that students understand *take something seriously enough, solve a problem* and *the environment* /ɪnˈvaɪərənmənt/.

Students work in pairs with someone from the same group. Students put the verbs in brackets in the correct active or passive form. Point out that there can sometimes be more than one possible answer.

If necessary, check answers with the class. Only check the words they need to fill in the gaps.

> **Student A** **1** take/are taking **2** do **3** are taught/are being taught **4** be made **5** will happen/is going to happen
>
> **Student B** **a)** is taken/is being taken **b)** has been done **c)** have been damaged **d)** do **e)** be solved

b) Reorganise the class so that a pair of students from group A works with a pair of students from group B. Students take turns to ask and answer their questions. Encourage students to give reasons for their answers where possible.

c) Ask each group to tell the class some of the things they have discussed.

Finally, ask students what they think the future of the planet is and what they can do to help reduce global warming.

--- EXTRA PRACTICE AND HOMEWORK ---

Ph **Vocabulary Plus** 8 Weather conditions p184 (Instructions p175)

Ph **Class Activity** 8A Passive knowledge p156 (Instructions p126)

8 Review Exercises 1 and 2 SB p67

CD-ROM Lesson 8A

Workbook Lesson 8A p40

8B Recycle your rubbish

Vocabulary containers
Grammar quantifiers: *a bit of, too much/many,*
(not) enough, plenty of, etc.
Help with Listening quantifiers
Review weather; food

QUICK REVIEW ●●●

This activity reviews weather vocabulary. Students work on their own and write five weather words that are connected to them. Put students into pairs. Students compare words and tell their partner why they have chosen these words, as in the example. Ask students to share interesting answers with the class.

Vocabulary Containers

 a) Students do the exercise on their own or in pairs, then check their answers in **V8.2** SB p132.

Check answers with the class (see **V8.2** SB p132). Note that some products may come in different containers in some countries.

Point out that we usually use *a tin* for food (*a tin of tomatoes*) and *a can* for drink (*a can of cola*). Also point out that *marmalade* is made from citrus fruit (oranges, lemons, etc.) and *jam* is made from soft fruit (strawberries, blackberries, etc.).

Highlight that in the UK *crisps* (US: *chips*) are thin, cold fried potatoes that are often sold in bags. In the UK *chips* (US: *French fries*) are hot, fried potatoes that are often eaten with meals. Point out that we say *a box of chocolates* but *a bar of chocolate*, and that we say *sweets* in British English and *candy* in American English.

Model and drill the complete phrases (*a bottle of milk, a bag of crisps,* etc.). Pay particular attention to the pronunciation of *jar* /dʒɑː/, *honey* /ˈhʌniː/, *biscuits* /ˈbɪskɪts/, *marmalade* /ˈmɑːməleɪd/, *chocolates* /ˈtʃɒkləts/ and *crisps* /krɪsps/. Point out that we say the weak form of *of* /əv/ in these phrases. Also highlight that the stress on *carton* is on the first syllable, not the second.

b) Students do the exercise in pairs. You can ask students to close their books while they are being tested.

c) Students do the exercise in new pairs. Ask students to think of at least one more thing for each container. Check answers with the class.

> **Possible answers** a bottle of wine; a bag of rice, a tin of sardines; a box of matches; a can of cola; a carton of tomato juice; a jar of olives; a packet of pasta

Listening and Grammar

 Pre-teach *recycle* /riːˈsaɪkl/ and *recycling* /riːˈsaɪklɪŋ/, and check students remember *a law* /lɔː/. Drill these words with the class.

Students discuss the questions in groups. If possible, include students of different nationalities in the same group.

Ask students to share answers with the class.

 a) Focus students on the picture. Ask students to cover the vocabulary boxes in **1a)**. Students work on their own or in pairs and write down all the containers and products they can see in the picture, for example *a bottle of lemonade*. Set a time limit of two minutes.

Check answers with the class and find out which student or pair has the most phrases.

> a bottle of tomato ketchup; a bottle of olive oil; a bottle of lemonade; a bag of sweets; a bag of potatoes; a tin of tuna; a tin of cat food; a tin of beans; a box of chocolates; a carton of orange juice; a jar of honey; a jar of jam; a packet of biscuits; a packet of soup; a packet of crisps

b) Focus students on the picture again. Tell students that Val and her boyfriend, Pete, are visiting Val's brother, James.

R8.3 Give students time to read sentences 1–6, then play the recording (SB p151). Students listen and choose the correct answers. Students check answers in pairs. Check answers with the class.

> 1 don't have anything 2 doesn't recycle any 3 15% 4 90% 5 tins 6 is

 a) Pre-teach *a recycling bin* (a large container in the street where you can recycle bottles, cans, etc.) and *a recycling box* (a small container in your house in which you put things that can be recycled).

R8.3 Give students time to read sentences 1–12. Play the recording again. Students listen and write who says each sentence.

> **EXTRA IDEA**
> • Ask students to work in pairs and decide who says sentences 1–12 before they listen again. Students can then listen and check their answers.

b) Students check their answers in pairs. Check answers with the class.

> 2 Val 3 Pete 4 James 5 Val 6 Pete 7 Val 8 Val 9 Pete 10 Val 11 James 12 Val

> **EXTRA IDEA**
> • Students look at the picture again and decide which things James can recycle.

Help with Grammar *Quantifiers*

 5 **a)–d)** Students do the exercises in pairs, then check their answers in [G8.2] SB p133.

🖊 While students are working, draw the table from **5b)** on the board so that you are ready to check their answers. Check answers with the class.

- **a) Countable nouns** tins; recycling bins; plastic bottles; people; friends
- **Uncountable nouns** pasta; sugar; milk; rubbish; stuff; paper; information; progress

- **b)** Focus students on the table on the board. Elicit which words in blue in **4a)** go in each column and complete the table (see the table in [G8.2] SB p133).
- Remind students that we can say *There aren't any biscuits.* or *There are no biscuits.* and *There isn't any milk.* or *There's no milk.*
- Point out that *not many, hardly any* and *not much* have a negative meaning. *Several, a few, a bit of* and *a little* have a positive meaning. *Several* is usually more items than *a few.*
- Also highlight that *loads of* is more informal than *a lot of* and *lots of.*
- Highlight the word order with *not enough* and *enough*:
  not + enough + noun: There aren't enough places.
  not + adjective + enough: It isn't big enough.
  enough + noun: There's enough milk.
  adjective + enough: That's hot enough.

- **c)** We usually use *some* in positive sentences: *I've found some coffee.*
- We usually use *any* in negative sentences and questions: *There isn't any sugar. Is there any milk?*
- We don't usually use *much* or *many* in positive sentences: *There's a lot of stuff here.* not ~~There's much stuff here.~~ *I've got lots of cups* not ~~I've got many cups.~~
- Check students remember that we use *some* and *any* with plural countable nouns (*biscuits, beans,* etc.) and uncountable nouns (*pasta, milk,* etc.).
- Remind students that we often use *some* in questions with *Would you like … ?: Would you like some coffee?*

Help with Listening *Quantifiers*

- This Help with Listening section focuses on how we say quantifiers and reviews sentence stress, linking and weak forms.

 6 **a)** [R8.4] Play the recording (SB p151). Students listen and write the sentences. Point out that they will hear each sentence twice before they start.

b) Students do the exercise on their own. Point out that contractions (*there's*, etc.) are two words before they start.

c) Students compare sentences in pairs and underline the quantifiers. Check the sentences with the class.

Ask students to turn to R8.4, SB p151. Play the recording again. Students listen and notice the stress and linking in each sentence. Also highlight the weak form of *of* /əv/.

> I think there's <u>a bit of</u> milk in the fridge. (11 words)
> We have<u>n't</u> got <u>enough</u> bags of crisps. (8 words)
> There's <u>hardly any</u> food in the cupboard. (8 words)
> He's got <u>a lot of</u> tins of cat food. (10 words)
> We need to get <u>a few</u> packets of biscuits. (9 words)
> There's <u>lots of</u> coffee and <u>plenty of</u> cups. (9 words)

 7 [R8.5] [P] Play the recording (SB p151). Students listen and practise, copying the linking and sentence stress.

 8 **a)** Students do the exercise on their own. Check answers with the class.

> **2** too much **3** hardly any **4** a few **5** a bit of **6** plenty of **7** enough **8** some **9** too many

b) Students work on their own and tick the sentences in **8a)** that are true for them.

c) Students do the exercise in pairs. Encourage students to ask follow-up questions if appropriate. Ask students to share one or two of their sentences with the class.

Get ready … Get it right!

 9 Pre-teach *cycle lane* and check students remember the other words/phrases in the box.

Focus students on the examples below the box and ask students what the quantifiers are in each sentence (*n't enough, too much*).

Students work on their own and write four good things and four bad thing about the town/city they are in now. Encourage them to use the ideas in the box or their own ideas, and the quantifiers from **5b)**.

10 **a)** Put the students into groups of three or four. Students take turns to say their sentences. The other students say whether they agree or disagree, giving reasons for their answers.

When students have discussed all of their sentences, they choose the two best and the two worst things about the town/city there are in now.

b) Ask each group to tell the class their two best and two worst things about the town/city there are in now.

Finally, ask the class to decide what they think is the best and the worst thing about the town/city.

┌─ **EXTRA PRACTICE AND HOMEWORK** ─
Ph **Class Activity** 8B The airport p157 (Instructions p126)
8 Review Exercises 3 and 4 SB p67
CD-ROM Lesson 8B
Workbook Lesson 8B p41

8C Dangers at sea

QUICK REVIEW ●●●
This activity reviews types of container. Students do the activity in pairs. Check students' answers by saying the containers in **1a)** on SB p62 and eliciting things that can come in each container.

> **Vocabulary** word formation (2): prefixes and opposites, other prefixes and suffixes
> **Skills** Listening: Shark attack!; Reading: Saving Jesse's arm
> **Help with Listening** linking (3): review
> **Review** the passive; Past Perfect; character adjectives

Listening

1 Students discuss the questions in groups. Ask students to share interesting answers with the class.

2 **a)** Focus students on the photo and use this to pre-teach *shark, attack* and *bite*. Also pre-teach *oxygen* /ˈɒksədʒən/.

b) Tell students that they are going to listen to a TV news report.

R8.6 Give students time to read questions 1–4, then play the recording (SB p151). Students listen and answer the questions. Check answers with the class.

> **1** A British tourist has been attacked by a shark off the coast of Texas. **2** Dead zones are areas in the ocean where there isn't enough oxygen, so all the fish die. **3** People./Too much pollution in the sea. **4** About 150.

c) Give students time to read sentences 1–7, then play the recording again. Students listen and choose the correct information in each sentence. Students check answers in pairs. Check answers with the class.

> **1** eight **2** quite near **3** leg **4** very big **5** half **6** bad **7** aren't

Help with Listening Linking (3): review

- This Help with Listening section reviews consonant-vowel links and linking with /w/, /j/ and /r/ sounds, which were first introduced in lessons 3C and 4C.

3 **a)** Focus students on the sentence from the news report. Students do the exercise on their own.

Check the answers with the class. Use the example sentence to highlight the consonant-vowel link and the three extra linking sounds /w/, /j/ and /r/.

> We usually link words that end in a consonant sound with words that start with a vowel sound.
>
> When a word ends in a vowel sound and the next word also starts with a vowel sound, we often link these words with a /w/, /j/ or /r/ sound.

─── EXTRA IDEA ───
- Students can refer back to the introductory bullet point in the Help with Listening box on SB p33 to find out when we use /w/, /j/ and /r/ sounds.

b) Focus students on the sentences from the beginning of the news report. Students work in pairs and draw the links, adding extra linking sounds if necessary.

c) Students turn to R8.6, SB p151 to check their answers.

You can check answers by playing the beginning of R8.6 again, pausing after each sentence to highlight the various types of linking.

> A British tourist has been‿attacked by‿/j/‿a shark‿off the coast‿of Texas, making‿it the‿/j/‿eighth shark‿attack‿in the‿/j/‿USA this year. We now go‿/w/‿over live to Freeport for‿/r/‿a special report from‿our North‿American correspondent, Andrew‿/w/‿Evans. Andrew,‿/w/‿I‿/j/‿understand the man didn't do‿/w/‿anything unusual to cause this‿attack.

d) **R8.6** Play the whole recording again. Students listen, read and notice the different types of linking.

Reading and Vocabulary

4 **a)** Be prepared with definitions, examples, etc. to pre-teach the vocabulary in the box, or bring in dictionaries for students to check the meanings themselves. Tell students that *estimate* and *harm* can be verbs or nouns. Also point out that *harm* is an uncountable noun.

Model and drill the words. Pay particular attention to the pronunciation of *conscious* /ˈkɒnʃəs/ and *strength* /streŋθ/. Note that *estimate* is pronounced /ˈestɪmeɪt/ if it is a verb and /ˈestɪmət/ if it is a noun.

b) Focus students on the title of the article. Point out that this is a true story. Students say what they think happened to Jesse. Don't tell them if they are correct at this stage.

c) Students read the article and decide if their predictions were correct. Check the answer with the class.

> Jesse's arm was bitten off by a shark. He was taken to hospital, where his arm was reattached.

5 Students do the exercise on their own. Early finishers can check answers in pairs. Check answers with the class.

> **1F** The shark bit off **the whole of** Jesse's arm. **2F A park ranger** shot the shark. **3F A volunteer firefighter** got Jesse's arm from inside the shark. **4T 5T**

Help with Vocabulary Word formation (2): prefixes and opposites, other prefixes and suffixes

6 a)–c) Focus students on the introductory bullet point and check students know what a prefix and a suffix are. Students do the exercises on their own or in pairs, then check their answers in **V8.3** SB p132. Check answers with the class. You may wish to check the answer to **6a)** briefly before students move on to **6b)**.

- **a)** We often use the prefixes *un-*, *dis-*, *im-*, *in-* and *ir-* to make opposites of words.
- Elicit examples of words with these prefixes from the article (*unconscious, disappeared, impossible, incorrect, irresponsible*).
- Point out that we can use these prefixes to make opposites of adjectives (*unconscious*, etc.) and verbs (*disappear*, etc.).
- Point out that adjectives beginning with *p* usually take the prefix *im-* (*possible* → *impossible*, etc.) and adjectives beginning with *r* usually take the prefix *ir-* (*responsible* → *irresponsible*, etc.)

- **b)** unbelievable; impatient; unselfish; dishonest; inconsiderate; impolite; disorganised; irregular; unreliable; disloyal; immature; unambitious; informal; dissimilar; insensitive; unhelpful
- Model and drill the words. Point out that prefixes aren't usually stressed.

7 a)–c) Students do the exercises on their own or in pairs, then check their answers in **V8.4** SB p132.

✐ While students are working, draw the table from **7a)** on the board so that you are ready to check their answers.

Check answers with the class. You may wish to check the answer to **7a)** briefly before students move on to **7b)**.

- **a)** ✐ Check the table on the board by eliciting the answers from the class (for the examples, see the words in pink in the table in **V8.4** SB p132). Check students understand the meanings of the prefixes and suffixes.
- **b)** underpaid; repaid, overpaid; rewrite; painful, painless; oversleep, sleepless; undercharge, recharge, overcharge; careful, careless; remarry; successful; replay, playful; underuse, reuse, overuse, useful, useless
- Check the meaning of any words you think your students might have problems with (for example people might overcharge you in a shop, etc.).
- ✐ You can elicit the answers and write them in the correct place in the table on the board.
- Also highlight that the opposite of *successful* is *unsuccessful*, not ~~successless~~.
- Note that *unhelpful* means 'not helpful'. *Helpless* means 'not able to do things for yourself or protect yourself': *A baby is helpless without its mother*.

EXTRA IDEAS

- Students work in pairs and take turns to test each other on the opposites in **6**. One student says the adjective, for example *honest*, and his/her partner says the opposite, for example *dishonest*.
- ✐ Write the following sentence on the board: *I was underpaid/overpaid last month, so I complained to my boss.* Ask students which word is correct (*underpaid*). Put students into pairs. Each pair writes six similar sentences with the words from **7**. Students swap sentences with another pair and choose the correct words in their sentences.

---

8 a) Tell students they are going to tell other people in the class about a frightening or exciting experience they have had. Give students a minute or two to think of an appropriate story. Encourage students to think of a true story if possible. If they are having problems, tell them that they can invent a story instead. Students shouldn't reveal if their stories are true or not to the class.

Students work on their own and decide what they are going to say, based on the prompts or their own ideas. While students are working, monitor and help them with new language and vocabulary.

b) Put students into groups of three or four. Students take turns to tell their stories. While students are working, monitor and help them with any problems. Don't interrupt students too much at this stage.

After each story, students ask questions to find out more information about the story and guess if it is true or not.

EXTRA IDEA

- Before doing **8b)**, students can practise telling their story in pairs. This will give students extra 'rehearsal time' before they tell the story in groups, as well as giving shy students more confidence.

c) Ask students to tell the class about the best story in each group. Finally, the class can decide what was the best story in the class.

EXTRA IDEA

- Students write their story for homework. These can be collected next class and displayed around the room for other students to read. Alternatively, correct the stories they have written for homework and give them back to students in the following class. Students can then write a final version of their stories.

EXTRA PRACTICE AND HOMEWORK

Ph **Class Activity** 8C Beginnings and endings p159 (Instructions p127)

8 Review Exercise 5 SB p67

CD-ROM Lesson 8C

Workbook Lesson 8C p43

8D Be careful!

Real World warnings and advice
Review prefixes and suffixes; *should*

QUICK REVIEW ●●●

This activity reviews prefixes and suffixes. Students work on their own and write eight words with prefixes or suffixes, as in the examples. ✍ If your students need some extra help, write the following prefixes and suffixes on the board before they begin: *un-, dis-, im-, in-, ir-, under-, re-, over-, -ful, -less*. Put students into pairs. Students take turns to say sentences with their partner's words, as in the example. Ask students to share some of their sentences with the class.

1 Focus students on pictures A–C. Students work in pairs and discuss what the people in each picture are going to do. Students also think of one possible danger for each situation.

Ask students to share their ideas with the class.

2 **a)** Be prepared with definitions, examples, pictures, etc. to pre-teach the vocabulary in the box, or bring in dictionaries for students to check the meanings themselves.

Note that *the outback* refers to the areas in Australia that are far away from towns and cities, especially in the desert area in central Australia.

Model and drill the words/phrases. Pay particular attention to the pronunciation of *bear* /beə/ and *calm* /kɑːm/.

b) Students do the activity in pairs or with the whole class. Note that there can be more than one possible answer for some words/phrases.

> **Possible answers** a bear C; the outback B; dive A; cross a river B/C; petrol A/B; a spare map B/C; stay calm A; a kangaroo B; shiver A/C

c) R8.7 Tell students they are going to listen to three conversations. Play the recording (SB p152). Students listen and match conversations 1–3 to pictures A–C. Check answers with the class.

> 1C 2B 3A

d) Give students time to read questions 1–6, then play the recording again. Students listen and answer the questions. Students check answers in pairs. Check answers with the class.

Ask students which of the three trips they would like to go on. Encourage students to give reasons for their answers.

> **1** Plenty of warm clothes and a spare map. **2** Make yourself look as big as possible. **3** Where you are going and when you expect to be back. **4** When it starts to get dark. **5** Stay calm. **6** Every two minutes.

Real World Warnings and advice

3 **a)–c)** Focus students on the introductory bullet point to check students understand *warnings*.

Students do the exercises on their own or in pairs, then check their answers in RW8.1 SB p133. Check answers with the class.

> - **a)** a) asking for advice b) giving advice c) giving warnings d) responding to advice/warnings
> - **b)** After *If I were you, I'd ...* and *You'd better ...* we use the **infinitive**: *If I were you, I'd take plenty of warm clothes. You'd better come up immediately.*
> - After *It's a good idea ...* and *Don't forget ...* we use the **infinitive with to**: *It's a good idea to take a spare map. Don't forget to tell them when you expect to be back.*
> - After *Whatever you do ...* we use the **imperative** (usually the negative imperative): *Whatever you do, don't lose your partner.*
> - Highlight that *If I were you, I'd take plenty of warm clothes* is a second conditional. Remind students that we often miss out the first clause in these sentences when giving advice: *I'd take plenty of warm clothes.*
> - Also remind students that we often use *in case* to give reasons why we're doing something.
> - Point out that after *Be careful* we can also use *of* + noun: *Be careful of kangaroos.*
> - Also tell students that *you'd better = you had better*.

4 R8.8 P Play the recording. Students listen and practise. Check they copy the sentence stress correctly. Play the recording again if necessary.

You can ask students to turn to RW8.1 SB p133. They can then follow the sentence stress while they listen and practise.

5 **a)** Check students remember *the tube* and pre-teach *pickpocket*. Focus students on sentences 1–8, which give advice for people visiting the UK. Students do the exercise on their own.

b) Students check their answers in pairs. Check answers with the class.

> **2** Make sure **3** Whatever you do, **4** If I were you, I'd **5** It's a good idea **6** Be careful **7** Don't **8** Look out for

6 **a)** Students do the exercise on their own. While students are working, monitor and check their sentences for accuracy.

b) Put students into groups. If possible, include students of different nationalities in the same group.

Students compare sentences. If all your students are from the same country, they decide if they agree or disagree with the other students' sentences. If your students are from different countries, they decide how many of the other students' sentences are also true for their country.

Finally, ask students to share the most important warnings or pieces of advice with the class.

--- EXTRA IDEA ---
• If you have a multilingual class, ask students to work in pairs with a student from a different country in **6b)**. Ask students to imagine that they have just arrived in their partner's country. Students take turns to give their partner advice/warnings about their country.

♪ Ask students to turn to p101 and look at *Stormy Weather*. This song was first recorded by the American blues singer, Ethel Waters, in 1933. It was also recorded by Billie Holiday, Frank Sinatra and Diana Ross.

1 Students discuss the questions in groups. Ask students to share interesting answers with the class.

2 a) R8.9 Give students time to read the song, then play the recording. Students listen and cross out the extra word in each line 1–19. Play the recording again if necessary.

b) Students check answers in pairs. Play the recording again, pausing after each line for students to check answers.

2 blue 3 living 4 down 5 completely 6 There's 7 old
8 very 9 now 10 Just 11 here 12 away 13 probably
14 ever 15 us 16 hot 17 all 18 again 19 on

3 Students do the exercise on their own before checking in pairs.

Check answers with the class.

Model and drill the words, paying particular attention to the pronunciation of *bare* /beə/ and *weary* /'wɪəriː/.

1d) 2c) 3b) 4a) 5e)

4 a) Check students remember *cheer yourself up* (= make yourself happy).

Students do the exercise on their own.

b) Students discuss their ideas in groups and find out which ways are the most popular.

Ask students to share these answers with the class.

--- EXTRA PRACTICE AND HOMEWORK ---
8 Review SB p67
CD-ROM Lesson 8D
Workbook Lesson 8D p44
Workbook Reading and Writing Portfolio 8 p78
Progress Test 8 p214

8 Review

See p30 for ideas on how to use this section.

1a)

```
S G O W S C K P B C
H Y L P T L N G L V
U S T O R C G A L F
R H M T R H Y L F L
R O H U M I D E O O
I W B O I L I N G S
C E P C F L O O D V
A R Z Z R Y A E J G
N F R E E Z I N G S
E I Q R E B O L I N
```

2 2 will be caused/are going to be caused 3 were hit
4 be taught 5 are held 6 will be introduced/are going to be introduced
3a) See V8.2 SB p132.
5a) 5c) See V8.3 and V8.4 SB p132

Progress Portfolio

See p30 for ideas on how to use this section.

9 Look after yourself

Student's Book p68–p75

9A Get healthy!

QUICK REVIEW ●●●
This activity reviews warnings and advice. Students do the first part of the activity on their own. Put students into pairs. Students compare sentences and decide what is the most important warning or piece of advice. Ask students to share their ideas with the class.

> **Vocabulary** health
> **Grammar** relative clauses with *who*, *that*, *which*, *whose*, *where* and *when*
> **Review** warnings and advice

Reading, Listening and Grammar

1 Pre-teach *a healthy diet* (when you eat a good balance of healthy food) and compare this with *go on a diet* (try to lose weight).

Students discuss the questions in groups. Ask each group to share interesting answers with the class.

> ┌─ **EXTRA IDEA** ─────────────────────────
> ● To revise food vocabulary, ask students to make a list of their favourite food. Students compare lists in pairs and see how many food items are the same.

2 a) Be prepared with definitions, examples, etc. to pre-teach the vocabulary in the box, or bring in dictionaries for students to check the meanings themselves. Note that the aim of these boxes is to highlight which words you need to pre-teach in order to help students understand the text that follows. The vocabulary in these boxes is not in the Language Summaries.

Model and drill the words. Pay particular attention to the pronunciation of *digest* /daɪˈdʒest/.

b) Focus students on the article. Ask students what they think the article is about (going on a fast and drinking only juice).

R9.1 Play the recording. Students read and listen to the article. Check answers with the class.

> The journalist felt healthier after her retreat because she felt more relaxed than she'd been for years and she'd lost 3 kilos.

3 a) Students do the exercise on their own, then check their answers in pairs. Check answers with the class.

> 1F You drink **fruit and** vegetable juice on the retreat. 2T 3 Louise **was doing the retreat.** 4T 5F Joanne **had an awful headache and felt as if she was getting a cold** on day two of the retreat. 6T 7T

b) Students discuss the questions in pairs. Ask each pair to share their ideas with the class. Find out how many students would like to go on a retreat like the one in the article.

Help with Grammar Relative clauses with *who, that, which, whose, where* and *when*

4 a)–c) Focus students on the introductory bullet point and check students understand what a relative clause is.

Students do the exercises on their own or in pairs, then check their answers in **G9.1** SB p135. Check answers with the class.

> ● **a)** a) who; that **b)** that; which **c)** where **d)** whose **e)** when
> ● Point out that we usually use *who* for people (but *that* is also correct), and we usually use *that* for things (but *which* is also correct).
> ● Highlight that we don't use *what* in relative clauses: ~~The food what we usually eat …~~ . We can use *what* to mean 'the thing/things that': *Now I'm much more careful about what I eat.* (= the things that I eat).
> ● **b)** 1 The subject of *eats* in sentence A is *that*. 2 The subject of *eat* in sentence B is *we*.
> ● We can leave out *who*, *that* or *which* when it isn't the subject of the relative clause.
> ● Tell students that we never leave out *whose* in relative clauses.
> ● Point out that we can usually leave out *where* if we add a preposition at the end of the relative clause: *That's the café where I met my wife.* → *That's the café I met my wife in.*
> ● Also highlight that can usually leave out *when* if the time reference is clear: *Monday's the day (when) I play tennis.* If the time reference isn't clear, we must use *when*: *This was also when I started getting really hungry.*

5 a) Students do the exercise on their own, then check answers in pairs. Check answers with the class.

> 1 that 2 who/that 3 who/that 4 that/which 5 who/that 6 that/which 7 whose 8 where 9 when 10 where

b) Students do the exercise on their own. Check answers with the class.

> We can leave out *who*, *that* or *which* in sentences 1, 4 and 6.

c) Students do the exercise on their own.

d) Students compare sentences in groups and find out how many are the same. Ask students to tell the class which sentences are the same for all the students in the group.

Vocabulary Health

6 a) Students choose the correct words/phrases in pairs.

b) R9.2 Play the recording. Students listen and check their answers. Check answers with the class. Don't tell students the meanings of the other words at this stage.

Tell students that *A&E* stands for 'Accident and Emergency'. In the UK this department is also called *the casualty* /'kæʒʊəlti/ *department*, or just *casualty*: *Mark's had a car accident. They've taken him to casualty.*

Highlight that we also say *allergic* /ə'lɜ:dʒɪk/ *to something*: *My sister is allergic to eggs.*

Model and drill the words. Pay particular attention to the pronunciation of *surgeon* /'sɜ:dʒən/, *asthma* /'æsmə/ and *allergy* /'ælədʒi/. Note that only the main stress in words/phrases is shown in vocabulary boxes and the Language Summaries.

> 1 A surgeon
> 2 An operating theatre
> 3 Asthma
> 4 A specialist
> 5 The A&E department
> 6 An allergy

7 a) Focus students on the six incorrect words in **6a)** (*a GP, a surgery, an infection, a prescription, a ward, a migraine*).

Students do the exercise on their own. Point out that the words from **6a)** go in the first gap in each sentence and that *who, that*, etc. go in the second gap. Early finishers can check their answers in pairs.

b) Students check their answers in V9.1 SB p134. Check answers with the class.

Ask students in which sentence we can leave out the relative pronoun (sentence 5). You can point out that we can also leave out *where* in sentence 4 if we add a preposition to the end of the relative clause: *A surgery is a building or an office you can go **to** and ask a GP or a dentist for medical advice.*

Highlight that *GP* is short for 'general practitioner'.

Model and drill the words. Pay particular attention to the pronunciation of *surgery* /'sɜ:dʒəri/ and point out that *migraine* can be pronounced /'maɪgreɪn/ or /'mi:greɪn/.

> 1 A migraine; that/which 2 A ward; where 3 A GP; who/that; who/that 4 A surgery; where 5 A prescription; (that/which) 6 An infection; that/which

8 Students do the exercise in pairs, as shown in the speech bubbles. Encourage students to use relative clauses in their definitions.

Get ready … Get it right!

9 Put students into two groups, group A and group B. Students in group A turn to SB p105 and students in group B turn to SB p110. Check they are all looking at the correct exercise.

a) Put students into pairs with someone from the same group. Students write sentences with relative clauses to define words/phrases 1–8, as shown in the example. Note that they are not allowed to use the words/phrases in their definitions.

If students don't know the words/phrases, they can check them in a dictionary. Note that all this vocabulary has appeared in earlier units of the Student's Book.

While students are working, monitor and help them with their definitions. Don't check their sentences with the class at this stage.

b) Reorganise the class so that a pair from group A is working with a pair from group B. Students take turns to say their sentences and guess the other pair's words. You can allow pairs to have two or three guesses for each word.

While students are working, monitor and correct any mistakes you hear. Ask each group to tell the class which pair guessed more words correctly.

Finally, check the definitions for the words with the whole class.

> **Possible answers**
> **Group A** 2 A place where you put your car at night. 3 A person who/that doesn't eat meat or fish. 4 A thing (that/which) you put your head on when you're in bed. 5 A house that/which only has one floor. 6 A machine that/which freezes your food. 7 A person who/that sells houses. 8 A thing on your computer screen that/which you click on.
>
> **Group B** b) A machine that dries your hair. c) A place where you put rubbish./A thing (that/which) you put rubbish in. d) A house that is not attached to other houses. e) A person who/that likes football. f) A place where you put things at the top of your house. g) A machine that/which cooks or heats up food very quickly. h) A person who/that works too hard.

— EXTRA IDEA —
- Review relative clauses in a later class by playing Hot Seats (p21).

— EXTRA PRACTICE AND HOMEWORK —
Ph **Class Activity** 9A Fighting fit p160 (Instructions p127)
9 Review Exercises 1 and 2 SB p75
CD-ROM Lesson 9A
Workbook Lesson 9A p45

9B Good news, bad news

Vocabulary news collocations

Grammar Present Perfect Simple active and passive for recent events

Help with Listening Present Perfect Simple active or passive

Review *just*, *yet*, *already*; relative clauses; Past Simple; health

Vocabulary News collocations

1 Students discuss the questions in pairs. Ask students to share answers with the class. You can also discuss any stories that are in the news at the moment.

2 **a)** Students do the exercise on their own, then check their answers in **V9.2** SB p134. Check answers with the class.

Point out that *accept* and *reject* are opposites. Also tell students that *protest* can be a verb or a noun: *We're protesting against the new pay offer. The protest soon became violent.* Highlight the different stress pattern on the verb (*protèst*) and the noun (*prótest*). Also tell students that a person who protests is called *a protèstor* and a person who demonstrates is called *a démonstrator*.

Highlight that we say *go on strike* and *be on strike*: *Ambulance drivers are going on strike at midnight. The factory's closed because everyone is on strike.* Model and drill the phrases, focusing on stress.

> discover something new; carry out a survey; suffer from an illness; take someone to hospital; take part in a demonstration; publish results/a report; protest against something; meet a target; call off a strike

b) Students work in pairs and take turns to test each other on the collocations in **2a)**, as shown in the speech bubbles. You can ask students to close their books while they are being tested.

Listening and Grammar

3 **a)** Focus students on photos A–C and ask students to cover the speech bubbles on SB p70. Tell students the photos are of today's main news stories.

Students work in pairs and discuss what they think the news stories are about. Encourage students to use the words/phrases in **2a)** where possible or their own ideas.

--- EXTRA IDEA ---

● 📝 Elicit students' ideas and write them in three columns headed A, B and C on the board. Students can then listen and check their answers against the ideas on the board.

b) **R9.3** Play the recording of today's news (SB p152). Students listen and put photos A–C in the same order as the news stories. Check answers with the class.

> 1C 2B 3A

c) Give students time to read the speech bubbles. Play the recording again. Students listen and fill in the gaps in the speech bubbles. Students check answers in pairs. Check answers with the class.

> 2 waiting 3 progress 4 two and a half 5 UK 6 three
> 7 causes 8 six 9 actress 10 heart

Help with Grammar Present Perfect Simple active and passive for recent events

4 **a)–d)** Focus students on the introductory bullet point to remind students of one of the main uses of the Present Perfect Simple.

Students do the exercises on their own or in pairs, then check their answers in **G9.2** SB p135. Check answers with the class.

● **a)** 1 The first sentence: The health service. The second sentence: A new report on allergies. 2 has failed 3 has ... been published 4 We make the Present Perfect Simple active with: subject + *'ve* (= *have*)/*haven't* or *'s* (= *has*)/*hasn't* + past participle. We make the Present Perfect Simple passive with: subject + *'ve* (= *have*)/*haven't* or *'s* (= *has*)/*hasn't* + *been* + past participle.

● Point out that we often use passive verb forms in news reports and newspaper articles.

● Remind students that we must use the Past Simple active or passive when we say the exact time something happened: *She was taken to hospital two days ago.*

● **b)** **Present Perfect Simple active** has failed; haven't met; 've made; has ... carried out; haven't ... seen; 've ... heard; has died

● **Present Perfect Simple passive** has ... been reduced; has ... been published; hasn't been published

89

- **c)** We use *just* to say something happened a short time ago.
- We use *yet* to say something hasn't happened, but we think it will happen in the future.
- We use *already* to say something happened some time in the past, maybe sooner than we expected.
- Remind students that we use *still* to say that something started in the past and continues to the present.
- We only use *just* and *already* in positive sentences and questions. We put these words before the past participle: *has **already** been reduced*, *we've **just** heard*.
- We only use *yet* in negative sentences and questions. We put *yet* at the end of the sentence or clause: *We haven't met our targets **yet**.*
- We only use *still* in negative sentences with the Present Perfect Simple active and passive: *That survey **still** hasn't been published*. not ~~That survey still has been published~~. We put *still* before the auxiliary.

Help with Listening Present Perfect Simple active and passive

- This Help with Listening sections helps students to hear the difference between the Present Perfect Simple active and passive.

5 **a)** R9.4 Focus students on the example sentences. Play the recording. Students listen and notice the weak forms of *has* /həz/, *been* /bɪn/ and *have* /həv/.

b) R9.5 Play the recording (SB p152). Students listen and decide if the verbs are in the Present Perfect Simple active (A) or passive (P).

Play the recording again, pausing after each sentence to check students' answers.

has just been published (P); has just published (A); have been taken (P); have taken (A); hasn't met (A); haven't been met (P); have already rejected (A); has already been rejected (P)

6 R9.5 P Play the recording again. Students listen and practise, copying the sentence stress and weak forms.

7 **a)** Students do the exercise on their own before checking answers in pairs.

b) R9.6 Play the recording. Students listen and check their answers.

Play the recording again, pausing after each verb form to check the answers with the class.

2 have been arrested 3 has been taken 4 has been called off 5 has accepted 6 have found 7 have been discovered 8 has just arrived 9 has already sold

8 Students do the exercise on their own, as in the example.

2 The Prime Minister has **just** arrived. 3 The relatives haven't been told **yet**. 4 He has **already** been questioned by the police. 5 Three men have **just** been arrested. 6 Has the match finished **yet**? 7 The results **still** haven't been published.

Get ready … Get it right!

9 Put students into two groups, group A and group B. Students in group A turn to SB p104 and students in group B turn to SB p109.

a) Tell students that they are going to be newsreaders. Students work with a partner from the same group and choose the correct auxiliaries in their news summaries. If necessary, check the auxiliaries only with the class.

Student A 1 has 2 have 3 have been 4 have been
5 has 6 has just 7 have 8 has been
Student B 1 have been 2 has 3 have just been
4 have been 5 has just 6 has already been 7 has

b) Students practise reading the news summary to their partner from a). Allow time for each student to read their summary at least twice. Encourage students to read the summary with natural rhythm and stress.

c) Reorganise the class so that a student from group A is working with a student from group B.

Give student Bs time to read questions 1–4. Student As then read their news summaries without stopping. Student Bs answer their questions. Students aren't allowed to look at their partner's books.

Tell students not to check their answers yet.

d) Students swap roles. Give student As time to read their questions. Student Bs then read their news summaries and student As answer their questions.

e) Students work with their partner and check their answers.

Finally, check answers with the class and find out who got all the answers right.

Student A 1 Seventeen. 2 Yes, they have. (Three men have just been arrested.) 3 For the opening of his new film. 4 Over 20 million. **Student B** 1 Texas. 2 Over 50. 3 Next year. 4 No, we don't.

EXTRA PRACTICE AND HOMEWORK

Ph **Class Activity** 9B Perfect circles p161 (Instructions p127)
9 Review Exercises 3 and 4 SB p75
CD-ROM Lesson 9B
Workbook Lesson 9B p46

9C Faking it

QUICK REVIEW ●●●
This activity reviews the Present Perfect Simple active and passive. Students do the first part of the activity on their own, as in the examples. Put students into groups. Students take turns to tell the other students their news and ask follow-up questions. Encourage students to use the Present Perfect Simple active and passive when giving news, and the Past Simple to give more information. Ask each group to share one interesting piece of news with the class.

Vocabulary connecting words: *although*, *even though*, *despite*, *in spite of*, *however*

Skills Listening: How to spot a liar; Reading: Catch Me If You Can

Help with Listening British and American accents

Review Present Perfect Simple active and passive

Listening

1 Check students remember *lie*. Students discuss the questions in groups. Ask students to share interesting answers with the class.

2 a) Be prepared with definitions, examples, etc. to pre-teach the vocabulary in the box, or bring in dictionaries for students to check the meanings themselves.
Model and drill the words. Point out the silent 'c' in *muscles* /ˈmʌsəlz/.

b) Focus students on photos A–D. Discuss if the person is lying or telling the truth in each photo with the whole class. Don't tell students the answers at this stage.

c) Tell students that they are going to listen to a radio interview with Dr Miriam Richards, a body language expert.
R9.7 Play the recording (SB p152). Students listen and check whether the woman in photos A–D in **2b)** is lying or not. Check answers with the class.

> **A** She's telling the truth (this is a real smile). **B** She's lying (her eyes are going left). **C** She's telling the truth (she's looking up). **D** She's lying (she's touching her nose and covering her mouth).

3 a) Students do the exercise in pairs.

b) **R9.7** Play the recording again. Students listen and check their answers to **3a)**. Check answers with the class.

> **1** 80% **2** more **3** often smile a lot **4** left **5** right **6** mouth

Help with Listening British and American accents

- This Help with Listening section helps students to hear the difference between British and American accents.

4 a) Give students a few moments to read the words in 1–5. Point out that in each set of words there are letters in **bold**. Tell students they are going to listen to how we say these letters differently in a British and an American accent. They will hear the British accent first.

R9.8 Play the recording. Students listen and notice the different ways we say the letters in **bold**.
Highlight that the vowel sounds in 1–3 are usually said differently in British English (UK) and American English (US). 1 *hot* UK /hɒt/; US /hɑt/ 2 *saw* UK /sɔː/; US /sɑː/ 3 *aunt* UK /ɑːnt/; US /ænt/. Point out that the letter 'r' is usually pronounced in American English (as in 4), whereas in British English the letter 'r' isn't usually pronounced (unless it is followed by a vowel sound). Also highlight that in American English, a 't' between two vowel sounds is pronounced more like a 'd' (as in 5).

b) **R9.9** Play the recording (SB p153). Students listen and decide which accent they hear first.
Play the recording again, pausing after each pair of sentences to check students' answers.

> **1** British **2** American **3** American **4** British **5** British **6** American

c) **R9.7** Ask students to turn to R9.7, SB p152. Play the recording of the interview again. Students listen and notice the difference between the interviewer's British accent and Dr Richards's American accent. Tell students that the voices on these recordings are standard British and American accents, and point out there is a wide variety of regional accents in both countries.

Reading and Vocabulary

5 a) Focus students on the photos in the article on SB p73. Students guess what the connection is between the two photos. Check answers now or after **5c)**. Note that *Abagnale* is pronounced /ˌæbənˈjɑːli/ and *Jr* is short for 'junior'. In the USA, when a father and son have the same first name, the son is usually called Joe Jr, etc.

> The first photo is of Frank Abagnale Jr. The second photo shows Leonardo DiCaprio in the film *Catch Me If You Can*, which is about Frank Abagnale Jr's life.

b) Be prepared with definitions, examples, etc. to pre-teach the vocabulary in the box. Note that *a con artist* is a person who deceives other people by making them believe something false or making them give money away. *A bad cheque* is a cheque that cannot be cashed. Also point out that *the FBI* stands for the Federal Bureau of Investigation, one of the national police forces in the USA.

Model and drill the words/phrases with the class. Pay particular attention to the pronunciation of *fraud* /frɔːd/, *cheque* /tʃek/, *overdrawn* /əʊvəˈdrɔːn/ and *FBI* /ef biː ˈaɪ/.

c) Students read the article and find out how many different jobs Frank Abagnale Jr has had and what he does now. Check answers with the class. Also check the answer to **5a)** if you haven't already done so.

> He has been a pilot, a doctor, a lawyer and a sociology lecturer. He now runs a successful business that gives advice to companies on how to stop fraud and he also gives lectures to the FBI for free.

6 a) Students do the exercise on their own. Early finishers can check answers in pairs. Check answers with the class.

> **1** Because he wrote bad cheques. **2** Because his hair was already going grey. **3** He found out that pilots could fly for free as guests on other airlines.
> **4** A lawyer (he passed his law exams the third time he took them). **5** Miami and France. **6** Five years.

b) Students discuss the questions in groups. Ask students to share their answers with the class.

Help with Vocabulary Connecting words: *although, even though, despite, in spite of, however*

7 a) 🖊 Focus students on the example sentence or write it on the board. Ask students how many clauses there are (two) and to underline or point out the connecting word (*Although*). Ask students how you would write this as two sentences (*Frank was rich. He was lonely and unhappy.*). Point out that the first sentence has a positive meaning and the second sentence has a negative meaning.

b)–d) Students do the exercises on their own or in pairs, then check their answers in V9.3 SB p134. Check answers with the class.

- **b)** *Although* /ɔːlˈðəʊ/, *even though* /ðəʊ/, *despite*, in *spite of* and *however* are similar in meaning to *but*.
- We use *although*, *even though*, *despite* and *in spite of* to contrast **two clauses in the same sentence**.
- We use *however* to contrast **two sentences**.
- Point out that *even though* is usually stronger than *although*.
- In spoken English we often use *though* instead of *although/even though*. We usually put *though* at the end of a sentence: It *was a lovely meal. I didn't like the wine, though.*
- We also say *despite the fact that* + clause: *We got lost, despite the fact that we had two different maps.*
- **c)** After *despite* and *in spite of* we usually use a noun or verb+ing: *In spite of/Despite* **his age**, *people believed he was a pilot. In spite of/Despite* **being so young**, *people believed he was a pilot.*

- After *although* and *even though* we usually use a clause: *He moved to Atlanta and got a job as a doctor, although/even though he didn't have any medical training.*
- Point out that we can put *although*, *even though*, *despite* and *in spite of* at the beginning or in the middle of a sentence: *I went out, even though I was tired. = Even though I was tired, I went out.*
- Also highlight that we usually put *however* at the beginning of a sentence.
- We use a comma (,) after the first clause in sentences with *although*, *even though*, *despite* and *in spite of*. We also use a comma after *However*.

8 Focus students on the example. Highlight that *felt* in the first sentence changes to *feeling* in the rewritten sentence because *despite* is usually followed by a noun or verb+*ing*.

Students rewrite the rest of the sentences on their own.

While students are working, monitor and help them with any problems.

Students check answers in pairs. Check answers with the class.

> **2** Robin slept really well, in spite of the noise./In spite of the noise, Robin slept really well. (Note that the clauses can be reversed in all the answers apart from sentence 4.) **3** Even though I don't get paid very much, I enjoy my job. **4** Erica was well-qualified. However, she didn't get the job. **5** We enjoyed the concert, even though there weren't many people there. **6** They watched TV all night, despite having to work the next day. **7** Even though the teacher explained it twice, I still didn't understand it.

9 a) Students do the exercise on their own. Tell students that they can write one or two words only to remember each of the four things.

b) Ask students if they can remember how to tell if someone is lying. If necessary, remind them of the following signs from the interview in **2c)**: avoiding eye contact or making more eye contact than usual, smiling a lot (but without using the muscles round the eyes), looking to the left, looking down or straight ahead, covering their mouths, touching their noses.

Put students into groups of four. Students take turns to tell the group their four things. Other students in the group can ask one question about each thing to try and find out if the person is lying. When each student has finished talking about his/her four things, the other three students then decide which two things he/she is lying about.

When students have finished, ask each group to decide who the best and worst liar was, and why.

c) Ask students to tell the class who the worst liar in each group was and why they could tell he/she was lying.

Finally, ask students who was the best liar in each group.

EXTRA PRACTICE AND HOMEWORK

9 Review Exercise 5 SB p75
CD-ROM Lesson 9C
Workbook Lesson 9C p48

EXTRA IDEA

- Finish the class by saying two true and two false sentences about yourself and ask students to decide when you are lying.

 # 9D At the doctor's

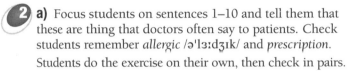

Real World at the doctor's
Vocabulary health problems, symptoms and treatment
Review Present Perfect Continuous

QUICK REVIEW ●●●
This activity reviews parts of the body. Students work in their own and write all the parts of the body that they know. Set a time limit of two minutes. Students compare lists in pairs to find out who has the most words. Students then work with their partner and take turns to point to a part of the body. Their partner says the word.

 1 a) Students do the exercise on their own or in pairs before checking new words/phrases in **V9.4** SB p134.

Note that only new words/phrases are included in the dictionary box in the Language Summary.

Check students understand the difference between *a runny nose* and *a blocked-up nose*. Point out that *flu* is short for *influenza*.

Highlight that *hay fever* is a type of *allergy*, usually to pollen. Also tell students that *wheezy* is an adjective and *sneeze* can be a verb or a noun. Teach students that when other people *sneeze*, we usually say *Bless you!*

Note that *be sick* has two meanings: 'be ill' or 'vomit/throw up'. In American English, *be sick* is more common than *be ill*: *Sorry, I can't come to work today. I'm ill.* (UK) *I'm sick.* (US).

Point out that we don't usually add an *-s* to make the plural of *paracetamol*: *Take two paracetamol every four hours.* You can teach students that the opposite of *have diarrhoea* is *be constipated*, which is a false friend in some languages.

Model and drill the words/phrases. Highlight the pronunciation of *antibiotics* /ˌæntɪbaɪˈɒtɪks/, *diarrhoea* /daɪəˈriːə/, *throat* /θrəʊt/ and *stomach ache* /ˈstʌmək eɪk/. Also point out that *temperature* /ˈtemprətʃə/ is three syllables, not four, and that the stress on *hay fever* is on the first word, not the second.

EXTRA IDEA ●●●

- Do **1a)** as a Know, Might Know, Don't Know activity (p21).

b) Focus students on groups 1–3 and the examples. Check students understand *symptoms* and *treatment*. Students do the exercise in pairs.

🖎 While students are working, draw a three-column table on the board with three headings: *health problems*, *symptoms* and *treatment*.

c) Students check their answers in **V9.4** SB p134–p135. Check answers with the class and fill in the table on the board. Note that some words/phrases, such as *a stomach ache*, could be included in groups 1 and 2.

1 asthma; an allergy; hay fever; flu; a migraine; a virus; food poisoning; an infection **2** a runny nose; a rash; wheezy; be sick; diarrhoea; a sore throat; sneeze; a temperature; throw up; a stomach ache; a blocked-up nose **3** antibiotics; painkillers; pills; penicillin; paracetamol

2 a) Focus students on sentences 1–10 and tell them that these are thing that doctors often say to patients. Check students remember *allergic* /əˈlɜːdʒɪk/ and *prescription*. Students do the exercise on their own, then check in pairs.

b) **R9.10** Play the recording. Students listen and check their answers. Check answers with the class.

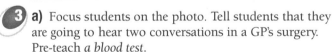

2 feeling 3 allergic 4 eaten 5 back 6 taking
7 symptoms 8 look 9 temperature 10 prescription

3 a) Focus students on the photo. Tell students that they are going to hear two conversations in a GP's surgery. Pre-teach *a blood test*.

R9.11 Play the recording (SB p153). Students listen and answer the questions. Check answers with the class.

Patient 1 Symptoms: a terrible stomach ache, throwing up, diarrhoea. The doctor thinks he's got food poisoning.
Patient 2 Symptoms: chest hurts, really bad headaches, sneezing. The doctor thinks he's got a virus.

b) Give students time to read sentences a)–h), then play the recording again. Students listen, tick the true sentences and correct the false ones. Students check answers in pairs. Check answers with the class.

a)T b)F His children cooked him **and his wife** a meal for **their wedding anniversary.** c)T d)F He **doesn't have** to come back to see the doctor again. e)T f)F He started feeling ill **3 days ago.** g)T h)F He gives him a prescription for some **painkillers.**

Real World At the doctor's

4 **a)–c)** Students do the exercises on their own or in pairs, then check their answers in [RW9.1] SB p135. Check answers with the class.

- **a)** 2a) 3d) 4e) 5b) 6g) 7j) 8f) 9h) 10i)
- **b)** We use *I keep ...* and *I can't stop ...* for things that happen **lots of times**. We don't want these things to happen: *I keep waking up at night*.
- *After I keep ...* and *I can't stop ...* we use **verb+ing**: *I can't stop coughing*.
- Remind students that we can only say *(a) stomach ache, a headache, backache, (a) toothache* and *earache*. For other parts of the body, we say: *My (chest) hurts.* or *I've got a pain in my (chest).* not *I have (chestache)*.

5 [R9.12] [P] Play the recording (SB p153). Students listen and practise, copying the sentence stress correctly.

6 Students do the exercise on their own, then check answers in pairs. Check answers with the class.

2 throw up 3 hay fever 4 a temperature 5 food poisoning 6 headache 7 a migraine 8 a sneeze

7 **a)** Focus students on the beginning of the conversation between a doctor and a patient. Students work in pairs and write the first half of their conversation. Tell students that they should write about the patient's symptoms only. Encourage them to use language from **2** and **4a)** in their conversations.

b) Ask students to swap papers with another pair. Give students a minute or two to read the other pair's conversation. Students then finish the conversation by suggesting treatment for the patient's symptoms.

c) Students practise the conversation they finished in **7b)** with their partner until they can remember it.

d) Reorganise the class so that the pairs of students who swapped papers are sitting in groups of four. Each pair takes turns to role-play the conversation for the other pair. Students decide if they agree with the other pair's suggestions for treatment, giving reasons for their answers. Ask a few pairs to role-play their conversations for the class.

8 Put students into pairs, student A and student B. Student As turn to SB p106 and student Bs turn to SB p111.

a) Students work on their own and read the information about the two conversations they are going to have. Tell students they can make notes for each conversation, but they shouldn't write out exactly what they are going to say.

b) Students role-play the conversations with their partner. Student A starts conversation 1 and student B starts conversation 2.

c) Ask students to tell the class about their symptoms and the treatment their doctors suggested. Also find out if students were happy with their doctor's advice and ask them to give reasons for their answers.

Finally, you may wish to teach students *hypochondriac* /ˌhaɪpəˈkɒndrɪæk/ (a person who always worries about their health, even when they aren't ill).

EXTRA PRACTICE AND HOMEWORK

[Ph] **Vocabulary Plus** 9 Injuries and health problems p185 (Instructions p175)

[Ph] **Study Skills** 4 Collocations p194 (Instructions p190)

[Ph] **Class Activity** 9D Noughts and crosses p162 (Instructions p128)

9 Review SB p75

CD-ROM Lesson 9D

Workbook Lesson 9D p49

Workbook Reading and Writing Portfolio 9 p80

Progress Test 9 p216

---

9 Review

See p30 for ideas on how to use this section.

1a) 1 that/which 2 who/that 3 where 4 whose 5 that/which 6 that/which 7 when

1b) Sentences 1 and 5.

2a) 2 patient 3 ward 4 asthma 5 surgeon 6 allergy 7 (A&E) department 8 migraine 9 prescription

3a) 1 protest 2 take part 3 reject 4 meet 5 call off 6 carry out

4 1 have been carried out → have carried out 2 have been injured ✓ 3 has been called off → has been called off 4 have been accepted → have accepted 5 has been increased → has increased 6 has published → has been published 7 has spent ✓ 8 has welcomed → has been welcomed

5 1 Despite/In spite of 2 Although/Even though 3 However 4 despite/in spite of 5 although/even though

Progress Portfolio

See p30 for ideas on how to use this section.

Student's Book p76–p83

10A The anniversary

Vocabulary Contacting people

1 Students do the exercise on their own, then check their answers in **V10.1** SB p136. Check answers with the class.
Highlight that *get hold of* implies difficulty and is often used with *manage* or *can't/couldn't*: *Did you manage to get hold of Mrs Edwards?*
Point out that we can say *keep in touch with someone* or *stay in touch with someone*, and teach students *get back in touch with someone* (communicate with someone again after a long time.
Also point out that we can say *be/lose/keep/get in touch with someone* or *be/lose/keep/get in contact with someone*: *I'm still in touch/contact with my old boss.*
Model and drill the phrases.
Note that only the main stress in words/phrases is shown in vocabulary boxes and the Language Summaries.

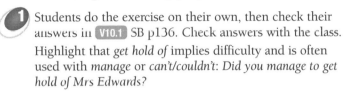

2 give 3 leave; call 4 let 5 're/are 6 lost 7 keep
8 heard; get

2 Students do the exercise in pairs.
Ask each pair to share interesting answers with the class.

Listening and Grammar

3 a) Check students understand *a marriage* /ˈmarɪdʒ/ (the relationship between a husband and wife) and compare it to *a wedding* (the ceremony when two people get married). Students write five things that they think make a successful marriage, as in the examples.

b) Put students into pairs to compare their lists. Encourage students to give reasons why the have chosen the things on their lists. Each pair then chooses the five most important things from both lists.

c) Put the class into groups, or finish the activity with the whole class. Students agree on a final list of five things people need for a successful marriage.

If students have been working in groups, ask each group to tell the class their top five things and write them on the board. Students can then choose a final list of five things from all the things on the board.

4 a) Focus students on the picture of a wedding. Students match the words in the box to the people in the picture. Check answers with the class.
Point out that *the bride* and *the groom* are the man and woman getting married. In British weddings the groom usually has a *best man*, who looks after the wedding ring and makes a speech at the reception. The bride usually has one or more *bridesmaids*, who help her prepare for the wedding.

the bride: Peggy; the groom: Tom;
the best man: Derek; the bridesmaid: Brenda

b) Tell students they are going to listen to Peggy talking to her son, Leo, about her wedding anniversary
R10.1 Give students time to read questions 1–3, then play the recording (SB p153). Students listen and check their answers. Check answers with the class.

1 No, they're not. 2 They want to organise a party.
3 Because they want to invite all the people who came to their parents' wedding.

c) Put students into pairs. Students read the summary of the conversation and try to correct five mistakes. Don't check their answers at this stage.

d) Play the recording again. Students listen and check their answers to **4c)**. Check answers with the class.

… married for **25** years … Derek Bradley, and his **wife**, Brenda, moved to **the USA** many years ago. Peggy **doesn't know** how to get in touch with them. She's **still in touch** with Trevor Jones …

— **EXTRA IDEAS** —
● If you think your students will find **4c)** difficult, play the recording again and ask them to correct the mistakes while they listen.
● If your class are finding the recording difficult, ask them to look at R10.1, SB p153. Play the recording again. Students listen, read and check their answers.

Help with Grammar *was/were going to, was/were supposed to*

 a)–d) Students do the exercises on their own or in pairs, then check their answers in G10.1 SB p137. Check answers with the class.

- **a)** 1 Yes, they did.
  2 No, they didn't.
  3 Yes, they did.
  4 No, they aren't.
  5 Yes, he did.
  6 No, he didn't.
  7 Yes, he did.
  8 No, she didn't.

- **b)** We use *was/were going to* to talk about plans we made in the past which didn't happen, or won't happen in the future.
- We use *was/were supposed to* to talk about things we agreed to do, or other people expected us to do, but we didn't do.
- Tell students that we often use *was/were going to* or *was/were supposed to* to apologise for not doing something. We usually give a reason: *Sorry, I was going to call you back last night, but I didn't get home until late.*
- Note that *was/were going to* and *was/were supposed to* are quite similar in meaning and native speakers sometimes confuse the two forms.

- **c)** After *was/were going to* and *was/were supposed to* we use the infinitive: *It was going to be a surprise party. I was supposed to call you back.*
- Point out that we can also *was/were going to* and *was/were supposed to* in negative sentences and questions.

 Focus students on the examples to highlight that we usually use the weak forms of *was* /wəz/ and *were* /wə/ in sentences with *was/were going to* and *was/were supposed to*. R10.2 P Play the recording (SB p154). Students listen and practise. Check students copy the sentence stress and weak forms correctly.

 a) Students do the exercise on their own. Check answers with the class.

2f) 3a) 4g) 5e) 6c) 7d)

b) Focus students on the example. Students do the exercise on their own. Early finishers can check their sentences in pairs. Check answers with the class.

2 Peggy and Tom were going to call Trevor and Sheila, but they lost their phone number.
3 Leo was supposed to try and find the Bradleys' address on the Internet, but his computer wasn't working.
4 Karen was going to get her parents a present on Monday, but she couldn't find her credit card.
5 Leo was going to buy himself a new suit last week, but he didn't have enough money.
6 Leo was supposed to get in touch with Jane Lewis, but he lost her phone number.
7 Leo's parents/Tom and Peggy were supposed to go through go through their old address books, but they couldn't find them.

Get ready … Get it right!

 Students do the exercise on their own. Tell students to write words or phrases, as in the example, not complete sentences.

 a) Put students into pairs. Students take turns to tell their partner about the things on their list, as in the speech bubbles. Encourage students to ask follow-up questions and continue each conversation for at least 30 seconds if possible.

While students are working, monitor and correct any mistakes you hear.

b) Finally, ask students to tell the class their partner's best reason for not doing one of the things on his or her list.

┌─ EXTRA IDEA ─────────────────────
- At the beginning of the next class, write the following prompt on the board: *I was going to hand in my homework today, but … .* Give students a few moments to think of an interesting or unusual excuse for not handing in their homework. Go around the class and elicit students' sentences. The class decides which is the most original excuse.
└──────────────────────────────────

┌─ EXTRA PRACTICE AND HOMEWORK ────
Ph **Class Activity** 10A Excuses, excuses! p164 (Instructions p128)
10 Review Exercises 1 and 2 SB p83
CD-ROM Lesson 10A
Workbook Lesson 10A p50
└──────────────────────────────────

10B Who's that?

Vocabulary describing people
Grammar modal verbs (2): making deductions
Review contacting people; state and activity verbs

QUICK REVIEW ●●●

This activity reviews vocabulary for contacting people. Students do the first part of the activity on their own. Put students into pairs. Students take turns to tell their partners about the people on their list. Encourage students to ask questions about the people if possible. Ask students to tell the class about one person on their list.

Vocabulary Describing people

1 a) Students do the exercise on their own, then check new words/phrases in **V10.2** SB p136. Check answers with the class (see **V10.2** SB p136).

Teach students the verb *dye*: *I'm going to dye my hair.*

Check students understand that when a man is losing his hair we say: *He's going bald.* If he has no hair, we just say: *He's bald.* For people whose hair is turning grey we can also say: *He/She's going grey.*

Point out that *jewellery* is an uncountable noun.

Tell students that when we use more than one adjective to describe someone's hair, we usually use the order 'length, style, colour': *She's got long, straight, brown hair.*

Also point out that we often use *in his/her teens/early twenties/mid-thirties/late forties*, etc. to talk about someone's approximate age. We use a hyphen (-) with *mid-twenties*, etc. but not with *early forties, late fifties*, etc.

Highlight that we use *The person/man/woman/one with …* + (red) hair, glasses, a beard, etc., but *The person/man/woman/one in …* + clothes: *She's the woman with long wavy hair and glasses. He's the one in a blue suit.*

Model and drill the words/phrases in **V10.2** SB p136. Pay particular attention to the pronunciation of *dyed* /daɪd/, *striped* /straɪpt/ and *jewellery* /ˈdʒuːəlri/.

b) Focus students on the picture of Tom and Peggy's 25ᵗʰ wedding anniversary party. Ask students what they remember about Tom and Peggy from lesson 10A.

Focus students on the speech bubbles and ask who the person is describing (2). Also teach the phrase: *You mean him/her?*

Students work in pairs and take turns to describe the people, using words/phrases from **1a)** and their own ideas. Their partner guesses who he/she is describing.

While students are working, monitor and check they are using the language from **1a)** correctly.

--- EXTRA IDEA ---
- Ask students to draw their family tree. Put students into pairs. Students work in pairs and take turns to describe members of their family using the language from **1a)**.

Listening and Grammar

2 a) **R10.3** Play the recording (SB p154). Students listen and match the names to people 1–7 in the picture, and find out where Peggy's husband, Tom, is.

Students check answers in pairs, giving reasons for their choices. Check answers with the class.

Also check which people are talking on the recording (Karen, Peggy, Jane, Leo and Trevor). Ask students which people in the picture are Karen and Leo. (Karen and Leo are standing at the back of the picture. Leo is wearing a striped shirt and glasses. Karen is wearing a long dress and has her hair in a ponytail.)

> Brenda 4 Jane 3 Derek 1 Nick 6 Trevor 7 Sheila 5
> Tom is in the bathroom (practising his speech).

--- EXTRA IDEA ---
- Ask students to look back at the picture of Peggy and Tom's wedding on SB p76. Students work in pairs and describe how the people have changed in 25 years.

b) Give students time to read sentences 1–10. Check students understand *a speech*.

Play the recording again. Students listen and decide who said each sentence: Peggy, Karen or Leo.

c) Students check answers in pairs. Check answers with the class.

> 2 Karen 3 Peggy 4 Leo 5 Karen 6 Leo 7 Peggy 8 Leo
> 9 Leo 10 Peggy

Help with Grammar Modal verbs (2): making deductions

3 a) Ask students if sentences 1–10 in **2b)** talk about the past, the present or the future (the present).

b) Students do the exercise on their own or in pairs. Check answers with the class.

> b) 3; 10
> c) 4; 5; 8
> d) 2; 7
> e) 6

c)–f) Students do the rest of the exercises on their own or in pairs, then check their answers in **G10.2** SB p137. Check answers with the class.

- **c)** We use *must* to talk about something that we believe is true. **2b):** sentences 3 and 10.
- We use *could, may* or *might* to talk about something that we think is possibly true. **2b):** sentences 1, 4, 5 and 8.
- We use *can't* to talk about something that we believe isn't true. **2b):** sentences 2 and 7.
- When we know something is definitely true, or is definitely not true, we don't use a modal verb. **2b):** sentences 9 and 6.
- To illustrate the point, ask students to compare these two sentences: *Leo's in the dining room* (I know this because I saw him go in there). *Leo must be in the dining room* (I can't see him anywhere else so I am making a deduction).
- Point out that we don't use *can* or *mustn't* to make deductions: *It could be him.* not *It can be him. He can't be a millionaire.* not *He mustn't be a millionaire.*
- You call also tell students that *could* and *might* are more common than *may*.

- **d)** Sentences 2, 4, 5, 6, 8 and 10 are talking about states. Sentences 1, 3, 7 and 9 are talking about something happening now.

- **e)** To make deductions about states we use: modal verb + **infinitive**.
- To make deductions about something happening now we use: modal verb + *be* + **verb+ing**.

4 R10.4 **P** Play the recording. Students listen and practise. Check they copy the sentence stress. Play the recording again if necessary.

5 Check that students remember who Karen is (Peggy and Tom's daughter).
Students do the exercise on their own before checking in pairs. Check answers with the class.

> 1 could 2 may 3 can't 4 must 5 might 6 must
> 7 can't 8 could; may

6 Students do the exercise on their own. Remind students that they must use either the infinitive or a form of *be* + verb+*ing*. Check answers with the class.

> 2 be doing 3 know 4 love 5 be working 6 be losing
> 7 need

7 **a)** R10.5 Tell students they are going to hear six short recordings of sounds and voices. Play the six recordings. Students listen and write sentences with *must, may, might, could* or *can't* about what they think is happening in each recording. Pause after each recording to allow students time to write. Play the six recordings again if necessary.

b) Students compare sentences in groups and find out if any of their deductions are the same. If they aren't the same, students discuss which of the group's sentences are correct.

c) Play the six recordings again, pausing after each recording to check students' sentences. Say whether you think each sentence is correct.

> **Possible answers** 2 Someone must be cooking sausages/frying something. 3 He might be late./He must be stuck in a traffic jam. 4 They could be watching a football match. 5 They must be at work./They can't know each other very well. 6 Someone may be heating up a ready meal/cooking something in a microwave.

Get ready … Get it right!

8 Focus students on the picture. Tell students that all these things belong to people at the party.
Students work on their own and decide who they think owns each thing.
✏️ Elicit the names of the people at the party and write them on the board before students begin (Tom, Peggy, Karen, Leo, Derek, Brenda, Trevor, Sheila, Nick, Jane).

9 **a)** Students compare answers in groups. Students discuss who they think each thing belongs to, using modal verbs of deduction. Encourage students to give reasons for their deductions, as in the example.
Note that students must use modals of deduction in their discussions, even if they believe they know the correct answer, as they don't know for certain who the things belong to.
While students are working, monitor and correct any mistakes you hear.

b) Students turn to SB p141 to check their answers. Finally, ask the class how many answers they got right.

> **baseball cap:** Nick Bradley; **wedding photos:** Peggy; **glasses case:** Brenda Bradley; **speech:** Tom; **earrings:** Jane Lewis; **wedding ring:** Sheila Jones; **football key ring:** Leo; **driving test book:** Karen; **London book:** Brenda Bradley; **wallet:** Derek Bradley; **watch:** Trevor Jones

---

EXTRA PRACTICE AND HOMEWORK

Ph **Class Activity** 10B Where's Robin? p165 (Instructions p129)
10 Review Exercises 3 and 4 SB p83
CD-ROM Lesson 10B
Workbook Lesson 10B p51

Vocabulary phrasal verbs (3)
Skills Reading: For better, for worse; Listening: Prenuptial agreements
Help with Listening /t/ and /d/ at the end of words
Review describing people

 QUICK REVIEW ●●●
This activity reviews vocabulary for describing people and modal verbs of deduction. Students write descriptions of three people in the class on their own, as in the example. Make sure students don't include the person's name in their sentences. Put students into pairs. Students take turns to say their sentences. Their partner guesses who the person is, using modal verbs of deduction, as in the example.

Reading and Vocabulary

1 Students discuss the questions in groups. If possible, include students from different countries in the same group. Ask students to share their ideas with the class.

─ EXTRA IDEAS ─
- If you have a multilingual class, ask students to describe a typical wedding in their country in pairs or groups.
- Alternatively, students can describe the last wedding they went to.

2 a) Focus students on the magazine article. You can point out that the title 'For better, for worse', is taken from the vows that people make when they get married: *I (groom/bride) take you (bride/groom) to be my (wife/husband), to have and to hold from this day forward; for better, for worse, for richer, for poorer, in sickness and in health, to love and to cherish, till death do us part.*
Students do the exercise on their own. Early finishers can check answers in pairs. Check answers with the class.

| 1 fourth 2 went 3 had 4 has 5 Fewer |

b) Students do the exercise on their own. Check answers with the class.
Ask students if any of the numbers surprised them. If appropriate, you can also ask students about the divorce rate in their own countries.

A typical wedding costs about £16,000.
A typical wedding lasts six hours.
A typical wedding costs about £2,600 an hour.
The average cost of a divorce is £15,000.
In 1971 there were 459,000 weddings in the UK.
In 2001 there were 286,000 weddings in the UK.
The divorce rate in the UK is 53%.
The divorce rate in Italy is 12%.

c) Focus the students on the phrasal verbs in **bold** in the article. Students work on their own and match them to meanings 1–10. Encourage students to guess the meaning of the phrasal verbs from the context where possible.
Remind students to write the infinitives of the verbs.

d) Students check their answers in **V10.3** SB p136. Check answers with the class.
Tell students that we can say *split up* or *break up.*

2 get over 3 go up 4 look up 5 point out 6 put off
7 fall out 8 come up with 9 split up 10 come across

Help with Vocabulary Phrasal verbs (3)

3 a) Students read about the four types of phrasal verbs.
 Alternatively, write the examples on the board and go through the four types of phrasal verbs with the class, highlighting the position of the object for phrasal verbs types 2, 3 and 4.

b)–c) Students do the exercise in pairs, then check their answers in **V10.4** SB p136. Check answers with the class.

- **b)** TYPE 1 split up; go up TYPE 2 come across sth TYPE 3 put sth off; point sth out TYPE 4 come up with sth
- Point out that we can sometimes add a preposition to some type 1 phrasal verbs to make them type 4 phrasal verbs: *I've never **fallen out with** my brother. Georgina has just **split up with** her boyfriend.*
- Note that if the object in a type 3 phrasal verb is long, we put it at the end: *He pointed out **some problems in the report**.* not ~~He pointed some problems in the report out~~.

─ EXTRA IDEA ─
- Write these phrasal verbs on the board in random order: *come back, log on, get back, set off* (type 1 phrasal verbs); *deal with, go through, look after* (type 2); *tidy up, pick up, sort out* (type 3); *look forward to, put up with, go out with* (type 4). Students work in pairs and decide if the phrasal verbs are type 1, 2, 3 or 4.

4 Put students into pairs, student A and student B. Student As turn to SB p106 and student Bs turn to SB p111. Check they are all looking at the correct exercise.

a) Students do the exercise on their own.
Check the answers with the class. Only check the words students need to fill in the gaps, so that the students in the other group don't hear the questions they are about to be asked.

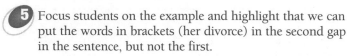

Student A 1 split up 2 get over 3 coming up with
4 get out of 5 looked up 6 put … off

Student B a) get out of b) fallen out c) get over
d) gone up e) point … out f) come across

b) Students work with their partner and take turns to ask
and answer the questions. Encourage students to ask
follow-up questions if possible.

5 Focus students on the example and highlight that we can
put the words in brackets (her divorce) in the second gap
in the sentence, but not the first.

Students do the exercise on their own before checking in
pairs. Check answers with the class. Ask students to give
reasons for their answers by saying what type of phrasal
verb is in each sentence.

2 ✓; ✓ 3 ✓; ✗ 4 ✗; ✓ 5 ✓; ✓ 6 ✓; ✗ 7 ✗; ✓ 8 ✓; ✓ 9 ✓; ✗

Listening

6 a) Focus students on the photos and ask students what
they know about the people. Also ask students what these
two couples have in common (they both got divorced).

Boris Becker is a former world number 1 tennis player
from Germany. He won six Grand Slam tournaments
and in 1985 he became the youngest ever winner of
Wimbledon at the age of 17. He married Barbara Feltus
in 1993, but they got divorced in 2001.
Steven Spielberg is an American film director and
producer. He directed *Jaws, E.T., Indiana Jones and the
Temple of Doom, Jurassic Park, War of the Worlds* and
Saving Private Ryan. He married actress Amy Irving in
1985, but they got divorced in 1989.

b) Be prepared with definitions, examples, etc. to pre-
teach the vocabulary in the box, or bring in dictionaries
for students to check the meanings themselves.
Model and drill the words. Highlight the pronunciation of
legal /ˈliːgəl/, *guarantee* /ˌgærənˈtiː/ and *court* /kɔːt/.

c) Check students understand *radio phone-in* (a radio
programme where members of the public phone in to give
their opinions or to ask an expert questions about a
particular topic).

R10.6 Play the recording (SB p154). Students listen and
answer the questions. Check answers with the class. Tell
students that *a prenuptial agreement* is sometimes called
a prenup.

1 A prenuptial agreement is like a divorce contract that
couples sign before they get married. They agree how
they'll divide up their property and money if they ever get
divorced. 2 Yes, she does. She says that if both the husband
and wife agree to follow the prenuptial agreement when
they get divorced, then they don't need a lawyer at all.

d) Give students time to read sentences 1–5, then play
the recording again. Students listen, tick the true
sentences and correct the false ones.

1F Most couples **don't** usually get half of everything
they own. 2T 3F Boris Becker and Barbara Feltus were
married for **seven** years. 4F Amy Irving got $100
million when she got divorced. 5F You **don't** need a
lawyer to deal with a prenuptial agreement.

Help with Listening /t/ and /d/ at the end of words

- This Help with Listening section focuses on when we
say /t/ and /d/ at the end of words in natural spoken
English and when we leave these sounds out.

7 a) Focus students on the sentences from the recording.
Students do the exercise on their own or in pairs, as in
the examples.

✏ While students are working, write the sentences on
the board so that you are ready to check their answers.

b) R10.6 Play the beginning of the recording again.
Students listen and check their answers.

Play the recording again, pausing after each sentence.
Elicit students' answers and circle or cross out each *t* or
d in **bold** on SB p81 in the sentences on the board.

Alison, firs(t) of all, we shoul**d** star**t** with the mos(t) obvious
question – wha(t) exactly is a prenuptial agreement?

Well, it's like a divorce contrac**t** couples sign before
they ge**t** married. They agree how they'll divi(d)e up
their property an**d** money if they ever ge**t** divorced.

c) Students choose the correct word in the rule on their
own. Check the answer with the class.

Point out that the /t/ and /d/ sounds that are pronounced
in the example sentences link to the vowel sound at the
beginning of the next word (first_of, etc.).

We don't usually hear /t/ or /d/ sounds at the end of
words when the next word starts with a consonant
sound.

d) Ask students to turn to R10.6, SB p154. Play the
whole recording again. Students listen and notice when
we don't say the /t/ and /d/ sounds at the end of words.

8 Students discuss the questions in groups. If possible,
include men and women in each group.

Finally, ask students to share their ideas and opinions
with the class.

┌─ **EXTRA PRACTICE AND HOMEWORK** ─
Ph **Vocabulary Plus** 10 Moods and relationships p186
(Instructions p176)
Ph **Class Activity** 10C Go up the ladder p166
(Instructions p129)
CD-ROM Lesson 10C
Workbook Lesson 10C p53

10D Do you mind?

Real World asking for, giving and refusing permission
Help with Listening intonation (3): asking for permission
Review phrasal verbs

QUICK REVIEW ●●●

This activity reviews phrasal verbs. Students work on their own and make a list of eight phrasal verbs they know. Put students into pairs. Students swap papers and take turns to say a sentence for each of the phrasal verbs on their partner's list. Students decide if their partner's sentences are correct. While students are working, monitor and help them with any problems. Ask a few students to tell the class one of their sentences.

1 Check students remember *relatives* (all the people in your family). Students discuss the questions in groups. Ask each group to share interesting answers with the class.

2 **a)** Focus students on the pictures. Ask students who Peggy and Tom are (the couple who had a 25th wedding anniversary party in lesson 10B) and what they remember about Derek, Brenda and Nick Bradley (Derek Bradley was Tom's best man and Brenda was Peggy's bridesmaid. They now live in New York with their teenage son, Nick). Tell students that Derek, Brenda and Nick are staying with Peggy and Tom after the party.

R10.7 Give students time to read sentences a)–f), then play the recording (SB p154). Students listen and fill in the gaps.

b) Put students into pairs. Students check their answers to 2a) and match conversations 1–3 to pictures A–C. Check answers with the class.

> a) emails b) books c) photos d) girlfriend
> e) sandwich f) washing
> 1C 2B 3A

3 **a)** Check students remember *give/refuse permission*.
Focus students on responses 1–6 from the conversations. Students work on their own and decide if each response is giving permission or refusing permission.

b) Students do the exercise on their own.

c) **R10.7** Play the recording again. Students listen and check their answers to 3a) and 3b). Check answers with the class.

> **3a)** Responses 2, 4 and 5 give permission.
> Responses 1, 3 and 6 refuse permission.
> **3b)** a)3 b)4 c)1 d)5 e)2 f)6

Real World Asking for, giving and refusing permission

4 **a)–e)** Students do the exercises on their own or in pairs, then check their answers in **RW10.1** SB p137. Check answers with the class.

- **a)** 3 infinitive 4 Past Simple 5 infinitive 6 Present Simple
- Point out that we use phrases 1–6 in **4a)** to ask for permission to do something.
- Also point out that *could, may* and *can* are modal verbs and are therefore followed by an infinitive.
- *Is it OK if I…* and *Do you mind if I ….* are followed by the Present Simple, not the infinitive, as *I* is the subject of the *if* clause. You can illustrate this by eliciting how you can ask permission for other people to do things: *Is it OK if Nick uses your computer?*
- Also point out that *Would you mind if I gave my girlfriend a call?* is a second conditional and is a very polite way to ask for permission.
- We can also use *Could I … ?* or *Is it all right if I … ?* to ask for permission: *Could I borrow your pen? Is it all right if I use your phone?*
- **b)** 1 Yes, of course. 2 No, not at all.
- **c)** *Would you mind if I … ?*
- Highlight that we usually give permission by saying: *Yes, of course (you can/it is, etc.); Go ahead.; Help yourself.*
- *Do you mind if I … ?* and *Would you mind if I … ?* mean 'Is it a problem if I do this?'. To give permission for these phrases we usually say: *No, not at all.*
- Point out that *Actually, I'd rather you didn't, if you don't mind.* is a very polite way to refuse permission.
- **d)** 1 No, we don't. 2 Yes, we do. 3 Sorry/Actually, … .
- Tell students that we don't usually say *no* to refuse permission because it isn't polite. We usually give a reason instead.

Help with Listening Intonation (3): asking for permission

- This Help with Listening section focuses on the difference between polite and impolite intonation patterns when asking for permission.

5 **R10.8** Play the recording. Students listen and decide which question sounds more polite, a) or b). Play the recording again. Pause after each pair of sentences to check students' answers. Use the example to point out that when we are being polite, our voice starts higher and moves up and down more. A flat intonation pattern makes the person sound either rude or bored when asking for permission and is less likely to get a positive response.

> 2b) 3b) 4a) 5a) 6b)

6 **R10.9** **P** Play the recording (SB p155). Students listen and practise.

Check students copy the polite intonation when they ask for permission. Play the recording again if necessary.

--- EXTRA IDEA ---

- Students work in pairs and think of three things they would like to ask you permission for. Students ask you their questions. You decide whether to give or refuse permission, giving reasons where appropriate.

 7 a) Students do the exercise on their own. Check answers with the class. Model and drill the sentences if necessary.

> 1 May I see what you've written? 2 Can I use your dictionary for a moment? 3 Do you think I could borrow some money? 4 Do you mind if I take a photo of you? 5 Is it OK if I borrow your CD-ROM for a few days? 6 Would you mind if I used your mobile to call the USA?

b) Put students into pairs. Students take turns to say the sentences in **7a)**. His/Her partner decides whether to give or refuse permission. If students refuse permission, they must give a reason.

Encourage students to use polite intonation when they ask permission.

While students are working, monitor and correct their intonation where necessary.

Ask a few pairs to practise their requests and responses in front of the class.

 8 Put students into pairs, student A and student B. Student As turn to SB p105 and student Bs turn to SB p110.

a) Students work on their own and read the information about the two conversations. Students then decide what they want to say in each conversation.

While students are working, monitor and help them with any problems. Encourage students to use a different phrase for each request. Also remind students that if they want to refuse permission, they must give a reason.

b) Students work with their partners and role-play the conversations. While students are working, monitor and correct any mistakes you hear.

c) Students tell the class which things their partner refused permission for and the reasons they gave.

Finally, you can ask one or two pairs to role-play their conversations for the class.

 Ask students to turn to p101 and look at *I'm Not in Love*. This song was first recorded by the British band 10CC / ˌten siː ˈsiː/ in 1975. It was also recorded by the American singer Tori Amos and the British band Westlife.

1 Students do the exercise on their own or in pairs. Check answers with the class.

> 2d) 3c) 4f) 5h) 6a) 7b) 8g)

 2 a) **R10.10** Give students time to read the song, then play the recording. Students listen and fill in the gaps. Play the recording again if necessary.

b) Students check answers in pairs. Play the recording again, pausing after each line for students to check their answers.

> 2 going 3 because 4 think 5 see 6 much 7 make 8 two 9 picture 10 hides 11 back 12 much 13 forget 14 going 15 because 16 think

 3 Students discuss the questions in groups. Ask students to share interesting ideas with the class.

--- EXTRA PRACTICE AND HOMEWORK ---

10 Review SB p83
CD-ROM Lesson 10D
Workbook Lesson 10D p54
Workbook Reading and Writing Portfolio 10 p82
Progress Test 10 p218

10 Review

See p30 for ideas on how to use this section.

1a) 1 got 2 heard 3 get 4 kept 5 lost 6 'm/am 7 give

2a) 1 agreement with another person 2 personal plan 3 agreement with another person 4 agreement with another person 5 personal plan

2b) 1 was supposed to 2 was going to 3 was supposed to 4 was supposed to 5 was going to

4 1 isn't; might be 2 must be; is 3 can't be; must be

Progress Portfolio

See p30 for ideas on how to use this section.

11 All part of the job

Student's Book p84–p91

11A Any messages?

QUICK REVIEW ●●●

This activity reviews ways of asking for, giving and refusing permission. Put students into pairs, but don't let them talk to each other yet. Students do the first part of the activity on their own. Students then work with their partners and take turns to ask for, give or refuse permission. Remind students that when they refuse permission, they must give a reason. Ask students to tell the class one or two things their partners gave them permission to do.

Vocabulary things people do at work
Grammar reported speech: sentences
Help with Listening /h/ in *he*, *his*, *him* and *her*
Review verb forms

Vocabulary Things people do at work

1 Students do the exercise on their own, then check their answers in **V11.1** SB p138. Check answers with the class.

Check students understand that *unsocial hours* are times when most people don't work, for example evenings, nights and weekends.

Point out that you can *do overtime* or *work overtime*.

Also check students understand that *run* in this context means *manage*.

Note that the person in charge of a public company is usually called *the managing director* (UK) or *the CEO* (= *Chief Executive Officer*, US).

Highlight that we usually use *customers* to talk about people who buy things from shops, restaurants and businesses. We usually use *clients* to talk about people who pay money for services from lawyers, banks, etc.

Model and drill the phrases. Highlight the pronunciation of *audition* /ɔːˈdɪʃən/, *finances* /ˈfaɪnænsɪz/, *shifts* /ʃɪfts/ and *clients* /ˈklaɪənts/. Also point out that the stress on *ŏrganise* is on the first syllable, not the third.

Note that only the main stress in words/phrases is shown in vocabulary boxes and the Language Summaries.

> work unsocial hours; sort out people's problems; organise conferences; do overtime; go for an audition; run a department; be responsible for the finances; deal with customers/clients; arrange meetings; work shifts; be in charge of a company

> ── EXTRA IDEA ──
> • Students work in pairs and take turns to test each other on the collocations. One student says the words/phrases from B, for example *conferences*, and his/her partner says the whole collocation, for example *organise conferences*.

2 a) Students do the exercise on their own.

b) Put students into pairs. Students take turns to tell their partner about the people whose names they wrote down in **2a)**. Encourage students to use phrases from **1** in their conversations and to ask follow-up questions if possible. You can also ask each pair to decide which person has the most interesting job.

Ask students to tell the class about some of the people they discussed.

Listening and Grammar

3 Focus students on the photo. The two people in the picture are Max and Gabi. Max is the boss of On The Box, a company that makes TV programmes, and Gabi is his PA (personal assistant).

Tell students they are going to listen to Gabi talking to an actress called Fiona on the phone.

R11.1 Give students time to read questions 1–4, then play the recording (SB p155). Students listen and answer the questions. Check answers with the class.

> 1 He's in a meeting all day. 2 She's in hospital.
> 3 She was in a car accident and she's broken her leg.
> 4 She's going to ask him to call Fiona back in the morning.

4 **R11.1** Give students time to read sentences 1–8, then play the recording again. Students listen and fill in the gaps. Students check answers in pairs. Check answers with the class.

> 2 accident 3 month 4 operation 5 Friday
> 6 programme 7 soon 8 Max

5 a) Focus students on the photo again. Tell the class that it is now the next day and Gabi is giving Max his messages from the previous day.

R11.2 Give students time to read sentences a)–h), then play the recording (SB p155). Students listen and put the sentences in the order Gabi says them.

Check answers with the class. You can also ask students what Gabi is going to do to solve the problem (she's going to find three people who can come in for auditions tomorrow morning).

> 2d) 3e) 4h) 5g) 6b) 7f) 8c)

b) Students do the exercise on their own before checking in pairs. Check answers with the class.

> 1g) 2a) 3h) 4d) 5e) 6b) 7f) 8c)

Help with Grammar Reported speech: sentences

 6 a)–c) Students do the exercises on their own or in pairs, then check their answers in **G11.1** SB p139. Check answers with the class.

- **a)** Present Continuous → Past Continuous; Present Perfect Simple → Past Perfect; Past Simple → Past Perfect; *am/is/are going to* → *was/were going to*; *will* → *would*; *can* → *could*; *must* → *had to*.
- Remind students that we use reported speech when we want to tell someone what another person said. We usually change the verb form in reported speech.
- Highlight that modal verbs *could*, *should*, *would*, *might* and *ought to* don't change in reported speech. The modal verb *may* changes to *might*: "*I may be late.*" *He said he might be late.*
- Tell students that the Past Simple doesn't have to change to the Past Perfect. It can stay the same: "*I met him in 2003.*" *She said she met him in 2003.*
- You can also point out that we don't have to change the verb form if the reported sentence is about something general, or something that is still in the future: "*I love classical music.*" → *I told him I love classical music.* "*John's going on holiday in June.*" → *I told her that John's going on holiday in June.*

- **b)** We never use an object (*me*, *her*, etc.) with *say*: *She said (that)* ... not *She said me (that)* ... .
- We always use an object (*me*, *her*, etc.) with *tell*: *She told me (that)* ... not *She told (that)* ... .
- We don't have to use *that* after *say* and *tell* in reported speech: *She told me (that) she'd broken her leg.*
- Pronouns (*I*, *he*, etc.) and possessive adjectives (*my*, *his*, etc.) usually change in reported speech: "*We can't come to your party.*" → *She told me that they couldn't come to my party.*
- We often change time expressions in reported speech: *tomorrow* → *the next day*; *next week* → *the following week*; *last week* → *the week before*, etc.

 7 R11.3 P Play the recording. Students listen and practise. Check students are copying the sentence stress and the weak form of *that* /ðət/ correctly.

 8 a) Tell the class that Gabi is now giving Max some other messages she took yesterday. Focus students on the example. Point out that they must use the verb *say* or *tell* in brackets when they write the sentences in reported speech.

Students do the exercise on their own, then check answers in pairs.

b) **R11.4** Play the recording (SB p155). Students listen and check their answers. Check answers with the class. Note that *that* is optional in all answers.

> **2** Carl told me (that) he was going to be in New York next week/the following week. **3** Sid said (that) he hadn't understood your email. **4** Linda Wise said (that) she couldn't come to Monday's meeting. **5** Mrs Lee told me (that) the designs would be ready on Monday. **6** Ted Black said (that) he was having a party on Saturday. **7** Ted Black said (that) he wanted to talk to you about a new project. **8** Your ex-wife told me (that) she'd/she had sold the house.

Help with Listening /h/ in *he*, *his*, *him* and *her*

- This Help with Listening section helps students to understand when we don't say the /h/ at the beginning of short words like *he*, *his*, *him* and *her*.

 9 a)–b) Focus students on the beginning of the conversation and give students a few moments to read it.

R11.4 Play the beginning of the recording. Students listen and circle each **h** in **bold** that they hear. Play the recording again if necessary.

Students check answers in pairs, then choose the correct words in the rules in **9b)**. Check answers with the class.

Point out that when *he*, *his*, *him* or *her* follow a word that ends in a consonant sound, we often don't say the /h/. If the previous word ends in a consonant sound, these words often link together (*said he*, *call him*, etc.). This can make these words difficult to hear in natural spoken English.

> **a)**
> GABI Well, Mr Hall said **h**e had to talk to you.
> MAX OK, I'll call **h**im later. What's **h**is number?
> GABI **H**e only gave me **h**is mobile number. Here it is.
> MAX What does **h**e want, anyway? I talked to **h**im last week.
> GABI Apparently **h**is wife wants **h**er script back.
>
> **b)** We usually hear /h/ in *he*, *his*, *him* and *her* if it follows a vowel sound. We don't usually hear /h/ in *he*, *his*, *him* and *her* if it follows a consonant sound.

c) Ask students to turn to R11.4, SB p155. Play the whole of the recording again. Students listen and notice when we don't say /h/ in *he*, *his*, *him* and *her*.

Get ready ... Get it right!

 10 Focus students on the prompts in the box and the examples. Students write four true sentences and four false sentences about themselves, using the prompts or their own ideas. Tell students to write their sentences in random order, not in two groups of four.

a) Put students into pairs. Students take turns to say their sentences and guess if their partner's sentences are true or false. Before they begin, tell students that they will need to remember their partner's sentences for the next part of the activity. To help them do so, they can write one word only for each sentence.

b) Reorganise the class so that students are working with a new partner. Students take turns to tell each other their first partner's sentences using reported speech, as in the speech bubbles. Their new partner guesses if the sentences are true or false.

Finally, ask students how many sentences they guessed right. Students can share any interesting or surprising things they found out about their classmates.

EXTRA PRACTICE AND HOMEWORK

Ph **Class Activity** 11A Work dominoes p167 (Instructions p129)
11 Review Exercises 1 and 2 SB p91
CD-ROM Lesson 11A
Workbook Lesson 11A p55

11B How did it go?

QUICK REVIEW ●●●

This activity reviews jobs vocabulary. Students work on their own and write all the words for jobs that they know. Set a time limit of three minutes. Students compare lists in pairs to find out who has the most jobs, then tell their partner about anyone they know who has the jobs on either list. Ask students to share any interesting or unusual jobs with the class. Note that students use their lists of jobs again in **1b)**.

Vocabulary adjectives to describe jobs
Grammar reported speech: questions, requests and imperatives
Review reported speech: sentences; verb forms

Vocabulary Adjectives to describe jobs

1 a) Students work on their own and tick the adjectives they know, then do the exercise in **V11.2** SB p138. Students check their answers in pairs. Check answers with the class.
Highlight that we can also say *I work full-time/part-time*. Point out that we can say *a rewarding job* or *a satisfying job*. Also highlight that *lonely* has a negative meaning. Compare these two sentences: *I was alone* (1 was on my own). *I was lonely* (I was on my own and unhappy about it).
Model and drill the words, focusing on stress. Pay particular attention to the pronunciation of *temporary* /ˈtempərəri/, *glamorous* /ˈglæmərəs/ and *dull* /dʌl/.

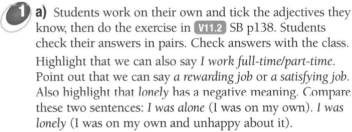

V11.2 2 rewarding 3 stressful 4 challenging 5 part-time
6 full-time 7 repetitive 8 temporary 9 permanent 10 dull
11 glamorous 12 well-paid 13 badly-paid 14 lonely

b) Ask students to look at the list of jobs they wrote in the quick review. Students match one adjective from **1a)** to each job. Encourage students to use all the adjectives if possible.

c) Put students into the same pairs as in the quick review. Students compare lists and say whether they agree with their partner's choice of adjectives. Discuss any adjectives students disagree about with the class.

EXTRA IDEA

• If you didn't do the quick review, ask students to work in pairs and think of one job for each adjective in **1a)**. Students can compare their lists in pairs.

---

2 a) Students do the exercise on their own.

b) Put students into groups. Students take turns to say why they chose the jobs.
Ask each group to share their ideas with the class.

Listening and Grammar

3 a) Focus students on the title of the lesson and tell students that we usually say *How did it go?* to people after they have had an interview or have done an exam.
Students discuss the questions in pairs. Ask students to share their ideas and experiences with the class.

b) Focus students on the photo and ask if they recognise any of the people (Max and Gabi, from lesson 11A). Tell students that the other woman, Eva, is having an audition for a part in a TV programme. Ask students why Max and Gabi need to find another actress quickly (in lesson 11A, the actress who was going to be in the TV programme phoned to say she had broken her leg).
R11.5 Give students time to read sentences 1–6, then play the recording (SB p156). Students listen and fill in the gaps.
Check answers with the class.

2 three 3 job 4 parts 5 acting 6 next week

c) Play the recording again. Students listen and answer the questions in **3b)**.
Students check answers in pairs. Check answers with the class.

1 Not at the moment./No, she isn't. 2 Maybe. 3 She played a nurse. 4 She was a schoolteacher. 5 The London School of Drama. 6 Yes, she is.

4 **a)** Tell students that they are going to listen to Eva telling her boyfriend, Joe, about the audition.

R11.6 Give students time to read sentences a)–f), then play the recording (SB p156). Students listen and put the sentences in the order Eva says them. Check answers with the class.

> 2f) 3c) 4e) 5b) 6d)

b) Students do the exercise on their own. Check answers with the class.

> 1a) 2f) 3c) 4e) 5b) 6d)

Help with Grammar Reported speech: questions

5 **a)–c)** Students do the exercises on their own or in pairs, then check their answers in **G11.2** SB p139. Check answers with the class.

- **a)** We **don't use** the auxiliaries *do*, *does* or *did* in reported questions: *He asked if I had any acting work.* not *He asked if I did have any acting work.*
- We use *if* or *whether* when we report questions **without** a question word: *First he asked me if/whether I was working at the moment.*
- We **sometimes** use an object (*me*, *him*, etc.) with *ask*: *He asked (me) whether I was available to start next week.*
- The changes in the verb forms in reported questions are **the same as** reported sentences: *"What other parts have you had recently?"* → *He asked me what other parts I'd had recently.*
- Remind students that we use reported questions when we want to tell someone what another person asked us.
- **b)** We make reported *Wh-* questions with: *He asked (me)/He wanted to know* + question word + subject + verb.
- We make reported *yes/no* questions with: *He asked (me)/He wanted to know* + *if* or *whether* + subject + verb.
- Point out that the word order in reported questions is the same as in a positive sentence: *I asked her where her brother was.* not *I asked her where was her brother.*
- Also highlight that we don't use question marks with reported questions.

6 **R11.7** **P** Play the recording. Students listen and practise. Check students copy the sentence stress.

7 **a)** Focus students on sentences 1–10 and the cartoons. Tell students that these are real questions that people have asked in interviews. Go through the example with the class. Students do the exercise on their own.

b) Students compare answers in pairs, then decide which question is the funniest. Check answers with the class.

2 She asked him what his star sign was. 3 He asked him if/whether it was a problem if he was angry most of the time. 4 She asked them why they weren't in a more interesting business. 5 He wanted to know if/whether he had to wear a suit for the next interview. 6 He wanted to know which job he was applying for. 7 She wanted to know if/whether she could come back when she found her glasses. 8 She wanted to know why she was here/there. 9 He asked her if/whether the company would pay to look after his horse. 10 He asked him if/whether he had been in prison too.

8 Check students remember what happened to Eva (she went for an audition). Tell students that Max phoned Eva later the same day to tell her that she's got the job.

R11.8 Give students time to read questions 1–4, then play the recording (SB p156). Students listen and answer the questions. Check answers with the class.

1 She has to go to the offices of On The Box for a meeting. 2 At ten o'clock. 3 The director and all the other actors. 4 For the next three months, at least.

Help with Grammar Reported speech: requests and imperatives

9 **a)–c)** Students do the exercises on their own or in pairs, then check their answers in **G11.3** SB p139. Check answers with the class.

- **a)** The first sentence is a request. The second and third sentences are imperatives.
- **b)** To report **requests**, we use *asked* + object + (*not*) + infinitive with *to*: *"Can you come to a meeting on Monday?"* → *He asked me to come to a meeting on Monday.* Point out that it is also correct to report the complete request: *He asked me if I could come to a meeting on Monday.*
- To report **imperatives**, we use *told* + object + (*not*) + infinitive with *to*. *"Be at our offices at ten."* → *He told me to be at their offices at ten. "Don't accept any more work."* → *He told me not to accept any more work.* Highlight the position of *not* when we report negative imperatives.
- You can tell students that we also use *asked* + object + (*not*) + infinitive with *to* to report invitations: *"Would you like to go with me?"* → *He asked me to go with him.*

10 Students do the exercise on their own, then check answers in pairs. Check answers with the class.

2 She told him to call her at lunchtime. 3 She asked him to pick her up after the meeting. 4 She told him not to worry about her. 5 She asked him to book a table at their favourite restaurant. 6 She told him not to tell anyone about the job yet. 7 She asked him to help her learn her lines.

Get ready … Get it right!

11 Allow students to choose a partner, or put students into pairs yourself. If possible, put students in pairs with someone they don't know very well.

Students write six questions to ask their partner, using the prompts or their own ideas. They should write questions that they don't know the answer to. Students are not allowed to talk to their partner at this stage of the activity. While students are working, monitor and check their questions for accuracy.

12 **a)** Students work with their partners and take turns to ask and answer their questions. Make sure all students make notes on their partner's answers, as they will need them for the final stage of the activity.

b) Reorganise the class so that students are working with a different partner. Students take turns to tell their new partner about their conversation with their first partner in **12a)**. Students should report the questions and the answers, as in the speech bubble.

Tell students that they can report the six questions their first partner asked and also the six questions they asked him/her (twelve questions in total).

While students are working, monitor and correct any mistakes you hear in the reported questions. Encourage students to discuss any interesting information and ask follow-up questions where appropriate, rather than just report the questions one by one.

c) Finally, ask students to tell the class two interesting things they found out about their first partner.

EXTRA PRACTICE AND HOMEWORK

Ph **Vocabulary Plus** 11 Working life p187 (Instructions p176)

Ph **Class Activity** 11B Teach your own language p168 (Instructions p130)

11 Review Exercises 3 and 4 SB p91

CD-ROM Lesson 11B

Workbook Lesson 11B p56

11C Undercover

QUICK REVIEW ●●●
This activity reviews reported sentences and questions. Students do the first part of the activity on their own. Put students into pairs. Students take turns to tell each other about their conversations using reported speech, as in the example. Ask one or two students to tell the class about interesting conversations they had yesterday.

Reading and Vocabulary

1 Check students understand *police drama* and *detective story*. Students discuss the questions in groups. Ask students to share interesting answers with the class.

2 **a)** Be prepared with definitions, examples, etc. to pre-teach the vocabulary in the box, or bring in dictionaries for students to check the meanings themselves. Point out that *cop* is informal for *police officer* and check students understand *undercover cop* (a police officer who pretends to be someone else in order to find out information about criminals). Note also that the meaning of *bug* in the article is a listening device, not an insect.

b) Focus students on the title of the website article and the photos. Ask students which company made the TV programme *Undercover* (On The Box) and the name of the actress who appears in both photos (Eva).

Students read the article and match the people's names to their roles in the TV programme.

Students check their answers in pairs and decide who they can see in the photos. Check answers with the class.

Vocabulary verb patterns (2): reporting verbs
Skills Reading: Undercover's success; Listening: Episode 5 of Undercover
Help with Listening missing words
Review reported speech

1c) 2e) 3a) 4f) 5b) 6d)
Photo on SB p88 Kat, Rupert and Gloria
Photo on SB p89 Dom and Kat

---

c) Students read the article again and answer the questions. Early finishers can check their answers in pairs.

Check answers with the class. Note that students discuss what they think is going to happen in the next episode of *Undercover* in **6a)**, so don't start this discussion here.

---

1 At a London art gallery. 2 Because Kat put a bug in the phone in Rupert's private study. 3 Gloria. 4 Dom is in love with Kat, but she isn't in love with him. 5 Kat is going to have dinner with Dom, and Hendrik is going to deliver three of his statues to Rupert's warehouse.

---

3 Students tick the verbs they know, then do the exercise in V11.3 SB p138. Students can check their answers in the article on SB p88–p89. Check answers with the class.
Model and drill the verbs, focusing on stress.

V11.3 2 offer 3 admit 4 refuse 5 promise 6 agree
7 suggest 8 remind 9 warn 10 threaten

Help with Vocabulary Verb patterns (2): reporting verbs

 4 **a)–b)** Students do **4a)** on their own, then check their answers in `V11.4` SB p138. Check answers with the class.

- **a)** **remind**, **warn** + object + (*not*) + infinitive with *to*; **refuse**, **promise**, **agree**, **threaten** + (*not*) + infinitive with *to*; **suggest** + verb+*ing*
- Use the examples in the article to highlight the verb patterns in the table: *Rupert invited her to have dinner*, etc.
- Also highlight that verb forms in other clauses still change as normal: *He threatened to kill him if anything went wrong.*
- Note that when we use these reporting verbs, we don't have to report every word people say. It's more important to report the idea: *"Don't forget to turn off the TV."* → *She reminded them to turn off the TV.* *"Yes, OK, it's true. I was the person who crashed your car."* → *He admitted crashing her car.*
- Point out that some reporting verbs can have more than one verb pattern. For example after *promise*, *agree*, *admit* and *suggest* we can use *that* + clause: *Kat promised (Dom) that she would go out with him. Dom admitted that he was madly in love with Kat.*
- Highlight how we make these verb forms negative and point out that we often use *not* with *warn*: *He warned Hendrik not to tell anyone about their plan.*

 5 **a)** Ask students to briefly summarise what happened in episode 4 of *Undercover*.

Focus students on the two conversations from that episode. Students work on their own and put the sentences in **bold** in reported speech. Do the first one or two with the class if necessary.

b) Students check answers in pairs. Check answers with the class.

1 Dom suggested going to the Ritz. **2** He offered to book a table. **3** He invited Kat to come/go to Paris next weekend/the following weekend. **4** He admitted saying some stupid things sometimes. **5** Kat agreed to talk about Paris after dinner. **6** Rupert warned Hendrik not to be late. **7** Hendrik promised to be there on time. **8** Rupert reminded him to watch out for the cops. **9** Hendrik threatened to tell the police everything he knows/knew. **10** Rupert refused to believe him.

 6 **a)** Put students into groups. Students discuss what they think is going to happen in episode 5 of *Undercover*.

 Elicit students' ideas and write them on the board for checking in **6b)**.

b) `R11.9` Play the recording (SB p156). Students listen and decide if any of the ideas on the board are correct. Check answers with the class.

---

c) Give students time to read sentences 1–8, then play the recording again. Students listen and decide if the sentences are true or false.

Students check answers in pairs. Check answers with the class.

1T	**2**F	**3**F	**4**T	**5**F	**6**T	**7**F	**8**T

Help with Listening Missing words

- This Help with Listening section shows students that we often miss out words in spoken English when the meaning is clear.

 7 **a)** Focus students on the beginning of episode 5 of *Undercover*. Students read the conversation and notice the missing words. Ask students what kind of words we often miss out (the verb *be*, pronouns, articles, prepositions and positive auxiliaries).

b) `R11.9` Ask students to turn to R11.9, SB p156. Students listen to the first two parts of episode 5 of *Undercover* again and notice the missing words.

 8 Focus students on sentences 1–10 in **bold** in R11.9, SB p156. Students work in pairs and take turns to say the sentences in reported speech, as in the speech bubble. Students should do this as a speaking activity, not a writing activity. Check answers with the class.

2 Darren suggested calling Kat.
3 Glenn reminded Darren to turn on the camera when they arrived.
4 Hendrik offered to put them/the statues in Rupert's car himself.
5 Hendrik invited Rupert to come and visit him in Amsterdam.
6 Rupert promised to buy some more of his/Hendrik's statues.
7 Gloria threatened to kill Kat if she turned around.
8 Kat admitted working for the SCS.
9 Gloria refused to help the police.
10 Gloria warned Kat not to say a word.

 9 **a)** Students work in the same pairs as in **8** and decide what happened at the end of episode 5 of *Undercover*. Encourage students to include all the characters, if possible.

— EXTRA IDEA —
- To help students with ideas, write all the characters' names on the board. Ask the class to tell you each person's location and current situation, and write this information on the board next to each name. Students then do **9a)** in pairs.

b) Students work in pairs and write a summary of what happened at the end of episode 5, using at least five reporting verbs from **3**. While students are working, help them with any problems and check they are using the reporting verbs correctly.

c) Students swap articles with another pair. Students read the summary and decide which ending is the best.

Finally, ask students to tell the class the main points of the ending they have read. The class can then decide which ending is the best.

— EXTRA IDEA —

* Students can write their summaries in **9b)** for homework. The articles can be displayed around the room for other students to read. Students can then decide which ending they think is the best.

— EXTRA PRACTICE AND HOMEWORK —

 Class Activity 11C Spy school p169 (Instructions p130)

11 Review Exercise 5 SB p91

CD-ROM Lesson 11C

Workbook Lesson 11C p58

11D It's my first day

QUICK REVIEW ●●●

This activity reviews reporting verbs. Students do the activity in pairs. If you have some students who weren't at the last class, put them in groups with students who were. If your students can't remember the character's names, write them on the board (see **2b)** on SB p88). Ask students to share what they remember about the programme with the class.

Real World checking information
Help with Listening contrastive stress
Review reporting verbs; requests

1 Students discuss the questions in groups. Ask students to share interesting answers with the class.

2 **a)** Focus students on the photo. Tell students that Nicola is working as a temp (a temporary assistant) for the company On The Box and today is her first day.

Ask students who else works for this company (Max and Gabi from lessons 11A and 11B) and what TV programme this company has made (*Undercover*).

R11.10 Give students time to read sentences 1–6, then play the recording (SB p157). Students listen and choose the correct words/phrases.

1 Max 2 wants 3 to 4 on holiday 5 the BBC 6 the week

b) Focus students on Nicola's notepad and give them a few moments to read it.

Play the recording again. Students listen and fill in the gaps on Nicola's notepad.

Students check answers in pairs. Check answers with the class.

2 CBN TV 3 Thursday 4 VA329 5 12.15 6 Groener
7 16ᵗʰ 8 Paris 9 07866 554390

— EXTRA IDEA —

* If your class are finding the recording difficult, ask them to look at R11.10, SB p157. Play the recording again. Students listen, read and check their answers.

Real World Checking information

3 **a)–c)** Students do the exercises on their own, then check answers in **RW11.1** SB p139. Check answers with the class.

* **a)** 2 with 3 didn't 4 say 5 mean 6 could 7 spelt 8 talking 9 catch 10 give
* **b)** **a)** Sentences 1, 3, 4, 6, 9 and 10 ask someone to repeat information. **b)** Sentences 2, 5, 7 and 8 check that the information you have is correct.
* Tell students that we can say *I didn't quite catch that.* or *I didn't quite get that.*

4 **R11.11** Play the recording (SB p157). Students listen and practise. Check that students copy the polite intonation correctly. Play the recording again if necessary.

Help with Listening Contrastive stress

* This Help with Listening section focuses on how we usually put the main stress on information that we want to check or correct.

5 **a)** Focus students on the introductory bullet point and check they understand it.

R11.12 Play the recording. Students listen and mark the main stresses in each sentence. Check answers with the class.

Highlight that Nicola stresses *fifty* as this is information she is unsure about. Mr Cramer stresses *fifty* as this is incorrect information and stresses *fifteen* as this is correct information.

NICOLA   And it arrives at twelve fifty.
MR CRAMER   No, not twelve fifty, twelve fifteen.

b) R11.13 Play the recording (SB p157). Students listen and write which words, letters or numbers have the main stress.

Play the recording again, pausing after each pair of sentences to check answers with the class.

> See R11.13, SB p157.

c) Ask students to look at R11.13, SB p157. Students work in pairs and practise saying the pairs of sentences they listened to in **5b)**.

While students are working, monitor and check they are stressing the correct words.

 6 a) Students do the exercise on their own. Check answers with the class.

> **2** mean **3** get **4** say **5** talking **6** give **7** that **8** with **9** with

b) Focus students on the sentences in **bold** in the conversations in **6a)**. Students work on their own and decide which words, letters or numbers are said with contrastive stress.

c) R11.14 Play the recording (SB p157). Students listen and check their answers.

Play the recording again, pausing after each sentence to check the answers with the class.

> See R11.14, SB p157.

d) Put students into pairs. Students practise the conversations in **6a)**. Encourage students to practise each conversation until they can remember it.

While students are working, monitor and check they are stressing the correct words.

Ask a few pairs of students to role-play the conversations for the class.

7 Put students into pairs, student A and student B. Student As turn to SB p106 and student Bs turn to SB p111. Check they are all looking at the correct exercise.

a) Students read the information and underline the main points, as in the examples. Students then plan what they are going to say in their phone conversations. Encourage students to make notes, but not to write out the whole conversation word for word.

While students are working, monitor and help them with any problems. Students are not allowed to look at each other's books at any stage of the activity.

b) Students work with their partners. Student As phone student Bs and leave a message.

Encourage student Bs to check information where necessary, using language from lesson 11D. While students are working, monitor and correct any mistakes you hear.

c) Students swap roles so that student Bs phone student As and leave a message.

d) Students take turns to check their partner's message to see if he/she has written down the correct information.

Finally, ask how many students wrote down all the information in the message correctly.

> **EXTRA IDEA**
> * Reorganise the class so that each student A is working with a different student B. Students repeat the activity with a different partner to give them extra fluency practice.

> **EXTRA PRACTICE AND HOMEWORK**
> **11 Review** SB p91
> **CD-ROM** Lesson 11D
> **Workbook** Lesson 11D p59
> **Workbook** Reading and Writing Portfolio 11 p84
> **Progress Test 11** p220

11 Review

See p30 for ideas on how to use this section.

> **1 1** have; organise; sort out; do **2** run; deal with; 'm/am; arrange
>
> **3a)–b)** rewarding; stressful; glamorous; lonely; temporary; challenging; demanding; permanent; badly-paid; repetitive
>
> **4** He asked/wanted to know ... **2** ... if/whether I liked the area I'm living in now. **3** ... which country I wanted to visit. **4** ... if I could have pets where I live. **5** ... if/whether I was going to do anything special this weekend. **6** ... who my oldest friend was. **7** ... what I did/had done last weekend. **8** ... if/whether I'd be able to have a holiday this year.

> **5a) 2** Ann asked him to get her a beer./Ann asked for a beer. **3** Ann/She refused to let him pay this time. **4** Ben admitted being a bit short of cash./Ben admitted that he was a bit short of cash. **5** Ben invited Ann to go to the cinema on Friday. **6** Ann told Ben not to tell Lil/her. **7** Ben promised not to tell Lil/her. **8** Ann threatened not to speak to him again if he did.

Progress Portfolio

See p30 for ideas on how to use this section.

12 Real or imaginary

12A   I wish!

QUICK REVIEW ●●●

This activity reviews ways of checking information. Students do the first part of the activity on their own. Students can invent the names and addresses if they wish. ✎ While students are working, write the phrases from **RW11.1** SB p139 on the board. Put students into pairs. Students take turns say the names and addresses to each other. Their partner writes them down. Encourage students to use the language on the board to check information where necessary. Students then check the names and addresses with their partner.

Vocabulary informal words and phrases
Grammar wishes
Review state and activity verbs; second conditional

---

c) Give students time to read sentences 1–5, then play the recording again. Students listen and fill in the gaps. Check answers with the class.

> 1 dishwasher 2 with you 3 broke 4 party 5 match

Help with Grammar Wishes

Vocabulary Informal words and phrases

1 **a)** Students do the exercise in pairs before checking their answers in **V12.1** SB p140.

Check answers with the class (see **V12.1** SB p140).

Point out that *broke* in this context is an adjective, not a verb. Also teach students that *hang around* and *be off* are type 1 phrasal verbs (they don't have an object). Note that we can also say *be off to …* to mean 'be going to a place': *I'm off to Brazil next month.*

Highlight that *fancy* is followed by a noun, a pronoun or verb+*ing* and *can't be bothered* is followed by the infinitive with *to*. Point out that the phrases ending in prepositions (*feel up to, have a go at, be into, could do with, be sick of*) can be followed by a noun, a pronoun or verb+*ing*.

Model and drill sentences 1–12 with the class. Note that only the main stress in words/phrases are shown in vocabulary boxes and the Language Summaries.

b) Students do the exercise on their own.

c) Students do the exercise in the same pairs. Encourage students to ask follow-up questions. Students should try to keep each conversation going for at least 20 seconds.

Ask students to tell the class about one or two conversations they had.

Listening and Grammar

2 **a)** Focus students on photos A–E. Students work in pairs and discuss what they think the people in each photo are talking about.

Ask students to share their ideas with the class. Don't tell students the answers at this stage.

b) **R12.1** Play the recording (SB p157). Students listen and match the conversations to the photos. Check answers with the class.

> 1E 2A 3C 4D 5B

3 **a)–d)** Students do the exercises on their own or in pairs, then check their answers in **G12.1** SB p141. Check answers with the class.

- **a)** The sentences talk about the present.
- **b)** 1 No, she hasn't. 2 Yes, she does.
- Use this example to highlight that we often use sentences with *I wish …* to talk about imaginary situations in the present. We often use it to talk about the opposite of what is true or real: *I wish we had a dishwasher* (The speaker hasn't got a dishwasher now, but she wants one).
- Highlight that even though the sentences talk about the present, we use a past verb form.
- **c)** To make wishes about states we use *wish + Past Simple*: *I wish we weren't so broke.*
- To make wishes about activities happening now we use *wish + Past Continuous*: *I wish you were coming to the match with me.*
- To make wishes about abilities or possibilities we use *wish + could + infinitive*: *I wish I could come with you.*
- To make wishes about obligations we use *wish + didn't have to + infinitive*: *I wish we didn't have to go to this party.*
- Point out that we can say *I wish I/he/she/it was …* or *I wish I/he/she/it were …* : *I wish I was/were taller.*
- Also highlight that we often use the second conditional to give reasons for wishes: *I wish we had a dishwasher. If we had one, I wouldn't spend my life washing up.*
- Note that students often confuse *I wish* and *I hope*. Point out that we use *I wish* for imaginary situations and *I hope* for real possibilities. *I wish you were coming to the party* (I know that you aren't coming = imaginary situation). *I hope you're coming to the party* (I think that you might come = real possibility).
- We can also make sentences with *wish* with *you/he/she/we/they*: *He wishes he lived somewhere hotter.*

4 R12.2 P Play the recording (SB p158). Students listen and practise. Check students copy the sentence stress correctly.

5 **a)** Students do the exercise on their own. Check answers with the class.

> 1 could 2 didn't have to 3 was/were 4 had 5 were doing
> 6 liked 7 could 8 were having

b) Students work in pairs and match the sentences in **5a)** to the people in the photos. Check answers with the class.

> 1 Wayne 2 Carrie 3 Ashley 4 Fran 5 Charlie/Zoë
> 6 Ashley 7 Wayne 8 Charlie/Zoë

— EXTRA IDEA —

● Students work in pairs and match sentences 1–8 in **5a)** with the different uses of wishes in **3c)**.

6 Students do the exercise on their own, then check answers in pairs. Check answers with the class.

> 2 I wish I wasn't/weren't sitting in a traffic jam. 3 I wish we didn't have to get up early every day. 4 I wish I could remember her phone number. 5 I wish my husband wasn't/weren't working late. 6 I wish I knew how to sail.
> 7 I wish we had enough money to buy a new car.

7 **a)** Focus students on the example. Ask students what type of conditional this is (a second conditional).

Students do the exercise on their own, then check answers in pairs. Check answers with the class.

> **b)** 'd come; didn't have **c)** wasn't/weren't; 'd be
> **d)** could; 'd get **e)** 'd take; didn't have to
> **f)** wouldn't have to; lived **g)** knew; 'd ask

b) Remind students that we often use second conditionals to give reasons for wishes.

Students do the exercise on their own. Check answers with the class.

> 1b) 2c) 3f) 4g) 5e) 6a) 7d)

Get ready … Get it right!

8 **a)** Check students understand all the prompts. Students do the exercise on their own.

b) Students write second conditionals to explain how their life would be different if their wishes in **8a)** came true, as in the example.

9 **a)** Students do the activity in groups of three or four. Encourage students to ask follow-up questions and extend the conversations, as shown in the speech bubbles.

When each group has finished, ask them to decide which are the most unusual or surprising wishes.

b) Students take turns to tell the class about the most unusual or surprising wishes in their group.

Finally, students can decide on the most unusual or surprising wish in the whole class.

┌─ EXTRA PRACTICE AND HOMEWORK ─
│ Ph **Class Activity** 12A Wish list p170
│ (Instructions p131)
│ **12 Review** Exercises 1 and 2 SB p98
│ **CD-ROM** Lesson 12A
│ **Workbook** Lesson 12A p60

12B Important moments

QUICK REVIEW ●●●

This activity reviews wishes and second conditionals. Students do the first part of the activity on their own. Highlight the examples before they begin. Put students into pairs. Students take turns to tell their partner about their wishes and reasons. Ask students to share their partner's interesting or surprising wishes with the class.

> **Vocabulary** phrases with *get*
> **Grammar** third conditional
> **Help with Listening** third conditional
> **Review** wishes; second conditional; travel phrases

Vocabulary Phrases with *get*

1 **a)** Focus students on the table. Tell the class that *get* in English has many different meanings.

Students work on their own and tick the phrases they know. If students don't know some of the phrases, they can check them in the Language Summary after doing **1b)**.

b) Students work on their own and fill in the gaps in the table with the phrases in the box. Point out that there are three phrases for each box.

Students check their answers in V12.2 SB p140. Check answers with the class (see V12.2 SB p140).

Check students understand *get to know someone* (learn more about a person by spending time with them) and compare this with *meet someone* and *know someone*: *I met Tony on holiday five years ago. We spent two weeks in the same hotel and got to know each other quite well. I also know his brother, Michael* (I've met him and I know who he is).

Ask students how children at school can *get into trouble* (by being rude, fighting, etc.).

Point out that we can use other adjectives with *get* (*get married, get annoyed,* etc.). Highlight that we also use *get* to mean *buy*: *Could you get me some bread from the shops?*

Model and drill the phrases with the class.

c) Students work in pairs and write other phrases with *get* that they know, as in the examples.

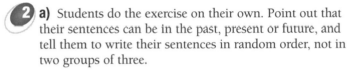 Elicit students' ideas onto the board and check the whole class understands what each phrase means.

> **Possible answers** get upset; get tired; get excited; get engaged; get divorced; get ready; get something right/wrong; get bored; get embarrassed; get (back) to sleep; get home; get ill/sick; get asthma; get a cold/flu; get over something; get up; get dressed; get sacked/fired; get arrested

2 a) Students do the exercise on their own. Point out that their sentences can be in the past, present or future, and tell them to write their sentences in random order, not in two groups of three.

While students are working, monitor and help with any problems or new vocabulary.

b) Put students into pairs. Students swap papers and decide which three of their partner's sentences are false. Students check their ideas with their partner to see how many they have guessed right.

Listening and Grammar

3 a) Focus students on photos A–C. Students discuss what they think were the most important moments in these people's lives with the class or in pairs. Don't tell students the answers as this stage.

b) Tell students that they are going to listen to the people in the photos talking about important moments in their lives.

R12.3 Give students time to read sentences 1–6, then play the recording (SB p158). Students listen and choose the correct answers. Students check answers in pairs. Check answers with the class.

> **1** at a party **2** lost her passport **3** lost her job **4** the country **5** an aggressive **6** a bike

4 a) Students do the exercise on their own or in pairs.

b) R12.3 Play the recording again. Students listen, check their answers to **4a)** and put the sentences in the order they hear them. Check answers with the class.

> **4a)** **Sandy** said sentences a) and c). **Miranda** said sentences b) and e). **Barry** said sentences d) and f).
> **4b)** 1a) 2c) 3b) 4e) 5d) 6f)

Help with Grammar Third conditional

5 a)–d) Students do the exercises on their own or in pairs, then check answers in G12.2 SB p141. Check answers with the class.

- **a)** **1** The past. **2** No, he didn't. **3** Yes, he did. **4** Imaginary.
- Use the example sentence to show students that we use the third conditional to talk about **imaginary** situations in the **past**. They are often the opposite of what really happened: *If I'd stayed at home, I wouldn't have met my wife* (he didn't stay at home and so he met his wife).

- **b)** We make the third conditional with: *if* + subject + Past Perfect, subject + *'d* (*would*)/*wouldn't* + *have* + past participle.

- **c)** **1** No, it isn't. **2** Yes, it is.
- Point out that we use a comma (,) when the *if* clause is first in the sentence: *If she hadn't lost her passport, she'd have flown home that day.* = *She'd have flown home that day if she hadn't lost her passport.*
- Tell students that we can use *could have* in the main clause of the third conditional to talk about ability: *If I'd been there, I could have helped you.*
- We can also use *might have* in the main clause of the third conditional to mean 'would have perhaps': *If you hadn't got lost, we might have got there on time.*
- Note that we don't usually use *would* in the *if* clause: *If I'd known, I'd have told you.* not ~~If I would have known, I'd have told you.~~

Help with Listening Third conditional

- This Help with Listening section helps students to understand the third conditional in natural spoken English.

6 a) R12.4 Focus students on the examples before playing the recording. Students listen and read the sentences. Highlight the way we say the contractions *I'd, wouldn't* and *hadn't*, and the weak form of *have* /əv/.

b) R12.5 Play the recording (SB p158). Students listen and write the sentences. Play the recording again if necessary. Ask students to check answers in pairs.

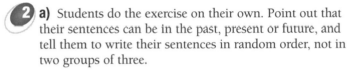 Play the recording again, pausing after each sentence to elicit students' answers and write them on the board. Check that all the contractions are included in each sentence.

> **1** They'd have come if they'd wanted to. **2** I'd have called you back if you'd left a message. **3** If I'd had some money, I'd have gone out last night. **4** We wouldn't have gone out if we'd known. **5** If I'd had more time, I'd have finished it.

7 R12.6 **P** Play the recording (SB p158). Students listen and practise. Check students copy the stress, contractions and weak form of *have* /əv/ correctly. Play the recording again if necessary.

You can also ask students to turn to R12.6, SB p158. They can then follow the sentence stress and weak forms of *have* as they listen and practise.

 8 **a)** Focus students on the example. Students do the exercise on their own.

Check answers with the class.

> 2 hadn't got; wouldn't have done
> 3 'd/would have stayed; hadn't lost
> 4 'd/had gone; wouldn't have seen
> 5 'd/would have got; hadn't decided

b) Students do the exercise in pairs. Check answers with the class.

> 1A 2B 3B 4A 5C

— **EXTRA IDEA** —

- Ask students to look again at the sentences in **8a)** and say what actually happened using *because* or *so*. For example sentence 1: *Sandy and Paula met each other because his friend introduced them.* Students can also do this for the sentences they wrote down in **6b)**.

 9 **a)** Students do the exercise on their own. While students are working, monitor and help them with any problems. Early finishers can check answers in pairs.

b) Students compare answers in pairs. Check answers with the class.

2 They wouldn't have got lost if they'd taken a map.
3 If Roberta hadn't been exhausted, she'd have gone out.
4 If Sally hadn't been ill, she'd have gone to school.
5 Mark wouldn't have got depressed if he hadn't lost his job.

 Get ready … Get it right!

10 **a)** Focus students on the prompts. Students work on their own and think about five important moments in their lives.

b) Students write third conditional sentences about their five important moments from **10a)**. While students are working, monitor and correct any mistakes you see.

11 Put students in pairs. Students take turns to tell each other about the important moments in their lives. They should include the sentences they prepared in **10b)** in their conversations. Encourage students to ask follow-up questions if possible.

Finally, ask students to share their most important moment with the class.

— **EXTRA PRACTICE AND HOMEWORK** —

Ph **Vocabulary Plus** 12 Phrasal verbs for plans p188 (Instructions p176)
Ph **Class Activities** 12B *get* stories p172 (Instructions p131)
12 Review Exercises 3 and 4 SB p98
CD-ROM Lesson 12B
Workbook Lesson 12B p61

 # 12C Superheroes

Vocabulary word formation (3): word families
Skills Listening: The life of Stan Lee; Reading: The real Spider-Man
Help with Listening sentence stress and weak forms: review
Review third conditional

QUICK REVIEW ●●●

This activity reviews the third conditional. Students do the first part of the activity on their own, as in the example. Put students into pairs and ask them to swap sentences. Students take turns to make third conditionals from their partner's sentences, as in the example. Ask each student to tell the class one of their third conditional sentences about their partner.

Listening

 1 Pre-teach *superheroes* (imaginary characters from comics, TV or films who fight evil, help people and save the world) and *superpowers* (special abilities that superheroes have).

Students discuss the questions in groups.

Ask students to share their answers with the class.

1 Spider-Man's superpowers include the ability to climb up the sides of buildings, super strength, and an ability to sense danger with his 'spider sense'.
2 **Possible answers** Superman (he can fly); The Incredible Hulk (he has super strength); The Fantastic Four (Mr Fantastic can stretch; Invisible Girl can become invisible; The Human Torch can fly and become a ball of fire; The Thing is made of rock and has super strength)
3 Stan Lee created the Spider-Man character and wrote the original Spider-Man comics.

- Find photos or illustrations of other superheroes from magazines or the Internet, for example Superman, The Incredible Hulk, The Fantastic Four, Batman, Wonder Woman, The X-Men, etc. Put the pictures on the board so that students can discuss them in **1**.

2 a) Be prepared with definitions, examples, etc. to pre-teach the vocabulary in the box, or bring in dictionaries for students to check the meanings themselves.

Point out that *a fly* is a type of *insect*. Model and drill the words, playing particular attention to the pronunciation of *crawl* /krɔːl/.

b) Tell students that they are going to listen to a radio interview with the writer, Robin Bell, who has just written a book about Stan Lee.

R12.7 Give students time to read sentences a)–e), then play the recording (SB p158). Students listen and put the topics in order. Check answers with the class.

> 1a) 2c) 3b) 4e) 5d)

c) Give students time to read sentences 1–6. Play the recording again. Students listen and decide if the sentences are true or false. Students check answers in pairs. Check answers with the class. If the sentences are false, ask students to explain why.

> 1T 2F He saw **a fly** crawling up a wall. 3F He also thought of **Insect-Man, Crawling-Man** and **Mosquito-Man**. 4F He **has the same problems as other young people**. 5T 6F He's usually a **hot-dog** seller.

Help with Listening Sentence stress and weak forms: review

- This Help with Listening section reviews the work on sentence stress and weak forms that students have done in **face2face** Intermediate.

3 a) Put students into pairs. Focus students on the beginning of the interview. Students decide which words are stressed and which words are said in their weak forms.

While students are working, write the beginning of the interview on the board ready for checking.

- Ask students to look at the Help with Listening sections on SB p16 and SB p56 again to remind them which words are usually said in their weak forms.

b) R12.7 Play the recording. Students listen and check their answers. Play the recording again, pausing after each sentence and eliciting students' answers. Mark the stress on the sentences on the board and write in the weak forms.

> Hellŏ and /ən/ welcome to /tə/ What Are /ə/ You /jə/ Reading?, the programme that /ðət/ looks at /ət/ what's new in the world of /əv/ publishing. With me in the studio is Robin Bell, whose new book, *Superhero*, tells the story of /əv/ Spider-Man's creator, Stan Lee. Welcome to /tə/ the programme.

c) Ask students to turn to R12.7, SB p158. Play the whole recording again. Students listen and notice the sentence stress and weak forms.

Reading and Vocabulary

4 a) Focus students on the photo of Alain Robert on SB p97. Find out if students have heard of him and ask what he is doing in the photo (climbing up the side of a tall building).

b) Be prepared with definitions, examples, etc. to pre-teach the vocabulary in the box, or bring in dictionaries for students to check the meanings themselves.

Model and drill the words. Point out that the stress on *skyscraper* is on the first syllable, not the second.

c) Students read the article and match the topics to paragraphs 1–5.

Check answers with the class.

> a)2 b)1 c)4 d)3 e)5

d) Students read the article again and answer the questions. Early finishers can check answers in pairs.

Check answers with the class.

Ask students for their reactions to the article and their opinion of Alain Robert.

> 1 Because he'd forgotten his keys. 2 Because they said he'd never climb again after a bad fall, but he was back on a mountain after only six months. 3 Because he climbs without ropes or protective equipment. 4 Because he usually climbs without permission. 5 He climbed the highest skyscraper in Venezuela dressed as Spider-Man. 6 Because it is a form of relaxation and it gives him a sense of what is important on Earth.

- Ask students to go to Alain Robert's website to find out more about his life and the buildings he has climbed.

Help with Vocabulary Word formation (3): word families

5 a)–d) Students do the exercises on their own or in pairs, then check their answers in V12.3 SB p140.

While students are working, draw the table from **5a)** on the board so that you are ready to check their answers. Check answers with the class.

- **a)** Focus students on the table on the board. Elicit which words from the article go in each column and complete the table (see the table in V12.3 SB p140).

- **b)** Focus students on the table again and elicit which are the suffixes for each noun and adjective. Underline these suffixes on the board.

- **c)** We use these suffixes to make nouns: *-ment, -ion, -ence, -ation.*
- We use these suffixes to make adjectives: *-ing, -ed, -able, -ive, -ful, -less.*
- Point out that sometimes the verb and the noun are the same: *They really **care** about the environment* (verb). *He puts a lot of **care** into his work.* (noun).
- Highlight that we often use *-able* to mean 'can': *It's a very enjoyable film.* = people can enjoy this film. *He's very dependable.* = you can depend on him.
- Remind students that we use *-ful* to mean 'with'. We use *-less* to mean 'without'.

6 **a)–b)** Students do the exercise in pairs, then check their answers in V12.4 SB p140. Check answers with the class.

- **a)** See the table in V12.4 SB p140.
- Point out that we often don't include the final *-e* on verbs when we add suffixes: *create → creation, pollute → pollution, confuse → confusing*, etc.

7 Give students a few minutes to learn the verb families in V12.3 and V12.4 SB p140.

Students do the activity in pairs. One students says a verb from **5a)** or **6a)** and his/her partner says the other words in the word family. Students should close their books while they are being tested.

8 **a)** Students work in groups and create their own superhero. Students can choose their hero's superpowers from the ideas in the box or invent their own.

Check students understand the phrases in the box before they begin and teach any new phrases if necessary.

b) Students continue working in their groups. Each group continues to develop their superhero's character based on the prompts. Make sure that all students take notes at this stage, as each student will be describing the group's superhero to other students in the next stage of the activity.

While students are working, monitor and help them with ideas and new language.

c) Reorganise the class so that students from different groups are sitting together. Students take turns to describe their superhero to the other people in the group. When all the students in the group have described their superhero, they decide which they think is the best.

Finally, ask students to tell the class about the best superhero in their group.

┌─ **EXTRA IDEA** ────────────
- For homework, students can draw a picture and write a description of their superhero. These can be collected next class and displayed around the room for other students to read.
└────────────────────────

┌─ **EXTRA PRACTICE AND HOMEWORK** ─
12 Review SB p98
CD-ROM Lesson 12C
Workbook Lesson 12C p63
Workbook Reading and Writing Portfolio 12 p86
Progress Test 12 p222
└────────────────────────

12 Review

See p30 for ideas on how to use this section.

1b) **2** (Name) is off on holiday soon. **3** (Name) is sick of working so hard. **4** (Name) is (really) into photography. **5** (Name) doesn't feel up to going out midweek. **6** (Name) would like to have a go at snowboarding. **7** (Name) could do with a holiday.

2a) **2** had **3** knew **4** didn't have to **5** could **6** had **7** was/were

3a) See V12.2 SB p140.

4 **2** hadn't met; wouldn't have moved **3** 'd/would have passed; 'd/had studied **4** had been; wouldn't have broken

5a) **Nouns** care; entertainment; creation
Verbs care; prefer; disappoint
Adjectives attractive; relaxed
Care can be both a noun or a verb.

5b) verb	noun	adjective
attract	attraction	attractive
care	care	careful, careless
entertain	entertainment	entertaining
prefer	preference	preferable
disappoint	disappointment	disappointed, disappointing
relax	relaxation	relaxing, relaxed
create	creation	creative

Progress Portfolio

See p30 for ideas on how to use this section.

End of Course Review

- The aim of this activity is to review language that students have learned throughout the course in a fun, student-centred way. The activity takes about 30–45 minutes.

  Check students understand *a counter, throw a dice, land on a square, move forward/back* and *have a rest*.

  Give students time to read the rules on SB p98 and answer any questions they may have.

  Ask students what happens when a student lands on a Grammar or Vocabulary square for the first time (they answer question 1 only).

  Ask what happens when a second student lands on the same square (they answer question 2).

  Also check what happens when a third student lands on the square (they can stay there without answering a question).

  Put students into groups of four and give a dice and counters to each group (or students can make their own counters).

  Ask a student with a watch in each group to be the time keeper for the group. He/She should time students when they land on a Keep Talking square and have to talk about a topic for 40 seconds.

  Students take turns to throw the dice and move around the board.

  If a student thinks another student's answer to a question on a Grammar or Vocabulary square is wrong, he/she can check in the Language Summaries in the Student's Book, or ask you to adjudicate.

  While students are working, monitor and help with any problems.

  The first student to get to *FINISH* is the winner. Students can continue playing until three students have finished.

  If one group finishes early, ask them to look at all the squares they didn't land on and answer the questions.

1 1 good at; nervous about; interested in; upset about (by) 2 keen on; fed up with; worried about; scared of (by)

2 1 How long has he been living in London? 2 How long have you had your car?

5 1 hot → boiling; surprised → amazed; tired → exhausted/shattered; bad → terrible/awful 2 big → huge/enormous; cold → freezing; small → tiny; difficult → impossible

6 1 If I **was/were** younger, I'd go back to university. 2 Could you tell me what time the class **starts**?

8 1 See `V7.2` SB p130. 2 See `V9.4` SB p134.

10 1 travel first class; go on a cruise; get off a bus 2 go on a trip; travel on your own; get a taxi home

12 1 *Seem* and *own* usually describe states. *Watch* and *eat* usually describe activities. 2 *Prefer* and *need* usually describe states. *Buy* and *cook* usually describe activities.

15 1 didn't you 2 does he

16 1 *keep* + verb+ing (*keep doing*); *need* + infinitive with *to* (*need someone to do*); *make* + object + infinitive (*make someone do*); *will* + infinitive (*will do*) 2 *let* + object + infinitive (*let someone do*); *seem* + infinitive with *to* (*seem to do*); *would* + infinitive (*would do*); *finish* + verb+ing (*finish doing*)

19 1 I've **visited** six countries so far. 2 He's been working here **for** two years.

21 1 My car has been stolen. 2 My house is being repainted.

22 1 sadness; danger; popularity; health 2 difficulty; kindness; patience; possibility

25 1 have a lie-in; do (some) gardening; go clubbing 2 work long hours; meet/hit deadlines; work/do overtime

27 1 *You mustn't go.* = You're not allowed to go.; *You don't have to go.* = It's not necessary for you to go, but you can if you want. 2 *I'll see him tonight.* = I decided to do this at the time of speaking.; *I'm seeing him tonight.* = I already have an arrangement with him.

29 1 See `V2.2` SB p116. 2 See `V4.2` SB p122.

30 1 I wish I had a car. 2 I wish I didn't have to go to a meeting tomorrow.

32 1 do a course; make money; make up your mind; do exercise 2 make a noise; do the shopping; make progress; do an exam

34 1 He/She asked (him/her) what he/she was doing. 2 He/She asked (him/her) if/whether Jim was going to the party.

36 His car's not as **old** as mine. 2 This house is the same size **as** ours.

38 1 painless; incorrect; uncommon; impolite 2 irresponsible; useful; disappear; unreliable

Photocopiable Materials

Class Activities

Instructions

There are 35 Class Activities worksheets (p132–p172). These worksheets give extra communicative speaking practice of the key language taught in the Student's Book. Each activity matches a lesson in the Student's Book, for example, *1A Our free time* matches lesson 1A, and *1B Celebrity match* matches lesson 1B, etc. There are three activities for units 1–11 and two activities for unit 12.

The Class Activities can be used as extra practice when you have finished the relevant lesson or as review activities in the next class or later in the course.

Many of the activities involve students working in pairs or groups. When you have an odd number of students, you can:

- ask two lower-level students to share a role card.
- give two role cards to a stronger student.
- vary the size of the groups.

1A Our free time p132

Language

Question forms; weekend activities

Activity type, when to use and time

'Find someone who' activity. Use any time after lesson 1A. 15–25 minutes.

Preparation

Photocopy one worksheet for each student.

Procedure

- Give each student a copy of the worksheet. Explain that they are going to try to find someone in the class who answers *yes* to each question. Focus students on the example. Students work on their own and write the other nine questions. Check questions with the class. Drill these questions if necessary.

- Students move around the room and ask their questions. If students are not able to leave their seats, they should ask as many students as they can sitting near them. When they find a student who answers *yes* to a question, they write the student's name in the second column on the worksheet. Students then ask a follow-up question based on the prompts in the third column. Encourage students to talk to as many different people as possible. Students only need to find one person who answers *yes* to each question. Demonstrate this stage of the activity with the whole class before students begin. With a low-level class you may also want to check the follow-up questions with the class before they begin.

- When students have finished, they work in pairs and tell their partners what they have learned about their classmates. Finish the activity by asking each student to tell the class two interesting things they have found out.

> 2 Do you chat to people online?
> 3 Are you reading a good book at the moment?
> 4 Did you go to an exhibition last month?
> 5 Have you had people round for dinner this month?
> 6 Did you do some gardening at the weekend?
> 7 Did you have a lie-in last weekend?
> 8 Are you trying to get fit at the moment?
> 9 Did you meet up with friends last week?
> 10 Have you (ever) tried a dangerous sport?

1B Celebrity match p133–p134

Language

Likes and dislikes

Activity type, when to use and time

Information gap. Use any time after lesson 1B. 15–20 minutes.

Preparation

Photocopy one Student A worksheet and one Student B worksheet for each pair of students.

Procedure

- Pre-teach *celebrity*, *the centre of attention*, *knitting*, *antiques*, *butterfly*, *environment*, *spicy*, *scuba diving* and *bingo*. Drill these words/phrases with the class.

- Put students into two groups, A and B. Give each student a copy of the appropriate worksheet. Elicit the names of the celebrities pictured on both worksheets and write them on the board. Elicit what the students know about each celebrity.

- Put students into pairs with someone from the same group. Students try to match the celebrities with their likes and dislikes.

- Reorganise the class so that a student from group A is working with a student from group B. Students are not allowed to look at each other's worksheets.

- Students take turns to read out their answers to their new partner, who tells them whether they are correct or incorrect. Before they begin, point out that each student has the answers to his/her partner's sentences at the bottom of his/her worksheet.

- Elicit from the class who had the highest score and discuss any surprising information students discovered.

- Ask students to turn over their worksheets. Students work in their pairs and see what they can remember about each celebrity.

1D Make it snappy! p135

Language

Question tags

Activity type, when to use and time

'Snap' game. Use any time after lesson 1D. 10–15 minutes.

Preparation

Photocopy one set of Sentence cards and **two** sets of Question tag cards for each group of three students. Cut into separate sets and shuffle each set.

Procedure

- Put students into groups of three. If you have extra students, have one or two groups of four. Give a set of Sentence cards to one student (A) in each group and ask them to put the cards face-down in a pile in front of them.

- Give a complete set of Question tag cards to students B and C in each group. Ask students to spread their cards out in front of them face-up so they can see all fifteen cards.

- Student A turns over the first Sentence card and reads out the sentence only (not the answer), for example *He's very tall.* Students B and C try to find the correct Question tag card (*isn't he?*) and give it to Student A, saying the question tag out loud at the same time. The first student to give Student A the correct card wins both cards as a 'trick'.

- The game ends when Student A has finished all the Sentence cards. The student (B or C) with the most 'tricks' wins.

- Students can shuffle the sets of cards and repeat the game, with Student B turning over the Sentence cards.

2A World rules p136

Language

Modal verbs (1); *be able to*, *be allowed to*, *be supposed to*

Activity type, when to use and time

Quiz. Use any time after lesson 2A. 15–25 minutes.

Preparation

Photocopy one worksheet for each student.

Procedure

- Pre-teach *primary school*, *do military service*, *mow the lawn*, *vote*, *tip waiters/waitresses* and *burn*.

- Put students into teams of three or four. Give a copy of the worksheet to each student. Explain that all the sentences are about different rules around the world.

- Students work with their partners and choose the correct answers in each sentence.

- Check answers with the class. Give each team one point for each correct answer. The team with the most points wins.

- Finish the activity by asking students what the rules for military service, voting, tipping, etc. are in their country/countries, and (if appropriate) whether they agree with these rules.

---

1 can't (you must be 17 years old) 2 have to 3 aren't allowed to 4 don't have to 5 aren't allowed to 6 mustn't 7 couldn't 8 are allowed to 9 can't 10 have to 11 shouldn't 12 are supposed to 13 aren't allowed to 14 have to 15 weren't allowed to

2B Opening night p137–p138

Language

Present Continuous and Present Simple

Activity type, when to use and time

Role play and gap-fill activity. Use any time after lesson 2B. 20–30 minutes.

Preparation

Photocopy one set of role cards for every twelve students and one What do you remember? worksheet for each student. Cut the role cards into twelve separate cards.

Procedure

- Tell students they are at the opening party of a new restaurant in London. Give each student a role card and allow them time to read and memorise the information. Give out the cards in random order. If you have more than 12 students, you can give out duplicate cards without affecting the outcome of the activity. If you have fewer than 12 students, omit the later role cards and delete the later sentences on the What do you remember? worksheet.

- 🖊 Elicit these questions and write them on the board: *Where are you from? What do you do? What are you doing in London? What do you do in your free time?*

- Explain that students must meet all of the other guests and find out as much as they can about each of them. Tell students that they must try to remember what they hear because they will be asked to use this information after the party.

- Students move around the room and talk to the other guests. Encourage students to ask the questions on the board when they meet new people.

- When students have finished, put them in pairs and give each pair a copy of the What do you remember? worksheet. Ask students to fill in the gaps with the appropriate information and choose the correct verb form in italics. Point out that the first gap in each sentence is a student's name.

- Check answers with the class. Give students one point for each correct piece of information and one point for each correct verb form. The pair with the most points wins.

---

a) is opening ... restaurant b) New York ... is visiting c) goes ... exhibitions d) writes ... food e) is studying ... chef f) usually directs ... horror g) is doing ... clubbing h) Los Angeles ... is making i) plays volleyball j) chef ... is doing k) plays ... piano l) pop singer ... is writing

2C The absolutely amazing game! p139

Language

Gradable and strong adjectives; adverbs

Activity type, when to use and time

Board game. Use any time after lesson 2C. 20–30 minutes.

Preparation

Photocopy one board for each group of three or four students. You also need a dice for each group and a counter for each student.

Procedure

- Put students into groups of three or four. Give each group a copy of the board, a dice and counters (or students can make their own counters). Ask a student with a watch in each group to be the timekeeper.

- Students take turns to throw the dice and move around the board. When they land on a sentence square, they must choose the correct word and say the complete sentence. If a student gets the sentence wrong, he/she must move back to his/her previous square.

- If a student thinks that another student's answer is wrong, he/she should ask you to adjudicate.

- When a student lands on a *Talk about* square, he/she must talk about the topic for 30 seconds. If he/she stops talking before 30 seconds is up, he/she must move back to his/her previous square.

- The first student to reach the FINISH square wins. If groups finish early, students can go through the squares in order and take turns to say the correct sentences. They can also discuss the topics in the *Talk about* squares they didn't land on during the game.

> 1 terrified 3 happy 5 good 7 big 9 shattered
> 10 absolutely 13 incredibly 16 delicious 17 difficult
> 21 absolutely 23 surprised 25 absolutely 26 terrible
> 28 big 30 beautiful 32 furious 33 absolutely

3B The world's greatest traveller p140

Language

Present Perfect Continuous and Present Perfect Simple

Activity type, when to use and time

Pairwork role play. Use any time after lesson 3B. 20–30 minutes.

Preparation

Photocopy one worksheet for each pair of students. Cut into separate role cards.

Procedure

- Put the students into two groups, A and B. Give a copy of the Traveller role card to each student in group A and a copy of the Interviewer role card to each student in group B. If you have an odd number of students, have an extra interviewer.

- Explain that the interviewers in group B are going to interview the travellers in group A for a TV documentary series called *Around the World*.

- Students work on their own and follow the instructions on their role cards. Encourage the travellers to use their imagination when preparing their roles and to think of interesting information they can tell the interviewer about each topic. Also check interviewers' questions for accuracy and help them with any problems. Encourage students to make questions with the Present Perfect Continuous and Present Perfect Simple where possible. With a low-level class, interviewers can prepare questions in pairs.

- Reorganise the class so that one interviewer is sitting with one traveller. Students do the role play in pairs. Encourage the interviewer to greet the traveller and make him/her feel comfortable before beginning the interview.

- When students have finished the role play, ask the interviewers to tell the class a few interesting things about the travellers they have just talked to. The class can then decide who is 'the world's greatest traveller'.

3C Suffix dominoes p141

Language

Suffixes for adjectives and nouns

Activity type, when to use and time

Dominoes. Use any time after lesson 3C. 15–25 minutes.

Preparation

Photocopy one set of dominoes for each pair of students. Cut into sets and shuffle each set.

Procedure

- Put students into pairs. Give one set of dominoes to each pair. Students share out the dominoes equally. Students are not allowed to look at each other's dominoes.

- One student puts a domino on the table. His/Her partner puts another domino at either end of the first domino so that the word and the suffix make a new word. Students continue taking turns to put dominoes at either end of the domino chain.

- If a student thinks the word and suffix don't match, he/she can challenge his/her partner. If the match is incorrect, the student must take back the domino and the turn passes to his/her partner. If students can't agree, they should check in V3.3 SB p120 or ask you to adjudicate.

- When a student can't put down a domino, the turn automatically passes to his/her partner. The game continues until one student has put down all his/her dominoes or until neither student can make a correct match. The student who finishes first, or who has the fewer dominoes remaining, is the winner.

- Early finishers can take turns to make sentences with the new words.

3D Memory maze p142

Language
Review of lessons 1A–3D

Activity type, when to use and time
Maze game. Use any time after lesson 3D. 15–25 minutes.

Preparation
Photocopy one worksheet for each student.

Procedure
- Put students into pairs. Give each student a copy of the worksheet.
- Ask students to look at the START sentence and decide if it is correct or incorrect. If they think it is correct, they should follow the solid arrow to sentence 1. If they think it is incorrect, they should follow the dotted arrow to sentence 2. (See key on worksheet.) Elicit that the START sentence is correct and direct the students to sentence 1.
- Students work with their partner and decide if sentence 1 is correct or incorrect. Students then follow the arrows accordingly. They can reach FINISH only by guessing the accuracy of each sentence correctly. If they make any errors, they will eventually be led back to an earlier position in the maze. If students get 'trapped' in this way, they should go back to START and try again.
- While students are completing the maze, monitor to ensure they know what to do and help where necessary.
- When students have finished, elicit the correct route and ask them to correct any incorrect sentences.
- Go through any squares not already dealt with and elicit if the sentences are correct or incorrect. If they are incorrect, elicit the correct sentence.

> The correct maze route is:
> START, 1, 4, 5, 7, 10, 11, 13, 12, 17, 14, 18, FINISH.
> 1 ✗ They**'re working** in the library at the moment.
> 2 ✗ They can't stand **watching** soap operas. 3 ✗ John's been working as a teacher **for** three years. 4 ✗ All of my friends **have** got mobile phones. 5 ✓ 6 ✓ 7 ✗ I was **absolutely/really** exhausted when I got home. 8 ✗ You **don't have to** wear a suit to work if you don't want to.
> 9 ✓ 10 ✓ 11 ✗ Don't bother **visiting** the museum because it's not open today. 12 ✓ 13 ✗ Sue's really frightened **of** the dark. 14 ✗ **Who visited** your parents last weekend?
> 15 ✓ 16 ✓ 17 ✓ 18 ✗ Sarah has a lot of **confidence**.

4A Celebrity engagement p143

Language
Past Simple and Past Continuous

Activity type, when to use and time
Role play. Use any time after lesson 4A. 25–35 minutes.

Preparation
Photocopy one worksheet for each pair of students. Cut into separate role cards.

Procedure
- Pre-teach *a celebrity*, *the media*, *engagement*, *a publicity stunt* and *propose to someone*.
- Elicit some famous celebrity couples from the class. Ask students if they think these people are in love or if they are in these relationships in order to get publicity.
- Divide the class into two equal groups, reporters and celebrities. If you have extra students, put them in the reporters group. If possible, have an equal number of men and women in the celebrities group. Give a copy of the appropriate worksheet to each student.
- Give students time to read the newspaper article at the top of their worksheets. Check students understand the situation by asking comprehension questions to check the main points of the story.
- Divide each group into pairs. If possible, put a man and a woman together for each pair of celebrities (Sam Kennedy and Alison Price). Note that you need an **equal number of pairs** of reporters and celebrities, so have one or two groups of three reporters if necessary.
- Students work in their pairs and prepare questions or answers based on the prompts. While they are working, check the reporters' questions for accuracy. Also check that all reporters are writing the questions, as they will be interviewing the celebrities separately. Encourage the celebrities to make their stories match as closely as possible, as they have to persuade the reporters that they really want to get married and haven't just got engaged for the publicity.
- Match up a pair of reporters with a pair of celebrities. Reorganise the class so that each reporter can interview each celebrity separately. Reporters interview the celebrities and make brief notes on their answers.
- When they have finished, students go back to their original pairs. Celebrities discuss the questions they were asked and whether they answered each question correctly. Reporters compare answers and decide if they think the celebrity couple are really in love or if the engagement is just a publicity stunt.
- Finally, ask reporters to tell the class if they believe that the couple are in love, giving reasons for their answers.

4C Rainforest adventure p144

Language
Past Simple; Past Continuous; Past Perfect

Activity type, when to use and time
Story-telling activity. Use any time after lesson 4C. 20–40 minutes.

Preparation
Photocopy one worksheet for each student.

Procedure
- Give each student a copy of the worksheet. Ask students to read the introduction at the top of the worksheet and check students understand the situation.

- Put students into pairs. Tell students that they are going to invent a story about what happened to Tom and Sally in the rainforest. Students work with their partner and discuss the questions in turn. Students write their ideas in the appropriate boxes next to each question. Encourage students to write brief notes, not complete sentences.

- When students have finished, ask them to practise telling their story to each other. This 'rehearsal stage' gives students time to work out how to tell their story and will increase students' confidence. Students can make any additional notes on their worksheet during this stage. Encourage students to use the Past Simple, Past Continuous and Past Perfect in their stories where appropriate.

- Reorganise the class so that students from different pairs are working together. Students take turns to tell their story, using the notes on their worksheets as prompts. Alternatively, this stage can be done by putting two pairs together and asking each pair to tell the story in turn.

- Students work with their partners and write the story. Alternatively, students can write the story for homework.

- Students read each other's stories and decide which one they think is the best.

4D Adjective crossword p145

Language

Adjectives to describe character and behaviour

Activity type, when to use and time

Paired crossword. Use any time after lesson 4D. 15–20 minutes.

Preparation

Photocopy one worksheet for each pair of students. Cut into two separate worksheets.

Procedure

- Divide the class into two groups, A and B. Give each student a copy of the appropriate worksheet. Point out to students that all the words in the crossword describe character and behaviour.

- Students work in pairs with a partner from the same group and check they know the meanings of all the words on their worksheet. With a low-level class, ask students to prepare clues for each of their words. Students can check any words they don't know in **V4.2** SB p122 and **V4.4** SB p123.

- Put students into pairs so that a student from group A is working with a student from group B. Students are not allowed to look at each other's worksheets. Check that students understand how to refer to words in a crossword, for example, *3 across* and *1 down*.

- Students then take turns to give clues for the words on their crossword, for example *1 down: this type of person likes giving presents*. Students are not allowed to use the words themselves, but they can give the first letter of the word if their partners are having difficulty remembering it.

- When students have finished, they check their completed crosswords and their spelling with their partner.

5A House hunting p146

Language

Comparatives and superlatives

Activity type, when to use and time

Role play. Use any time after lesson 5A. 15–25 minutes.

Preparation

Photocopy one worksheet for each student. Cut out the Properties to let advertisement. Cut each set of role cards into separate cards.

Procedure

- Pre-teach *modernised, marina, facilities, security system* and *keep fit*.

- Put the class into groups of four. Give a different role card to each student. Tell students that each group has decided to share a house or flat.

- Give each group a copy of the advertisement. Allow students time to read the advertisement and decide which house or flat they would like to live in.

- Students work with their partners and discuss which house or flat they want to rent. Tell students that they must compare the houses and flat for rent and agree which one is the best for all of them. Encourage them to use comparatives and superlatives, for example *I prefer the third-floor flat because it's more modern than the others*. Students discuss the houses/flat until they come to an agreement.

- Finally, students take turns to tell the class which house/flat they chose and how they came to their decision.

5B Look into the future p147

Language

The future: *will*, *be going to*, Present Continuous

Activity type, when to use and time

'Find someone who' activity. Use any time after lesson 5B. 15–25 minutes.

Preparation

Photocopy one worksheet for each student.

Procedure

- Give a copy of the worksheet to each student. Students work on their own and choose the correct future form for each sentence in the first column. Students can check answers in pairs. Check answers with the class.

- Explain that students are going to try to find someone who answers *yes* to each question. Elicit the questions that students will need to ask, for example *1 Are you going to do some shopping after class?*, etc. Encourage students to use *Do you think you'll ...* for questions 3, 5 and 8. With a low-level class you may want to check and drill all the questions before continuing.

- Students move around the room and ask the questions. If students are not able to leave their seats, they should ask as many students as they can sitting near them. When they find a student who answers *yes* to a question, they write the student's name in the second column on the worksheet. Encourage students to talk to as many different people as possible. Students only need to find one person who answers *yes* to each question.

- When students have written the person's name in the second column, they should then ask follow-up questions based on the prompts in the third column. Point out that not all of these follow-up questions are about the future, so students will need to decide which verb form they should use in each question. With a low-level class you may also want to check these follow-up questions with the class before they begin.

- When students have finished, they work in pairs and tell their partner what they have found out about their classmates. Finish the activity by asking each student to tell the class two interesting things they have found out.

> 1 is going to do 2 is meeting 3 will live 4 is having
> 5 will want 6 is working 7 is going 8 will be
> 9 is going to buy 10 is going

5C Who said what? p148

Language
Verb patterns

Activity type, when to use and time
Sentence completion and mingle. Use any time after lesson 5C. 15–20 minutes.

Preparation
Photocopy one worksheet for every seven students in the class. Cut into 14 sentence cards.

Procedure
- ✎ Write *I'd rather ... than ... .* on the board and elicit possible ways to complete the sentence.

- Give two sentence cards to each student. Ask the students to complete the sentences with true information about themselves. Tell students that they must use an appropriate verb form after the verb in **bold**, not a noun or a pronoun. Have some spare cards in case some students can't think of an appropriate way to complete their card. Students are not allowed to look at each other's cards.

- Collect all of the sentence cards, place them into a bag and mix them up. With larger classes, divide the class into groups and have a bag for each group.

- ✎ Elicit the question students would need to ask for the sentence on the board: *Would you rather … than ... ?*

- Ask each student to pick out one sentence from the bag. Explain that they are going to try to find the person in the class who wrote the sentence. If they pick their own sentence, they should put it back in the bag and pick a different sentence. Students prepare a question to find out who wrote the sentence they picked out.

- Students then move around the room asking their question. Remind students that they may find someone who answers *yes* to their questions, but did not write the sentence. Students can check they have the correct person by asking *Did you write this sentence?*

- When students have found the correct person, they pick another sentence from the bag. The activity continues until all the sentences have gone. The student who finds out who wrote the most sentences wins.

- When students have finished, they work in pairs and tell their partners what they have learned about their classmates.

6A Men and women p149

Language
make and *do*

Activity type, when to use and time
Discussion activity. Use any time after lesson 6A. 15–25 minutes.

Preparation
Photocopy one worksheet for each student.

Procedure
- Pre-teach *a member of the opposite sex, avoid doing something* and *admit doing something*. Also point out that *avoid* and *admit* are followed by the verb+*ing* form.

- Give a copy of the worksheet to each student. Students work on their own and fill in the gaps with the correct form of *make* or *do*. Check answers with the class.

- Students work on their own again and choose *men* or *women* in each sentence.

- Put students into groups of four. If possible, include men and women in each group. Students take turns to discuss their sentences, giving reasons for their opinions. Encourage students to come to an agreement on each sentence if possible.

- When they have finished, ask students to tell the class which sentences they all agreed with, giving reasons for their ideas.

> 1 do 2 making 3 do 4 doing 5 making 6 make
> 7 doing 8 made 9 doing 10 making 11 making 12 do

6C Synonyms bingo p150

Language
Synonyms

Activity type, when to use and time
Bingo game. Use any time after lesson 6C. 15–20 minutes.

Preparation
Photocopy one worksheet for every four students in the class. Cut into four separate bingo cards.

Procedure

- Give each student a bingo card. Allow students a few minutes to check they know the synonyms for all the words/phrases on their card. Students can check any words/phrases they don't know in **V6.3** SB p128. Students are not allowed to write the synonyms on their cards.

- Explain that you are going to say some words/phrases. When students hear a word or phrase which has the same meaning as a word or phrase on their card, they cross it out. The first student to cross out all the words on his/her card shouts *Bingo!*

- Read out the words/phrases in **bold** in the tables below in random order. When you say a word, put a tick next to it so you don't say it twice. Continue saying words until a student shouts *Bingo!* and wins the game. If necessary, you can check his/her card against the tables.

- If you want to play the game again, distribute new cards and read out the synonyms in random order. Alternatively, students work in pairs and read out their words to each other. Their partner says the synonym.

choose	pick	**concerned**	worried
satisfied	content	**frightened**	scared
lucky	fortunate	**make a decision**	make up your mind
behave	act	**try to do**	have a go at doing
notice	spot		
by chance	accidentally	**talk**	chat
attitude	approach	**nice**	pleasant
sure	certain	**enormous**	huge
deal with	cope with	**pleased**	glad
show	reveal	**wonderful**	brilliant
		terrible	awful

6D Round the board p151–p152

Language

Review of lessons 4A–6D

Activity type, when to use and time

Board game. Use any time after lesson 6D. 20–30 minutes.

Preparation

Photocopy one board, one set of Vocabulary cards and one set of Grammar cards for each group of four students. Cut the Vocabulary cards and Grammar cards into sets. Shuffle each set. Each group also needs a dice and counters.

Procedure

- Put students into groups of four. Give each group a copy of the board, a set of Vocabulary cards and a set of Grammar cards, dice and counters (or students can make their own counters). Students should place the cards face-down in two separate piles in the appropriate places in the middle of the board.

- Check students understand that they can go round the board as many times as they like, and that they collect 500 points every time they pass the *Start* square. Students will need a pen and paper to keep a record of their points during the game. Tell students that they all start the game with 500 points.

- Students take turns to throw the dice and move around the board. When a student lands on a square that says Vocabulary card or Grammar card, he/she turns over the top card of the appropriate pile and reads out the question to the group. He/She must then answer the question. If he/she answers the question correctly, he/she **wins** the number of points on the square. If he/she doesn't answer the question correctly, he/she **loses** the number of points on the square. He/She then puts the card at the bottom of the appropriate pile.

- If students think that another student's answer is wrong, they can check in the Language Summaries in the Student's Book or ask you to adjudicate.

- Students always stay on the square they landed on, whether they win or lose points. Students don't have to leave the game if they have a negative number of points. They should keep playing to try to win more points.

- The game can continue as long as you wish. You can set a time limit before students start playing. Alternatively, students can continue playing until they've answered all the Grammar and Vocabulary cards. The student with the most points when the game finishes wins.

Vocabulary cards

1 appeared; live 2 on; in 3 a cellar is under a house, a loft is in the roof of a house; you put your car in a garage, you work in a study 4 concerned; certain; act 5 going up; go 6 do; make; do; make 7 See **V4.2** and **V4.4** SB p122–p123. 8 up; out 9 a terraced house shares a wall with houses on both sides of it, a detached house doesn't; a bungalow has one storey, a cottage is a small house, usually in the country 10 herself; ourselves 11 to be; staying 12 in; at 13 pick; fortunate; by chance 14 out; through 15 Possible answers: a shirt; a tyre; a box; a belt 16 do; make; make; do

Grammar cards

1 As soon as **I get** home, I'll call you. I won't do anything until **I talk** to him. 2 was driving; had 3 to; to/from 4 It's (much) **more** exciting than I thought. He's the **most** amazing person I've met. 5 got; realised; had stolen 6 In the first sentence, the person arranged to meet Jim before speaking. In the second sentence, the person decided to meet Jim at the time of speaking. 7 Is your phone the same **as** Gary's? No, his isn't as **old** as mine. 8 I **didn't use to** watch TV a lot. I **hadn't** met him before. 9 I **met** John while I **was living** in Rome. What **were you** doing when I called? 10 We'll come **unless we're busy**. We won't go **unless you come with us**. 11 called; was watching 12 The first sentence is always true. The second sentence talks about one specific time in the future. 13 in case; If 14 Where **did you use** to live when you were young? I **went** to the 2004 World Cup final. 15 bigger; further/farther; worse; happier 16 cleaning; get

7A Guess my name p153

Language
Ability: *be able to, manage, have no idea how, be good at*, etc.

Activity type, when to use and time
Writing activity. Use any time after lesson 7A. 15–25 minutes.

Preparation
Photocopy one worksheet for each student. Write a number in the box at the bottom of the worksheet for each student in your class. For example if you have 16 students, write 1–16 on the worksheets. Shuffle the worksheets.

Procedure
- Give a copy of the worksheet to each student. The worksheets should **not** be given out in number order. Tell students that they are not allowed to write their names on the worksheet.
- Students work on their own and complete the worksheet about themselves and people they know. Tell students that they can fill in the gaps with general abilities, for example finding things, making people laugh, organising things, etc., as well as sports, musical abilities, skills, school subjects, etc. Remind students to use the correct verb form in each gap.
- Collect in the completed worksheets and shuffle them. Put the worksheets up around the room. Put students into pairs. Each pair moves around the room and guesses who wrote each worksheet. They should make a note of the number of each worksheet and the name of the student they think wrote it. Students continue until they have read all the worksheets.
- Check answers with the class and find out which pair guessed the most worksheets correctly. You can also ask students to say what they thought was the most surprising or interesting thing they read.
- Alternatively, shuffle the worksheets and redistribute them in random order. Students read the new worksheet and decide who wrote it. Students check answers with the class by reading out the worksheet and saying who they think wrote it.

7B The conditional game p154

Language
Second conditional; first conditional; future time clauses

Activity type, when to use and time
Board game. Use any time after lesson 7B. 20–30 minutes.

Preparation
Photocopy one board for each group of three or four students. You also need a dice for each group and a counter for each student.

Procedure
- Pre-teach *a cartoon character, a member of the opposite sex* and *a ghost*.
- Put the class into groups of three or four. Give each group a copy of the board, a dice and counters (or students can make their own counters). Point out that some squares require first conditionals or sentences with future time clauses, and some squares require second conditionals.
- Students take turns to throw the dice and move around the board. When a student lands on a sentence square, he/she must complete the sentence correctly in order to stay on the square.
- If a student can't complete the sentence correctly, he/she must move back to his/her previous square. If students think another student's sentence is wrong, they can ask you to adjudicate.
- If a student lands on *Move forward/back 2/3 squares* or *Throw again*, he/she does as the square says and then completes the sentence of the square he/she lands on.
- If a student lands on a square which another student has already landed on, he/she must complete the sentence with a different ending.
- The game ends when one student reaches the *Finish* square. If one group finishes early, they can finish the sentences they didn't land on during the game.

7C Article auction p155

Language
Use of articles: *a, an, the*, no article

Activity type, when to use and time
Auction game. Use any time after lesson 7C. 20–30 minutes.

Preparation
Photocopy one worksheet for each pair of students.

Procedure
- Pre-teach *auction* /ˈɔːkʃən/ and check students understand how an auction works.
- Put students into pairs. Give a copy of the worksheet to each pair. Focus students on the sentences on the worksheet. Tell students that some sentences are correct and some are incorrect.
- Students work in their pairs and decide if the use of articles in each sentence is correct. If they think a sentence is incorrect, they must decide what the correct sentence is. Point out that the incorrect sentences can have one or two mistakes. Tell students not to share their ideas with other pairs, as they will be competing against each other later. You can set a time limit of five or ten minutes.
- Explain that students can now bid for these sentences at an auction. Tell each pair that they have £1,000 to spend and that they can only bid in multiples of £50 (£50, £100, etc.). Auction the sentences to the class by inviting bids for each sentence in turn. When you have no further bids, you can say *Going, going, gone!*

- When a pair buys a sentence, they must say whether they think the sentence is correct, or tell you the correct version of the sentence, before they are allowed to own it. If a pair gets the sentence wrong, they lose the money they have bid, but do **not** get the sentence. You can then auction the same sentence again.

- When a pair buys a sentence, they deduct the price from the £1,000 in the *Money left* box on their worksheet. If they buy a sentence, but don't get the sentence correct, they must still deduct the money they spent. Students can spend only £1,000 during the whole auction.

- The pair that collects the most sentences wins.

> 1 ✓ 2 She works for a department store in **the** centre of Madrid. 3 ✓ 4 Many people from the USA go to ~~the~~ Hawaii on holiday. 5 ✓ 6 The Smiths' flat is much bigger than **the** last place I lived in. 7 This is the third time I've asked you to tidy up **the** living room! 8 ✓ 9 ✓ 10 My sister has been **a** doctor at the City Hospital for about ten years. 11 Did your parents go to ~~the~~ university after they left ~~the~~ school? 12 ✓ 13 If you ever get a computer virus, you shouldn't send ~~the~~ emails. 14 ✓ 15 ~~The~~ Australian people are very friendly when they meet ~~the~~ foreigners. 16 Vatican City is **the** smallest country in ~~the~~ Europe. 17 If your monitor isn't working, turn off **the** computer and wait **a** minute. 18 ✓

8A Passive knowledge p156

Language
The passive

Activity type, when to use and time
Pairwork quiz. Use any time after lesson 8A. 15–20 minutes.

Preparation
Photocopy one worksheet for each pair of students. Cut into two separate worksheets.

Procedure
- Put students into groups of four. Divide each group into two pairs, pair A and pair B. Give a copy of Quiz A to each student in pair A and a copy of Quiz B to each student in pair B. Students are not allowed to show their quizzes to the other pair in their group.

- Students work in their pairs and put the verb in brackets in each question in the correct passive form. Check answers with the class. Only check the passive verb forms, so that the other pair in each group doesn't hear the questions they are about to be asked. Each pair gets one point for each correct passive verb form and a bonus point if all six answers are correct.

- Students work in their groups of four. Each pair takes it in turns to ask the other pair a question from their quiz. Students read out their questions and the three possible answers. If the other pair gets an answer correct, they get two points. Before they begin, tell students that the words/phrases in **bold** are the correct answers.

- When both pairs have asked all their questions, students in each pair add up their points from both parts of the activity. The pair with the most points wins.

- Finally, you can teach students that *a calf* is a baby cow, *a cub* is a baby lion, bear, etc. and *a foal* is a baby horse.

> **Quiz A**
> 1 was invented 2 is called 3 was married 4 are spoken 5 were written 6 will be held/is going to be held
>
> **Quiz B**
> 1 was married 2 will be held/are going to be held 3 was invented 4 has been stolen 5 is/was played 6 is called

8B The airport p157–p158

Language
Quantifiers; discussion language

Activity type, when to use and time
Debate. Use any time after lesson 8B. 30–45 minutes.

Preparation
Photocopy one set of six role cards for each group of six students. Cut into separate cards.

Procedure
- Pre-teach *unemployment*, *wildlife*, *a residents' association* (an organisation that represents local people) and *in favour of something*.

- Divide the class into six groups. Give each student in group A a copy of the Student A role card, each student in group B a copy of the Student B role card, etc. Try to choose confident students to be the chairpeople (group F).

- **Extra students:** If you have one or two extra students, put them in group E. If you have three extra students, put them in groups A, B and E. If you have four extra students, put them in groups A, B, C and D. If you have five extra students, put them in groups A, B, C, D and E. Note that students A and B are against the airport, students C and D are for the airport, while student E is undecided.

- Give students time to read the introduction on their cards and check they have understood the situation.

- Students work in their groups and follow the instructions on their role cards. Encourage students to use quantifiers (*not much, too much, not enough, plenty of, hardly any,* etc.) if possible. Chairpeople work together and plan the introduction and questions.

- While students are working, write the discussion language from RW6.1 SB p129 on the board.

- Rearrange the class so that students are sitting in groups of six, with one student A, one student B, etc. in each group. If you have extra students, distribute them equally amongst the groups. Try to ensure that each group contains an equal number of A/B students and C/D students. Focus students on the language on the board and remind them to use this during the meeting.

- Ask the chairpeople to start their meetings. Allow the meetings to proceed uninterrupted if possible, but try to ensure everyone has an opportunity to speak. Allow about 15 minutes for this stage of the activity. While students are talking, you can note down mistakes and examples of good language to discuss at the end of the activity.
- At the end of the meetings, each chairperson conducts a vote on whether the airport should be built or not. Ask each chairperson to share his/her group's conclusions with the class.

8C Beginnings and endings p159

Language
Prefixes and suffixes

Activity type, when to use and time
Pelmanism. Use any time after lesson 8C. 10–20 minutes.

Preparation
Photocopy one worksheet for each group of three students. Cut into sets. Shuffle each set.

Procedure
- Put the class into groups of three students. Give each group a set of cards. Ask them to put the cards face-down in front of them, with the smaller cards on one side and the bigger cards on the other.
- Students take it in turns to turn over one small card and one big card. If a student thinks that the two cards make a word, he/she makes a sentence which includes this word. If the two cards match and the sentence is correct, the student keeps the pair of cards and has another turn. If the two cards don't match, the student puts both cards back on the table face-down in exactly the same place.
- If a student thinks that one of his/her partner's words or sentences is not correct, he/she can challenge him/her. If it is incorrect, the student must put back the cards and the turn passes to the next student. If students can't agree, they can check in V8.3 and V8.4 SB p132 or ask you to adjudicate.
- The activity continues until all the cards are matched up. The student who collects the most cards is the winner.
- If a group finishes early, students can take turns testing each other by saying the words on the big cards. The other students say what prefixes and suffixes can be used with each word.

9A Fighting fit p160

Language
Relative clauses with *who*, *that*, *which*, *whose*, *where* and *when*

Activity type, when to use and time
Information gap. Use any time after lesson 9A. 15–25 minutes.

Preparation
Photocopy one worksheet for each pair of students. Cut into two separate worksheets.

Procedure
- Check students understand *a fat-free diet*, *a fasting programme* (a way of controlling your weight by fasting at regular intervals), *jogging* and *a jogger*. Also check students understand the difference between the verb *weigh* /weɪ/ and the noun *weight* /weɪt/.
- Put students into pairs, A and B. Give students a copy of the appropriate worksheet.
- Students work on their own and fill in the gaps with *who*, *that*, *which*, *whose*, *where* or *when*. Check answers with the class. Only check the words they need to fill in the gaps, so that the other students don't hear the sentences they are about to discuss.
- Students work with their partner. Students share their information and fill in the table at the bottom of their worksheets. Students are not allowed to look at their partner's worksheets. ✎ While students are working, copy the table onto the board ready for checking.
- Check answers with the class by eliciting the answers from the students and writing them on the table on the board.

STUDENT A **1** when **2** who/that **3** who/that; where **4** who/that **5** whose **6** that/which **7** who/that

STUDENT B **a)** where **b)** that/which **c)** who/that **d)** whose **e)** who/that **f)** who/that **g)** when

	David	Mick	Richard	Susie	Anna
Weight now	75 kg	90 kg	80 kg	70 kg	85 kg
Exercise	walking	cycling	swimming	yoga	jogging
Type of diet	fasting programme	juice diet	fat-free diet	organic diet	meat-free diet

9B Perfect circles p161

Language
Present Perfect Simple active and passive for recent events

Activity type, when to use and time
Information gap. Use any time after lesson 9B. 15–25 minutes.

Preparation
Photocopy one worksheet for each student.

Procedure
- Give each student a copy of the worksheet. Tell students to read the prompts in the box and then write ten short answers in the circles at the bottom of the worksheet. Students should write single words or short phrases, for example *Marta*, *Madrid*, *bought a new bike*, etc., not complete sentences. They can write their answers in any order they want, but not in the same order as the prompts.
- When students have finished, ask them to fold their worksheets in half. Put students into pairs. Students swap worksheets with their partner.

- Students take turns to ask questions to discover why their partner has written the words/phrases in the circles, for example *Why have you written Marta?* The other student must answer with the correct form of Present Perfect Simple active or passive, for example *Because she's just started a new job.* Encourage students to ask follow-up questions for each point, for example *How do you know Marta? What's her new job? When did she start working there?*, etc.

- Finally, ask each pair to tell the class two or three things they discussed.

9D Noughts and crosses p162–p163

Language

Review of lessons 7A–9D

Activity type, when to use and time

Noughts and crosses board game. Use any time after lesson 9D. 20–30 minutes.

Preparation

Photocopy one Board 1/Team A question sheet for half the number of students in your class and one Board 2/Team B question sheet for the other half. Cut each worksheet into separate boards and question sheets.

Procedure

- Ask students if they know the game noughts /nɔːts/ and crosses. ✏ If not, draw a noughts and crosses grid on the board. Explain that the aim of the game is to win squares by answering questions. The first team to get a line of three across the board, horizontally, vertically or diagonally wins.

- Put students into groups of four or six. Divide each group into two teams: team A and team B. Give each group a copy of the Board 1 worksheet.

- Give each student in each team A a copy of the Team A question sheet and each student in each team B a copy of the Team B question sheet. Students are not allowed to look at the other team's question sheet. Students toss a coin to decide who starts.

- The teams take it in turns to choose a square on Board 1. For example team A chooses vocabulary. Team B then reads the first question in the vocabulary section of their question sheet. If team A answers correctly, they win the square and draw a cross or a circle on it. If the answer is incorrect, the square remains available (team B doesn't get the square). Point out that the answers to the questions are in brackets on the question sheets.

- The first team to get a line of three squares on Board 1 wins the first game. Students can then play on Board 2. If students run out of questions in a particular category, they can ask any question from the other categories instead.

- Groups that finish early can ask each other the unanswered questions on their worksheet.

10A Excuses, excuses! p164

Language

was going to, *was supposed to*; Present Perfect Simple

Activity type, when to use and time

Information gap. Use any time after lesson 10A. 15–25 minutes.

Preparation

Photocopy one worksheet for each pair of students. Cut into separate worksheets.

Procedure

- Pre-teach *invitations*, *catering*, *disposable camera* and *decorations*.

- Put students into pairs. Give each student a copy of the appropriate worksheet.

- Give students a minute or two to read the first paragraph on the worksheets. Check students understand that they are organising a party with their partner and that they have already agreed who is going to do what.

- Focus students on the first list on their worksheets and ask who was supposed to do these things (their partner was). Students work on their own and make questions with the Present Perfect Simple + *yet* about the phrases in **bold**, as in the example. Before they begin, point out to students that they do **not** use the phrases in brackets (*last week*, *two weeks ago*, etc.) in their questions.

- Focus students on the second list on their worksheets and ask who was supposed to do these things (they were). Students work on their own and tick two more things they've done, then think of good excuses why they haven't done the other things. Encourage students to be imaginative when thinking of their excuses, and tell them they can't just use *I forgot.* as an excuse!

- Students work with their partner and take turns to ask each other their questions. For example student A asks: *Have you given out the invitations yet?*. If student B hasn't done this, he/she should give an excuse, using *was going to* and the time phrase in brackets, for example: *I was going to give the invitations out last class, but I left them on the bus.* Tell students to put a tick or a cross next to the things their partner has or hasn't done and to make brief notes on their partner's excuses.

- Put students into new pairs. Students take turns to tell their new partner what their old partner hasn't done, using *was supposed to*: *Marco was supposed to give out the invitations last class, but he left them on the bus.* They can also tell their new partner what they haven't done, and why: *I was supposed to pay for the club a week ago, but someone stole my credit card.*

- Finally, ask students to share the best excuses they heard with the class.

10B Where's Robin? p165

Language
Modal verbs (2): making deductions

Activity type, when to use and time
Information gap. Use any time after lesson 10B. 15–25 minutes.

Preparation
Photocopy one worksheet for every four students. Cut into four separate information cards.

Procedure
- Remind students of the wedding anniversary party in lesson 10B of the Student's Book. Ask students whose party it is (Tom and Peggy's) and how long they have been married (25 years). Also ask who suggested the party (Tom and Peggy's children, Leo and Karen).
- Tell the class that it is now 8 p.m. on the evening of the party, but Karen's boyfriend, Robin, still hasn't arrived. The students are going to help Karen work out where he is.
- Divide the students into groups of four. Give each student a different information card. If you have extra students, have some groups of five and ask two students to share one information card.
- Focus students on sentences 1–4 on their cards. Students work on their own and make deductions about each situation, using the verbs in brackets. If necessary, remind students to use *must/could/may/might/can't + be* + verb+*ing* for deductions about something happening now.
- Give students a minute or two to read the extra information on their cards. Students then work in their groups and take turns to tell each other their deductions. When each student makes a deduction, another student in the group must respond using the extra information at the bottom of his/her card. For example student A might say *He might be writing a report at work*. Student C should respond *He can't be writing a report. He finished it at five o'clock*. If necessary, demonstrate this with the class before students begin.
- Students continue making deductions until they work out what Robin is doing now. Check the answer with the class.

Robin is in the town square watching his favourite football team on a big TV.

10C Go up the ladder p166

Language
Phrasal verbs

Activity type, when to use and time
Board game. Use any time after lesson 10C. 15–25 minutes.

Preparation
Photocopy one worksheet for each group of three or four students. You also need a dice for each group and a counter for each student.

Procedure
- Put the students into groups of three or four. Give each student a copy of the snakes and ladders board, a dice and counters (or students can make their own counters).
- Students take turns to throw the dice and move around the board. When they land on a square, they must say the complete sentence, including the correct form of the phrasal verb. Point out that there is one space for each letter of the phrasal verbs, that the first letter is already given and that an oblique (/) indicates a new word. If a student gets the sentence wrong or can't remember the correct phrasal verb, he/she must move back to his/her previous square. Note that all the phrasal verbs practised in the activity are from V10.3 , V3.1 and V5.2 in the Language Summaries in the Student's Book.
- If students land at the bottom of a ladder, they must complete the sentence correctly before they are allowed to go up it. They don't have to complete the sentence at the top of the ladder. If they land on the head of a snake, they must always go down the snake to its tail. They don't have to complete the sentence at the bottom of a snake.
- If a student thinks another student's answer is wrong, he/she should ask you to adjudicate.
- If a student lands on a square that has already been answered, he/she must say the completed sentence again to check that he/she has been listening!
- The first student to reach the *Finish* square is the winner. If groups finish early, they can go through the squares in order and take turns to say the missing phrasal verbs.

1 see … off 2 take out 3 go up 4 sort out 5 deal with 6 get over 7 put away 8 split up 9 come up with 10 look … up 11 bring … back 13 coming back 14 point out 15 Throw … away 16 put off 17 gave … away 18 pick … up 19 clear out 20 go through 22 came across 23 check out of 24 get back 26 put up with 27 tidy … up 28 fall out 29 get around 30 looking forward to 31 get out of 33 set off

11A Work dominoes p167

Language
Collocations connected to work

Activity type, when to use and time
Dominoes. Use any time after lesson 11A. 15–25 minutes.

Preparation
Photocopy one set of dominoes for each pair of students. Cut into sets and shuffle each set.

Procedure
- Put students into pairs. Give one set of dominoes to each pair. Students share out the dominoes equally. Students are not allowed to look at each other's dominoes.
- One student puts a domino on the table. His/Her partner puts another domino at either end of the first domino so that it makes a sentence.

- Encourage students to pay particular attention to the words/phrases in **bold** on the dominoes, which form work collocations when they are matched up correctly. Note that these collocations are taken from **V11.1** SB p138 and **V2.1** SB p116.

- Students continue taking turns to put dominoes at either end of the domino chain. If a student thinks the dominoes don't match, he/she can challenge his/her partner. If the match is incorrect, the student must take back the domino and the turn passes to his/her partner. If students can't agree, they should ask you to adjudicate.

- When a student can't put down a domino, the turn automatically passes to his/her partner. The game continues until one student has put down all his/her dominoes or until neither student can make a correct match. The student who finishes first, or who has the fewer dominoes remaining, is the winner.

- Early finishers can share the dominoes equally and take turns to test each other on the collocations in **bold**.

11B Teach your own language p168

Language

Reported speech: sentences and questions

Activity type, when to use and time

Role play. Use any time after lesson 11B. 30–40 minutes.

Preparation

Photocopy one worksheet for each pair of students. Cut into separate role cards.

Procedure

- Divide the class into two groups, A and B. Give each student a copy of the appropriate role card. If you have an extra student, make him/her an interviewer.

- Focus students on the advertisement and give them a minute or two to read it. Tell the class that students in group A are going to interview students in group B for jobs at this school.

- Put the interviewers into pairs. Students work together and follow the instructions on their worksheets. Encourage teachers to use their imagination.

- Reorganise the class so that one interviewer is sitting with one teacher. If you have an extra student, put one teacher with two interviewers. The interviewers then interview the teachers. Ask students to make brief notes at this stage, as they will need them for the next stage of the activity.

- Interviewers then work in their original pairs and compare notes on their interviews using reported speech, for example *I asked Paolo what language he taught and he told me he was a Spanish teacher.* Each pair of interviewers must choose which teacher they want to employ.

- Also put the teachers in pairs and ask them to discuss the interview, for example *She asked me what I did before I started teaching and I told her that I was a tour guide.*

- Finally, ask interviewers to tell the class who they want to employ, giving reasons for their decision.

11C Spy school p169

Language

Verb patterns: reporting verbs

Activity type, when to use and time

Mingle. Use any time after lesson 11C. 15–25 minutes.

Preparation

Photocopy one worksheet for each pair of students. Cut out the Spy memory test worksheet. Cut out one set of Sentence cards for every ten students in the class. Shuffle the cards. Discard the extra Sentence cards.

Procedure

- Pre-teach *follow someone* and *an embassy*. Also check students know what the CIA is, and teach students that MI6 is a similar organisation run by the British government.

- Tell students they have enrolled on a course at 'Spy school'. Their first task is to remember all the information that the other 'spies' in the class are going to tell them.

- Give each student a sentence card. If you have fewer than ten students, give stronger students two cards. If you have more than ten students, you can give out duplicate cards without affecting the outcome of the activity. Ask students to memorise their sentence. Students are not allowed to look at each other's cards.

- Students move around the room saying their sentences to each other. Each student must talk to everyone else in the room. Remind students that they need to remember the other students' sentences.

- Put students into pairs. Give a copy of the Spy memory test worksheet to each pair. Students work together and complete the worksheet. You can elicit sentence 1 from the class if necessary. Point out that there are prompts in the box on the worksheet in case students have forgotten some of the sentences. You can also set a time limit of three or five minutes.

- ✏ Elicit the sentences from the class and write them on the board. The students who got the most sentences correct are the best spies in the class.

1 (Name) invited me to (come and) work for the CIA.
2 (Name) promised to get me a job with the British Secret Service.
3 (Name) admitted reading all my private emails.
   or (Name) admitted he/she (had) read all my private emails.
4 (Name) offered to introduce me to the head of MI6.
5 (Name) warned me not to go home tonight (because I was being followed by a man in a black coat).
6 (Name) suggested writing a book about spying (together).
7 (Name) reminded me to change the password on my computer every day.
8 (Name) refused to tell me what his/her real name was.
9 (Name) threatened to kill me if I told anyone where I got my new passport.
10 (Name) agreed to meet me outside the American Embassy at midnight.

12A Wish list p170–p171

Language

Wishes; second conditional

Activity type, when to use and time

Mingle. Use any time after lesson 12A. 25–35 minutes.

Preparation

Photocopy one set of cards for every eight students. Cut into eight separate cards. You can make cuts between the pictures on each card to make tearing them off easier. Don't cut off the pictures.

Procedure

- Give one card to each student. If you have more than eight students, you can give duplicate cards without affecting the outcome of the activity. Tell students that sentences 1–3 on their cards are things they wish for. Point out that the pictures on the cards are wishes other students have.

- Students work on their own and complete the *I wish ...* sentences on their cards. While they are working, monitor and check their sentences for accuracy.

- Give students a few more minutes to think of good reasons for their wishes. Encourage students to use second conditionals if possible, for example *If I had a boat, I'd sail around the world.* Students can also express their reasons in other ways, for example *I've always wanted to learn how to sail.*

- Students move around the room telling each other their wishes and their reasons. If a student has a picture on his/her card that corresponds to the other student's wish, he/she grants the other student's wish, tears off the appropriate picture from his/her card and gives it to the other student. Teach the phrase *Your wish is granted!* before students begin.

- Students must try to find all three pictures that correspond to their wishes. Allow the activity to continue until most students have had their wishes granted.

- Finally, ask students to tell the class any wishes that haven't been granted and see if other students can help.

> **A 1** I wish I had a house with a swimming pool. **2** I wish I could speak five languages. **3** I wish I didn't have to start work at 6 a.m. **B 1** I wish I had a cottage in the country. **2** I wish I could get to sleep at night. **3** I wish I didn't have to work six days a week. **C 1** I wish I had a boat. **2** I wish I was/were a professional tennis player. **3** I wish I didn't have to drive 100 km to work every day. **D 1** I wish I could fly a plane. **2** I wish I had a million pounds. **3** I wish I was/were going to the Caribbean next week. **E 1** I wish I had a Harley Davidson motorbike. **2** I wish I was/were taller. **3** I wish I lived in New York. **F 1** I wish I could play the piano. **2** I wish I didn't have to cook for my family every day. **3** I wish I was/were a famous actor/actress. **G 1** I wish I was/were staying in a five-star hotel this month. **2** I wish I had a Ferrari. **3** I wish I was/were a famous pop star. **H 1** I wish I could go to the moon. **2** I wish I had a helicopter. **3** I wish I was/were swimming with dolphins now.

12B *get* stories p172

Language

Phrases with *get*

Activity type, when to use and time

Story-telling activity. Use any time after lesson 12B. 20–30 minutes.

Preparation

Photocopy one worksheet for each pair of students. Cut out the Story cards. Cut all the *get* cards into separate cards and put them all in a bag.

Procedure

- Check students remember *get arrested, get sacked, get hold of someone* and *get promoted.*

- Put the students into pairs. Give each pair a Story card. Tell students that they must invent a story about Mark or Laura's day.

- Ask each pair to take six *get* cards from the bag. If students take duplicate cards, they can swap them for another card. Tell the class that they must include these phrases with *get* in their story. To make the activity more challenging, ask students to take eight cards instead of six.

- Students work in their pairs and invent a story about Mark or Laura's day, including the phrases with *get* in their story where appropriate. During the activity, you can allow each pair to swap two *get* cards they don't want by putting them back in the bag and taking alternative cards. Encourage students to make notes on their stories, but students should not write the whole story.

- Reorganise the class so that a pair who has invented a story about Mark is working with a pair who has invented a story about Laura. Pairs take turns to tell their stories and then decide which story they like better.

- For futher practice, you can ask students to tell their story again to a different pair of students.

- Ask a few pairs to tell the class their stories. Finally, you can ask each pair to write the story in class or for homework. These stories can be put up around the room for other students to read.

Find someone who ...	Name	Follow-up questions
1 ... goes clubbing every week. Question: _Do you go clubbing every week?_		Where / go?
2 ... chats to people online. Question: _____		Who / chat to?
3 ... is reading a good book at the moment. Question: _____		What / read?
4 ... went to an exhibition last month. Question: _____		What / see?
5 ... has had people round for dinner this month. Question: _____		What / cook?
6 ... did some gardening at the weekend. Question: _____		How long / work for?
7 ... had a lie-in last weekend. Question: _____		What time / get up?
8 ... is trying to get fit at the moment. Question: _____		What / do?
9 ... met up with friends last week. Question: _____		What / do?
10 ... has tried a dangerous sport. Question: _____		Which / try?

Student A

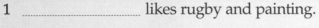

Star Magazine's Celebrity Gossip

Can you match these celebrities to their likes and dislikes?
There are two sentences for each celebrity.

Orlando Bloom

Nicole Kidman

Prince William

Michael Schumacher

1 .... likes rugby and painting.

2 .... can't bear computers.

3 .... thinks football and skiing are great.

4 .... can't stand being the centre of attention.

5 .... is keen on writing short stories.

6 .... loves dogs and knitting.

7 .... is very interested in photography and antiques.

8 Being famous gets on ....'s nerves.

9 .... isn't keen on butterflies.

10 .... doesn't like people taking her photograph.

Julia Roberts

Answers for Student B:

1 Leonardo DiCaprio thinks the environment is really important.

2 Queen Elizabeth II doesn't like spicy food at all.

3 David Beckham isn't keen on dancing.

4 Tom Cruise loves scuba diving and flying.

5 David Beckham thinks Spain, children and cars are great.

6 Queen Elizabeth II enjoys horseracing.

7 Journalists drive Russell Crowe crazy.

8 Russell Crowe really likes bingo.

9 Leonardo DiCaprio can't bear talking about his life.

10 Tom Cruise thinks people who are late for work are really annoying.

Star Magazine's Celebrity Gossip

Can you match these celebrities to their likes and dislikes? There are two sentences for each celebrity.

Queen Elizabeth II

Russell Crowe

Tom Cruise

Leonardo DiCaprio

David Beckham

1 .... thinks the environment is really important.

2 .... doesn't like spicy food at all.

3 .... isn't keen on dancing.

4 .... loves scuba diving and flying.

5 .... thinks Spain, children and cars are great.

6 .... enjoys horseracing.

7 Journalists drive .... crazy.

8 .... really likes bingo.

9 .... can't bear talking about his life.

10 .... thinks people who are late for work are really annoying.

1D Make it snappy! question tags

Sentence cards

He's very tall, (Answer: isn't he?)	**You haven't been there,** (Answer: have you?)	**You aren't a vegetarian,** (Answer: are you?)
She called you yesterday, (Answer: didn't she?)	**You like coffee,** (Answer: don't you?)	**We don't have a test,** (Answer: do we?)
He doesn't smoke, (Answer: does he?)	**You've studied French,** (Answer: haven't you?)	**We're going out tonight,** (Answer: aren't we?)
She didn't go to work, (Answer: did she?)	**He isn't very happy,** (Answer: is he?)	**She lives in Rome,** (Answer: doesn't she?)
They've already seen it, (Answer: haven't they?)	**I'm late,** (Answer: aren't I?)	**I've missed the train,** (Answer: haven't I?)

Question tag cards

isn't he?	**have you?**	**are you?**
didn't she?	**don't you?**	**do we?**
does he?	**haven't you?**	**aren't we?**
did she?	**is he?**	**doesn't she?**
haven't they?	**aren't I?**	**haven't I?**

CLASS ACTIVITIES:
PHOTOCOPIABLE

Instructions p119

© Cambridge University Press 2006   face2face Intermediate Photocopiable

135

1 You *must/ are allowed to/ can't* drive a car when you are 16 in the UK.

2 Children in Japanese primary schools *have to/ don't have to/ mustn't* clean their classrooms.

3 In Singapore you *can/ aren't allowed to/ should* eat chewing gum.

4 British men over the age of 18 *have to/ don't have to/ mustn't* do military service.

5 In Germany you *are able to/ aren't allowed to/ are supposed to* mow the lawn on a Sunday.

6 You *mustn't/ don't have to/ should* eat with your left hand in India.

7 One hundred years ago, women in the UK *were allowed to/ couldn't/ had to* vote.

8 You *can't/ are allowed to/ must* get married at 16 in the UK with your parents' permission.

9 You *can/ have to/ can't* vote in Japan if you're 19.

10 Turkish men over the age of 20 *have to/ should/ don't have to* do military service.

11 You *have to/ ought to/ shouldn't* tip waiters and waitresses in Iceland.

12 You *shouldn't/ are supposed to/ are able to* drive with your lights on during the day in Sweden.

13 In the USA you *can/ ought to/ aren't allowed to* burn your own money.

14 Brazilians over the age of 18 *have to/ don't have to/ ought to* vote.

15 In the 19th century, female teachers in the USA *had to/ were allowed to/ weren't allowed to* get married.

Instructions p119

2B Opening night Present Continuous and Present Simple

Role cards

STUDENT A
You're a famous chef from Paris. Today you're opening a new restaurant in London. You hope that everyone likes your food. You're very busy with work and don't have any free time at the moment.

STUDENT B
You're a writer from New York. You write love stories. At the moment you're visiting London to sell your new book. In your free time you love having people round for dinner.

STUDENT C
You're an opera singer from Scotland. You sing in famous opera houses around the world. You're visiting your brother in London for a few days. In your free time, you go to exhibitions – you love modern art.

STUDENT D
You're a journalist from Ireland. You write about food for a newspaper. You're staying with some friends in London at the moment. You take photographs in your free time.

STUDENT E
You're a student from Australia. You're studying to be a chef in London and working in a restaurant at the weekends. In your free time you travel around the UK.

STUDENT F
You're a film director from Mexico. You usually direct successful horror films in your own country, but at the moment you're filming the new James Bond film in London.

STUDENT G
You're a model from Japan. You're in London because you're doing the London Fashion Show this week. In your free time you meet up with friends and go clubbing.

STUDENT H
You're an actor from Los Angeles. You usually work in Hollywood, but at the moment you're living in London because you're making a comedy here. In your free time you go to the gym.

STUDENT I
You're a writer from Wales. You write about health food. At the moment you're in London because you're writing a book about traditional English food. In your free time you play volleyball.

STUDENT J
You're a chef from Italy. You usually work in a top hotel in Milan, but at the moment you're doing a course in London. In your free time you go mountain biking.

STUDENT K
You're a journalist from Canada. You write about restaurants for a Canadian website. You're visiting London to write about the opening of this new restaurant. In your free time you play the piano.

STUDENT L
You're a pop singer from London. You write your own music and play the guitar. You're writing your third album at the moment. In your free time you do judo and yoga.

What do you remember?

a) .... is a chef and *opens/is opening* a new .... today.

b) .... is a writer from .... and *visits/is visiting* London to sell his/her new book.

c) .... is an opera singer and he/she *goes/ is going* to .... in his/her free time.

d) .... is from Ireland and *writes/is writing* about .... for a newspaper.

e) .... is an Australian student and *studies/is studying* to be a ....

f) .... is from Mexico and *usually directs/is usually directing* successful .... films.

g) .... *does/is doing* the London Fashion Show this week and goes .... in his/her free time.

h) .... usually lives in .... but *makes/is making* a comedy in London at the moment.

i) .... is a health food writer and *plays/is playing* .... in his/her free time.

j) .... is an Italian .... and *does/is doing* a course in London at the moment.

k) .... is a journalist from Canada and *plays/is playing* the ....

l) .... is a British .... and *writes/is writing* his/her third album.

Instructions p119

2C The absolutely amazing game! gradable and strong adjectives; adverbs

(30) I've been to your country. It's very *beautiful/ gorgeous*, isn't it?	(31) MOVE BACK TWO SQUARES	(32) She was absolutely *angry/furious* because I forgot her birthday.	(33) Mark's mobile is *very/absolutely* tiny.	FINISH
(29) Talk for 30 seconds about a time when you were really frightened.	(28) My phone bill last month was incredibly *big/ enormous*.	(27) Talk for 30 seconds about an actor or actress that you think is excellent.	(26) The book is really good, but the film is absolutely *bad/terrible*.	(25) That TV show was *very/ absolutely* fabulous.
(20) Talk for 30 seconds about something you think is really delicious.	(21) When we got home, our clothes were *absolutely/very* filthy.	(22) Talk for 30 seconds about an incredibly beautiful place in your country.	(23) To be honest, I wasn't very *surprised/amazed* to hear the news.	(24) MOVE FORWARD THREE SQUARES
(19) MOVE FORWARD THREE SQUARES	(18) Talk for 30 seconds about an awful day you've had recently.	(17) I found the exam fairly *difficult/ impossible*.	(16) That ice cream was absolutely *tasty/delicious*.	(15) Talk for 30 seconds about a band or singer that you think is brilliant.
(10) My room is always *fairly/absolutely* freezing.	(11) Talk for 30 seconds about a book you think is absolutely wonderful.	(12) Talk for 30 seconds about the last time you were really exhausted.	(13) My mother's cooking is always *absolutely/ incredibly* good.	(14) MOVE BACK TWO SQUARES
(9) I've worked so hard today. I'm absolutely *tired/ shattered*.	(8) MOVE FORWARD THREE SQUARES	(7) I come from a fairly *big/huge* city.	(6) Talk for 30 seconds about something you're really interested in.	(5) The weather was extremely *good/fantastic*.
START	(1) I was absolutely *terrified/frightened* by that film!	(2) MOVE FORWARD TWO SQUARES	(3) When I see her, I always feel extremely *happy/delighted*.	(4) Talk for 30 seconds about a really brilliant film you've seen recently.

Instructions p120

face2face Intermediate Photocopiable

139

3B The world's greatest traveller Present Perfect Continuous and Present Perfect Simple

Traveller role card

You are the world's greatest traveller. A TV company wants to interview you for a documentary series called *Around the World*. Before the interview, complete this information about yourself.

- You've been travelling for .... years. You've been to .... countries so far.
- The most interesting country you've ever visited was .... You liked it so much because
  ....
- You've been writing travel books since ....
  You've written .... books so far. Your last book
  was about your trip to ....
  It's sold .... copies.
- At the moment you're living in ....
  You started living there .... months/years ago.
- Before that you lived in .... You lived there for .... months/years.
- When you travel you always take .... with you. You've had this since ....
- The strangest thing you've ever eaten was .... You ate this when you were in ....
- The best thing about travelling is ....

When you have finished, read the information again. Think of other things you can say about each topic.

- ✂ - - - - - -

Interviewer role card

You are a TV interviewer. You're going to interview the world's greatest traveller for a documentary series called *Around the World*. Look at this information and write questions to ask him/her.

- How long / travel?
  How long have you been travelling?
- How many countries / visit?
- What / be / interesting country / ever visit?
- Why / like it so much?
- How long / write / travel books?
- How many / books / write?
- What / be / last book about? How many copies / sell?
- Where / live / at the moment? How long / live / there?
- Where / live / before that? How long / live / there?
- What / always take with you when you travel? How long / have / it?
- What / strange / thing / ever eat? When / eat this?
- What / be / best thing about travelling?

When you have finished, think of three more questions you can ask.

face2face Intermediate Photocopiable   © Cambridge University Press 2006
Instructions p120

CLASS ACTIVITIES: PHOTOCOPIABLE

-able	rude	-y	popular
-ness	music	-ity	comfort
-al	polite	-able	sad
-ness	honest	-ness	tradition
-y	fashion	-al	ill
-able	tourist	-ness	modest
-y	difficult	-y	knowledge
-y	danger	-able	stupid
-ous	kind	-ity	tired
-ness	health	-ness	change

face2face Intermediate Photocopiable

KEY

You think the sentence is:

correct ⟶

incorrect ·····▶

START

Have you seen any good films lately?

① They work in the library at the moment.

② They can't stand watch soap operas.

③ John's been working as a teacher since three years.

④ All of my friends has got mobile phones.

⑤ He hasn't got a car, has he?

⑥ I'm really keen on football.

⑦ I was very exhausted when I got home.

⑧ You mustn't wear a suit to work if you don't want to.

⑨ Someone is picking me up from class today.

⑩ I think you ought to do more homework.

⑪ Don't bother visit the museum because it's not open today.

⑫ They've lived here for about ten years.

⑬ Sue's really frightened at the dark.

⑭ Who did visited your parents last weekend?

⑮ Are you looking forward to the weekend?

⑯ You can't smoke in here. It's not allowed.

⑰ I feel absolutely shattered.

⑱ Sarah has a lot of confident.

FINISH

Well done!

Instructions p121

Celebrity

ENGAGED – BUT IS THEIR LOVE REAL?

Film star Sam Kennedy and singer Alison Price have announced that they have just got engaged. Journalists and fans all over the world are shocked at the news, as the couple only met for the first time six weeks ago. People in the media are asking if they are really in love, or if their engagement is just a publicity stunt to help their careers. Tonight, Channel 44 reporters Alex Clark and Pat Morris will try to discover the truth about Sam and Alison's relationship when they interview the couple separately live on TV.

You are Sam Kennedy or Alison Price. A journalist from Channel 44 is going to interview you. Make notes on these things to help you in the interview.

- where you first met
- what you were both wearing
- what you talked about
- which film/album you were working on at the time
- where you went on your first date
- if reporters were following you that evening
- how many times you met after that
- what Alison was doing when Sam proposed to her
- why you decided to get married so quickly
- if you are going to allow reporters at the wedding
- if you are planning to make a film/album together
- other things you want to tell the media/your fans

Reporter

ENGAGED – BUT IS THEIR LOVE REAL?

Film star Sam Kennedy and singer Alison Price have announced that they have just got engaged. Journalists and fans all over the world are shocked at the news, as the couple only met for the first time six weeks ago. People in the media are asking if they are really in love, or if their engagement is just a publicity stunt to help their careers. Tonight, Channel 44 reporters Alex Clark and Pat Morris will try to discover the truth about Sam and Alison's relationship when they interview the couple separately live on TV.

You are Alex Clark or Pat Morris. You are going to interview Sam Kennedy or Alison Price. Write questions to ask about these things.

- where Sam and Alison first met
- what they were both wearing
- what they talked about
- which film/album they were working on at the time
- where they went on their first date
- if reporters were following them that evening
- how many times they met after that
- what Alison was doing when Sam proposed to her
- why they decided to get married so quickly
- if they are going to allow reporters at the wedding
- if they are planning to make a film/an album together
- any other questions you want to ask

CLASS ACTIVITIES: PHOTOCOPIABLE

Last year four British students, Tom Edwards, Sally Fisher, Jack Harris and Hilary Richards, went to the Amazon rainforest on holiday. They went to stay in a guest house in a small village for a few days. One day, Tom and Sally decided to go for a walk in the rainforest ...

	write your ideas here
What time did Tom and Sally set off?	
What did they take with them?	
Why didn't Jack and Hilary go with them?	
What did Tom and Sally find while they were walking through the rainforest?	
How long had it been there?	
Who had it belonged to?	
What did they do with it?	
Why did they get lost on the way back to the village?	
What had they forgotten to take with them?	
What did they do when it got dark?	
What happened while they were trying to sleep?	
What did they do next?	
How did they survive in the rainforest after that?	
How did Jack and Hilary find them?	
What were Tom and Sally doing when Jack and Hilary found them?	
How long had they been in the rainforest?	
What did they do when they got back to the guest house?	

Instructions p121

4D Adjective crossword adjectives to describe character and behaviour

Student A

Student B

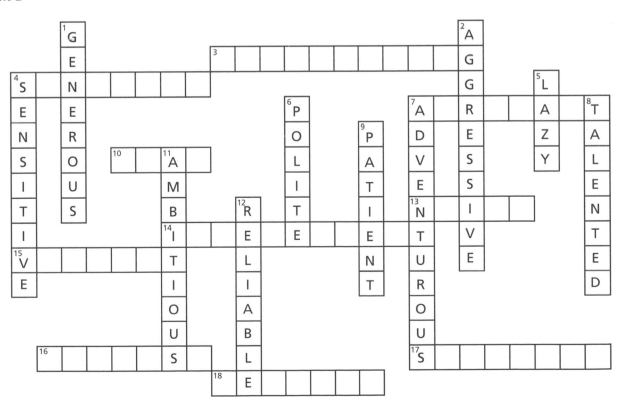

Instructions p122   © Cambridge University Press 2006   face2face Intermediate Photocopiable

PROPERTIES TO LET

Hill Road, Newton

Attractive detached house: Four bedrooms, two bathrooms, two reception rooms and large kitchen. Recently modernised. Big garden. Single garage and parking space for two cars. Situated next to the local primary school. Only a 15-minute walk from town centre. £1,200 per month.

Woodlands, Newton

Very spacious semi-detached house: Four bedrooms, two bathrooms, large living room and kitchen. Front and back garden. Garage and parking for two cars. Close to the local sports field and park (0.5 km), 10-minute walk to town centre. £1,300 per month.

Stone Street, Newton

200-year-old detached cottage: Four bedrooms (two double, two single), main bedroom with en-suite bathroom, family bathroom, living room and large family kitchen. Garden and double garage. Situated in a quiet area of Newton with beautiful views of the countryside. 10-minute drive to town centre. £1,500 per month.

Marina Rise, Newton

New third-floor flat: Three double bedrooms with en-suite bathrooms, one single bedroom. Beautiful view overlooking the marina. All modern facilities, newly fitted kitchen. Three parking spaces. Next to local sports centre. Security system. 15-minute walk to town centre. £1,400 per month.

Student A
You're a lawyer and you work in the town centre. In your free time you love doing sport and cooking for friends. You don't have a car so you walk or cycle to work.

Student B
You work for the post office. You have to get up early every morning and you sleep during the afternoon. You have a car and a motorbike. You love going for walks.

Student C
You're a student at the university in the town centre. You need somewhere quiet to study. In your free time, you like driving your old sports car and playing tennis.

Student D
You're a gardener. You travel to lots of different places in the area for your job and you have a big van. You enjoy keeping fit. You have a dog called Zak.

Instructions p122

5B Look into the future the future: *will, be going to*, Present Continuous

Find someone who ...	Name	Follow-up questions
1 ... *is going to do/will do* some shopping after class.		What / buy? Which shops / usually go to?
2 ... *is meeting/will meet* someone for a coffee or a drink after class.		Who / meet? Where / go?
3 ... *will live/is living* abroad sometime in the future.		Where would / like to live? Why / want / live there?
4 ... *will have/is having* lunch with his/her parents next Sunday.		Where / live? How often / have lunch with them?
5 ... *will want/is wanting* to study another language in the future.		Which language / want to study? Why / want / speak that language?
6 ... *is working/will work* at the weekend.		Where / work? What time / have to get up?
7 ... *will go/is going* to the cinema or the theatre next weekend.		Which film or play / see? Who / go with?
8 ... *is being/will be* a student at this school next year.		Why / learn / English? Where / study last year?
9 ... *is going to buy/is buying* some new clothes in the next few weeks.		What / buy? Which shops / go to?
10 ... *is going/will go* to a wedding next month.		Whose wedding / go to? What / wear?

5C Who said what? verb patterns

I'd rather _____ than _____ .	I need _____ _____ next week.
I sometimes **help** _____ (who?) _____ (what?)	I **could** _____ when I was _____ years old.
I'd **like** _____ _____ next year.	I **started** _____ about _____ years ago.
I **plan** _____ _____ in a few years' time.	I often **ask** _____ (who?) _____ (what?).
I hate it when _____ (who?) **keep(s)** _____ .	Last year I **decided** _____ _____ .
My parents used to **make** me _____ _____ .	I'm **trying** _____ _____ at the moment.
I really **enjoy** _____ _____ at the weekend.	I sometimes **forget** _____ _____ .

face2face Intermediate Photocopiable   © Cambridge University Press 2006

Instructions p123

6A Men and women *make* and *do*

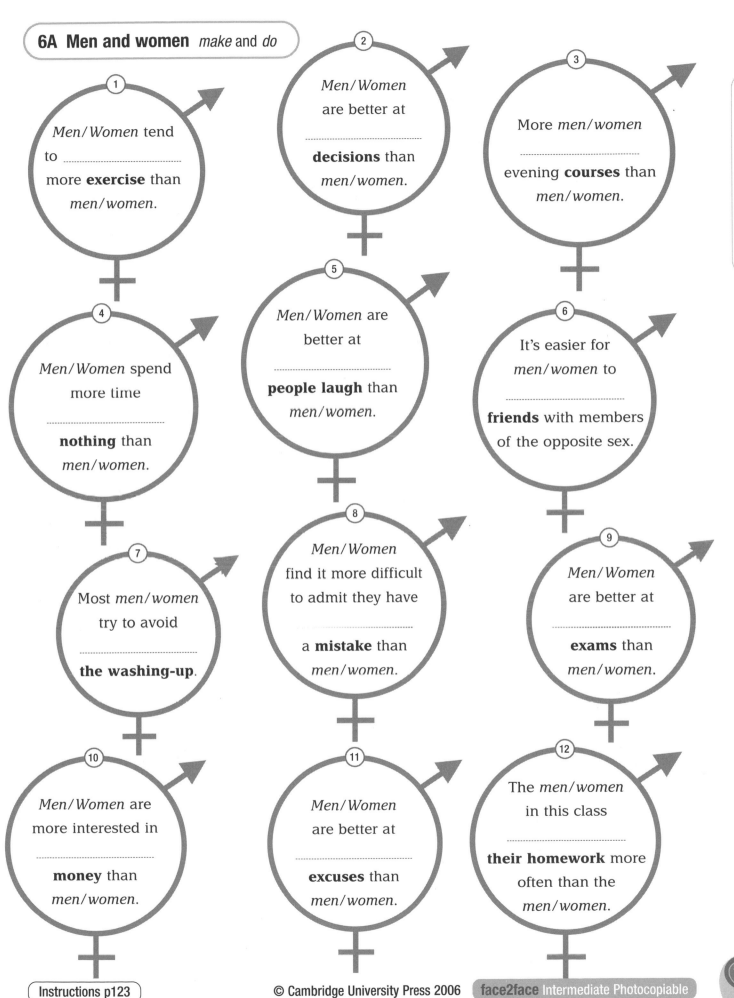

1 *Men/Women* tend to .... more **exercise** than *men/women*.

2 *Men/Women* are better at .... **decisions** than *men/women*.

3 More *men/women* .... evening **courses** than *men/women*.

4 *Men/Women* spend more time .... **nothing** than *men/women*.

5 *Men/Women* are better at .... **people laugh** than *men/women*.

6 It's easier for *men/women* to .... **friends** with members of the opposite sex.

7 Most *men/women* try to avoid .... **the washing-up**.

8 *Men/Women* find it more difficult to admit they have .... a **mistake** than *men/women*.

9 *Men/Women* are better at .... **exams** than *men/women*.

10 *Men/Women* are more interested in .... **money** than *men/women*.

11 *Men/Women* are better at .... **excuses** than *men/women*.

12 The *men/women* in this class .... **their homework** more often than the *men/women*.

face2face Intermediate Photocopiable

Student A

pleasant	act	approach
spot	huge	have a go at doing
worried	certain	glad
pick	scared	cope with
make up your mind	reveal	accidentally

Student B

fortunate	brilliant	worried
certain	cope with	pleasant
chat	spot	pick
content	huge	approach
glad	awful	reveal

Student C

spot	glad	worried
accidentally	pick	chat
have a go at doing	awful	fortunate
content	brilliant	scared
act	make up your mind	approach

Student D

act	awful	make up your mind
fortunate	scared	huge
pleasant	accidentally	have a go at doing
brilliant	reveal	chat
cope with	certain	content

Instructions p123

6D Round the board Review of lessons 4A–6D

START (You get 500 points every time you pass this square.)

Vocabulary card 250

Grammar card 100

Throw again!

Vocabulary card 150

Each person in the game gives you 250 points!

Grammar card 100

Grammar card 200

The person on your left gives you 500 points!

Grammar card 250

VOCABULARY CARDS

Vocabulary card 250

Give the person on your right 300 points!

Vocabulary card 200

Grammar card 150

Give the person on your left 300 points!

GRAMMAR CARDS

Vocabulary card 300

Vocabulary card 300

Miss a turn!

Grammar card 150

Grammar card 100

Give 250 points to each person in the game!

Vocabulary card 250

The person on your right gives you 500 points!

Grammar card 300

Vocabulary card 150

Double your points!

© Cambridge University Press 2006   face2face Intermediate Photocopiable

151

6D Round the board Review of lessons 4A–6D

Vocabulary cards

V1 Choose the correct word.
REM *did/appeared*
on TV last week.
Have you seen them play
live/alive?

V2 Which preposition?
Elton John is going ....
tour soon.
We live .... a rough
neighbourhood.

V3 What's the difference?
a cellar and *a loft*
a garage and *a study*

V4 Say a synonym
for these words/phrases.
worried
sure
behave

V5 Say the correct forms
of the verbs.
Prices keep (go up).
My parents made me (go)
to bed early.

V6 Do we use *make* or *do*
with these words?
an exam, progress, a course,
a mistake

V7 Say eight adjectives
that describe character
or behaviour
in 30 seconds.

V8 Fill in the gaps in
these sentences.
John, can you tidy ....
your room, please? I want to
clear .... the garage today.

V9 What's the difference?
a terraced house and
a detached house
a bungalow and *a cottage*

V10 Fill in the gaps with
a reflexive pronoun.
She made this ....
We decorated our
house ....

V11 Say the correct forms
of the verbs.
This seems (be) correct.
I don't mind (stay).

V12 Which preposition?
My brother lives ....
the suburbs.
I'd like to have
a go .... sailing.

V13 Say a synonym
for these words.
choose lucky accidentally

V14 Fill in the gaps in
these sentences.
I've sorted .... all my books.
I went .... all my drawers
but couldn't find my watch.

V15 Say one thing that is made
from these materials.
cotton rubber
cardboard leather

V16 Do we use *make* or *do*
with these phrases?
someone a favour,
a mess of something,
up your mind, some work

Grammar cards

G1 Correct these sentences.
As soon as I'll get
home, I'll call you.
I won't do anything
until I'll talk to him.

G2 Put the verbs in the Past
Simple or Past Continuous.
While I (drive) home last
night I (have) an accident.

G3 Which preposition?
My new flat is similar ....
my old one.
My car is different ....
my sister's.

G4 Correct these sentences.
It's much exciting than
I thought.
He's the more amazing
person I've met.

G5 Put the verbs in the
Past Simple or Past Perfect.
When they (get) home,
they (realise) that someone
(steal) their TV.

G6 What's the difference
between these sentences?
I'm meeting Jim at six.
I'll meet Jim at six.

G7 Correct these sentences.
Is your phone the same
than Gary's?
No, his isn't as older as mine.

G8 Make these sentences
negative.
I used to watch TV a lot.
I'd met him before.

G9 Correct these sentences.
I was meeting John while
I lived in Rome.
What you were doing
when I called?

G10 Say these sentences
again with *unless*.
We'll come if we aren't busy.
We won't go if you don't
come with us.

G11 Put the verbs in the Past
Simple or Past Continuous.
Tony (call) me while I (watch)
the football on TV.

G12 What's the difference
between these sentences?
I watch TV if I'm tired.
I'll watch TV if I'm tired.

G13 Choose the correct word/phrase.
I have two alarm clocks
if/in case I oversleep.
If/In case he's not here soon,
we'll go without him.

G14 Correct these sentences.
Where used you to live
when you were young?
I used to go to the 2004
World Cup final.

G15 Spell the comparative form
of these adjectives.
big, far, bad, happy

G16 Say the correct verb forms.
It's a thing for (clean)
cookers.
My kids tend to (get)
quite loud.

GUESS MY NAME

When I was child, I was quite good at ....

.... and I was also able to ....

quite well, but I was completely useless at ....

.... I also found .... very

difficult. However, I could .... better

than some of the other kids at school and I'd learned how ....

.... by the age of .... I also managed

to pass my .... when I was ....

These days I think I'm quite good at ....

.... and I'm not bad at ....

either. Unfortunately I have no idea how .... , and most

of my friends think I'm terrible at ....

And I still don't know how .... !

Some of my friends are actually quite talented. For example, my friend

.... is brilliant at ....

.... And as for my family, my ....

.... is able to .... quite

well, but my .... hasn't got a clue how

.... !

Student number ....

153

| **30**
If I lived in the USA, … | → | **31**
MOVE BACK 2 SQUARES | → | **32**
If I could see into the future, … | → | **33**
As soon as the class finishes, … | → | **FINISH** |

| **29**
If I saw a ghost, … | **28**
I'll study English until … | **27**
If I had a time machine, … | **26**
If I live to be 100, … | **25**
If I were famous, … |

| **20**
I'll do your homework for you if … | **21**
If I was a member of the opposite sex, … | **22**
MOVE FORWARD 3 SQUARES | **23**
After this course finishes, … | **24**
If I needed £100,000 quickly, … |

| **19**
THROW AGAIN | **18**
If I had more free time, … | **17**
I'll cook dinner for you if … | **16**
If I saw someone stealing, … | **15**
If I could live anywhere in the world, … |

| **10**
If I was a cartoon character, … | **11**
I'll do some shopping before … | **12**
I wouldn't be frightened if … | **13**
If it doesn't rain at the weekend, … | **14**
MOVE BACK 2 SQUARES |

| **9**
If I were a type of animal, … | **8**
MOVE FORWARD 3 SQUARES | **7**
If I can't come to the next class, … | **6**
When I get home tonight, … | **5**
If I was president of the world, … |

| **START** | **1**
If I lost my wallet/purse, … | **2**
THROW AGAIN | **3**
If I were a colour, … | **4**
I'll feel more relaxed when … |

Instructions p125

7C Article auction use of articles: *a*, *an*, *the*, no article

1 Most families in the UK have a DVD player.

2 She works for a department store in centre of Madrid.

3 The head of the company was sent to prison for two years.

4 Many people from the USA go to the Hawaii on holiday.

5 That band's singer has the most beautiful eyes I've ever seen.

6 The Smiths' flat is much bigger than last place I lived in.

7 This is the third time I've asked you to tidy up a living room!

8 Children in Germany start school when they are six years old.

9 Footballers earn too much money and don't do much work.

10 My sister has been doctor at the City Hospital for about ten years.

11 Did your parents go to the university after they left the school?

12 I used to have a BMW and a Volvo, but I preferred the BMW.

13 If you ever get a computer virus, you shouldn't send the emails.

14 I went to the only school in the village where I lived.

15 The Australian people are very friendly when they meet the foreigners.

16 Vatican City is smallest country in the Europe.

MONEY LEFT £1,000

17 If your monitor isn't working, turn off a computer and wait minute.

18 He lives in the biggest house in the street.

© Cambridge University Press 2006 face2face Intermediate Photocopiable

8A Passive knowledge the passive

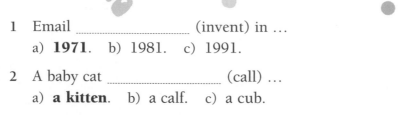

Quiz A

1 Email _____ (invent) in …
   a) **1971**.   b) 1981.   c) 1991.

2 A baby cat _____ (call) …
   a) **a kitten**.   b) a calf.   c) a cub.

3 The American actress Marilyn Monroe _____ (marry) …
   a) twice.   b) **three times**.   c) four times.

4 More than 300 languages _____ (speak) in …
   a) China.   b) Peru.   c) **Indonesia**.

5 The books *1984* and *Animal Farm* _____ (write) by …
   a) Oscar Wilde.   b) **George Orwell**.   c) Agatha Christie.

6 The 19th football World Cup took place in 2002. The 25th football World Cup _____ (hold) in …
   a) **2026**.   b) 2028.   c) 2030.

- ✂ - - - -

Quiz B

1 King Henry VIII of England _____ (marry) …
   a) three times.   b) five times.   c) **six times**.

2 The 28th Olympic Games took place in 2004. The 35th Olympic Games _____ (hold) in …
   a) 2030.   b) **2032**.   c) 2034.

3 The telephone _____ (invent) by …
   a) Thomas Edison.   b) John Logie Baird.   c) **Alexander Graham Bell**.

4 The painting *Mona Lisa* _____ (steal) … in the last hundred years.
   a) **once**.   b) twice.   c) three times.

5 In the film *Titanic*, Rose Dewitt Bukater _____ (play) by …
   a) **Kate Winslet**.   b) Julia Roberts.   c) Gwyneth Paltrow.

6 A baby dog _____ (call) …
   a) a cub.   b) a foal.   c) **a puppy**.

face2face Intermediate Photocopiable   © Cambridge University Press 2006

Instructions p126

Student A: Environmentalist

The government is planning to build an airport 3 miles from a town called Tayford (population 13,500). The town is 500 years old and is surrounded by beautiful countryside. In the summer it's very popular with tourists. However, there is quite a lot of unemployment in the town, particularly during the winter. At the moment the nearest airport is in Bristol, 46 miles away. There is going to be a meeting in the town tonight to decide if they should build the airport or not.

You are from the local environmental group, Keep Tayford Green, and you are against the airport. Think of at least five reasons why they shouldn't build the airport. Use these ideas or your own.

pollution   new roads   local wildlife   noise   number of tourists   countryside

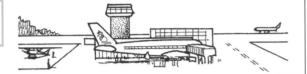

The airport will cause too much pollution.

Student B: Local resident (North Tayford)

The government is planning to build an airport 3 miles from a town called Tayford (population 13,500). The town is 500 years old and is surrounded by beautiful countryside. In the summer it's very popular with tourists. However, there is quite a lot of unemployment in the town, particularly during the winter. At the moment the nearest airport is in Bristol, 46 miles away. There is going to be a meeting in the town tonight to decide if they should build the airport or not.

You are the head of North Tayford Residents' Association and you are against the airport. Think of at least five reasons why they shouldn't build the airport. Use these ideas or your own.

noise at night   number of tourists   cars   prices in local shops   historic buildings   new buildings

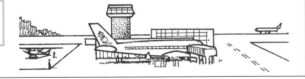

There'll be too much noise at night.

Student C: Local resident (South Tayford)

The government is planning to build an airport 3 miles from a town called Tayford (population 13,500). The town is 500 years old and is surrounded by beautiful countryside. In the summer it's very popular with tourists. However, there is quite a lot of unemployment in the town, particularly during the winter. At the moment the nearest airport is in Bristol, 46 miles away. There is going to be a meeting in the town tonight to decide if they should build the airport or not.

You are the head of South Tayford Residents' Association and you are in favour of the airport. Think of at least five reasons why the airport is a good idea. Use these ideas or your own.

unemployment   new jobs   number of tourists   restaurants   new buildings   going on holiday

There's too much unemployment in Tayford at the moment.

Student D: Local businessperson

The government is planning to build an airport 3 miles from a town called Tayford (population 13,500). The town is 500 years old and is surrounded by beautiful countryside. In the summer it's very popular with tourists. However, there is quite a lot of unemployment in the town, particularly during the winter. At the moment the nearest airport is in Bristol, 46 miles away. There is going to be a meeting in the town tonight to decide if they should build the airport or not.

You are the head of the Tayford Business Association and you are in favour of the airport. Think of at least five reasons why the airport is a good idea. Use these ideas or your own.

jobs during the winter   hotels   number of tourists   shops
new roads   new businesses

There aren't enough jobs during the winter at the moment.

Student E: Local government officer

The government is planning to build an airport 3 miles from a town called Tayford (population 13,500). The town is 500 years old and is surrounded by beautiful countryside. In the summer it's very popular with tourists. However, there is quite a lot of unemployment in the town, particularly during the winter. At the moment the nearest airport is in Bristol, 46 miles away. There is going to be a meeting in the town tonight to decide if they should build the airport or not.

You are the head of the local government in Tayford. You are not sure if the airport is a good idea or not. Think of questions to ask the other people at the meeting about the airport. Use these ideas or your own.

local wildlife   jobs   pollution   new roads   number of tourists
new businesses

Will the airport have much effect on local wildlife?

Student F: Chairperson

The government is planning to build an airport 3 miles from a town called Tayford (population 13,500). The town is 500 years old and is surrounded by beautiful countryside. In the summer it's very popular with tourists. However, there is quite a lot of unemployment in the town, particularly during the winter. At the moment the nearest airport is in Bristol, 46 miles away. There is going to be a meeting in the town tonight to decide if they should build the airport or not.

You work for the government and you are going to be the chairperson at the meeting.

- Write a short introduction to the meeting. Welcome everyone and say what the meeting is about. Then ask all the people to introduce themselves.
- Think of questions to ask about the airport, for example *Will the airport create too much traffic?*
- During the meeting, make sure everyone has a chance to speak and ask questions. Remember, you are in control of the meeting.

Instructions p126

dis-	honest	re-	marry
dis-	appear	under-	estimate
un-	selfish	re-	write
un-	reliable	over-	sleep
ir-	responsible	-ful	hope
im-	possible	-ful	harm
in-	sensitive	-less	care
in-	considerate	-less	pain

© Cambridge University Press 2006 face2face Intermediate Photocopiable

159

9A Fighting fit relative clauses with *who, that, which, whose, where* and *when*

Student A

1 David weighed 92 kg three months ago. That was _____ he began dieting. Now he weighs 75 kg.
2 The person _____ swims regularly is on a fat-free diet.
3 The person _____ weighs 70 kg goes to a gym _____ she can do yoga.
4 The man _____ goes cycling weighs 90 kg.
5 The person _____ weight is 10 kg less than Anna's is on a fasting programme.
6 Susie only eats food _____ is organic, including meat. She doesn't go jogging.
7 The person _____ weighs the least is Susie. She weighs 70 kg.

	David	Mick	Richard	Susie	Anna
Weight now					
Exercise					
Type of diet					

Student B

a) Richard goes to a swimming pool _____ he can exercise every morning.
b) One of the women is on a diet _____ is meat-free.
c) Mick is the man _____ only drinks juice.
d) The person _____ weight is 80 kg at the moment is on a fat-free diet.
e) The person _____ walks regularly is on a fasting programme.
f) The person _____ weighs the most is Mick. He weighs 90 kg.
g) The jogger weighed 100 kg in June. That was _____ she began dieting. Now she weighs 85 kg.

	David	Mick	Richard	Susie	Anna
Weight now					
Exercise					
Type of diet					

Instructions p127

Write short answers to ten of these prompts in the circles below.
Don't write them in this order.

- someone famous who's been in the news recently
- something that's just happened in your country
- someone you know who's just started a new job
- something you've already done this week
- something you have to do this week, but haven't done yet
- the name of someone you've already spoken to today
- a TV programme you've seen this week
- something interesting you've been told recently
- a film that's just been released that you'd like to see
- someone who's been interviewed on TV recently
- something unusual or interesting that you've been given recently
- a book that's just been published that you'd like to read
- a place you've been to recently that you enjoyed visiting
- the name of someone you know who's just got married or engaged
- a film that's been shown on TV recently

fold

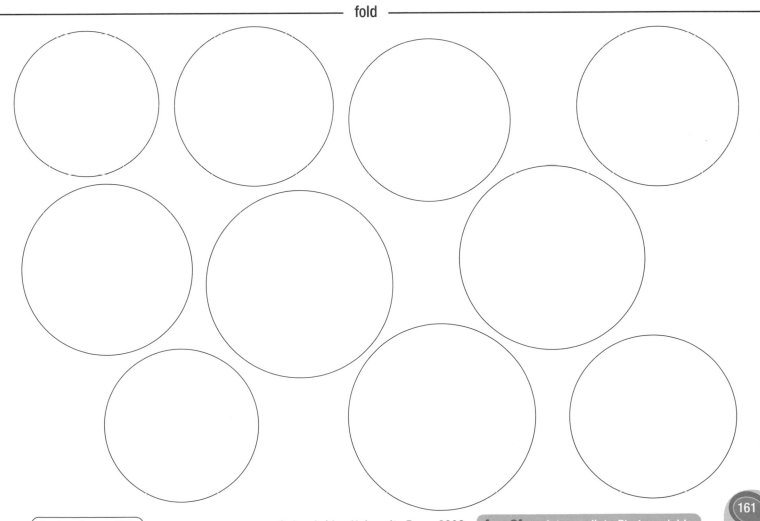

Board 1

THE PASSIVE	INDIRECT QUESTIONS	CONDITIONAL SENTENCES
ABILITY	RELATIVE CLAUSES	QUANTIFIERS
VOCABULARY	ERROR CORRECTION	ARTICLES

✂

Team A question sheet

THE PASSIVE	INDIRECT QUESTIONS	CONDITIONAL SENTENCES
Put the sentence into the passive. 1 A storm has hit the *USA.* (*The USA has been hit by a storm.*) 2 Brazil won the 2002 World Cup. (*The 2002 World Cup was won by Brazil.*) 3 They're repairing my car. (*My car is being repaired.*)	**Complete the indirect question.** 1 Where is he from? Do you know … (*where he's from?*) 2 Did she ask him? Could you tell me … (*if/whether she asked him?*) 3 When does it start? Can you tell me … (*when it starts?*)	**Which is correct?** 1 If I see him, I'll tell him. *or* If I saw him, I'll tell him. (*see*) 2 I'd buy a car if I can drive. *or* I'd buy a car if I could drive. (*could*) 3 I won't go unless we get a taxi. *or* I won't go unless we don't get a taxi. (*we get*)
ABILITY	**RELATIVE CLAUSES**	**QUANTIFIERS**
Which is correct? 1 I have no idea how … to cook/cooking. (*to cook*) 2 I find it difficult … read maps/ to read maps. (*to read maps*) 3 I'm good at … play golf/playing golf. (*playing golf*)	**Fill in the gap in this sentence.** 1 She's the girl _____ parents own the Italian restaurant. (*whose*) 2 That's the restaurant _____ I had lunch. (*where*) 3 This is the watch _____ I got for my birthday. (*that/which*)	**Which is correct?** 1 I haven't got many money. *or* I haven't got much money. (*much*) 2 There are no chairs. *or* There are any chairs. (*no*) 3 I've got plenty time. *or* I've got plenty of time. (*plenty of*)
VOCABULARY	**ERROR CORRECTION**	**ARTICLES**
In 20 seconds say … 1 six nouns connected with computers. (*see* **V7.1**) 2 six types of bad weather. (*see* **V8.1**) 3 eight types of electrical equipment. (*see* **V7.3**)	**Correct this sentence.** 1 This exercise is unpossible. (**im**possible) 2 I'm hopeless at cooking the Italian food. (*cooking the Italian food*) 3 Can you tell me when will he be back? (*when he will be back*)	**Complete the sentence with the correct article or no article.** 1 My sister works for _____ company in town. (*a*) 2 He's _____ best singer in my family. (*the*) 3 I started _____ school when I was five. (*no article*)

Instructions p128

Board 2

ARTICLES	CONDITIONAL SENTENCES	RELATIVE CLAUSES
VOCABULARY	ERROR CORRECTION	THE PASSIVE
QUANTIFIERS	INDIRECT QUESTIONS	ABILITY

✂

Team B question sheet

THE PASSIVE	INDIRECT QUESTIONS	CONDITIONAL SENTENCES
Put the sentence into the passive. 1 They make Fiats in Italy. (*Fiats are made in Italy.*) 2 Steven Spielberg directed E.T. (*E.T. was directed by Steven Spielberg.*) 3 Someone has stolen my bag. (*My bag has been stolen.*)	**Complete the indirect question.** 1 Where does Jo live? Can you tell me … (*where Jo lives?*) 2 When did it open? Do you know … (*when it opened?*) 3 Is this your car? Could you tell me … (*if/whether this is your car?*)	**Which is correct?** 1 If I find your wallet, I'll call you. *or* If I found your wallet, I'll call you. (*find*) 2 I'd go if I had time. *or* I'll go if I had time. (*I'd go.*) 3 I'll do it when I could. *or* I'll do it when I can. (*can*)
ABILITY **Which is correct?** 1 I'm useless at … swim/swimming. (*swimming*) 2 I managed … to find it/finding it. (*to find it*) 3 I haven't got a clue how … to do it./doing it. (*to do it*)	**RELATIVE CLAUSES** **Fill in the gap in this sentence.** 1 I know a lot of people _____ are famous. (*who/that*) 2 That's the man _____ car was stolen. (*whose*) 3 That's the place _____ I grew up. (*where*)	**QUANTIFIERS** **Which is correct?** 1 I speak a few Japanese. *or* I speak a little Japanese. (*a little*) 2 I have several time. *or* I have hardly any time. (*hardly any*) 3 There's a bit of rubbish. *or* There's not many rubbish. (*a bit of*)
VOCABULARY **In 20 seconds say …** 1 ten health problems or symptoms. (*see* **V9.4**) 2 six verbs connected with computers. (*see* **V7.2**) 3 six types of container. (*see* **V8.2**)	**ERROR CORRECTION** **Correct this sentence.** 1 This bill is too much. You've recharged me. (***over**charged*) 2 A new shopping centre will build here. (*will **be built***) 3 Could you give us an advice? (***some** advice*)	**ARTICLES** **Complete the sentence with the correct article or no article.** 1 Tom works at _____ hospital on Green Road. (*the*) 2 He's been working as _____ actor for two years. (*an*) 3 Have you ever been to _____ Mexico City? (*no article*)

Student B

You and your partner are organising a party in a local club for your classmates and their friends. Look at these things your partner was supposed to do and when he/she was supposed to do them (in brackets). Make questions with the Present Perfect Simple + *yet* for the things in **bold**.

- **book the club** (two weeks ago)
  Have you booked the club yet?
- **pay for the club** (a week ago)
- **ask your friend to organise the music** (last Friday)
- **buy the decorations** (last weekend)
- **ask your brother to video the party** (last night)
- **check what time the club opens and closes** (two nights ago)
- **get in touch with students who left last month** (last week)
- **organise some taxis home after the party** (yesterday)

Look at this list of things you agreed to do and when you were supposed to do them (in brackets). Tick two more things you've already done. Then think of good excuses for why you haven't done the other things.

- make the invitations (last week) ✓
- give out the invitations (last class)
- hire a band (last Saturday)
- organise the catering (two days ago)
- buy some disposable cameras for the party (yesterday)
- let the school director know where we're going (last Monday)
- organise some flowers for the party (last Wednesday)
- invite our teacher (at the end of the last class)

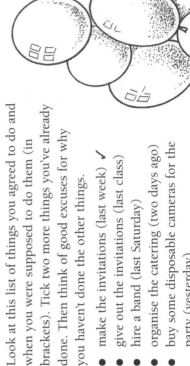

Student A

You and your partner are organising a party in a local club for your classmates and their friends. Look at these things your partner was supposed to do and when he/she was supposed to do them (in brackets). Make questions with the Present Perfect Simple + *yet* for the things in **bold**.

- **make the invitations** (last week)
  Have you made the invitations yet?
- **give out the invitations** (last class)
- **hire a band** (last Saturday)
- **organise the catering** (two days ago)
- **buy some disposable cameras for the party** (yesterday)
- **let the school director know where we're going** (last Monday)
- **organise some flowers for the party** (last Wednesday)
- **invite our teacher** (at the end of the last class)

Look at this list of things you agreed to do and when you were supposed to do them (in brackets). Tick two more things you've already done. Then think of good excuses for why you haven't done the other things.

- book the club (two weeks ago) ✓
- pay for the club (a week ago)
- ask your friend to organise the music (last Friday)
- buy the decorations (last weekend)
- ask your brother to video the party (last night)
- check what time the club opens and closes (two nights ago)
- get in touch with students who left last month (last week)
- organise some taxis home after the party (yesterday)

Instructions p128

10B Where's Robin? modal verbs (2): making deductions

Student A

Karen is at her parents' 25th wedding anniversary party. It's now 8 p.m., but her boyfriend, Robin, still hasn't arrived. Make deductions about Robin from this information. Use the verbs in brackets.

1 Robin had to finish writing a report at work. (write)
2 The traffic is really bad this evening. (be stuck)
3 Robin often meets his friend Lucy for coffee. (have)
4 He wants a new guitar and the music shop is usually open late. (buy)

Read this extra information.
- Robin bought a new mobile this afternoon.
- His friend Ken is away on business this week
- Visiting hours at the hospital are from 2 p.m. to 6 p.m.
- Hundreds of people are watching football on a big TV in the town square.

Student B

Karen is at her parents' 25th wedding anniversary party. It's now 8 p.m., but her boyfriend, Robin, still hasn't arrived. Make deductions about Robin from this information. Use the verbs in brackets.

1 Robin sometimes stays in the office until late. (be)
2 His cat didn't come home last night. (look for)
3 His mother is quite ill these days. (look after)
4 It's Karen's birthday tomorrow. (buy)

Read this extra information.
- Robin planned to travel to the party by train.
- He hurt his leg yesterday and the doctor told him not to do any exercise.
- His neighbour's dog is ill and isn't allowed to go out.
- The mechanic said he needed three days to fix Robin's car.

Student C

Karen is at her parents' 25th wedding anniversary party. It's now 8 p.m., but her boyfriend, Robin, still hasn't arrived. Make deductions about Robin from this information. Use the verbs in brackets.

1 Robin's grandmother is in hospital. (visit)
2 His train is often late. (still be)
3 He took his car to the garage this morning. (pick up)
4 He sometimes takes his neighbour's dog for a walk in the evening. (take)

Read this extra information.
- Robin finished writing his report at 5 p.m.
- A neighbour found his cat this morning.
- His friend Lucy is on holiday.
- All the trains are running on time today.

Student D

Karen is at her parents' 25th wedding anniversary party. It's now 8 p.m., but her boyfriend, Robin, still hasn't arrived. Make deductions about Robin from this information. Use the verbs in brackets.

1 Robin often visits his friend Ken after work. (visit)
2 He lost his mobile phone yesterday. (buy)
3 He goes to the gym most days. (be)
4 His favourite football team are playing this evening. (watch)

Read this extra information.
- Robin's office closes at 7.30 p.m.
- He bought Karen's birthday present last weekend.
- His mother is at the party and having a great time.
- The music shop closed early today.

(30) I'm really l _ _ _ _ _ _ / _ _ _ _ _ _ _ / _ _ my holiday.

(31) I don't like going to weddings. I always try to g _ _ / _ _ _ / _ _ them.

(32)

(33) I'm going to London tomorrow. I have to s _ _ / _ _ _ at 6 a.m.

FINISH

(29) What's the best way to g _ _ / _ _ _ _ _ _ your city?

(28) My sister and I don't get on very well. We often f _ _ _ / _ _ _ with each other.

(27) This room is a mess. Can you t _ _ _ it _ _ , please?

(26) My neighbour always plays loud music. I can't p _ _ / _ _ / _ _ _ _ it any more.

(25)

(20) I can't find my passport. I'll have to g _ / _ _ _ _ _ _ _ all my drawers.

(21)

(22) I c _ _ _ / _ _ _ _ _ _ this article in the newspaper yesterday.

(23) What time do we have to c _ _ _ _ / _ _ _ / _ _ the hotel?

(24) I'm going away for the weekend. I'll g _ _ / _ _ _ _ on Monday.

(19) We need to c _ _ _ _ / _ _ _ the spare room this weekend.

(18) I'd better go. I have to p _ _ _ Billy _ _ from the airport.

(17) I didn't need my old printer so I g _ _ _ it _ _ _ _ .

(16) Jo is ill, so she's going to p _ _ / _ _ _ the party until next weekend.

(15) We don't need this any more. T _ _ _ _ it _ _ _ _ .

(10) I don't know this word. I'll have to l _ _ _ it _ _ in a dictionary.

(11) I'm going to New York soon. I'll b _ _ _ _ you _ _ _ _ a present!

(12)

(13) Eve's in Brazil, but she's c _ _ _ _ _ / _ _ _ _ on Friday.

(14) Laura had to p _ _ _ _ / _ _ _ that Mark had forgotten her birthday.

(9) Tom has just c _ _ _ / _ _ / _ _ _ _ a great idea!

(8) I was really upset when my boyfriend s _ _ _ _ / _ _ with me.

(7) Sally, can you p _ _ / _ _ _ _ your toys, please?

(6) It took me ages to g _ _ / _ _ _ _ the flu.

(5) In this job I have to d _ _ _ / _ _ _ _ a lot of problems.

START

(1) Dave's going to Italy today. I'm going to the airport to s _ _ him _ _ _ .

(2) Could you t _ _ _ / _ _ _ the rubbish for me, please?

(3) Prices in our country g _ / _ _ every year.

(4) I really need to s _ _ _ / _ _ _ my study. I can't find anything!

Instructions p129

11A Work dominoes collocations connected to work

pressure at work at the moment.	I think we **have**	**good working conditions**.	I never manage to **meet**
deadlines.	I'm not very good at **sorting out**	**people's problems**.	I only have to **do**
overtime once a week.	Wendy's **going for**	**an interview** tomorrow.	I've been **running**
this department since September.	Mrs Earle is **responsible**	**for the finances**.	I have to **deal with**
customers every day.	Fiona always has to **arrange**	**meetings** for her boss.	Michael used to **work**
shifts when he was a police officer.	Tom's cousin is now **in charge**	**of this company**.	I always have to **take**
work home with me.	I really need to **take**	some **time off work**.	I think my boss **is a**
workaholic. He never leaves the office.	Most nurses **work**	very **long hours**.	My friend Abi **went for**
an audition last week.	Jane **organises**	**conferences** all over the country.	I don't want a job which **has a lot of**
responsibility.	I'm working so hard I don't **have**	any **time to relax**.	She**'s under** a lot of

Student B: Teacher

The Worldwide Language School teaches over forty languages to more than 1,000 students. We are looking for teachers of all languages to join our professional and hard-working teaching staff.

You should have at least two years' teaching experience and be able to work unsocial hours.

If you're looking for a challenging and rewarding career in teaching, email us at www.worldwidels.org for an application form.

You are an experienced teacher of your own language. You are going to be interviewed for a job at The Worldwide Language School.

Make notes on these things.

- which language you teach
- how long you've been a teacher
- what you did before you started teaching
- where you're working at the moment
- how long you've been there
- what you enjoy most about teaching
- if you have ever taught exam classes
- which other languages you can speak
- when you'd be able to start work

Make questions to ask the interviewer. Then write two more questions of your own.

- teach / hours / a / many / would / I / How / week ?
- *How many hours would I teach a week?*
- a / job / permanent / this / or / a / Is / temporary ?
- school / Does / your / have / classes / evening ?
- there / a / students / How / are / class / many / in ?
- the / be / What / salary / would ?

Student A: Interviewer

The Worldwide Language School teaches over forty languages to more than 1,000 students. We are looking for teachers of all languages to join our professional and hard-working teaching staff.

You should have at least two years' teaching experience and be able to work unsocial hours.

If you're looking for a challenging and rewarding career in teaching, email us at www.worldwidels.org for an application form.

You are one of the directors of The Worldwide Language School. You are going to interview a teacher for a job at your school.

Make questions with *you* from these prompts. Then write three more questions of your own.

- Which language / teach ?
- *Which language do you teach?*
- How long / be / teacher?
- What / do / before / start / teaching?
- Where / work / at the moment?
- How long / be / there?
- What / enjoy most / about teaching?
- ever / teach / exam classes?
- Which other languages can / speak?
- When would / be able / start work here?
- Have / got / questions?

Make notes on these things.

- number of hours teaching per week
- temporary or permanent job
- working hours
- number of students per class
- the average monthly salary

Instructions p130

11C Spy school verb patterns: reporting verbs

Sentence cards

1. Would you like to come and work for the CIA?

2. I'll get you a job with the British Secret Service, I promise.

3. Yes, it's true. I've read all your private emails.

4. I'll introduce you to the head of MI6, if you like.

5. Don't go home tonight. You're being followed by a man in a black coat.

6. Why don't we write a book about spying?

7. Don't forget to change the password on your computer every day.

8. I *won't* tell you what my real name is.

9. If you tell anyone where you got your new passport, I'll have to kill you.

10. OK. I'll meet you outside the American Embassy at midnight.

Spy memory test

What do you remember?

| the CIA   a black coat   a new passport   emails   password   real name |
| the head of MI6   a book   the American Embassy   the British Secret Service |

1 _____ invited _____

2 _____ promised _____

3 _____ admitted _____

4 _____ offered _____

5 _____ warned _____

6 _____ suggested _____

7 _____ reminded _____

8 _____ refused _____

9 _____ threatened _____

10 _____ agreed _____

Student A

1 I haven't got a house with a swimming pool.

I wish _____

_____ .

2 I can't speak five languages.

I wish _____

_____ .

3 I have to start work at 6 a.m.

I wish _____

_____ .

Student B

1 I haven't got a cottage in the country.

I wish _____

_____ .

2 I can't get to sleep at night.

I wish _____

_____ .

3 I have to work six days a week.

I wish _____

_____ .

Student C

1 I haven't got a boat.

I wish _____

_____ .

2 I'm not a professional tennis player.

I wish _____

_____ .

3 I have to drive 100 km to work every day.

I wish _____

_____ .

Student D

1 I can't fly a plane.

I wish _____

_____ .

2 I haven't got a million pounds.

I wish _____

_____ .

3 I'm not going to the Caribbean next week.

I wish _____

_____ .

Student E

1 I haven't got a Harley Davidson motorbike.

I wish ....

....

2 I'm not tall enough.

I wish ....

....

3 I don't live in New York.

I wish ....

....

Student F

1 I can't play the piano.

I wish ....

....

2 I have to cook for my family every day.

I wish ....

....

3 I'm not a famous actor/actress.

I wish ....

....

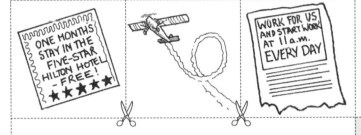

Student G

1 I'm not staying in a five-star hotel this month.

I wish ....

....

2 I haven't got a Ferrari.

I wish ....

....

3 I'm not a famous pop star.

I wish ....

....

Student H

1 I can't go to the moon.

I wish ....

....

2 I haven't got a helicopter.

I wish ....

....

3 I'm not swimming with dolphins now.

I wish ....

....

 face2face Intermediate Photocopiable

Story cards

Mark's had a really terrible day today.
What's his story?

Laura's had an absolutely fantastic day today.
What's her story?

get **cards**

get a (new) job	get a phone call from someone	get a message from someone	get a present for someone
get something to eat/drink	get home	get to work	get back from somewhere
get lost	get angry/annoyed	get fed up with something	get better/worse at something
get arrested	get on well with someone	get sacked	get hold of someone
get rid of something	get in touch with someone	get promoted	get engaged/married

Vocabulary Plus

Instructions

There are twelve Vocabulary Plus worksheets (p177–p188). These worksheets introduce additional vocabulary that is **not** presented in the Student's Book. The topic of each Vocabulary Plus worksheet is linked to the topic of the corresponding unit in the Student's Book. There is an answer key at the bottom of each worksheet, which can be cut off if necessary. You will need to photocopy one Vocabulary Plus worksheet for each student.

- Use them as extra vocabulary input in class. We suggest you cut off the answer keys and check the answers after each exercise.

- Give them for homework for students to use on their own. You can either leave the answer keys on the worksheets so students can check the answers themselves or cut them off and check answers at the beginning of the next class.

- When you have a mixed-level class, give them to students who finish longer speaking activities early. They can begin the worksheets in class and finish them for homework if necessary. You can then give the worksheet for homework to the other students at the end of the class.

1 -ed/-ing adjectives p177

Language

satisfied/satisfying, fascinated/fascinating, exhausted/exhausting, irritated/irritating, depressed/depressing, annoyed/annoying, frustrated/frustrating, entertained/entertaining, embarrassed/embarrassing, disappointed/disappointing

When to use and time

Use any time after lesson 1C. 20–30 minutes.

Procedure

1 **a)** Focus students on the article. Pre-teach *commute to work* and *meet deadlines*. Students read the article and answer the questions.

Check answers with the class (see answer key on worksheet). Ask students if they agree with the points made in the article.

b) Students do the exercise on their own or in pairs. Check answers with the class.

Check students understand the new words *fascinating* (very interesting), *exhausting* (very tiring) and *irritating* (annoying).

2 **a)–b)** Students do the exercises on their own or in pairs. Check answers with the class.

c) Students write the adjectives on their own. Check answers with the class. Model and drill the words, highlighting the pronunciation of *exhausted* /ɪgˈzɔːstɪd/ and *embarrassed* /ɪmˈbærəst/. Point out that *-ed* endings are pronounced as an extra syllable /ɪd/ after a /t/ sound (*irritated*, *frustrated*, etc.).

3 Students do the exercise on their own, then check answers in pairs. Check answers with the class.

4 Students do the exercise on their own before comparing sentences in groups of three or four. Finally, ask each group to tell the class two interesting things they have found out about other students.

2 Food and drink p178

Language

chewy, fizzy, fresh, ripe, sour, savoury, bitter, alcoholic, salty, off, still, sweet

When to use and time

Use any time after lesson 2B. 15–25 minutes.

Procedure

1 Students do the exercise in pairs or groups. Students can use dictionaries if necessary. Check answers with the class (see answer key on worksheet).

Point out that only fruit can be *ripe*, whereas other types of food (meat, vegetables, milk, etc.) can be *fresh*. Also point out that *still* is usually used with mineral water and that the opposite is *sparkling*. Also teach the verb *chew* /tʃuː/.

Model and drill the words, paying particular attention to *chewy* /ˈtʃuːi/, *sour* /sauər/ and *savoury* /ˈseɪvəri/. Check students understand the differences between similar words, (for example *savoury* and *salty*) by asking students to name another type of food or drink for each word.

Students can then work in pairs and test each other on the vocabulary. Students take turns to point to a picture and ask their partner to say the correct adjective.

2 Students do the exercise on their own before checking in pairs. Check answers with the class.

3 Students do the crossword in pairs. Check answers with the class.

4 Students do the exercise on their own before checking in pairs. Check answers with the class. Then students work in pairs and take turns to ask each other the questions.

3 Travelling by car p179

Language

run out of, fill up, speed up, catch up with, overtake, slow down, pull over, take a short cut, get lost, give someone a lift, map-read, get stuck

When to use and time

Use any time after lesson 3D. 15–25 minutes.

Procedure

1 Introduce the topic by asking how many students in the class can drive and whether they enjoy driving. Students do the exercise on their own before checking in pairs. Check answers with the class (see answer key on worksheet).

2 Students do the exercise on their own or in pairs. Check answers with the class. Point out that you can *run out of something* or *run out*, and *catch up with someone* or *catch up*. Also point out that we often get stuck in *traffic jams*. Model and drill the words/phrases. Students can work in pairs and test each other on the words/phrases and definitions. Alternatively, you can ask them to cover the text, look at the pictures and say what happened.

3 a) Students do the exercise on their own before checking answers in pairs. Check answers with the class.

b) Put students into groups. If possible, include at least one driver in each group. Students then take turns to ask each other the questions in **3a)**.

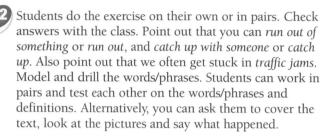

4 Compound adjectives for character p180

Language

good-natured, narrow-minded, strong-willed, bad-tempered, well-behaved, broad-minded, weak-willed, over-confident, hard-working, self-centred

When to use and time

Use any time after lesson 4B. 15–25 minutes.

Procedure

1 Students do the exercise in pairs. Check answers with the class (see answer key on worksheet). Point out that the prefix *over-* means 'too' and the prefix *self-* means 'about yourself'. Also highlight that we only use *well-behaved* about children or pets.

Model and drill the words. Point out that compound adjectives are generally stressed on the second word, not the first (*good-natured*, *strong-willed*, etc.) and highlight that the *-ed* endings in *broad-minded* and *narrow-minded* are pronounced /ɪd/ because they follow a /d/ sound.

Students can then work in pairs and test each other on the vocabulary by taking turns to read a definition and asking their partner to say the correct compound adjective.

2 a)–b) Students do the exercises on their own or in pairs. Check answers with the class.

3 Students do the exercise on their own before checking in pairs. Check answers with the class.

4 Students do the exercise on their own. Students can then compare answers in groups, giving reasons for their choices. Finally, ask a few students to share their answers with the class.

5 Shopping p181

Language

sale, (50%) off, from (£250), bargain, discounts, products, branch, stock, refund, goods

When to use and time

Use any time after lesson 5C. 20–30 minutes.

Procedure

1 Focus students on the advertisement for Collins department store and ask what kind of things the store sells. Students do the exercise in pairs. Check answers with the class (see answer key on worksheet). Point out that if something is *for sale*, it means you can buy it, and if it is *in a sale*, it means it is cheaper than usual. Also point out that *stock* is an uncountable noun and *goods* is a plural noun. Teach the phrase *It's (not) in stock*.

Model and drill the new words, paying particular attention to the pronunciation of *bargain* /ˈbɑːɡɪn/. Teach students that the stress is on the first syllable of *refund* when it is a noun and the second syllable when it is a verb.

2 Check students understand *receipt* /rɪˈsiːt/. Students do the exercise in pairs. Check answers with the class.

3 a) Students do the exercise on their own before checking in pairs. Check answers with the class.

b) Students work in pairs or groups and ask each other the questions. Finally, ask students to tell the class one or two things they found out about other students.

6 Antonyms p182

Language

delicious/disgusting, optimistic/pessimistic, brave/cowardly, spicy/mild, spacious/cramped, satisfied/dissatisfied, delighted/horrified, gorgeous/hideous, increase/decrease, include/exclude

When to use and time

Use any time after lesson 6C. 20–30 minutes.

Procedure

1 a) Students work on their own or in pairs and check they know the meaning of the words a)–j). Tell students not to write on the lines at this stage. Note that all these words are in units 1–5 of **face2face** Intermediate.

b) Students do the exercise on their own, then check answers in pairs. Check answers with the class (see answer key on worksheet). Check students understand that *include* and *exclude* are verbs and *increase* and *decrease* can be nouns and verbs. All the other words are adjectives. Point out that *delicious*, *disgusting*, *delighted*, *horrified*, *gorgeous* and *hideous* are all strong adjectives, so we say *absolutely delicious*, etc., not ~~*very delicious*~~. Also teach students the nouns *an optimist* and *a pessimist*.

Model and drill the words. Pay particular attention to the pronunciation of *spacious* /ˈspeɪʃəs/, *gorgeous* /ˈgɔːdʒəs/, *hideous* /ˈhɪdiəs/ and *horrified* /ˈhɒrɪfaɪd/, and point out that *cramped* is one syllable, not two.

Students can then work in pairs and test each other on the opposites. For example student A says *satisfied* and student B replies *dissatisfied*.

 2 Students do the exercise on their own before checking in pairs. Check answers with the class.

 3 a) Students do the exercise on their own before checking in pairs. Check answers with the class.

b) Students work in pairs or groups and take turns to ask each other the questions. Ask students to share interesting answers with the class.

7 Machines p183

Language
anti-virus software, rewind, pay-as-you-go, a firewall, charge, a contract, surf, a search engine, pause, fast forward, top up

When to use and time
Use any time after lesson 7B. 20–30 minutes.

Procedure

1 a) Students do the exercise on their own. Check answers with the class (see answer key on worksheet). Point out that *rewind*, *charge*, *surf*, *pause*, *fast forward* and *top up* are verbs and that *software* is an uncountable noun. Ask students which *search engines* they know (Google, Yahoo, etc.). Check students remember *a charger* (a machine for charging your mobile phone). You can also teach students *a top-up card* (a card you use to top up your mobile phone) and *a button* (for example a fast-forward button on a remote control).

Model and drill the new words/phrases.

b) Students do the exercise on their own before checking answers in pairs. Check answers with the class.

2 Students do the exercise on their own before checking answers in pairs. Check answers with the class.

3 a) Students do the exercise on their own or in pairs. Check answers with the class.

b) Put students into pairs or groups. Students take turns to ask each other the questions from **3a)**. Encourage students to ask follow-up questions if possible. Finally, ask students to share interesting answers with the class.

8 Weather conditions p184

Language
foggy/fog, misty/mist, cloudy/cloud, sunny spells, fine, heavy snow/rain, warm, humid/humidity, drizzle, light showers, frosty/frost, icy/ice, hail, overcast, stormy/storm, high temperatures

When to use and time
Use any time after lesson 8A. 20–30 minutes.

Procedure

 1 Students do the exercise in pairs. Check answers with the class (see answer key on worksheet).

Teach students that *fog* is thicker than *mist*. Also teach students that *frost* is the ice that forms on the ground overnight, and that *drizzle* and *light rain* are synonyms.

Model and drill the new words, paying particular attention to the pronunciation of *humid* /ˈhjuːmɪd/, *icy* /ˈaɪsi/ and *temperature* /ˈtemprətʃə/. Students can then work in pairs and test each other on the vocabulary by taking turns to point to a picture and asking *What's this?*

 2 Students do the exercise in pairs. Check answers with the class. Point out the different stress patterns on *hu̇mid* and *humi̇dity*.

 3 Students do the exercise on their own before checking in pairs. Check answers with the class.

 4 a) Focus students on the two weather maps. If necessary, check students know where the UK, France, Germany and Spain are on the maps. Students do the exercise on their own. Check answers with the class.

b) Students do the exercise on their own. Early finishers can check answers in pairs. Check answers with the class.

 5 Put students into groups. If possible, include students from different countries in each group. Students discuss the questions in their groups. Ask students to share any interesting or surprising answers with the class.

9 Injuries and health problems p185

Language
sprain your wrist, twist your ankle, have a black eye, have a stiff neck, have a bad back, have swollen ankles, (my shoulder) aches, (my finger)'s sore, (I've) hurt (my knee), have a pain in your chest

When to use and time
Use any time after lesson 9D. 15–25 minutes.

Procedure

 1 a) Students do the exercise on their own or in pairs. Check answers with the class (see answer key on worksheet).

Point out that you can *twist* or *sprain your ankle*, but you *sprain your wrist*, not ~~twist your wrist~~. Also highlight the collocation *a stiff neck*. Point out that *ache* and *hurt* are verbs, *sore* and *swollen* are adjectives, and *pain* is a noun. You can also teach students the verb *swell* (*swelled*, *swollen*).

Model and drill the new words and phrases, paying particular attention to the pronunciation of *wrist* /rɪst/, *swollen* /ˈswəʊlən/ and *aches* /eɪks/. Check students can hear the difference between *ankle* /ˈæŋkəl/ and *uncle* /ˈʌŋkəl/.

b) Students work in pairs and take turns to test each other on the vocabulary by pointing to a picture and asking *What's he/she saying?*

2 Students do the exercise on their own or in pairs. Check answers with the class.

3 Students do the exercise on their own before checking in pairs. Check answers with the class.

4 **a)** Students do the exercise on their own. Check answers with the class.

b) Put students into pairs or groups. Students take turns to ask each other the questions in **4a)**. Finally, ask students to tell the class two interesting things they have found out.

10 Moods and relationships p186

Language
be in a bad/good mood, feel down, feel sorry for sb, cheer sb up, be separated from sb, look up to sb, look down on sb, get back together (with sb), have a row (with sb), make up (with sb), move out

When to use and time
Use any time after lesson 10C. 20–30 minutes.

Procedure

1 **a)** Students read the emails and answer questions 1–3. Check answers with the class (see answer key on worksheet).

b) Students do the exercise on their own or in pairs. Check answers with the class and highlight the different prepositions in the phrases. Check students understand the difference between a *separated* married couple (they live apart but are still married) and a *divorced* couple. Tell students that you can *cheer someone up* or *cheer up*: *I was very down last night, but I've cheered up now.* Model and drill the phrases. Pay particular attention to the pronunciation of *row* /raʊ/.

2 Students do the exercise on their own before checking answers in pairs. Check answers with the class.

3 **a)** Students do the exercise on their own. Check answers with the class.

b) Students take turns to answer the questions in **3a)** in pairs or groups. Ask each group to share interesting answers with the class.

11 Working life p187

Language
a career, job satisfaction, an income, freelance, involve, get a pay rise, a day off, maternity leave, get fired, be made redundant, resign, retire

When to use and time
Use any time after lesson 11B. 20–30 minutes.

Procedure

1 Focus students on the photo and ask them to guess what Sandra's job is. Students read the text and answer the questions. Check answers with the class (see answer key on worksheet).

2 Students do the exercise on their own. Early finishers can check answers in pairs. Check answers with the class.

Check students understand the difference between *a career* and *a university course*. Teach students that we use *on* with *maternity leave*: *I'm on maternity leave at the moment.* Also highlight that we can say *get fired* or *get sacked*, and check students understand the difference between *get fired* and *be made redundant*.

Model and drill the words/phrases, paying attention to the pronunciation of *career* /kəˈrɪə/ and *resign* /rɪˈzaɪn/.

Students can then work in pairs and test each other on the vocabulary by saying a definition and asking their partner to say the word or phrase.

3 **a)** Students do the exercise on their own before checking in pairs. Check answers with the class.

b) Put students into groups. If you have a multilingual class, put different nationalities in the same group. Students take turns to ask each other the questions. Encourage students to ask follow-up questions if possible.

12 Phrasal verbs for plans p188

Language
end up, fall through, let someone down, get round to, set out, put up with, work (something) out, get on

When to use and time
Use any time after lesson 12B. 15–25 minutes.

Procedure

1 Students do the exercise on their own before checking in pairs. Check answers with the class (see answer key on worksheet). Point out that *end up* and *get round to* are often followed by a verb+*ing* form (*end up/get round to doing something*) and that *set out* is always followed by the infinitive with *to* (*set out to do something*). Also highlight that *work out* is often followed by a question word (*work out why/what/who*, etc.) and is often used with *can't* or *couldn't*: *I can't work out what to do.* Highlight that we often use the preposition *with* with *get on*: *How are you getting on with your new job?* Model and drill the phrasal verbs.

2 Students do the exercise on their own before checking in pairs. Check answers with the class.

3 **a)** Students do the exercise on their own before checking in pairs. Check answers with the class.

b) Put students into pairs. Students take turns to ask each other the questions in **3a)**. Encourage students to ask follow-up questions if possible. Finally, ask students to share any interesting answers with the class.

1 *-ed*/*-ing* adjectives

1 **a)** Read the article about happiness. Which activities do the people in the survey like? Which do they hate?

b) Write adjectives 1–11 from the article in the table.

positive meaning	negative meaning
satisfied	

2 **a)** Look again at the article. Which adjectives 1–11 in the article describe:

a) how people feel? *1*

b) the thing, situation, place or person that causes the feeling?

b) Complete the rules with *-ing* or *-ed*.

- We use _____ adjectives to describe how people feel.

- We use _____ adjectives to describe the thing, situation, place or person that causes the feeling.

c) Write the *-ed* or *-ing* adjective for each word in 1b).

satisfied → satisfying

How to measure happiness

Scientists have found a new way to measure happiness: they can calculate how [1]**satisfied** people are with their everyday lives by giving positive and negative points for typical activities. In a [2]**fascinating** survey, scientists discovered that commuting to work is the activity that people find most [3]**exhausting** and [4]**irritating**. Many people feel [5]**depressed**, [6]**annoyed** and [7]**frustrated** when they have to do housework and meet deadlines at work. In general, the most [8]**entertaining** activity is relaxing with friends and the most [9]**satisfying** is spending time with family. However, some parents were [10]**embarrassed** to say that looking after children didn't always make them happy. Finally, you may be [11]**disappointed** if you think that a higher salary will bring greater happiness. In fact, one scientist suggests that organising your time well might be the best way to improve your quality of life.

3 Complete the adjectives with *-ed* or *-ing*.

1 Eileen has been working twelve hours a day for the last week. She's absolutely *exhausted* .

2 I can't bear being without my family. I find it very *depress___* .

3 Please don't shout so loudly. You're making me really *embarrass___* .

4 Juan must be very *frustrat___* . He's just failed his driving test again.

5 I can't stand waiting in queues. It's really *irritat___* .

6 My history of art course is absolutely *fascinat___* .

7 I'm afraid I was extremely *disappoint___* by the results of these tests.

8 Marek doesn't earn much but he finds his job very *satisfy___* .

9 You must go and see that new film. It's extremely *entertain___* .

10 I'll be very *annoy___* if they don't reply to my letter.

4 Write three sentences about you with *-ed* adjectives and three sentences with *-ing* adjectives.

I often feel exhausted after a long day at work.
Waiting for buses is really annoying.

2 Food and drink

1 Match the adjectives to pictures 1–12.

chewy fizzy ☐ fresh ☐
ripe ☐ sour ☐ savoury ☐

bitter ☐ alcoholic ☐ salty ☐
off ☐ still ☐ sweet ☐

2 Cross out the incorrect word.

1 Bread and cakes can be *fresh/fizzy*.
2 Milk and meat can be *off/ripe*.
3 Cola and lemonade are *chewy/fizzy*.
4 Crisps and nuts are *savoury/sour*.
5 Wine and beer are *alcoholic/savoury*.
6 Bananas and apples can be *salty/ripe*.
7 Milk and fruit can be *fresh/still*.
8 Mineral water can be *savoury/still*.
9 Coffee can be *bitter/salty*.
10 Sweets can be *still/chewy*.

3 Do the crossword.

ACROSS

2 You have to be over 18 to buy … drinks.
4 These bananas are too green. I only like … ones.
5 This soup's too … . I can't eat it.
6 Let's buy some … snacks like crisps and nuts for the party.
8 I can't eat lemons. They're too … .
9 … drinks are bad for your teeth.
10 I eat … fruit for breakfast every day.

DOWN

1 I don't like black coffee because it's too … . I prefer apple juice.
3 These sweets are really … . My mouth is starting to ache!
6 Have we got anything … , like chocolate?
7 This milk smells terrible. I think it's … .
8 I'll have some … mineral water, please.

4 Fill in the gaps with the correct word. Then answer the questions for yourself.

~~still~~ savoury fresh (x 2) sweet off bitter

1 Do you prefer ...*still*... or sparkling mineral water?
2 How often do you eat _____ fruit?
3 How often do you eat _____ snacks, like crisps?
4 How do you know if meat is _____ ?
5 Do you usually buy _____ milk?
6 Do you have something _____ for dessert every day?
7 Do you think coffee is too _____ without sugar?

VOCABULARY PLUS: PHOTOCOPIABLE

3 Travelling by car

 1 Read the story and put pictures A–D in order.

Last Saturday it was my mum's 70th birthday so we went on a family trip to Paris for the weekend. My wife Viv and I – and the kids, of course – set off early for the airport, with my parents driving in front in their own car. Soon I realised we were going to **run out of** petrol, so I phoned them on their mobile and explained that we would **fill up** at the next garage.

When we left the garage, we **speeded up** to **catch up with** mum and dad, but suddenly a police car **overtook** us and I had to **slow down** and **pull over**. Luckily the police officer only gave me a warning, so I apologised and we set off again. By now the traffic was terrible, so we decided to **take a short cut**. Unfortunately, we **got lost** and didn't know where we were. We stopped a young man to ask the way and because he was going in the same direction, we **gave him a lift**. He was able to **map-read** so we got to the airport in time, but there was no sign of my mum and dad. They **got stuck** in a traffic jam after we lost them, so we all had to catch a later flight. Although it was difficult getting to Paris, we still had a great weekend.

 2 Match the word/phrases in **bold** in the story in 1 to definitions a)–1). Write the infinitive form of the verbs.

a) take someone where they want to go in a car
   give someone a lift

b) put petrol in a car ....

c) not be able to move forward or make progress
   ....

d) follow a quicker or shorter way to get somewhere
   ....

e) pass another car because it is going more slowly than you ....

f) understand a map ....

g) go faster ....

h) go slower ....

i) not know where you are ....

j) use all of something so there is nothing left
   ....

k) reach someone who is in front of you
   ....

l) stop at the side of the road ....

 3 a) Fill in the gaps with the correct form of the words/phrases from 2.

1 Have you ever _run out of_ petrol?

2 Do you .... if someone is driving too close behind you?

3 Do you usually .... in bad weather?

4 Do you wait until your car is nearly empty before you .... it .... ?

5 If you were following a friend and he or she was driving too fast, would you try to .... him/her?

6 Are you good at .... or do you always have to ask for directions?

7 Have you ever stopped to .... ? Where did he or she want to go?

8 Have you ever .... in a town that you don't know very well?

9 What do you do if you .... in a traffic jam?

10 Have you ever been asked to .... by a police officer?

11 If you were in a hurry, would you .... if you weren't sure which way to go?

12 Do other cars often .... you?

b) Answer the questions for you.

4 Compound adjectives for character

1 Match the words in **bold** to definitions a)–j).

1 [b] I'm not surprised Tomoko is so popular. She's very **good-natured** and easy to get on with.

2 [ ] Celine doesn't like anybody who's different to her. She's extremely **narrow-minded**.

3 [ ] I'm sure you could give up smoking. You're a very **strong-willed** person.

4 [ ] Jo is always **bad-tempered** in the morning. She hates getting up early.

5 [ ] I really love looking after my sister's children because they're so **well-behaved**.

6 [ ] I'd like to invite Nagi to join our discussion group. He's very **broad-minded** and is interested in different people and cultures.

7 [ ] Albert needs to lose weight, but he's too **weak-willed** to go on a diet.

8 [ ] I think Lucia is **over-confident** about passing her driving test. She hasn't practised at all.

9 [ ] Sonia will do well in her exams. She's a very **hard-working** student.

10 [ ] It's quite difficult to be friends with Tony these days. He's a bit **self-centred** and hasn't got time for anyone else.

a) not happy to accept new ideas or opinions different from your own

b) naturally friendly and doesn't get angry easily

c) behave in a quiet and polite way

d) interested only in yourself

e) too sure about yourself and your abilities

f) very determined to do what you want to do

g) always doing a lot of work

h) happy to accept ideas and ways of life different to your own

i) often annoyed, angry or impatient

j) not determined enough to succeed in what you want to do

weak-willed

hard-working

2 a) Write the words in **bold** from 1 in the table.

positive meaning	negative meaning
good-natured	

b) Which words in **2a)** are opposites?

3 Fill in the gaps with the words in **bold** from 1.

1 I should be studying for my exams next week, but I can't say no to invitations. I'm too _weak-willed_ .

2 My grandfather is always annoyed about something. He's quite ....

3 Elizabeth always listens to new ideas. She's very ....

4 Sam's a very .... boy. He always gets what he wants.

5 Our daughter is .... and polite to everyone.

6 My best friend gets on well with everyone. She's such a .... person.

7 Although Mark's my friend, he's only interested in himself. He's a bit ....

8 I think I was .... before my exams. I didn't do as well as I thought I would.

9 Sophie doesn't really like people who are different from her. I'm afraid she's a bit ....

10 Their son is a bit lazy, but their daughter is extremely ....

4 Choose adjectives from **2a)** to describe yourself.

---

1 2a) 3f) 4i) 5c) 6h) 7j) 8e) 9g) 10d) 2 a) **Positive:** strong-willed; well-behaved; broad-minded; hard-working **Negative:** narrow-minded; bad-tempered; weak-willed; over-confident; self-centred **b)** good-natured/bad-tempered; broad-minded/narrow-minded; strong-willed/weak-willed; broad-minded/narrow-minded 3 2 bad-tempered 3 broad-minded 4 strong-willed 5 well-behaved 6 good-natured 7 self-centred 8 over-confident 9 narrow-minded 10 hard-working

Instructions p174

1 Look at words 1–10 in the advertisement. Choose the correct meaning.

1 a) when a shop sells new things
  b) when a shop sells things cheaper than usual ✓
2 a) not included
  b) reduced
3 a) this price or more
  b) this price or less
4 a) something that is cheaper than usual
  b) something that is better quality than usual
5 a) the cheapest prices
  b) the amount prices are reduced by
6 a) things sold in a shop
  b) things given away free in a shop
7 a) a shop owned by a different company
  b) one of a number of shops that are part of the same company
8 a) the total number of things you can buy in a shop
  b) the biggest things in a shop
9 a) money that you get back when you return something you have bought
  b) a piece of paper you get when you buy something
10 a) things that you can buy
  b) things that are good to use

Collins summer ¹sale starts Saturday

men's fashion	up to 50% ²**off**
women's fashion	up to 25% off
luggage	up to 75% off
leather sofas	³**from** £250

Come to our city centre store and pick up a ⁴**bargain**! Take advantage of our amazing ⁵**discounts** on a huge range of ⁶**products**. Also available at a ⁷**branch** near you. All ⁸**stock** must go!

*No ⁹**refund** on ¹⁰**goods** bought in the sale.

 2 Fill in the gaps with words 1–10 from the advertisement.

1 Why not try our new range of skin-care ..*products*.. ? You won't be disappointed.
2 Our autumn .... starts on Monday. Everything must go!
3 I'm afraid we haven't got any blue suitcases in .... Shall I order one for you?
4 This TV I bought yesterday doesn't work. Can I have a .... ?
5 We haven't got any red shirts in this shop. I could find out whether another .... has any in red.
6 The garden centre has taken 20% .... the price of their garden furniture.
7 Green's is a great place to buy carpets. They give .... of at least 30% on orders over £500.
8 You must have a receipt if you want to return .... bought in this shop.
9 Beautiful hand-made leather belts .... only 10 euros.
10 I bought this designer suit in the sale for only £100. It was a real .... !

 3 a) Choose the correct word.

1 Is there a (branch)/sale of a big department store near you?
2 Have you ever bought anything that had 50% *from/off*?
3 Do you look for *refunds/discounts* when you're buying electrical equipment or clothes?
4 If you want something that's not in *stock/branch*, do you order it or go somewhere else?
5 What's the best *discount/bargain* you've ever bought?
6 Have you ever taken something back and asked for a *refund/bargain*?
7 What's the most interesting *product/stock* you've bought this year?

b) Answer the questions for you.

---

3 2 off 3 discounts 4 stock 5 bargain 6 refund 7 product

2 2 sale 3 stock 4 refund 5 branch 6 off / discounts 8 goods 9 from 10 bargain

1 2b) 3a) 4a) 5b) 6a) 7b) 8a) 9a) 10a)

face2face Intermediate Photocopiable

a) Tick the words a)–j) you know. Check other words with your teacher or in a dictionary.

a) delicious ....

b) optimistic ....

c) brave ....

d) spicy ....

e) spacious ....

f) satisfied ....

g) delighted ....

h) gorgeous ....

i) increase ....

j) include ....

b) Read sentences 1–10. Then write the words in **bold** next to their antonyms (opposites) a)–j).

1 By the way, these prices all **exclude** sales tax. That's 17% extra.

2 Running away was a very **cowardly** thing to do. Why didn't you stay and help us?

3 The amount of paid work men do in the UK is going to **decrease** in the next ten years.

4 I'd like to go and stay in a nicer hotel. This place is absolutely **hideous**.

5 Don't be so **pessimistic**! Everything will be all right in the end.

6 Is that a **mild** dish? I don't want anything too hot.

7 If you are **dissatisfied** with this product, we will give you your money back.

8 Our last flat had large rooms, but where we live now feels a bit **cramped**.

9 That meat looks **disgusting**. I don't think you should buy it.

10 Susan's mother was **horrified** when she discovered her daughter hadn't been to school.

| cramped | disgusting | horrified |

2 Tick the correct sentences. Correct the sentences that are wrong by changing the words in **bold**.

Pessimistic

1 ~~Optimistic~~ people find it difficult to see the positive side of things.

2 There used to be hardly any traffic on this road, but it has **decreased** in the last ten years.

3 I'm very **dissatisfied** with my working life. My job is really boring.

4 This food is burning my mouth – it's incredibly **mild**.

5 Have you met Eva's new boyfriend? He's **hideous**, the best-looking guy in the office.

6 Can I have some more soup? This is absolutely **delicious**.

7 We can fit seven people in our tent, but it'll be very **cramped**.

8 We were **delighted** to hear that you had such a terrible time.

9 The price of the hotel room **excludes** meals, but there are lots of good restaurants and bars nearby.

a) Fill in the gaps with words from 1a) and 1b).

1 Would you prefer to live in a ..*cramped*.. flat in the centre of town or a tiny cottage in the country?

2 Do you prefer spicy or .... dishes?

3 Have you ever been .... with the service you received in a restaurant?

4 Are you generally optimistic or .... ?

5 What would you do if you were invited to dinner at a friend's house and you thought the food was .... ?

6 Your best friend asks you what you think of her new dress. She thinks it's nice, but you think it's .... What do you say?

7 Has the amount of housework done by men in your country increased or .... in the last ten years?

8 Would you feel .... or delighted if you had to sing in public?

b) Answer the questions for you.

face2face Intermediate Photocopiable   © Cambridge University Press 2006   Instructions p174

VOCABULARY PLUS: PHOTOCOPIABLE

 1 **a)** Match these words/phrases to definitions 1–11.

anti-virus software 4	rewind ☐
pay-as-you-go ☐	a firewall ☐	charge ☐
a contract ☐	surf ☐	a search engine ☐
pause ☐	fast forward ☐	top up ☐

1 You do this when you look quickly at websites on the Internet for anything that interests you.
2 You can use one of these to help you find what you want on the Internet.
3 This stops other people accessing your computer.
4 This software stops viruses infecting your computer.
5 You do this if you want to watch part of a video or a DVD again.
6 You do this if you don't want to miss part of a video or a DVD when you go out of the room for a short time.
7 You do this to go quickly to the next part of a video or a DVD you want to watch.
8 You need to do this to your mobile phone when the batteries are dead.
9 You need to do this when you have no money in your mobile phone account.
10 You have to pay a monthly bill if you have this type of mobile phone agreement.
11 You need this type of mobile phone if you want to pay for each call.

b) Which words in 1a) talk about these things?
a) mobile phones
b) TVs
c) computers

2 Choose the correct words.

1 I usually use (*a search engine*)/*anti-virus software* when I want to *surf/top up* the Internet.
2 I didn't understand that bit. Can you *rewind/fast forward* it?
3 I've run out of credit on my mobile. I need to *top it up/ charge it*.
4 I use *a firewall/a search engine* to stop people finding out my bank details on my computer.
5 My *pay-as-you-go/charge* mobile is quite expensive. I think I'll get one with a monthly *top-up/contract*.
6 Can you *pause/fast forward* the video while I make a cup of tea? I don't want to miss anything.
7 This bit's really boring. Let's *rewind/fast forward* to the end.

3 **a)** Fill in the gaps with words/phrases from 1a).

1 If you don't understand something on a video or a DVD, do you __rewind__ it or just continue watching?
2 Do you usually _____ a video or a DVD if someone phones you while you're watching it?
3 Have you got a _____ mobile phone or have you got a contract?
4 How often do you _____ your mobile phone? Do you ever forget?
5 How often do you _____ the Internet? What are your favourite websites?
6 Which _____ do you use to help you find websites on the Internet?
7 Have you got any _____ or _____ to protect your computer from viruses and stop pop-ups*? If so, which one(s)?

* *pop-ups* advertising messages on your computer screen

b) Answer the questions for you.

VOCABULARY PLUS: PHOTOCOPIABLE

VOCABULARY PLUS: PHOTOCOPIABLE

1 Match words/phrases a)–l) to weather symbols 1–12.

a) foggy and misty *2*
b) cloudy with sunny spells
c) fine and sunny
d) heavy snow
e) warm and humid
f) drizzle and light showers

g) heavy rain
h) frosty and icy
i) hail
j) overcast
k) stormy
l) high temperatures

2 Fill in the gaps in the table.

adjective	noun
1 foggy	*fog*
2	mist
3	ice
4	frost
5 cloudy	....
6	humidity
7 stormy	....

3 Cross out the incorrect word.

1 light/~~sunny~~/heavy rain
2 high/warm/fine weather
3 high/stormy/low temperatures
4 light/low/heavy showers
5 a chilly/humid/high day
6 a foggy/drizzle/frosty morning

4 **a)** Read the weather forecasts and match them to the maps.

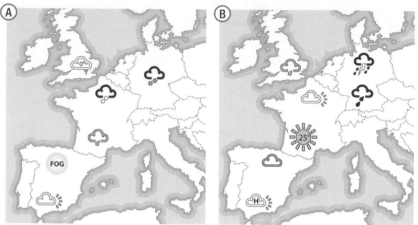

1

It's quite warm in the UK, but there's going to be ¹ *drizzle* and light ² .... for most of the day. In the north of France it's ³ .... with sunny spells, and ⁴ .... should reach 25°C in the south, where it's ⁵ .... and sunny. There's a lot of ⁶ .... weather in Germany, along with some ⁷ .... rain. The south of Spain will have a warm and ⁸ .... day, but it's going to remain ⁹ .... in the north.

2

It will be an extremely chilly day in the UK, and it will be rather ¹⁰ .... to begin with. It's very cold in France too, with the possibility of ¹¹ .... this afternoon in the north and some ¹² .... and light showers in the south. In Germany there's already ¹³ .... snow falling in the north. In northern Spain, there will be some ¹⁴ .... and fog in places, and in the south it will be ¹⁵ .... with some ¹⁶ .... spells in the afternoon.

b) Fill in the gaps in the weather forecasts with words from **1** and **2**.

5 Say what the weather is like: a) where you are today b) in your country in winter c) in your country in summer.

---

9 Injuries and health problems

 a) Match sentences a)–j) to pictures 1–10.

a) I've sprained my wrist. *4*
b) I've twisted my ankle.
c) I've got a black eye.
d) I've got a stiff neck.
e) I've got a bad back.
f) I've got swollen ankles.
g) My shoulder aches.
h) My finger's sore.
i) I've hurt my knee.
j) I've got a pain in my chest.

b) Cover the sentences in 1a). What is the person saying in each picture?

 Cross out the incorrect word.

1 sprain your *wrist/leg/ankle*
2 twist your *knee/chest/neck*
3 your *stomach/hair/elbow* aches
4 have a pain in your *chest/side/ache*
5 hurt your *nails/foot/hand*
6 have swollen *eyes/feet/teeth*

 Fill in the gaps with words from 1a).

1 A What have you done to your arm?
  B Oh, I've ..*sprained*.. my wrist.

2 Morgan was playing hockey and she
  .... her ankle.

3 Do you think Luis has been in a fight? He's got
  a .... eye.

4 I always get .... ankles when
  I fly long distances.

5 I'm sorry, I can't turn round. I've got a
  .... neck.

6 I can't walk very far. I've ....
  my foot.

7 I don't think I should lift that heavy suitcase.
  I've got a .... back.

8 A Let's play tennis.
  B I can't. My shoulder ....

9 I need to see a doctor immediately. I've got a
  .... in my chest.

10 I've just cut my finger and it's really
  ....

 **a)** Match the beginnings and endings of these questions.

1 Have you ever broken ⌐⌐⌐⌐ a) aches?
2 Have you ever sprained   b) in your chest?
3 Have you ever had a black c) a bone?
4 Do you ever get swollen   d) neck?
5 What do you do if your   e) yourself?
  back   f) your wrist or ankle?
6 What would you do if you   g) eye?
  had a bad pain   h) ankles?
7 Do you ever get a stiff
8 When was the last time
  you hurt

b) Answer the questions for you.

VOCABULARY PLUS:
PHOTOCOPIABLE

10 Moods and relationships

 1 **a) Read emails A and B. Answer these questions.**

1 What do Julia and her husband do?
2 What did they have a problem about?
3 Did they solve the problem?

A
from: Valerie R <valerie_r@...>

Hi Tom
You've met my sister, Julia, haven't you? She**'s** just **separated from** her husband and I **feel** really **sorry for** her. They met when she was a student at drama school. She used to **look up to** him because he was already a successful actor, but now she's getting more acting work than him. She said he **was** always **in a bad mood** and then they **had a row** about a film she wants to do – and the next day he **moved out**. She's **feeling** really **down** and I'd like to be able to **cheer** her **up** a bit, but I don't know what I can do. Any ideas?

Love Valerie

B
from: Valerie R <valerie_r@...>

Hi again
Guess what? I**'m in** such **a good mood**. My sister **has got back together** with her husband. She told me that he just didn't like the film she was going to do and **looked down on** the people she was working with, so she's agreed not to do it. Anyway, they**'ve made up** and now everything can go back to normal. It's so nice to see her happy again.

Lots of love Valerie

---

b) Match the phrases in bold in the emails to definitions 1–12. Write the infinitive form of the verbs.

1 feel unhappy *be in a bad mood*
2 feel happy
3 feel depressed
4 feel sympathy for someone because something bad has happened to them
5 make someone feel happy when they're depressed
6 live in a different place from your husband or wife, but not be divorced
7 admire and respect someone
8 think that someone is less important than you
9 to start a relationship again with someone that you broke up with
10 have an argument
11 become friends again after an argument
12 stop living in a particular place

2 **Fill in the gaps with the correct form of the words/ phrases from 1b).**

1 My father always <u>looks down on</u> people who don't have a job.
2 I was feeling .... after my boyfriend left me, but your lovely letter really .... me ....
3 Don't talk to Paul. He's in a really ....
4 I .... for Mark. Did you know he's .... from his wife? Apparently she .... a week ago and he's living on his own.
5 My brother and his wife split up last year, but now they've .... I'm so happy for them.
6 The people next door had a terrible .... last night. But I think they've .... because they both looked very happy today.
7 When I was a child, I used to .... my uncle Frank and I wanted to be just like him.
8 I'm usually in a .... on Friday afternoon because I love weekends.

3 **a) Match the beginnings and endings of the questions.**

1 How often are you in a   a) sorry for?
2 What's a good way to cheer   b) rows with?
3 Who do you look   c) someone up?
4 What do you do when   d) down?
   you're in
5 Which famous person   e) up with him/her?
   do you feel   f) a good mood?
6 What do you do when   g) up to?
   you're feeling   h) bad mood?
7 Is there someone you
   often have
8 Do you find it easy
   to make

b) Answer the questions for you.

---

1 a) 1 They're actors. 2 Julia's new film. 3 Yes, they did. b) 2 be in a good mood 3 feel down 4 feel sorry for someone 5 cheer someone up 6 be separated from someone 7 look up to someone 8 look down on someone 9 get back together (with someone) 10 have a row 11 make up 12 move out 2 down; cheered ... up 3 bad mood 4 feel sorry; separated; moved out 5 got back together 6 row; made up 7 look up to 8 good mood 3 a) 2c) 3g) 4f) 5a) 6d) 7b) 8e)

VOCABULARY PLUS: PHOTOCOPIABLE

face2face Intermediate Photocopiable   © Cambridge University Press 2006   Instructions p176

11 Working life

1 Read the text. What is Sandra's job now? Does she enjoy it?

Someone asked me recently if I thought it was important to have [1]**a career** that is well-paid. Personally, I think [2]**job satisfaction** is more important than a high [3]**income**. I started out doing jobs like cleaning and waitressing, but I'd always wanted to write so I did an evening course, and now I'm a [4]**freelance** journalist. My work [5]**involves** lots of research and I have to work long hours, but I love what I do. There are good and bad things about working freelance. I hardly ever [6]**get a pay rise**, I don't get paid if I take [7]**a day off**, and I didn't get [8]**maternity leave** when I had my two children. On the other hand, I can't really [9]**get fired** for missing a deadline or [10]**be made redundant** and I'll never need to [11]**resign**. Unfortunately, I'll probably never be able to [12]**retire** when I'm old either!

Sandra

2 Match words/phrases 1–12 in **bold** in the text to definitions a)–l). Write the infinitive form of the verbs.

a) when you lose your job because your employer no longer needs you

be made redundant

b) the feeling of pleasure you get when you know that your work is worth doing

c) doing pieces of work for several different organisations, rather than working for one organisation

d) stop working (usually when you're 60–65)

e) when you're told to leave your job (usually for doing something wrong or badly)

f) a period of paid holiday for a woman after she's had a baby

g) get paid more for doing a job than you did before

h) tell an employer that you want to leave a job

i) the amount of money you earn from working

j) include as part of the job

k) the job, or the series of jobs, that you do during your working life, especially if you continue to get better jobs and earn more money

l) a day's holiday

3 **a)** Fill in the gaps with words/phrases from 1.

1 Do you think job ___satisfaction___ is more important than a high .... ?

2 When did you last take .... during the week?

3 What age can people .... in your country?

4 Do you know anyone who has been made .... ?

5 Do you think it's better to work for an employer or work .... ? Why?

6 What does/did your father do? What does/did his work .... ?

7 Do you think it's important to have a .... ? Why?/Why not?

8 How much .... do women get in your country?

9 If you decided to .... , what would you say to your boss before you left?

10 Can you think of four reasons why people get .... from their jobs?

11 Do you think everyone should get a .... every year? Why?/Why not?

b) Answer the questions for you.

12 Phrasal verbs for plans

1 Match the phrasal verbs in **bold** in sentences 1–8 to definitions a)–h).

1 I hated school, so I never thought I'd **end up** being a teacher.
2 I was going to travel round the world with my friend last year, but our plans **fell through** when he got sick.
3 Minori worked incredibly hard in order to meet the deadline. She didn't want to **let** anyone **down**.
4 I'm so pleased I've finally **got round to** doing a photography course. I've been putting it off for ages.
5 When Tim started working there, he **set out** to become the best salesperson in the company by the end of the year.
6 Adam doesn't like the people he works with, but he **puts up with** them because he loves the job.
7 I'm almost thirty, but I'm still trying to **work out** what I want to do with my life.
8 I saw Tom last night. He said he was **getting on** very well in his new job.

a) fail to happen
b) accept or tolerate something even though you don't like it
c) finally be in a particular situation or place
d) disappoint someone because you haven't done what you said you were going to do
e) understand something or find the answer to something after thinking about it
f) start an activity with a particular aim
g) deal with a situation, usually successfully
h) do something that you have planned or wanted to do for a long time

2 Fill in the gaps with the correct form of the phrasal verbs from 1.

1 Nikolaus __set out__ to become a millionaire by the time he was thirty.
2 I recommended you for the job so please don't _____ me _____ .
3 I love living here, but I have to _____ a lot of noise from my neighbours.
4 A How are you _____ with that report?
  B Oh, I've nearly finished it.
5 Sarah is always busy and doesn't think she'll ever _____ doing her driving test.
6 When Mariko's plans to study in England _____ , she was very disappointed.
7 Pete wasn't very happy in Europe. He _____ going back to Australia after only six months.
8 I can't _____ the answer to question seven.

3 a) Choose the correct phrasal verb.

1 Have you ever made an important plan that got by/fell through at the last minute?
2 When was the last time a friend let you down/ended up?
3 Have you made up for/worked out what you want to do with the next ten years of your life?
4 How often do you achieve what you put up with/set out to do?
5 Is there something you've always wanted to do that you haven't got round to/get on yet?
6 What do you have to get round to/put up with that you don't like?
7 What do you think you'll end up/work out doing when you retire?
8 How are you setting out/getting on with your English?

b) Answer the questions for you.

---

1 2a) 3d) 4h) 5f) 6b) 7e) 8g) **2** 2 let ... down 3 put up with 4 getting on 5 get round to 6 fell through 7 ended up 8 work out **3** 2 let you down 3 worked out 4 set out 5 got round to 6 put up with 7 end up 8 getting on

face2face **Intermediate** Photocopiable © Cambridge University Press 2006 Instructions p176

VOCABULARY PLUS: PHOTOCOPIABLE

Study Skills

Instructions

There are four Study Skills worksheets (p191–p194). The aim of these worksheets is to help students become better and more independent learners. The worksheets are designed to be used in class, offering a change of pace and focus for both teacher and students. You will need to photocopy one Study Skills worksheet for each student.

1 Independent learning p191

Aim

To help students become more autonomous learners by raising awareness of ways of learning English outside the classroom.

When to use and time

Use any time after lesson 1B. 15–25 minutes.

Procedure

 Ask students what the four skills are (speaking, listening, reading and writing). Students read the conversation and answer the question. Check answers with the class.

> Ana practises reading and writing.
> Luis practises speaking and listening.

2 a) Focus students on the table and tell students that these are ways to improve their English outside the classroom. Pre-teach *graded readers*, *a personal diary*, *an e-pal*, *a pen pal* and *subtitles*. Students do the exercise on their own before checking in pairs. Check answers with the class. Ask students to tell the class some of the things in the table that they often/sometimes do.

> 1 Ana keeps a diary of what she has learned, reads English-language magazines and websites, and writes to an e-pal. Luis practises English with a conversation partner.

b) Students do the exercise in pairs. Elicit ideas from students and write them on the board. Students decide which they think are the most useful ideas.

3 a)–c) Students do the exercises on their own. Remind students to think about what they do outside the classroom as well as in their lessons.

4 Put students into groups. Students compare their answers to **3a)–c)**. Ask each group to share interesting answers with the class. Also ask students to tell the class what they are planning to do outside class to improve their English.

2 Using dictionaries for pronunciation p192

Aim

To help students use phonemic transcriptions in dictionaries to check pronunciation and word stress.

When to use and time

Use any time after lesson 4D. 20–30 minutes.

Preparation

A class set of monolingual dictionaries would be useful.

Procedure

 a) Focus students on the table. Tell students that these are the phonemic symbols for all the vowel sounds (including diphthongs) in standard British English. Students work in pairs and decide how we say the sounds. Encourage students to look at the example words if they don't know the symbols. Check students' pronunciation of each sound with the class, modelling and drilling difficult sounds as necessary.

b) Students work in the same pairs and write the words in the box under the correct phonemic symbols in the table in **1a)**. Encourage students to say the words aloud to each other to help them decide which symbols they match with. Don't check answers at this stage.

c) Ask students to turn to Student's Book p159 to check their answers. Check answers with the class.

2 a) Students do the exercise on their own before checking answers in pairs. Don't check answers at this stage. Note that all these words are in **V4.2** SB p122 and **V4.4** SB p123.

b) Students do the exercise on their own. Check answers with the class.

> b)12 c)1 d)8 e)3 f)10 g)4 h)9 i)11 j)7 k)2 l)6

c) Students do the exercise in pairs. Check answers with the class.

> 2 sensible 3 determined 4 reliable 5 independent
> 6 organised 7 responsible 8 aggressive 9 enthusiastic
> 10 considerate 11 bad-tempered 12 well-behaved

3 Tell the class that the words in **bold** in sentences a) and b) have the same spelling but have different meanings and pronunciation. Students do the exercise in pairs. Ensure each pair has at least one monolingual dictionary before they begin. Check answers with the class. Model and drill the words, highlighting the pronunciation of each pair.

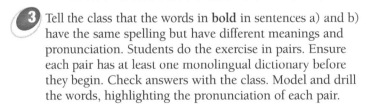

> 1b) **row** /rəʊ/ noun: a line of people or things 2a) **record** /'rekɔːd/ noun: the best, biggest, longest, etc. b) **record** /rɪ'kɔːd/ verb: store sounds on electronic equipment so you can listen to them again 3a) **minute** /'mɪnɪt/ noun: 60 seconds b) **minute** /maɪ'njuːt/ adjective: tiny 4a) **refuse** /rɪ'fjuːz/ verb: say or show that you don't want to do something b) **refuse** /'refjuːs/ noun (U) (formal): rubbish 5a) **wind** /wɪnd/ noun: air that moves across the earth b) **wind** /waɪnd/ verb: make something work by turning a key or handle 6a) **present** /'prezənt/ noun: a gift b) **present** /prɪ'zent/ verb: give something to somebody, usually at a formal ceremony

4 a) Students do the exercise on their own.

> 1 wind /wɪnd/ 2 minute /maɪˈnjuːt/ 3 row /raʊ/
> 4 present /ˈprezənt/ 5 record /rɪˈkɔːd/ 6 refuse /rɪˈfjuːz/
> 7 present /prɪˈzent/ 8 record /ˈrekɔːd/

b) Students check answers in new pairs and practise saying the words. Check answers with the class.

3 Developing reading skills p193

Aim

To raise awareness of useful reading strategies.

When to use and time

Use any time after lesson 7A. 15–25 minutes.

Procedure

1 Students discuss the questions in groups. Ask students to share interesting ideas with the class.

2 Students do the exercise on their own, then check answers in pairs. Check answers with the class. Check students understand *the gist* /dʒɪst/ (the general idea of a text) and the difference between *skimming* and *scanning*.

> a)2 b)3 c)5 d)1 e)4

3 a) Students do the exercise on their own.

b) Students compare answers in pairs. Ask students to share answers with the class.

4 a)–b) Do these exercises with the whole class. Set a time limit of 30 seconds to encourage students to read for gist.

c)–e) Students do the exercises on their own before checking in pairs. Check answers with the class. When checking **4d)**, teach the verb *stick* (*stuck, stuck*) and highlight the collocation *press a button*.

> **c)** The EasyFind 4-Way Key Tracker. About £40.
> **d) 1 rush** (v): go or do something very quickly
> **2 sticker** (n): a small piece of paper or plastic with writing or a picture on that you put on something
> **3 press** (v): push something (for example a button)
> **4 item** (n): an object/thing **5 range** (n): the distance that it is possible for something to travel
> **e) 1** It helps you to find things that you have lost.
> **2** You get a remote control and some stickers. **3** You put the stickers on the things you often lose. Press a button on the remote control and the sticker on the item makes a noise. **4** No, it doesn't.

5 a) Students do the exercise on their own.

b) Students check answers in pairs. Check answers with the class.

> a)3 b)2 c)4 d)1 e)5

4 Collocations p194

Aim

To raise awareness and provide practice of collocations.

When to use and time

Use any time after lesson 9D. 20–30 minutes.

Procedure

1 a) Check students remember what a collocation is. Students do the exercise on their own. Check answers with the class.

> 2e) 3a) 4c) 5b) 6h) 7j) 8i) 9g) 10f)

b) Focus students on the different types of collocations a)–e) and check students know what all the parts of speech mean. Students do the exercise on their own or in pairs. Check answers with the class.

> **a)** meet the deadline **b)** completely different; absolutely furious **c)** worried about; keen on **d)** sore throat; healthy diet **e)** hit single; hair dryer

2 a) Pre-teach *poetry*. Students do the exercise on their own. Check answers with the class.

> 2 very 3 house 4 bathroom 5 with 6 rock 7 heavy
> 8 make 9 of 10 doing

b) Students do the exercise on their own or in pairs. Check answers with the class.

> very tired b); semi-detached house d); en-suite bathroom d); pleased with c); rock concert e); heavy sleeper b); make friends a); scared of c); do a course a)

3 a) Focus students on the example. Students do the exercise on their own or in pairs. Check answers with the class.

> 2 medicine 3 exercise 4 on tour 5 a noise
> 6 a stomach ache

b) Students do the exercise on their own or in pairs. Check answers with the class.

> take medicine; do exercise; go on tour;
> make a noise; have a stomach ache

c) Students do the exercise in pairs. Check answers by eliciting students' answers and writing them on the board.

4 a) Students do the exercise on their own. Check answers with the class.

> 2 take 3 from 4 temperature 5 operating
> 6 painkillers/paracetamol 7 allergic

b) Students do the exercise in pairs. Finally, ask students to share interesting answers with the class.

STUDY SKILLS: INSTRUCTIONS

1 Read the conversation between two students. Which skills do Ana and Luis practise outside the classroom?

ANA   What do you do to learn English at home?

LUIS   Well, I meet a friend once a week, an English friend who wants to learn Spanish, and we speak in English for half an hour and Spanish for half an hour.

ANA   That's a great idea! How did you meet?

LUIS   I put up a notice in the university. What about you?

ANA   Well, I'm a very hard worker, you know! So I always do my homework and I keep a diary of what I learn in every lesson. It helps me remember everything we've done.

LUIS   Wow, that's good.

ANA   I also read a lot in English.

LUIS   What kinds of things do you read?

ANA   I buy English magazines like *Hello!* and read the articles about famous people. I also have an e-pal who I write to. Her name's Hannah, she's Swedish and her English is brilliant.

LUIS   How often do you write to her?

ANA   Oh, about once a week. And I also read English news websites on the Internet. The BBC website is my home page.

LUIS   You do a lot more than me. You'll probably be fluent by the end of the year!

2 **a)** Look at the table of ways to improve your English outside the classroom. Answer these questions.

1 Which things do Ana and Luis do?

2 Which things do you often/sometimes do?

reading	writing	listening	speaking
Read English-language magazines and newspapers.	Write a personal diary.	Watch English-language programmes on TV (with subtitles).	Listen to CDs and repeat what you hear.
Borrow graded readers from your school.	Keep a diary of what you have learned.	Listen to English on the Internet or the radio.	Find a conversation partner.
Visit English-language websites.	Do the writing lessons in the Reading and Writing portfolio in the **face2face** Workbook.	Watch English-language films with or without subtitles.	Use the **face2face** CD-ROM to record yourself speaking.
Read English books.	Write to e-pals, pen pals and friends from previous courses	Listen to songs in English.	Speak English to other students in the break.

b) Work in pairs. Add one more idea to each column.

3 **a)** What did you read, listen to, write or talk about in English last week? Write your answers in the table.

in the classroom	outside the classroom

b) Which of these things did you enjoy the most/least? Why?

c) Look again at the table in **2a)**. Choose two things from the table that you will try to do next week.

4 Work in groups. Compare answers to **3a)–c)**.

© Cambridge University Press 2006   **face2face** Intermediate Photocopiable

STUDY SKILLS: PHOTOCOPIABLE

2 Using dictionaries for pronunciation

1 **a)** Work in pairs. Look at the table. How do we say these phonemic symbols?

/ə/ father	/æ/ apple	/ʊ/ book	/ɒ/ on	
/ɪ/ in	/i/ happy	/e/ bed	/ʌ/ cup	
/ɜː/ her	/ɑː/ arm	/uː/ blue	/ɔː/ born	/iː/ eat
/eə/ chair	/ɪə/ near	/ʊə/ tour	/ɔɪ/ boy	
/aɪ/ nine	/eɪ/ eight	/əʊ/ go	/aʊ/ out	

b) Write the words in the box under the correct symbol in the table in **1a**).

got   easy   ago   shirt   too   could   cat   swim
any   walk   car   meet   under   mature   eye
brown   where   noisy   day   over   we're

c) Check on p159 of the Student's Book.

2 **a)** Mark the stress on these words.

1 adventurous
2 sensible
3 determined
4 reliable
5 independent
6 organised
7 responsible
8 aggressive
9 enthusiastic
10 considerate
11 bad-tempered
12 well-behaved

b) Match phonemics a)–l) to words 1–12 in **2a**).

a) /ˌɪndɪ'pendənt/ 5   g) /rɪ'laɪəbl/
b) /ˌwelbɪ'heɪvd/   h) /ɪnˌθjuːzi'æstɪk/
c) /əd'ventʃərəs/   i) /bæd'tempəd/
d) /ə'gresɪv/   j) /rɪ'spɒnsəbl/
e) /dɪ'tɜːmɪnd/   k) /'sensɪbl/
f) /kən'sɪdərət/   l) /'ɔːgənaɪzd/

c) In dictionaries the main stress in a word is usually shown with /'/ before the stressed syllable. Look at the phonemics a)–l) again in **2b**) and check your answers to **2a**).

3 Work in pairs. Use your dictionary and write the pronunciation, part of speech and definition for both uses of the words in **bold** in sentences a) and b).

1 a) I had a **row** with my best friend.
   ...*/raʊ/ noun: a loud, angry argument*...
   b) We sat in the front **row** of the cinema.

2 a) He holds the world **record** for 100 metres.

   b) He's going to **record** a new album next year.

3 a) She missed the train by one **minute**.

   b) The model animals he made were **minute**.

4 a) I **refuse** to go to that restaurant again.

   b) The lorry left a pile of **refuse** in the street.

5 a) The weather forecast said there would be strong **wind** and rain.

   b) Don't forget to **wind** the clock.

6 a) Did you get a **present** when you left your job?

   b) They're going to **present** her with a prize.

4 **a)** Fill in the gaps in these sentences. Use the words in bold in **3**.

1 I couldn't sleep last night. The _____ outside was too noisy.
2 I can't read Johanna's letter. Her writing is _____ .
3 I've never heard my parents have a _____ .
4 What was the best _____ you got for your last birthday?
5 The teacher is going to _____ us when we do the speaking exercise.
6 If you ask Michael to help you, he'll probably _____ . He's very unhelpful.
7 They're going to _____ Dr Evans with an award at this year's conference.
8 What a great race – and it's a new world _____ !

b) Work in new pairs. Check your answers to **4a**). How do you pronounce the words?

Instructions p189

3 Developing reading skills

1 Work in groups. Discuss these questions.

1 What do you read in your language?

2 Do you read in English outside class? If so, what do you read?

3 What was the last thing you read in English?

2 Match the types of reading a)–e) to reading skills 1–5.

a) ☐ read a long magazine article very quickly

b) ☐ decide whether to read an article from the title and the pictures

c) ☐ read a unit in a textbook you are studying for an exam

d) ☐ understand unknown words in a story

e) ☐ read a TV guide to find what time your favourite programme is on

1 guessing the meaning of words from the context

2 reading to get a general idea (the gist) of what a text is about (skimming)

3 predicting what a text is about before you read it

4 looking through a text quickly to find the information you want (scanning)

5 reading a text carefully for detailed understanding

3 a) Tick how you deal with words you don't know when you are reading.

1 I don't worry about them.

2 I guess the meaning of each word.

3 I underline them and look them up at the end.

4 I choose four or five important words and look them up.

b) Work in pairs. Compare answers.

4 a) Look at the picture and the title of the article. What do you think the article is about?

b) Read the article quickly. Were you correct?

c) Find the name of the product and how much it costs.

d) Find words 1–5 in the article. Can you guess what they mean?

e) Read the article again and answer questions 1–4.

1 What does the key finder do?

2 What do you get when you buy one?

3 How does it work?

4 Does the thing you've lost have to be in the house?

Where are my keys?

The remote control, your reading glasses, your mobile phone and house keys have one thing in common – they're easily lost. This always seems to happen at the worst possible moment, just as you are ¹**rushing** to catch a plane or a train, or when you're trying to get to a meeting on time.

Now you can get some electronic help and buy a key finder. The EasyFind 4-Way Key Tracker includes a hand-held remote control and some small circular ²**stickers** that you put on your keys. This new improved key finder sends a digital radio message out to the stickers. Finding the lost item is easy: ³**press** the button on the remote control and the sticker will make a noise, which tells you where the lost ⁴**item** is. This makes it much easier to find things that are lost outside, in the garden or in the street, because it has a ⁵**range** of up to 25 metres.

The EasyFind 4-Way Key Tracker costs about £40 and is in the shops now.

5 a) Match 4a)–e) to reading skills 1–5 in **2**.

b) Work in pairs. Compare answers.

Instructions p190 © Cambridge University Press 2006 **face2face** Intermediate Photocopiable

4 Collocations

1 **a)** Collocations are two or more words that often go together. Match the beginnings and endings of these sentences.

1 I've got a **sore** d)
2 I've decided to **accept**
3 Tom and I are **completely**
4 They've never had a **hit**
5 Jenny's **worried**
6 Have you seen my **hair**
7 They're not going to **meet**
8 You should eat a **healthy**
9 They've cancelled the meeting. I'm **absolutely**
10 I'm quite **keen**

a) **different**.
b) **about** her job.
c) **single**.
d) **throat**.
e) **the offer**.
f) **on** sailing.
g) **furious**.
h) **dryer**?
i) **diet**.
j) **the deadline**.

b) Match the collocations in bold in **1a)** to these patterns.

a) verb + noun *accept the offer*
b) adverb + adjective
c) adjective + preposition
d) adjective + noun
e) noun + noun

2 **a)** Choose the correct word.

1 Would you mind *making/doing* me a big **favour**?
2 I was *very/absolutely* **tired** when I got home.
3 My parents live in a **semi-detached** *flat/house*.
4 We've got a lovely **en-suite** *bathroom/bedroom*.
5 Janet was **pleased** *with/of* her exam results.
6 Have you ever been to a *rock/poetry* **concert**?
7 My husband is a very *heavy/fast* **sleeper**.
8 Ellen finds it difficult to *know/make* **friends**.
9 I didn't know you were **scared** *for/of* mice.
10 Jack didn't enjoy the **course** he was *doing/learning*.

b) Match the collocations in **2a)** to the types of collocations a)–e) in **1b)**.

do someone a favour a)

3 **a)** Cross out the word/phrase that <u>isn't</u> a collocation of the verb in **bold**.

1 **have** *a massage/a lie-in/~~dressed~~/time to relax*
2 **go** *clubbing/medicine/to exhibitions/home*
3 **make** *exercise/money/a decision/an excuse*
4 **get** *on a bus/back to sleep/into a car/on tour*
5 **do** *an exam/a noise/the housework/nothing*
6 **take** *somebody to hospital/a stomach ache/ a nap/part in something*

b) Which verbs in **3a)** collocate with the words/phrases you crossed out?

get dressed

c) Work in pairs. Think of two more words/phrases that go with the verbs in bold in **3a)**.

4 **a)** Look at the words in **bold** and complete the collocations about health.

1 Do you g*et.* **hay fever** in the summer?
2 Do you usually t............................. **antibiotics** if you get an infection?
3 Do you know anyone who **suffers** f............................. asthma?
4 When was the last time you had a **high** t............................. ?
5 Have you ever been inside an o............................. **theatre**?
6 Do you **take** p............................. when you get a headache or a migraine?
7 Are you a............................. **to** penicillin?

b) Work in pairs. Ask and answer the questions in **4a)**. Ask follow-up questions if possible.

face2face Intermediate Photocopiable   © Cambridge University Press 2006

Instructions p190

Progress Tests

Instructions

The Progress Tests (p200–p223) are designed to be used after students have completed each unit of the Student's Book. Each Progress Test checks students' knowledge of the key language areas taught in the unit. Some exercises and questions may also test students' knowledge of language taught in previous units. It is helpful for students to have done the Review section at the end of each unit before doing a Progress Test. You can also encourage students to revise for the test by reviewing the relevant Language Summary in the back of the Student's Book and by doing exercises for that unit on the CD-ROM and in the Workbook. Note that Progress Test 6 and 12 also contain a listening section.

- Allow students 40 minutes for Progress Tests 1–5 and 7–11, and 50 minutes for Progress Tests 6 and 12. You may wish to adjust this time depending on your class.

- Photocopy one test for each student. Students should do the tests on their own. You can either check the answers with the whole class at the end of the test or collect in the tests and correct them yourself. Keep a record of the test scores to help you monitor individual students' progress and for report writing at the end of the course.

- Progress Tests can also be given as homework.

Listening tests

There is a listening section in Progress Tests 6 and 12 only. The corresponding recording scripts (R6.10 and R12.8) are in the Answer Key for the tests. Both R6.10 and R12.8 have two separate sections. Focus on one section of the recording at a time. Allow students time to read through the questions for that section in the Progress Test before you start. Play that section of the recording without stopping and allow students to answer the questions. Then play the recording again without stopping. Repeat this procedure for the other section.

Answer Key and Recording Scripts

Progress Test 1 p200

1 2 visit 3 tidy up 4 have 5 go 6 have 7 chat 8 do 9 go 10 have 11 meet

2 (2 marks each) 2 How long has Eve lived/been living in her flat? 3 What is Nick watching at the moment? 4 What happened when you got home last night? 5 What does Andrew normally do at the weekend? 6 What are Tom and Ann doing now? 7 When did she start coming to this school? 8 How many cars have you had in your life? 9 Where did they go on holiday last year? 10 Who came to your party last weekend? 11 What do/did your children usually have for dinner? 12 How often did you go to the beach when you were a child?

3 2 stand/bear 3 keen 4 nerves 5 mind 6 crazy/mad 7 all 8 interested 9 really

4 2 They **aren't playing** … 3 Alice **doesn't live** … 4 **None** of my friends … 5 John **hasn't been** … 6 **No one** in my family … 7 I **don't usually** … 8 **Neither** of my sisters **has** … 9 They **haven't seen** … 10 I **didn't see** … 11 **I'm not going** …

5 (2 marks each) 2 upset 3 frustrated 4 embarrassed 5 nervous 6 glad 7 depressed 8 concerned 9 scared 10 stressed 11 shocked

6 2 with 3 with 4 about 5 by 6 with 7 at 8 with 9 of 10 with 11 about

7 (2 marks each) 3 didn't we 4 Yes, we did 5 No, I haven't 6 doesn't he 7 Yes, he does 8 have they 9 Yes, they have 10 aren't they 11 No, they aren't 12 aren't I

Progress Test 2 p202

1 2 time 3 meet/hit 4 working 5 work/do 6 time 7 hours 8 under 9 home 10 spending

2 2 was able to 3 ought to 4 mustn't 5 weren't allowed to 6 should 7 are supposed to 8 doesn't have to 9 can 10 have to 11 aren't allowed to; can

3 2 freezer 3 grill; frying pan 4 baking 5 microwave 6 boils; saucepan 7 fridge 8 blender 9 oven

4 2 broccoli 3 lamb 4 carrots 5 peas 6 an aubergine 7 courgettes 8 beans 9 a rubbish bin 10 a toaster

5 (2 marks each) 2 'm not doing 3 Does … know 4 is growing 5 Do … like 6 isn't eating 7 spend 8 taste 9 Is … cooking 10 do … weigh

6 2 dirty 3 exhausted/shattered 4 delicious 5 happy 6 fascinated 7 huge/enormous 8 terrified 9 good 10 furious 11 beautiful 12 impossible 13 freezing 14 small 15 boiling

7 2 wide 3 asleep 4 light 5 nap 6 off 7 insomnia 8 fast

8 2 a bit of a problem 3 how awful 4 why you're upset 5 have you tried 6 I've tried that 7 why don't you 8 it's worth a try 9 you ought to 10 a good idea 11 I'd ask 12 might try that

9 2 You shouldn't ~~to~~ work … 3 ✓ 4 … was **absolutely** brilliant/very **good**. 5 … a great **cook**. 6 ✓ 7 ✓ 8 … to **anyone** at the party. 9 ✓ 10 … fed up **with** my job. 11 I **didn't have to** ~~to~~ get up …. 12 … places **have you** been to?

Progress Test 3 p204

1 (2 marks each) 2 deal with 3 set off 4 put up with 5 brought … back 6 get around 7 see … off 8 looking forward to 9 check out of 10 getting back; pick … up

2 2 get 3 went on 4 going on 5 get 6 get 7 travels 8 gone/been on 9 travelled 10 to go on 11 travel

3 (2 marks each) 2 studied 3 became 4 has been 5 started 6 has also appeared 7 made 8 has presented 9 made 10 has visited 11 have followed

4 2 directed 3 since 4 known 5 I've been living 6 for 7 had 8 read

5 2 ever 3 just 4 yet 5 recently 6 never 7 the second time 8 ago 9 this evening 10 before

6 2 healthy 3 laziness 4 honesty 5 kindness 6 knowledgeable 7 comfortable 8 adventurous 9 fame 10 musical 11 natural 12 confidence 13 popularity

7 2 really must 3 good to know 4 it's worth 5 the best way 6 best to take 7 sounds good 8 bother 9 what about 10 you should definitely 11 you know any 12 I wouldn't recommend 13 that's really useful

8 2 ... your **trip/journey** to Scotland? 3 ... India **for** three months. 4 ✓ 5 ... time I**'ve eaten** fish ... 6 ... very **touristy** town. 7 ✓ 8 ✓ 9 You **don't have to** wear ... 10 ... last year, **didn't** you? 11 ✓

Progress Test 4 p206

1 2 release 3 appear 4 done 5 see 6 have 7 going 8 had 9 been

2 (2 marks each) 2 were touring 3 was waiting 4 threw; was walking 5 Did ... see 6 was sleeping 7 interviewed; were getting 8 were ... doing

3 (2 marks each) 2 Did ... use to 3 didn't use to 4 used to 5 used to

4 2 Reliable 3 Ambitious 4 Generous 5 Sensible 6 Brave 7 Mean 8 Stubborn 9 Confident 10 Practical 11 Arrogant 12 Sensitive 13 Aggressive 14 Enthusiastic 15 Rude 16 Violent 17 Spoilt

5 2 had ever got 3 fell 4 realised 5 had broken 6 needed 7 had already used 8 hadn't brought 9 tried 10 had to 11 was 12 had died 13 walked 14 wasn't 15 had fallen 16 didn't know 17 wasn't able to 18 found 19 made 20 reached 21 had already burned

6 2 can 3 quite 4 times 5 a few 6 to laugh 7 on 8 bit 9 speaking 10 considerate 11 rather

7 (2 marks each) 2 Where were you going when you had the accident? 3 How many books had he written by the time he retired? 4 Where did aspirin come from originally? 5 What was the doctor doing at 10 p.m.? 6 How long have you been waiting at this bus stop?

8 2 ✓ 3 ... TV **when** the phone ... 4 ✓ 5 I **went** to my sister's wedding ... 6 ... put up **with** the noise. 7 ... bother **going** to ... 8 ✓ 9 ... to **seeing** you. 10 ... here **for** three years. 11 John's **gone** to ...

Progress Test 5 p208

1 2 a cottage 3 a terraced house 4 a bungalow 5 a semi-detached house 6 a detached house

2 2 take out 3 sort out 4 clear out 5 go through; throw away 6 tidy up; put away 7 give ... away

3 2 as 3 most 4 far/much 5 bit/little 6 less 7 least 8 as/so 9 than 10 the

4 (2 marks each) 2 I'm less adventurous than John. 3 I'm as tall as Julia. 4 Jo's the nicest person/woman I know. 5 Your mobile phone is different from/to mine. 6 My computer is similar to his. 7 My handwriting is worse than yours. 8 Leeds Castle is the most beautiful castle in England.

5 (2 marks each) 2 it'll be 3 won't take 4 They're bringing 5 I'll probably put 6 it's going to fit 7 I'll have to 8 going to get 9 you'll definitely need 10 I'm playing 11 I'll call

6 2 stuff 3 do you mean 4 you use it when 5 what's it called 6 can I help you 7 the word for them 8 made of 9 they've got 10 a thing for 11 can't remember what 12 what you're looking for

7 2 have 3 to help 4 to play 5 washing 6 get up 7 to learn 8 rising 9 to come 10 work 11 start 12 to go 13 try 14 to do 15 going 16 to be

8 2 rubber 3 cardboard 4 cotton 5 wood 6 glass 7 metal/steel 8 wool 9 leather

9 2 I live **on** the ... 3 It's **within** walking ... 4 ✓ 5 ... him **to** go home. 6 ✓ 7 They didn't **use** to live ... 8 ... tend **to be** quite noisy. 9 ✓ 10 ... the football **live**. 11 ✓

Progress Test 6 p210

R6.10 See p195 for Listening Test instructions.

1

a) ROB What are you doing on Saturday night, Jill? You usually go clubbing, don't you?

JILL Yes, I do, but unfortunately, I've hurt my foot, so that's no good. I should really tidy up the flat, but I think I'm going to have a quiet night in and watch an old film instead.

b) JANE Have you found a new place to live yet, Steve?

STEVE We're still looking, actually. My wife fell in love with an old cottage we saw last week. It was gorgeous, but it needed a lot of repairs. Then this morning we saw a terraced house, which was tiny but in a good neighbourhood, and a larger semi-detached house in the suburbs. Um, I preferred the smaller one, I think.

c) JAN I don't know what to get Mum for her birthday. I was thinking of buying her some perfume. What do you think?

MAY Well, she loves things that smell nice, but isn't that what you always get her?

J Um, I suppose it is. I saw a lovely cat in the market made of wood that she might like. Or there was also a really nice corkscrew that looked easy to use.

M That sounds good. You know how she likes practical things.

J Right. I'll get that then.

d) MUM Tim, can you give me a hand making dinner?

TIM OK. What do you want me to do?

M First, can you get some vegetables out of the fridge?

T There are a couple of aubergines. I love those.

M Yes, I know, but they'll take too long to cook. Are there any peppers?

T Um … oh yes, there are some here at the back.

M They'll be fine then, thanks.

T And what about these courgettes?

M Let's keep those to have with the roast lamb tomorrow.

2

Hi there, and welcome to the programme. Firstly, let me give you some information I've just received about the Beddington Bridge Music Festival, which takes place every year. Regular fans will remember that the festival happens over the third weekend of August – Friday to Sunday – near the village of Beddington. This year, though, it's going to start on the Thursday, which will give people the chance to have even more fun. There's a range of tickets to suit everyone, from one-day visitors to people who want to stay for the whole long weekend. You should book early because tickets are 30% off until the 30th June. From the 1st July until the festival starts on the 22nd August it will be full-price tickets only. This is a family-friendly event, so children under 16 are allowed in for half price and children below the age of 12 can go in free. Most festival-goers camp in the fields on the festival site, although there's some accommodation available in the nearby villages. Rooms tend to be quite expensive during festival time though, costing at least £50 per person. If you're driving there, there's a parking fee of £27 per car, or £35 if you have a van, for however long you stay. You can also get there easily by public transport – the nearest station is about 4 miles away. Oh, and motorbikes can park for free. Hot and cold food and drink are available on the festival site of course, and don't forget you can also get fantastic home-cooked breakfasts in the main square in the village. Anyway for more information check out the website, which is www.beddingtonfestival.com.

1 (2 marks each) a)2 b)1 c)1 d)3

2 (2 marks each) 2 third 3 Thursday 4 30th June 5 12 6 £35 7 motorbike 8 (main) square

3 2 make 3 making 4 does 5 do 6 make 7 making 8 done 9 makes 10 made 11 doing 12 made 13 doing

4 2 until 3 unless 4 as soon as 5 if 6 before 7 in case

5 2 herself 3 ourselves 4 themselves 5 myself 6 yourself/yourselves 7 itself 8 ourselves

6 (2 marks each) 2 don't leave; 'll miss 3 won't be able to; book 4 'll tidy up; do 5 don't do; put 6 'll call; 'm 7 want; don't go 8 'll take; 's 9 don't know; ask 10 Will … help; buy 11 won't move; gets

7 2 pick 3 fortunate 4 sure 5 pleasant 6 concerned 7 scared 8 satisfied 9 chat 10 acting 11 glad 12 huge 13 by chance 14 awful

8 2 I'm not sure I agree 3 can I say 4 go ahead 5 do you mind 6 can I just finish 7 of course 8 what's your opinion 9 absolutely 10 sure about that 11 that may be true

9 2 … text **each other** every day. 3 ✓ 4 **Do** you **agree** with me? 5 We must ~~to~~ see … 6 … much **confidence**. 7 ✓ 8 … big **as** yours. 9 ✓ 10 … sister **off** at … 11 ✓

Progress Test 7 p212

1 2 attachment 3 online 4 link 5 back-up copy 6 delete 7 click on 8 log on 9 download 10 create 11 password 12 broadband 13 icon 14 folder 15 keyboard 16 speakers

2 (2 marks each) 2 Mark's useless at playing football. 3 I find fixing problems on my computer very easy. 4 Rachel is good at speaking French. 5 I've no idea how to use a computer. 6 Robin hasn't (got) a clue how to play chess. 7 I wasn't able to swim when I was five. 8 Yolanda's no good at making cakes. 9 I managed to pass my exams (but they were very difficult).

3 (2 marks each) 2 would … visit; had 3 would be; lived 4 didn't have; 'd go 5 didn't work; 'd move 6 could; 'd be able to 7 was/were; 'd save 8 bought; 'd be 9 Would … do; didn't have 10 not be; wasn't/weren't

4 2 a dishwasher 3 a webcam 4 a hair dryer 5 central heating 6 a washing machine 7 a hand-held computer 8 an MP3 player 9 a GPS/sat nav 10 a scanner 11 a printer 12 a monitor

5 2 the 3 – 4 a 5 a 6 the 7 – 8 – 9 the 10 a 11 – 12 the 13 the 14 the 15 the 16 – 17 an 18 The 19 – 20 the 21 –

6 (2 marks each) 2 Have you any idea if John is coming to the meeting? 3 Do you think we should pick him up from the station? 4 Could you tell me whether Harry has left me a message? 5 Do you know what time the next train is going to arrive? 6 Can you tell me when Sarah will be back from lunch?

7 2 I'll **do** the shopping … 3 ✓ 4 … replied **to** the … 5 ✓ 6 … the **most** expensive … 7 … by **myself**. 8 … for **cleaning** computers. 9 … when **I** see it. 10 ✓ 11 I've **had** this …

Progress Test 8 p214

1 2 tornado 3 fog 4 lightning 5 hurricane 6 flood 7 shower 8 thunder 9 gale 10 heat wave 11 humid 12 freezing

2 2 was reported 3 have been recorded 4 will affect 5 are rising 6 should be taught 7 are affected 8 happened 9 are being kept 10 must be collected 11 will lose

3 (2 marks each) 2 The old man was taken to hospital by Mrs Burrows. 3 The virus writer hasn't been arrested yet. 4 A lot can be done to slow down global warming. 5 A number of men are being questioned (by the police). 6 Bananas are grown in the Caribbean. 7 This medicine must be taken twice a day. 8 A lot of countries are going to be affected by rising sea levels. 9 A baby was found outside the hospital (by a cleaner). 10 All students will be tested (by the school) at the end of term 11 Computers could be used instead of teachers in the future.

4 (2 marks each) 2 a bag/packet of crisps 3 a tin of cat food 4 a bottle of tomato ketchup 5 a packet of biscuits 6 a jar of (strawberry) jam

5 2 too much 3 a few 4 hardly any 5 loads of 6 no; enough 7 any 8 little

6 2 impatient 3 irresponsible 4 unhelpful 5 impossible 6 disorganised 7 unsuccessful 8 dishonest 9 impolite 10 inconsiderate

7 2 overcharge 3 overpaid 4 reuse 5 underestimate 6 recharge 7 painless 8 underused 9 careful

8 2 if I were you 3 in case 4 good idea 5 make sure 6 what should we do 7 you'd better 8 don't forget 9 do you think it's a good idea 10 shouldn't 11 whatever you do 12 be careful 13 don't 14 or else 15 that's really useful

9 2 ... better **recycle** those ... 3 ... out **for** bears ... 4 ... plenty **of** food ... 5 ✓ 6 ... when the film **starts**? 7 ✓ 8 ... to ~~the~~ prison ... 9 ... at **playing** tennis. 10 ✓ 11 I managed **to** find ...

Progress Test 9 p216

1 2 where 3 whose 4 that 5 where 6 that 7 that 8 where 9 whose 10 when 11 who

2 (2 marks each) 2 have been arrested 3 has been taken 4 have protested 5 has called off 6 has been accepted 7 has been published 8 has been carried out 9 have met 10 has been discovered 11 has suffered

3 (2 marks each) 2 John has just discovered the cause of his allergy. 3 His father has already been taken to hospital. 4 Hasn't she been seen by the specialist yet? 5 We've already been in the A&E department for six hours. 6 The doctor hasn't operated on the boy's leg yet. 7 The man who stole the painting still hasn't been arrested.

4 2 Although 3 in spite of 4 However 5 despite 6 even though 7 in spite of

5 (2 marks each) 2 Tania didn't speak very good French even though she had lived in Paris for a year. 3 I couldn't sleep despite being very tired. 4 We went out for a walk in spite of the snow. 5 I really enjoyed the party although there weren't many people there. 6 I've just been told by my doctor that I need an operation.

6 2 blocked-up nose 3 migraine 4 antibiotics 5 rash 6 food poisoning 7 surgeon 8 infection 9 wheeze 10 surgery 11 hay fever 12 ward 13 operating theatre 14 paracetamol 15 sneeze 16 throw up

7 2 hurts 3 symptoms 4 sick 5 temperature 6 prescription 7 should I take it 8 come back 9 haven't been feeling 10 stop coughing 11 throat 12 allergic to 13 how long have you been 14 have a look 15 pills 16 appointment

8 2 ✓ 3 ... do, **don't** go ... 4 ✓ 5 It's very **foggy** outside. 6 California **was** hit ... 7 ... how **to do** this. 8 ... where **Ian has** gone? 9 ... as **healthy** as ... 10 ✓ 11 ✓ 12 ... let me ~~to~~ stay ... 13 ✓

Progress Test 10 p218

1 2 went up 3 come up with 4 get out of 5 came across 6 pointed out 7 fell out 8 get over 9 split up 10 put off 11 look up

2 (2 marks each) 2 I think we should put it off for a week. 3 I couldn't get out of taking the exam. 4 I've never come across it before. 5 Why didn't you point it out to her? 6 We split up last year and I still haven't got over it. 7 She can't put up with the noise. 8 I didn't want to point it out to him but Tom was wrong.

3 2 jewellery 3 plain shirt 4 ponytail 5 going bald 6 striped tie 7 curly hair 8 flowery dress 9 shoulder-length hair 10 light ... jacket 11 dark ... jacket 12 glasses

4 (2 marks each) 2 was supposed to tidy up 3 were going to drive 4 was supposed to meet 5 were going to move 6 was going to give up 7 were supposed to call

5 2 with 3 back 4 from 5 in 6 in 7 with 8 of 9 with 10 up 11 with 12 in 13 up

6 (2 marks each) 2 can't be 3 must be having 4 must be coming 5 can't be 6 must speak 7 might be sleeping; may have 8 can't be watching; might be doing

7 2 ahead 3 I could 4 of course 5 open 6 not at all 7 mind 8 opened 9 I'd rather you didn't 10 can 11 yourself 12 may I 13 I'm afraid

8 2 ... Tom **borrows** your bike? 3 ✓ 4 ... well **despite/in spite of** the noise./... well although **it was noisy**. 5 He **still hasn't** called me. 6 ✓ 7 ✓ 8 ... person **who/that** hit me. 9 keep **getting** ... 10 ... is **incorrect**. 11 ✓ 12 ... you, **I'd/I wouldn't** go home.

Progress Test 11 p220

1 (2 marks each) 2 temporary 3 stressful 4 part-time 5 rewarding 6 repetitive 7 dull 8 glamorous 9 challenging 10 demanding

2 (2 marks each) 2 work 3 dealing with 4 organises 5 work 6 's/has been 7 'll/will run/are going to run 8 's/is going (to go) 9 had

3 (2 marks each) 2 Bill (that) there was going to be 3 (that) he couldn't visit 4 Bill (that) he wouldn't be able to go 5 (that) he wanted to have 6 Bill (that) Alice (had) visited 7 Joe (that) she hadn't talked to him 8 (that) she was getting 9 (that) he had to go

4 (2 marks each) 2 if/whether I had seen/saw Marian at the concert. 3 which other countries Fred had visited. 4 (me) if I could help her with the gardening/me to help her with the gardening. 5 who was taking Susan to the cinema. 6 how the children would get home after the party. 7 (me) if I had to go to London tomorow.

5 (2 marks each) 2 offered to give me a lift to the station. 3 suggested going to the cinema. 4 threatened to tell the police if I/he/she called her again. 5 reminded Jo to phone the bank. 6 warned Ian not to go in the park at night. 7 invited Sue to go to a party. 8 promised to give the money back. 9 refused to go to bed. 10 admitted he stole/had stolen the lady's bag.

6 2 catch 3 spelled 4 mean 5 talking about 6 sorry
7 could you say 8 can you give 9 get all 10 you give
11 is that

7 2 ✓ 3 ... responsible **for** the ... 4 ... me **not to** go ...
5 ... me **to** come ... 6 ✓ 7 ✓ 8 I looked **it up** on ...
9 ... might **be watching** TV ... 10 That **can't** be ... 11 ✓

Progress Test 12 p222

R12.8 See p195 for Listening Test instructions.

1
INTERVIEWER We're very pleased to welcome on *Arts Today* the actor Colin Waring.

COLIN Hello.

I Firstly, how did you become interested in acting?

C Well, my mother took me to the theatre when I was ten, to see a Shakespeare play that we were studying in English at school. That didn't really attract me though – the language was too old-fashioned, I suppose. Then one of my friends was in a local play and we all went along to watch. That was when I started thinking it might be something I could do too.

I Did you enjoy drama school?

C I loved it. Some of the teachers were very well-known actors and we were all a bit frightened of them! The most useful thing was being able to go and see all the new plays in London – we often got free tickets and I learned so much that way. The other students were great too and I made a lot of good friends there.

I What was your first acting job?

C Well, after drama school I worked part-time in a restaurant called The Rendezvous, you know, like actors do. Then I auditioned for a part in a play called *Secret Lives*, but I didn't get that, sadly. Then I was chosen to play a waiter in *Table for Two*, you know, the John Frank musical.

I You always say your first love is the theatre. Why is that?

C A lot of actors say it's the contact with a live audience, and that *is* exciting of course. But the thing I find most fascinating is that you're part of something that grows and changes – a play is never the same two nights in a row. Some people like playing their part in the same way every night, but I'd get rather fed up with that.

I Finally, any plans for the future?

C Well, I was offered a part in a new American detective film, but I didn't want to be away from home for that long. Then there's a new play directed by Ian Scott, but that would mean going on tour. So I'm going to do a TV serial, set near here – less travelling!

I Colin, thank you for talking to us.

C Thank you.

2
MARIE You're looking very well, Paul, have you had a holiday?

PAUL No, but I've just come back from a health retreat. I lived on just fruit and vegetable juice for a week.

M Wow! Didn't you feel hungry?

P Actually it wasn't too bad. Um, on Day 1, things were OK. There was a lot to do so I didn't notice I was hungry. I felt a lot worse the next day – bad headache and so on. After that it was great, though.

M So would you recommend going to a place like that?

P Oh yes, definitely. Some people do it regularly, every six months or so and, er, I'm thinking of doing it again in March. Anyway, you always look healthy. What are your tips?

M Well number one – don't miss breakfast. It's the most important meal of the day. I always have fruit, yogurt, that kind of thing.

P I tend to have a cooked breakfast – you know, eggs, beans, toast, sausages and then I can work without stopping until lunchtime.

M Wow, that's a lot. I hope you think about the quality of your food. I always buy organic eggs, vegetables and bread. I know they're more expensive, but I feel you get what you pay for.

P Are you a vegetarian?

M Well, when I was younger, I thought it was the right thing to do, both for my health and to protect animals. But now I eat a bit of everything – meat and fish included.

P Mm. So what sort of food do you prefer if you're eating out?

M It depends what I'm doing and who I'm with. I love spicy food, so Indian or Thai are always good choices.

P They're delicious, but a bit too hot for me. If I have the choice I go to my favourite restaurant just round the corner from my flat which serves great pasta – and it's quite cheap too.

M Sounds good to me!

1 (2 marks each) 1c) 2b) 3a) 4c) 5b)

2 (2 marks each) 1T 2T 3F 4T 5F 6F

3 2 into 3 going/coming 4 up 5 at 6 with 7 to
8 around/out 9 bothered 10 of 11 broke

4 2 had 3 were going/could go 4 didn't have to 5 could
6 were eating 7 didn't live 8 were 9 knew 10 had

5 2 enjoyable 3 pollute 4 care 5 disappointment
6 entertaining 7 creative 8 confusion 9 dependable
10 employ 11 protective 12 reservation

6 (2 marks each) 2 'll/'re going to get lost 3 getting into
trouble 4 get to know 5 got fed up with 6 'll get
something to eat 7 gets excited 8 'd/would get better
9 got rid of 10 getting on with 11 to get in touch with

7 (2 marks each) 2 hadn't left; 'd/would have gone
3 wouldn't have missed; 'd/had woken up 4 would have
become; hadn't failed 5 'd/had warned; wouldn't have
said 6 hadn't had; wouldn't have met 7 'd/would have
called; 'd/had had

8 2 few 3 in case 4 Although 5 going 6 gone 7 since
8 to tell 9 mustn't

9 2 She's **in** charge ... 3 He said ~~me~~ he .../He **told** me ...
4 ✓ 5 ... where **I lived**. 6 ... threatened **to take** me ...
7 ✓ 8 ... worth **visiting**. 9 ✓

Name _____ Score [100]

 1 Fill in the gaps with these verbs. You can use the verbs more than once.

| do chat visit tidy up have go meet |

1 I often _do_ some gardening at the weekend.
2 We usually _____ my grandmother on Sundays.
3 When did you last _____ the flat?
4 I think I'll _____ a quiet night in.
5 We often _____ clubbing with friends.
6 I never _____ a lie-in on Saturday mornings.
7 My sister and I often _____ to people online.
8 I really need to _____ some exercise.
9 We hardly ever _____ to exhibitions.
10 I sometimes _____ friends round for dinner.
11 Sam's going to _____ up with some friends.

[10]

 2 Make questions with these words.

1 Why / you / learn / English / this school?
   Why are you learning English at this school?
2 How long / Eve / live / her flat?
   ----
3 What / Nick / watch / at the moment?
   ----
4 What / happen / when you / get / home last night?
   ----
5 What / Andrew normally / do / the weekend?
   ----
6 What / Tom and Ann / do / now?
   ----
7 When / she / start / coming / this school?
   ----
8 How many cars / you / have / in your life?
   ----
9 Where / they / go / holiday last year?
   ----
10 Who / come / your party last weekend?
   ----
11 What / your children usually / have / dinner?
   ----
12 How often / go / the beach when / be / child?
   ----

[22]

3 Fill in the gaps with one word.

1 He loves his new MP3 player. He thinks it's _brilliant_ .
2 Tania hates mobile phone ring tones. She just can't _____ them.
3 I'm very _____ on cooking. It's a great way to relax.
4 Listening to other people's conversations really gets on my _____ .
5 Computer games are OK, I suppose. I don't _____ them.
6 My mum doesn't like loud music. It drives her _____ .
7 My sister loves exhibitions, but I don't like them at _____ .
8 I'm very _____ in sailing.
9 Janet _____ loves watching her children sleep.

[8]

4 Make these sentences negative by changing the words/phrases in **bold**.

1 I **like** watching sport on TV.
   I don't like watching sport on TV.
2 They**'re playing** tennis at the moment.
   ----
3 Alice **lives** with her parents.
   ----
4 **All** of my friends can drive.
   ----
5 John**'s been** to Italy before.
   ----
6 **Everyone** in my family likes football.
   ----
7 I **usually** go out on Friday evenings.
   ----
8 **Both** of my sisters **have** a car.
   ----
9 They**'ve seen** him before.
   ----
10 I **saw** Rupert last night.
   ----
11 I**'m going** out tonight.
   ----

[10]

⑤ Complete these adjectives.

1 I always feel extremely r*elaxed* after I've been swimming.

2 Wendy was u＿＿＿＿＿＿＿ about the news. She was crying after she heard it.

3 Rosie feels fr＿＿＿＿＿＿＿ when her boss doesn't listen to her.

4 He felt e＿＿＿＿＿＿＿ when my brother got angry and shouted at everyone.

5 Isabel is quite n＿＿＿＿＿＿＿ about the interview.

6 I'm very g＿＿＿＿＿＿＿ you all enjoyed the meal.

7 Edward was very d＿＿＿＿＿＿＿ when he heard that he didn't get the job.

8 Is everything OK, son? Your mother and I are quite c＿＿＿＿＿＿＿ about you.

9 After watching that horror film I was so s＿＿＿＿＿＿＿ I couldn't sleep.

10 Kate gets very s＿＿＿＿＿＿＿ when she has too much to do. She should calm down a bit.

11 I was sh＿＿＿＿＿＿＿ to hear that you lost your job.

[20]

⑥ Choose the correct word.

1 My cousin George is really good (at)/with/by football.

2 Veronica's getting fed up *for/with/by* working at the weekend.

3 Jonathan's boss was quite angry *with/about/on* him during the meeting.

4 My granddaughter is very worried *for/on/about* her driving test.

5 We were very surprised *of/on/by* the letter we received yesterday.

6 I don't think Joanne's very satisfied *with/on/at* her new mobile.

7 My brother is very bad *for/of/at* maths.

8 Dave is bored *for/about/with* his new course.

9 Tim's daughter is frightened *of/from/about* the dark.

10 My English teacher was very pleased *of/on/with* my test results.

11 We were really angry *with/by/about* what happened.

[10]

⑦ Read this conversation at a barbecue. Fill in the gaps with a question tag or a short answer.

A Hello. It's Caroline, [1] *isn't it* ?

B ✓ [2] *Yes, it is* . How are you?

A I'm fine, thank you. We met last summer, [3] ＿＿＿＿＿＿＿ ?

B ✓ [4] ＿＿＿＿＿＿＿ . It was at Steve's party, I think.

A That's right. Have you seen him recently?

B ✗ [5] ＿＿＿＿＿＿＿ . He's at university in Edinburgh.

A That's right. I remember now. He studies medicine, [6] ＿＿＿＿＿＿＿ ?

B ✓ [7] ＿＿＿＿＿＿＿ . He's in his second year. He's really enjoying it.

A What about his brothers? They haven't left school yet, [8] ＿＿＿＿＿＿＿ ?

B ✓ [9] ＿＿＿＿＿＿＿ , actually. They're working abroad.

A Oh yes, I remember. They're teaching English in Japan, [10] ＿＿＿＿＿＿＿ ?

B ✗ [11] ＿＿＿＿＿＿＿ , actually. They're working in Argentina now.

A Really? How interesting. Oh dear, I'm asking a lot of questions, [12] ＿＿＿＿＿＿＿ ? Tell me about yourself. What do you do?

[20]

Name _____ Score [100]

1 Fill in the gaps with the correct word.

1 Chris _is_ a workaholic. He never stops!
2 She hardly ever takes _____ off work.
3 I worked all night to _____ my deadline.
4 They have very good _____ conditions.
5 Nurses often have to _____ overtime.
6 Rob doesn't have enough _____ to relax.
7 My sister works very long _____ .
8 We're _____ a lot of pressure at work.
9 I always take work _____ in the evenings.
10 Jo is _____ a lot of time at work these days.

[9]

2 Choose the correct words.

1 I (must)/can't leave now or I'll miss my train.
2 My sister is very bright. She *was able to/can* read when she was three.
3 I know I *am allowed to/ought to* leave work earlier and relax more.
4 No one knows about this yet, so you *mustn't/don't have to* tell anyone.
5 Last year we *didn't have to/weren't allowed to* take more than two weeks' holiday in the summer.
6 You are working too hard. You *should/are able to* have a holiday.
7 We *can't/are supposed to* take an hour for lunch, but my boss takes a lot longer than that.
8 Sheila *doesn't have to/mustn't* go to London because the meeting is cancelled.
9 My brother *has to/can* drive to work now he's passed his driving test.
10 Do you *have to/must* work every weekend?
11 You *aren't allowed to/must* send personal emails at work. You *can/shouldn't* only send work emails.

[11]

3 Complete these words for ways of cooking and things in the kitchen.

1 We usually have r_oast_ chicken on Sundays.
2 It's useful to have a f_____ because you can keep food in it for months.
3 It's healthier to cook sausages under the g_____ , not in a f_____ p_____ .
4 My grandmother loves b_____ cakes and biscuits.
5 A lot of people have a m_____ because you can heat things up in it very quickly.
6 When the water b_____ , put the pasta in the s_____ .
7 Put that bottle of lemonade in the f_____ to keep it cold.
8 It's really quick to make soup in a b_____ .
9 Don't forget to put the chicken in the o_____ .

[10]

4 Write the words.

1 _beef_
2 _____
3 _____
4 _____
5 _____
6 _____
7 _____
8 _____
9 _____
10 _____

[9]

5 Put the verbs in brackets in the correct form of the Present Simple or the Present Continuous.

1 Many people _don't have_ (not have) time to cook.
2 I _____ (not do) anything at the moment. How can I help you?
3 _____ your husband _____ (know) how to cook pasta?

Answer Key p195

4 The international market for ready meals
_____ (grow) rapidly.

5 _____ you _____ (like) the
mushroom pizza? I made it myself.

6 Steve _____ (not eat) chips
at the moment because he's on a diet.

7 I _____ (spend) 20 minutes
every day cooking my main meal.

8 These vegetables _____
(taste) delicious.

9 _____ your mother _____ (cook)
soup? It smells wonderful.

10 How much _____ you _____
(weigh)?

[ ] 18

6 Complete the table of gradable and strong adjectives.

	gradable adjectives	strong adjectives
1	bad	*terrible*
2		filthy
3	tired	
4	tasty	
5		delighted
6	interested	
7	big	
8	frightened	
9		fantastic
10	angry	
11		gorgeous
12	difficult	
13	cold	
14		tiny
15	hot	

[ ] 14

7 Choose the correct word.

1 Do you remember your (dreams)/sleep?

2 The children are fast/wide awake.

3 I fell sleep/asleep on the train.

4 Tom is a very light/fast sleeper.

5 Gabi usally takes a nap/doze after lunch.

6 I dozed off/out in front of the TV.

7 When I have nightmares/insomnia, I don't sleep a wink.

8 Are the children fall/fast asleep?

[ ] 7

8 Fill in the gaps in the conversation with these words and phrases.

the matter   a good idea   have you tried
why you're upset   it's worth a try   I'd ask
why don't you   might try that   a bit of a problem
how awful   I've tried that   you ought to

JOHN   You look terrible, Lucy. What's [1] _the matter_ ?
LUCY   I've got [2] _____ . I think I'm
        going to lose my job.
JOHN   Oh no, [3] _____ ! What happened?
LUCY   My boss told me that he's disappointed with
        my work.
JOHN   Oh, dear. I can see [4] _____ .
        Are you working hard at the moment?
LUCY   Well, Mum's ill and I've had to have a few
        days off.
JOHN   So [5] _____ telling your boss
        about your mum?
LUCY   [6] _____ , but he doesn't listen.
JOHN   Hmm, [7] _____ write him a letter?
LUCY   Well, [8] _____ , I guess.
JOHN   Maybe [9] _____ give it to him
        on Friday so he can think about it over the
        weekend.
LUCY   Yes, that's [10] _____ .
JOHN   Also [11] _____ to talk to him
        about it on Monday.
LUCY   I [12] _____ . Thanks, John.

[ ] 11

9 Tick the correct sentences. Change the incorrect sentences.

                is doing
1 My sister ~~does~~ a cooking course at the moment.

2 You shouldn't to work too hard.

3 Our last exam was incredibly difficult.

4 That film was very brilliant.

5 My husband's a great cooker.

6 You've been to Chile, haven't you?

7 That music is getting on my nerves.

8 I didn't talk to no one at the party.

9 I can't stand washing up.

10 I'm really fed up of my job.

11 I hadn't to get up early yesterday because
   it was Sunday.

12 How many places you have been to?

[ ] 11

Name ⎯⎯⎯⎯⎯⎯⎯⎯⎯⎯⎯⎯⎯⎯⎯⎯⎯⎯⎯⎯ Score [100]

1 Complete the phrasal verbs.

1 I haven't c*hecked into* the hotel yet.

2 In my job I have to d⎯⎯⎯⎯ ⎯⎯⎯⎯ a lot of difficult customers.

3 Our flight was at 6 a.m., so we s⎯⎯⎯⎯ ⎯⎯⎯⎯ very early in the morning.

4 I can't p⎯⎯⎯⎯ ⎯⎯⎯⎯ ⎯⎯⎯⎯ the noise any longer. It's driving me crazy.

5 My sister b⎯⎯⎯⎯ me ⎯⎯⎯⎯ this little red bus from London as a souvenir.

6 The best way to g⎯⎯⎯⎯ a⎯⎯⎯⎯ Scotland is to hire a car.

7 When I flew to Australia, my parents came to the airport to s⎯⎯⎯⎯ me ⎯⎯⎯⎯ .

8 I'm really l⎯⎯⎯⎯ ⎯⎯⎯⎯ ⎯⎯⎯⎯ going on holiday next week.

9 You need to c⎯⎯⎯⎯ ⎯⎯⎯⎯ ⎯⎯⎯⎯ the hotel before midday.

10 Henry is g⎯⎯⎯⎯ ⎯⎯⎯⎯ from London at 7.30. Can you go and p⎯⎯⎯⎯ him ⎯⎯⎯⎯ from the station?

[20]

2 Fill in the gaps with the correct form of *travel*, *get* and *go on*.

1 I usually _*travel*_ light.

2 Tom and Meg should ⎯⎯⎯⎯ here by 6.30.

3 Last year I ⎯⎯⎯⎯ lots of business trips.

4 My parents are ⎯⎯⎯⎯ a Caribbean cruise next month.

5 We've missed the last bus. Let's ⎯⎯⎯⎯ a taxi home.

6 Be careful when you ⎯⎯⎯⎯ out of the car.

7 My boss always ⎯⎯⎯⎯ first class.

8 Have you ever ⎯⎯⎯⎯ a guided tour?

9 I ⎯⎯⎯⎯ around Brazil on my own last year.

10 I wouldn't like ⎯⎯⎯⎯ a package holiday.

11 They're business partners, but they always ⎯⎯⎯⎯ separately when they go to conferences abroad.

[10]

3 Read about Michael Palin. Put the verbs in brackets in the Present Perfect Simple or the Past Simple.

Michael Palin

Michael Palin, the British comedian and television presenter, [1] _was_ (be) born in 1943 in Sheffield. After leaving school he [2] ⎯⎯⎯⎯ (study) history at the University of Oxford. He first [3] ⎯⎯⎯⎯ (become) famous for his work in the comedy programme *Monty Python's Flying Circus*. Since then he [4] ⎯⎯⎯⎯ (be) one of the most popular comedians in the UK. After Monty Python, Palin [5] ⎯⎯⎯⎯ (start) writing comedy series such as *Ripping Yarns*, and in the last 20 years he [6] ⎯⎯⎯⎯ (also appear) in some very successful films.

In 1980 Palin [7] ⎯⎯⎯⎯ (make) his first travel documentary as part of the series *Great Railway Journeys of the World*. Since then, he [8] ⎯⎯⎯⎯ (present)

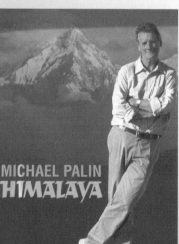

six successful series of TV travel programmes on television. For example, in 2004 he [9] ⎯⎯⎯⎯ (make) a series called *Himalaya*.

In his lifetime Michael Palin [10] ⎯⎯⎯⎯ (visit) every continent in the world and thousands of his fans [11] ⎯⎯⎯⎯ (follow) in his footsteps.

MICHAEL PALIN
HIMALAYA
As seen on
BBC

[20]

4 Choose the correct words.

1 We've been here (for)/since five years.

2 My uncle has *directed/been directing* 20 films in his life.

3 She's been to ten countries *for/since* she left school.

4 How long have you *known/been knowing* your teacher?

5 *I've been living/I lived* here since March.

6 We've been waiting at the bus stop *for/since* ages.

7 How long have you *had/been having* your car?

8 I've only *been reading/read* three books this year.

[7]

5 Fill in the gaps with these adverbs and time phrases.

> already   the second time   never   yet   this evening
> ago   before   ever   just   recently

1 She gave me a book for my birthday, but I've
  already read it twice.
2 A Have you .... been to India?
  B Yes, I have. I went there in 1998.
3 A What's the matter?
  B I've .... hit my head on the door!
4 I'm afraid I can't come tonight. They haven't
  repaired my car ....
5 She went to Rome a lot when she was young,
  but she hasn't been there ....
6 John's always been a vegetarian. He's
  .... eaten meat in his life.
7 This is .... my car has broken
  down on the motorway.
8 Nancy started work in Cardiff three months
  ....
9 My mum's already phoned me three times
  .... and it's only 7.30!
10 I'm sure I haven't seen that man .... ,
  but he says he knows me.

$\boxed{9}$

 6 Complete this table with nouns or adjectives.

	noun	adjective
1	fashion	*fashionable*
2	health	
3		lazy
4		honest
5		kind
6	knowledge	
7	comfort	
8	adventure	
9		famous
10	music	
11	nature	
12		confident
13		popular

$\boxed{12}$

 7 Fill in the gaps in this conversation with these words/phrases.

> tips   it's worth   that's really useful   what about
> the best way   sounds good   you should definitely
> you know any   I wouldn't recommend   bother
> really must   good to know   best to take

TIM You've been to Venice, haven't you? Have you
  got any [1] _tips_ for me?
ANN Well, there's so much to see, but you
  [2] .... have a coffee in St Mark's
  Square.
TIM That's [3] ....
ANN It's a bit expensive, but [4] ....
  sitting there for an hour.
TIM What's [5] .... to get around?
ANN It's [6] .... the vaporetti – the
  water buses. They're cheap and you get a good
  view of the canals.
TIM That [7] ....
ANN Another thing. Don't [8] ....
  going to the island of Murano. It takes a long
  time to get there and it isn't very interesting.
TIM Right, [9] .... places outside
  Venice?
ANN Um, [10] .... take a boat up the
  River Brenta to Verona. It's beautiful.
TIM Do [11] .... good places to eat?
ANN Well, [12] .... anywhere in the
  centre. Try to find a restaurant away from the
  touristy places.
TIM Thanks, Ann, [13] ....

$\boxed{12}$

 8 Tick the correct sentences. Change the incorrect sentences.
  lost
1 I've ~~been losing~~ my keys.
2 How was your travel to Scotland?
3 He's been in India during three months.
4 Uli's not here. She's gone to the supermarket.
5 This is the first time I eat fish and chips.
6 This is a very touristic town.
7 That film was absolutely incredible!
8 You're not supposed to wear jeans in the office.
9 You mustn't wear a suit, but you can if you want.
10 You went to France last year, haven't you?
11 Both of my brothers have got cars.

$\boxed{10}$

Answer Key p195   © Cambridge University Press 2006   face2face Intermediate Photocopiable

Name _____ Score [100]

1 Look at these questions from an interview with a rock star. Choose the correct words.

1 What time do you *go*/*do* onstage?
2 When are you going to *release*/*play* a new album?
3 When did you last *appear*/*be* on TV?
4 How many gigs have you *made*/*done* this year?
5 When did you last *see*/*go* another band play live?
6 Do you *release*/*have* an album in the charts?
7 When are you *being*/*going* on tour?
8 How many hit singles have you *had*/*done*?
9 Have your parents *been*/*had* to one of your concerts?

[8]

2 Put the verbs in brackets in the Past Simple or the Past Continuous.

1 My father *told* (tell) me to work hard.
2 The band wrote some new songs while they _____ (tour) Australia.
3 The promoter _____ (wait) for the band when the plane landed.
4 Someone _____ (throw) an egg at the singer while he _____ (walk) off the stage.
5 _____ you _____ (see) all the bands at the festival?
6 At 12 o'clock the band's singer _____ (sleep) in her hotel room.
7 A reporter _____ (interview) the group while they _____ (get) ready for the gig.
8 What _____ you _____ (do) at six o'clock yesterday?

[18]

3 Fill in the gaps with the correct form of *used to*.

1 The Rolling Stones *used to* be very famous in the 1960s.
2 _____ your parents _____ go to gigs together?
3 We _____ go abroad for holidays when I was little – it was too expensive.
4 My uncle _____ play the guitar.
5 I never _____ like rock music.

[8]

4 Write the adjectives.

1 S*elfish* people usually only think about themselves.
2 R_____ people always do what they promise to do.
3 A_____ people want to be very successful or powerful.
4 G_____ people give money and presents to other people.
5 S_____ people make good decisions based on reasons and facts.
6 B_____ people show no fear in dangerous situations.
7 M_____ people don't like spending money.
8 S_____ people won't change their minds when others want them to.
9 C_____ people are sure that they can do things successfully.
10 P_____ people are good at planning things.
11 A_____ people think they are better than other people.
12 S_____ people understand other people's feelings and problems.
13 A_____ people behave in an angry or violent way.
14 E_____ people show a lot of interest and excitement about something.
15 R_____ people aren't polite.
16 V_____ people try to hurt other people.
17 S_____ children behave badly because their parents always give them what they want.

[16]

PROGRESS TESTS: PHOTOCOPIABLE

face2face Intermediate Photocopiable   © Cambridge University Press 2006   (Answer Key p196)

5 Read about the climber Joe Simpson. Put the verbs in brackets in the Past Simple or the Past Perfect.

Joe Simpson's amazing adventure

In 1985 Joe Simpson and his friend Simon Yates ¹ _climbed_ (climb) the 6,344-metre-high mountain called Siula Grande in the Andes. No one ² _____ (ever get) to the top before by climbing up the west side. Unfortunately, Simpson ³ _____ (fall) on the way down. He soon ⁴ _____ (realise) that he ⁵ _____ (break) his leg. The two men ⁶ _____ (need) to get back to their camp quickly because they ⁷ _____ (already use) up all their gas to make water from snow. Also they ⁸ _____ (not bring) any extra food with them.

Yates ⁹ _____ (try) to lower Simpson down the mountain on a rope, but Yates couldn't hold him so in the end he ¹⁰ _____ (have to) cut the rope. The next day Yates ¹¹ _____ (be) sure that Simpson ¹² _____ (die) so, very sadly, he ¹³ _____ (walk) down the mountain alone.

However, Simpson, ¹⁴ _____ (not be) dead. He ¹⁵ _____ (fall) into a very deep hole and ¹⁶ _____ (not know) where he was. He ¹⁷ _____ (not be able to) walk because of his broken leg, but he ¹⁸ _____ (find) a way out of the hole and ¹⁹ _____ (make) his way down the mountain very slowly. He finally ²⁰ _____ (reach) the camp three days later. Yates ²¹ _____ (already burn) Simpson's clothes and was preparing to leave.

Simpson and Yates are still friends and their amazing story is told in the film *Touching the Void*.

☐ 20

6 A journalist is asking a local woman about the behaviour of young people. The woman is trying not to sound rude. Choose the correct words.

A What's your opinion ¹*on/of* the teenagers in your area?

B Well, they ²*must/can* be ³*quite/bit* rude at ⁴*times/sometimes*, particularly to older people.

A What do they do exactly?

B Well, you get ⁵*a few/most* who tend ⁶*laugh/to laugh* or make jokes when they see us.

A Do many of them behave like that?

B No, ⁷*on/in* the whole, most are just a ⁸*rather/bit* noisy.

A Do they have radios or CD players with them?

B Generally ⁹*speak/speaking*, that only happens at weekends.

A That's not very ¹⁰*inconsiderate/considerate*, is it?

B No, it's not. It's ¹¹*rather/absolutely* selfish, I think.

☐ 10

7 Make questions for these answers.

1 A What / Cleopatra use / her skin?
      What did Cleopatra use on her skin?
   B She used leaves from the aloe vera plant.

2 A Where / go / when / have / the accident?
      _____
   B I was walking home.

3 A How many books / write / by the time / retire?
      _____
   B Thirteen, I think. He stopped writing in 1989.

4 A Where / aspirin / come / from originally?
      _____
   B The bark of the willow tree.

5 A What / the doctor / do / at 10 p.m.?
      _____
   B He was treating a patient with heart problems.

6 A How long / wait / at this bus stop?
      _____
   B We've been here for half an hour.

☐ 10

8 Tick the correct sentences. Change the incorrect sentences.

1 I'm bored ~~about~~ *with* my job.

2 The patient made a complete recovery.

3 Kim was watching TV while the phone rang.

4 I knew I'd seen her before.

5 I used to go to my sister's wedding last year.

6 My mother couldn't put up the noise.

7 Don't bother go to the art gallery.

8 I've never travelled on my own.

9 We're looking forward to see you.

10 I've been living here since three years.

11 John's been to the station. He'll be back in a few minutes.

☐ 10

1 Write the types of homes.

1   <u>a three-</u>
    <u>storey house</u>

2 _____
   _____

3 _____
   _____

4 _____
   _____

5 _____
   _____

6 _____
   _____

☐ 5

2 Complete the phrasal verbs.

1 Do you want to c<u>ome</u> b<u>ack</u> later?

2 Could you t_____ o_____ the rubbish, please?

3 I need to s_____ o_____ my desk. I can't find anything.

4 I think I'll c_____ o_____ the garage this weekend.

5 I'm going to g_____ t_____ these boxes and t_____ a_____ anything I don't want.

6 Rebecca, could you please t_____ u_____ your room and p_____ a_____ all those clothes that are on the floor?

7 If you don't want it, why don't you g_____ it a_____ to someone?

☐ 8

3 Fill in the gaps with one word.

1 This room's <u>more</u> attractive than the other one.

2 I think he's the same age _____ me.

3 He's the _____ patient man I know. He never gets angry.

4 This house is _____ nicer than the one we saw yesterday. I really love it, don't you?

5 It's a _____ heavier, but not much.

6 It's _____ expensive than I expected. I thought I'd have to pay more.

7 It's the _____ spacious flat we've seen. All the others were a lot bigger.

8 The garden's not _____ big as I'd hoped.

9 It's got more space _____ our last house.

10 It's _____ smallest place we've seen.

☐ 9

4 Rewrite these sentences with the words in brackets.

1 I'm not as sensitive as him. (more)
   <u>He's more sensitive than me.</u>

2 John is more adventurous than me. (less)
   I _____

3 Julia and I are both 1.65 m tall. (as … as)
   I _____

4 I don't know anyone who's nicer than Jo. (nicest)
   Jo _____

5 My mobile phone isn't the same as yours. (different)
   Your _____

6 His computer is almost the same as mine. (similar)
   My _____

7 Your handwriting is better than mine. (worse)
   My _____

8 Leeds Castle is very beautiful. There isn't a more beautiful castle in England. (most)
   Leeds Castle _____
   _____

☐ 14

5 Read the conversation and choose the correct verb form.

SAM   When you start working from home next week, which room ¹(*are you going to work*)/ *are you working* in?

KIM   This bedroom, I think. It's nice and bright.

SAM   Do you think ²*it'll be/it's being* big enough?

KIM   Oh yes. My new desk ³*won't take/isn't taking* up much space.

SAM   That's good.

KIM   In fact, the shop has just phoned. ⁴*They'll bring/They're bringing* it round in half an hour.

SAM   Where are you thinking of putting it?

KIM   I'm not sure. ⁵*I'll probably put/I'm probably putting* it by the window.

SAM   I don't think ⁶*it's going to fit/it's fitting* there.

face2face Intermediate Photocopiable   © Cambridge University Press 2006   Answer Key p196

KIM   You're right. [7] *I'll have to/I'm having to* put it against that wall.

SAM   What about that bed? It's [8] *going to get/getting* in your way. Also [9] *you'll definitely need/you're definitely needing* some shelves for books and things. By the way, what time is it?

KIM   It's nearly six.

SAM   Is it? I must go. [10] *I'll play/I'm playing* football at half past.

KIM   Right. [11] *I'll call/I'm calling* you later. Bye.

☐ 20

6   **Fill in the gaps in the conversations with these words/phrases.**

> I'm looking for   made of   a thing for
> the word for them   they've got   stuff
> can't remember what   can I help you
> you use it when   what you're looking for
> what's it called   do you mean

1   A   Excuse me, [1] *I'm looking for* some [2] _____ to clean my clothes.

   B   Oh, [3] _____ washing powder?

   A   No, [4] _____ there's a mark on your shirt.

   B   Oh yes. It's over there on the bottom shelf.

   A   Thank you – [5] _____ in English?

   B   Stain remover.

2   A   Hello, [6] _____ ?

   B   Yes, please. I'm looking for those things for putting notices up. I've forgotten [7] _____ .

   A   Do you mean glue?

   B   No, they're [8] _____ metal and [9] _____ a round top.

   A   Oh yes – drawing pins. Here you are.

3   A   Hello. I need [10] _____ opening bottles. I [11] _____ it's called in English.

   B   Is this [12] _____ ? A corkscrew?

   A   Yes, that's it.

☐ 11

7   **Fill in the gaps with the correct form of the verbs in brackets.**

1   I like *buying* (buy) things on the Internet.

2   My boss let me _____ (have) the day off.

3   He asked me _____ (help) him move house.

4   Would you like _____ (play) tennis?

5   My son doesn't mind _____ (wash) the car.

6   My parents made me _____ (get up) early.

7   I forgot _____ (learn) the vocabulary.

8   The number of customers keeps _____ (rise).

9   Have you told him _____ (come)?

10   I'd rather _____ (work) at home.

11   My car wouldn't _____ (start) today.

12   Liz doesn't need _____ (go) to the meeting.

13   Should we _____ (try) a different restaurant?

14   We pay someone _____ (do) the gardening.

15   I really enjoy _____ (go) to exhibitions.

16   This seems _____ (be) the right place.

☐ 15

8   **What are these objects made of?**

1 *paper*	4 _____	7 _____
2 _____	5 _____	8 _____
3 _____	6 _____	9 _____

☐ 8

9   **Tick the correct sentences. Change the incorrect sentences.**

1   You must ~~going~~ *go* home now.

2   I live in the ground floor.

3   It's in walking distance of the shops.

4   My room's a lot more spacious than hers.

5   The police allowed him go home.

6   What had he done before you met him?

7   They didn't used to live in London.

8   Children tend being quite noisy.

9   I was working when you called.

10   We watched the football alive.

11   Who wanted to go to the cinema?

☐ 10

Name _____ Score ☐ 100

1 R6.10 **Listen to four conversations. Tick the correct pictures.**

a) What is Jill going to do on Saturday?

 ① ☐   ② ☐    ③ ☐

b) Which house does Steve like best?

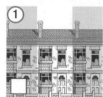 ① ☐    ② ☐    ③ ☐

c) Which present is Jan going to buy for her mother?

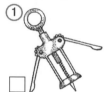 ① ☐   ② ☐   ③ ☐

d) Which vegetables is Tim's mother going to cook?

 ① ☐   ② ☐    ③ ☐

☐ 8

2 R6.10 **Listen to part of a radio programme about a festival. Fill in the missing information.**

BEDDINGTON BRIDGE MUSIC FESTIVAL

Dates
The festival takes place ¹ _every year_ on the ² _____
weekend in August.
This year the festival begins on a ³ _____ .

Prices
Adults: cheapest tickets available until ⁴ _____
Children under ⁵ _____ are allowed in free.
Parking costs a maximum of ⁶£ _____ per vehicle.
People arriving by ⁷ _____ can park for free.

Catering
Food is available at the festival site and in the ⁸ _____
in the village.

☐ 14

 PROGRESS TESTS: PHOTOCOPIABLE

3 **Fill in the gaps with the correct form of *make* or *do*.**

1 I love _doing_ nothing at the weekend.
2 Don't _____ a noise. The baby's asleep.
3 Gary's very good at _____ excuses when he arrives late for lessons.
4 My father usually _____ the washing-up.
5 George, can you _____ me a favour?
6 I couldn't _____ up my mind which CD to buy.
7 I think you're _____ progress this year.
8 Have you _____ your homework yet?
9 Maria always _____ me laugh.
10 I _____ dinner for my family last Saturday.
11 I'm _____ a course in photography.
12 Have you _____ an appointment yet?
13 I hate _____ the cleaning.

☐ 12

4 **Fill in the gaps with these words/phrases.**

| ~~after~~ if in case before as soon as until unless |

1 I'll see you _after_ I get back.
2 I'll stay here _____ I know that he's OK.
3 I think he'll leave his job _____ his boss gives him a pay rise.
4 He's going to buy a new car _____ he gets his first month's salary.
5 I'll go to the party with you _____ you come and pick me up.
6 I'm sure Frances will come to say goodbye _____ she leaves the country.
7 I think you should take some sandwiches _____ you get stuck in traffic.

☐ 6

5 **Fill in the gaps with the correct reflexive pronoun.**

1 My father likes to repair his car _himself_ .
2 She often goes away on holiday by _____ .
3 We really enjoyed _____ at the festival.
4 My parents look after the garden _____ .
5 I often make my children's clothes _____ .
6 Are you going to travel round the world by _____ ?
7 Please wash the car. It can't wash _____ , you know!
8 Both of us really know how to enjoy _____ .

☐ 7

© Cambridge University Press 2006   (Answer Key p196)

6 Fill in the gaps with the correct form of the verbs in brackets.

1 He'll _do_ it today if he _has_ (have) time.
2 If we _____ (not leave) now, we _____ (miss) the plane.
3 We _____ (not be able to) stay at our favourite hotel unless we _____ (book) it soon.
4 I _____ (tidy up) the house this afternoon if you _____ (do) the shopping.
5 If people _____ (not do) enough exercise, they _____ (put) on weight.
6 I've nearly finished. I _____ (call) you as soon as I _____ (be) ready.
7 If you _____ (want) a relaxing holiday, _____ (not go) to a big city.
8 I _____ (take) some sun cream with me tomorrow in case it _____ (be) very sunny.
9 If you _____ (not know) what to do, you must _____ (ask) a colleague.
10 _____ you _____ (help) me with this homework if I _____ (buy) you dinner this evening?
11 They _____ (not move) to London unless Bob _____ (get) a well-paid job.

[ ] 20

7 Fill in the gaps with a synonym of the words in brackets.

1 He thought the film was b_rilliant_ . (wonderful)
2 How do you p_____ your lottery numbers? (choose)
3 I'm very f_____ to work here. (lucky)
4 Are you s_____ it was him? (certain)
5 Staying at home on Friday night makes a p_____ change. (nice)
6 Why are you looking so c_____ ? (worried)
7 My aunt is s_____ of spiders. (frightened)
8 I'm quite s_____ with life at the moment. (content)
9 I often c_____ to my neighbours. (talk)
10 Didn't you think he was a_____ a bit strangely? (behaving)
11 I'm very g_____ to be here (pleased).
12 That house is absolutely h_____ . (enormous)

13 I met him b_____ c_____ on the train. (accidentally).
14 Flora thought the meal was a_____ . (terrible)

[ ] 13

8 Fill in the gaps in the conversations with these words/phrases.

wanted   absolutely   do you mind
that may be true   of course   go ahead
can I just finish   can I say   I'm not sure I agree
sure about that   what's your opinion

1
PAT You had something you [1] _wanted_ to say, Jim.
JIM Yes, I just wanted to say that it's much easier to learn a language when you're very young.
PAT [2] _____ , actually. Young children are still learning their own language so …
SUE Um, [3] _____ something here?
JIM Sure, [4] _____ .
SUE I started learning French when I was four, but …
PAT Sorry, [5] _____ if I interrupt?
SUE Pat, [6] _____ what I was saying?
PAT Yes, [7] _____ . Sorry.

2
MEG So [8] _____ of the new boss?
DAN I think he's a lot better than our last one.
MEG Yes, [9] _____ .
JOE I'm not [10] _____ . At least Mike was hard-working.
MEG Well, [11] _____ , but he was very rude.

[ ] 10

9 Tick the correct sentences. Change the incorrect sentences.

1 I always ~~do~~ mistakes in my maths tests. _make_
2 George and Fiona text themselves every day.
3 Soap operas really get on my nerves.
4 Are you agreeing with me?
5 We must to see that new Spielberg film.
6 Rose hasn't got much confident.
7 You haven't seen John recently, have you?
8 Our flat isn't as big than yours.
9 Are you doing anything this weekend?
10 I went to see my sister out at the station.
11 What were you doing when I called?

[ ] 10

Name _____ Score [100]

1 Write these computer words/phrases.

1 computer programmes: s*oftware*
2 something that is sent with an email: an a_____
3 connected to the Internet: o_____
4 a connection between parts of the Internet: a l_____
5 an extra copy of computer information: a b_____-_____ c_____
6 remove something from a computer's memory: d_____
7 press a button on the mouse in order to do something on a computer: c_____ o_____
8 connect your computer so you can start working: l_____ o_____
9 to copy information, music, etc. from the Internet onto your computer: d_____
10 make something new on the computer: c_____
11 a secret word that allows you to use a computer: a p_____
12 a fast connection to the Internet: b_____
13 a small picture on a computer screen: an i_____
14 a place to put documents on a computer so you can find them again easily: a f_____
15 you use this to write on a computer: a k_____
16 you can hear music from your computer through these: s_____

[15]

2 Rewrite these sentences using the words in brackets.

1 I'm able to do this easily. (can)
 I can do this easily
2 Mark doesn't know how to play football. (useless)
 _____
3 Fixing problems on my computer is very easy. (find)
 _____
4 Rachel can speak French well. (good at)
 _____
5 I don't know how to use a computer. (no idea)
 _____
6 Robin can't play chess at all. (clue)
 _____
7 I couldn't swim when I was five. (able)
 _____
8 Yolanda can't make cakes. (no good at)
 _____

9 I passed my exams, but they were very difficult. (manage)
 _____

[16]

3 Fill in the gaps in these second conditionals with the correct form of the verbs in brackets.

1 If I _won_ (win) a million pounds, I'_d buy_ (buy) an island in the Pacific.
2 Which countries _____ you _____ (visit) if you _____ (have) six months off?
3 Life _____ (be) so much easier if I _____ (live) nearer my work.
4 If we _____ (not have) air conditioning at home, I_____ (go) crazy.
5 If Sam _____ (not work) in London, he _____ (move) to the country.
6 If Jack _____ (can) find a better job, he _____ (be able to) buy a new car.
7 If I _____ (be) more computer literate, I _____ (save) myself a lot of time.
8 If he _____ (buy) a hands-free phone, I _____ (be) less worried about his driving.
9 _____ you _____ (do) less exercise if you _____ (not have) a dog?
10 I might _____ (not be) so bad-tempered if my job _____ (not be) so boring.

[18]

4 Write the words/phrases.

a DVD recorder

②
_____

③
_____

④
_____

⑤ _____

⑥
_____

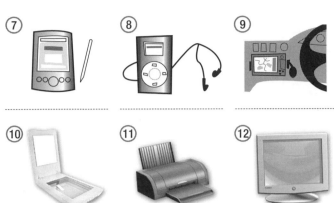

(7) _____

(8) _____

(9) _____

(10) _____

(11) _____

(12) _____

[11]

5 Read the biography of Bill Gates. Fill in the gaps with *a*, *an*, *the* or – (no article).

Bill Gates

Bill Gates is ¹ _the_ chairman of Microsoft, ² _____ worldwide leader in software. Born in 1955, Gates grew up in ³ _____ Seattle with his two sisters. Their father worked as ⁴ _____ lawyer. Gates went to ⁵ _____ small elementary school in Seattle and then went on to ⁶ _____ well-known Lakeside School. There, he discovered his interest in ⁷ _____ software and began programming ⁸ _____ computers at ⁹ _____ age of 13.

In 1973 Gates went to Harvard University. While at Harvard, Gates developed ¹⁰ _____ new type of ¹¹ _____ programming language called BASIC. Gates left Harvard before ¹² _____ end of his course to give his time totally to Microsoft, which was ¹³ _____ name he had given to ¹⁴ _____ company he'd started in 1975 with his friend Paul Allen.

In 1999 Gates wrote *Business @ the Speed of Thought*. This was ¹⁵ _____ first book he wrote and it shows how computer technology can solve ¹⁶ _____ business problems in new ways.

Gates and his wife, Melinda, run ¹⁷ _____ organisation called the Bill and Melinda Gates Foundation. ¹⁸ _____ aim of this organisation is to provide money in areas of ¹⁹ _____ global health and education. One project provides computers and Internet access to libraries in poor areas of ²⁰ _____ United States and ²¹ _____ Canada.

[20]

6 Put the words in order to make indirect questions.

1 mobile phone / is / you / where / Do / know / my?
   Do you know where my mobile phone is?

2 idea / coming / to / any / Have / if / John / the / meeting / is / you ?
   _____

3 you / we / up / station / Do / should / him / from / pick / think / the ?
   _____

4 message / me / you / left / has / a / me / Harry / Could / whether / tell ?
   _____

5 the / arrive / what / to / you / next / know / is / time / Do / train / going ?
   _____

6 when / you / back / tell / from / Sarah / Can / will / be / lunch / me ?
   _____

[10]

7 Tick the correct sentences. Change the incorrect sentences.

1 Keith is absolutely brilliant ~~in~~ *at* playing chess.
2 I'll make the shopping if you do the cleaning.
3 Do you mind if I interrupt?
4 I haven't replied at the manager's email yet.
5 We'll take you swimming if it doesn't rain.
6 That's the more expensive camera in the shop.
7 I like going to the cinema by yourself.
8 It's a thing for clean computers.
9 I'll believe it when I'll see it.
10 When do you usually do your homework?
11 I've been having this computer for a year.

[10]

Name .... Score [100]

1 Write the weather words/phrases.

1 very bad weather with lots of rain, snow or wind: a s*torm*

2 a very strong, dangerous wind that blows in a circle: a t_____

3 thick cloud just above the ground that makes it difficult to see: f_____

4 a very bright light in the sky during a storm: l_____

5 a violent storm with very strong winds: a h_____

6 a lot of water covering an area that is usually dry: a f_____

7 a short period of rain: a s_____

8 the loud noise that comes from the sky in a storm: t_____

9 a very strong wind: a g_____

10 a long period of unusually hot weather: a h_____ w_____

11 when the air is hot and wet: h_____

12 very cold: f_____

[11]

2 Choose the correct verb form.

1 Many houses in the town (were damaged)/ damaged by a serious flood in 2005.

2 More bad weather *reported/was reported* in Florida yesterday.

3 Extreme weather conditions *have recorded/ have been recorded* recently.

4 Global warming *will affect/will be affected* a lot more places in the future.

5 Sea levels *are rising/are being risen* around the world.

6 People *should teach/should be taught* how to save energy.

7 Many places *affect/are affected* by strong winds.

8 A strange thing *happened/was happened* in our street yesterday.

9 More records of temperature changes *are keeping/ are being kept* these days.

10 Tickets *must collect/must be collected* at reception.

11 More people *will lose/will be lost* their homes in the future.

[10]

3 Make these sentences passive. Use 'by + the agent' if necessary.

1 We give classes English homework twice a week.
   Classes are given English homework twice a week.

2 Mrs Burrows took the old man to hospital.
   ....

3 They haven't arrested the virus writer yet.
   ....

4 We can do a lot to slow down global warming.
   ....

5 The police are questioning a number of men.
   ....

6 They grow bananas in the Caribbean.
   ....

7 You must take this medicine twice a day.
   ....

8 Rising sea levels are going to affect a lot of countries.
   ....

9 A cleaner found a baby outside the hospital.
   ....

10 The school will test all students at the end of term.
   ....

11 They could use computers instead of teachers in the future.
   ....

[20]

4 Write the containers and the food items.

① *a box of chocolates*   ② ....   ③ ....

④ ....   ⑤ ....   ⑥ ....

[10]

5 Fill in the gaps with these words and phrases.

~~some~~ any enough loads of little
too much hardly any a few no

1 Would you like _some_ cake?
2 Chris spends _____ time working. He should have a holiday.
3 I can only say _____ words in Chinese.
4 I had _____ time to do my homework last night. I've only written 50 words.
5 My daughter's always on the phone. She's got _____ friends.
6 We've got two small pizzas, but _____ salad at all. That isn't _____ food for six people.
7 I can't see _____ potatoes in the cupboard either. I think we've run out.
8 There's a _____ milk left in the fridge. It should be enough for two coffees.

[8]

6 Write the opposites of these words.

1 usual   _unusual_
2 patient   _____
3 responsible   _____
4 helpful   _____
5 possible   _____
6 organised   _____
7 successful   _____
8 honest   _____
9 polite   _____
10 considerate   _____

[9]

7 Fill in the gaps by adding a prefix or suffix to the word in brackets.

1 Jimmy is absolutely _useless_ (use) at basketball. He's much too short.
2 I wouldn't go to that restaurant. They always _____ (charge).
3 I think footballers are _____ (paid). Some of them are millionaires.
4 Please don't throw that plastic bag away. I can _____ (use) it.
5 You shouldn't _____ (estimate) Susan. She's really very clever.
6 I need to _____ (charge) my mobile.
7 You needn't worry about the operation. It's completely _____ (pain).

8 That cottage is _____ (used). The owners only stay in it twice a year.
9 You need to be very _____ (care) with that. It might break.

[8]

8 Fill in the gaps in this conversation with these words/phrases.

~~could~~ don't forget that's really useful make sure
you'd better whatever you do shouldn't or else
good idea what should we do don't be careful
do you think it's a good idea in case if I were you

A We've never been walking in these mountains before. ¹ _Could_ you give us some advice?
B Well, ² _____ , I'd take a warm jacket ³ _____ it gets cold suddenly.
A That's a ⁴ _____ .
B And ⁵ _____ you take plenty of water. That's very important.
A So ⁶ _____ if we get lost?
B Um, ⁷ _____ take a mobile with you and ⁸ _____ to tell your family when you expect to be back.
A And ⁹ _____ to take a tent with us?
B Not really. You ¹⁰ _____ stay on the mountain at night, and ¹¹ _____ , don't walk around in the dark – you could easily have an accident. Also ¹² _____ when you come down – ¹³ _____ go too fast ¹⁴ _____ you'll fall.
A Thanks a lot, ¹⁵ _____ .

[14]

9 Tick the correct sentences. Change the incorrect sentences.

1 Vera's son ~~bit~~ *was bitten* by a shark.
2 You'd better recyling those bottles.
3 Watch out to bears when you go walking.
4 I've got plenty food in the house.
5 It's quite chilly this evening, isn't it?
6 Could you tell me when does the film start?
7 If I had a car, I'd be able to drive to work.
8 He was sent to the prison for 20 years.
9 I'm useless at play tennis.
10 What you would do if you lost your job?
11 I managed find some really cheap CDs.

[10]

Name _____ Score [100]

1 Choose the correct word.

1 I've met the doctor *which/who* looks after Sarah.

2 This is the hospital *where/which* my son works.

3 He's the man *who/whose* car was stolen.

4 I go to restaurants *that/where* serve organic food.

5 I met Adela in Ibiza, and that's *where/when* we fell in love.

6 That's the doctor *which/that* saved my son.

7 None of the people *that/where* I know are vegetarians.

8 I hate places *which/where* people are smoking.

9 That's the boy *whose/which* brother hit me.

10 That was the year *where/when* I lived in India.

11 Everyone knows *which/who* did it.

[10]

2 Fill in the gaps with the Present Perfect Simple active or passive of these verbs.

| take part | call off | meet | publish | discover |
| carry out | suffer | arrest | take | accept | protest |

Here are today's main stories.

About ten thousand people ¹ *have taken part* in a demonstration in London today against the latest National Health Service cuts. Ten people ² _____ and one police officer ³ _____ to hospital. This is the third time people ⁴ _____ against the government's plans in the last week.

The train drivers' union ASLEF ⁵ _____ _____ the one-day rail strike planned for next Thursday. The company's new pay offer of 5% ⁶ _____ by the union leader, Pat Jenkins.

A new report on street crime ⁷ _____ _____ . The report, which ⁸ _____ by the Metropolitan Police, shows that they ⁹ _____ the targets the government set last year.

The gene which controls sleep ¹⁰ _____ _____ in California. The discovery could help people who suffer from serious insomnia.

Finally, the singer Joe Stevens is in hospital after a heart attack. He ¹¹ _____ from heart problems for many years.

[20]

3 Put these words in the correct order.

1 given / GP / me / a / just / prescription / has / The .
   The GP has just given me a prescription.

2 discovered / John / of / the / allergy / has / cause / just / his .
   _____
   _____

3 father / to / already / has / been / hospital / taken / His .
   _____
   _____

4 seen / specialist / she / yet / been / the / Hasn't / by ?
   _____
   _____

5 already / the / six / We / A&E / been / hours / 've / in / department / for .
   _____
   _____

6 operated / The / yet / on / doctor / leg / the / hasn't / boy's .
   _____
   _____

7 been / The / hasn't / arrested / man / the / painting / stole / still / who .
   _____
   _____

[12]

4 Choose the correct words.

1 We had a great time *although/despite* the rain.

2 *Although/In spite of* Erich was very well-qualified, he couldn't find a good job.

3 Sheila enjoyed the concert *however/in spite of* her bad headache.

4 We had a great flat in London. *However/Even though*, we wanted to move to Oxford.

5 Fred decided to leave his job *although/despite* needing to earn some money.

6 He went to an all-night party *however/even though* he had a test the next day.

7 He was offered a job as a specialist *although/ in spite of* being unqualified.

[6]

PROGRESS TESTS: PHOTOCOPIABLE

⑤ Rewrite these sentences using the words in brackets.

1 I was exhausted. I went to the party. (although)
   Although I was exhausted, I went to the party.

2 Tania didn't speak very good French. She had lived in Paris for a year. (even though)
   _____

3 I couldn't sleep. I was very tired. (despite)
   _____

4 We went out for a walk. It was snowing. (in spite of)
   _____

5 I really enjoyed the party. There weren't many people there. (although)
   _____

6 My doctor has just told me that I need an operation. (been)
   _____

   [ ] 10

⑥ Write these words/phrases connected to health.

1 when your head is very hot: a t*emperature*

2 when you have to breathe through your mouth:
   a b_____ - _____ n_____

3 an extremely painful headache: a m_____

4 medicines which cure infections: a_____

5 a group of small red spots on the skin:
   a r_____

6 when bad food makes you ill: f_____
   p_____

7 a doctor who does operations: a s_____

8 a disease caused by bacteria or a virus:
   an i_____

9 when you breathe noisily and with difficulty:
   w_____

10 an office or building where you go to see a GP:
   a s_____

11 an illness caused by flowers or grass in the spring or summer: h_____ f_____

12 a big room with beds in a hospital:
   a w_____

13 the place where you have an operation:
   an o_____ t_____

14 a type of painkiller: p_____

15 you do this a lot when you have a cold:
   s_____

16 be sick, vomit: t_____ u_____

   [ ] 15

⑦ Fill in the gaps in these conversations between a doctor and a patient with these words/phrases.

> ~~problem~~   sick   stop coughing   haven't been feeling
> have a look   appointment   come back   prescription
> allergic to   how long have you been   should I take it
> symptoms   pills   temperature   throat   hurts

1

DR   Now, what seems to be the ¹ *problem* ?

MIA   My chest ² _____ .

DR   Have you got any other ³ _____ ?

MIA   Yes, I feel ⁴ _____ all the time.

DR   I'm just going to take your ⁵ _____ .
     Hmm, it's a bit high. Right, here's a
     ⁶ _____ for some medicine.

MIA   How often ⁷ _____ ?

DR   Three times a day. Then ⁸ _____ in
     a week if you're not feeling better.

2

ROB   I ⁹ _____ very well recently. I can't
      ¹⁰ _____ and I've got a sore ¹¹ _____ .

DR   Do you know if you're ¹² _____ anything?

ROB   I don't think so.

DR   And ¹³ _____ feeling like this?

ROB   For a few weeks now.

DR   Right, let me ¹⁴ _____ at you. … Hmm.
     I think you've got an allergy. Take these
     ¹⁵ _____ for a week.

ROB   Do I need to make another ¹⁶ _____ ?

DR   Not at the moment, no.

   [ ] 15

⑧ Tick the correct sentences. Change the incorrect sentences.

1 They ~~haven't been~~ there last year.   *didn't go*

2 I'm very careful about what I eat.

3 Whatever you do, not go in there.

4 If I were you, I'd go to bed immediately.

5 It's very fog outside.

6 California hit by a hurricane last night.

7 I haven't a clue how doing this.

8 Have you any idea where has Ian gone?

9 I'm not as healthier as I used to be.

10 Unless I change jobs soon, I'll be too old.

11 I've made a lot of progress this month.

12 My mum used to let me to stay up late.

13 He keeps making excuses.

   [ ] 12

Name _____ Score [100]

1 Fill in the gaps with the correct form of these phrasal verbs.

| tidy up   put off   go up   get out of   point out |
| look up   split up   come up with   fall out |
| get over   come across |

1 Could you please _tidy up_ your room?

2 The price of petrol _____ last year.

3 Alexandra has managed to _____ a solution.

4 I don't want to go, but I can't _____ it.

5 Ruth _____ these old photos while she was clearing out the cupboard.

6 I _____ that he had already borrowed my car twice this week.

7 Wendy and Richard _____ last week and they're still not speaking to each other.

8 It took me ages to _____ the operation.

9 I was going out with Heidi, but then we _____ last week.

10 If everyone's feeling ill, maybe we should _____ the meeting until next week.

11 Please _____ these words in the dictionary.

[10]

2 Put these words in the correct order.

1 really / forward / it / I'm / looking / to .
I'm really looking forward to it.

2 put / for / week / should / we / it / think / off / a / I .
_____

3 get / I / of / couldn't / the / out / taking / exam .
_____

4 before / never / across / 've / it / I / come .
_____

5 out / her / to / you / Why / point / didn't / it ?
_____

6 still / up / year / over / it / and / haven't / I / last / split / got / We .
_____

7 the / put / She / up / can't / noise / with .
_____

8 didn't / him / wrong / to / but / point / I / want / Tom / to / out / was / it .

[14]

3 Complete these words/phrases.

1 She's got s_traight_ h_air_ .

2 j_____

3 a p_____ s_____

4 She's got a p_____ .

5 He's g_____ b_____ .

6 a s_____ t_____

7 He's got c_____ h_____ .

8 a f_____ d_____

9 She's got s_____-l_____ h_____ .

10 a l_____ grey j_____

11 a d_____ grey j_____

12 g_____

[11]

4 Fill in the gaps with *was/were supposed to* or *was/were going to* and these verbs.

| ~~finish~~   move   give up   drive   tidy up   call   meet |

1 I _was going to finish_ the report this afternoon, but I ran out of time.

2 Jimmy _____ his room, but he watched TV instead. His mum was furious.

3 We _____ to the beach last weekend, but we couldn't get there because our car broke down.

4 Fiona _____ some important customers at 9 o'clock, but she overslept.

5 Lynn and Al _____ house, but in the end they decided to stay where they were.

6 I _____ smoking last weekend, but I've been under too much pressure at work.

7 We _____ Mr Lee back, but I forgot. He's going to be very angry.

[12]

face2face Intermediate Photocopiable   © Cambridge University Press 2006

Answer Key p198

5 Fill in the gaps with the correct preposition.

1 I'm very keen _on_ tennis.
2 I'd like to keep in touch _____ all my school friends.
3 Can you ask Jan to call me _____ when she comes in?
4 A Have you heard _____ your cousin lately?
   B Yes, I got an email yesterday.
5 I hadn't heard from Ian for ages. Then he got back _____ touch with me last month.
6 She's _____ her mid-twenties, I think.
7 He fell out _____ his boss.
8 Can you get hold _____ Mr Green for me?
9 Aki has just split up _____ her husband.
10 They had to divide _____ their property when they got divorced.
11 Who's the person _____ a beard?
12 Gloria's the one _____ a blue suit.
13 She's got very long hair, but she has to wear it _____ for work.

[ ] 12

6 Choose the correct modal verb and write the correct form of the verb in brackets.

1 JIM Do you know where Fred is?
   ANN I'm not sure. He *must/could* _be_ (be) in the sitting room with the other children.

2 TOM Is that George over there?
   MAY It *might/can't* _____ (be) him. That man's smoking and George has never smoked in his life.

3 CHRIS What's Mum doing?
   DAD She *can't/must* _____ (have) a bath. I can hear her radio in the bathroom.

4 FRAN Why aren't they here yet?
   JOE They *can't/must* _____ (come) by train. It's often late.

5 SAM Have you heard that John's going to train to be a teacher?
   BEN That *could/can't* _____ (be) true. He can't stand children.

6 JACK Usha's started another English course.
   SUE But why? She *might/must* _____ (speak) perfect English by now. She's been studying for 20 years!

7 FRED Why's Lucy in bed in the middle of the day?
   DAD She *might/can't* _____ (sleep) or she *must/may* _____ (have) a migraine.

8 EMMA What's Mum doing at the moment?
   NICK Well, she *can't/must* _____ (watch) the football with Dad, because she hates sport. She *can't/might* _____ (do) some shopping. Some people are coming round for dinner.

[ ] 18

7 Fill in the gaps in the conversations with these words or phrases.

| if can yourself of course opened open I'm afraid I'd rather you didn't ahead I could not at all may I mind |

A Is it OK ¹ _if_ I borrow your phone?
B Sure, go ² _____ .
A Do you think ³ _____ stay tonight?
B Yes, ⁴ _____ .
A Do you mind if I ⁵ _____ a window?
B No, ⁶ _____ . It is a bit warm in here, isn't it?
A Would you ⁷ _____ if I ⁸ _____ a window?
B Actually, ⁹ _____ . I'm quite cold.
A Mum, ¹⁰ _____ I have some more pasta?
B Help ¹¹ _____ .
A Um, ¹² _____ use your washing machine?
B Sorry, ¹³ _____ it's not working at the moment.

[ ] 12

8 Tick the correct sentences. Change the incorrect sentences.

1 Why didn't you point out the mistake ~~at~~ *to* her?
2 Is it OK if Tom borrow your bike?
3 I can't stop sneezing.
4 I slept very well although the noise.
5 He hasn't still called me.
6 Mark was taken to hospital yesterday.
7 Do you think he wants to come?
8 He's the person what hit me.
9 I keep get terrible headaches.
10 This answer is uncorrect.
11 Can you get me a jar of marmalade?
12 If I were you, I go home.

[ ] 11

© Cambridge University Press 2006 **face2face** Intermediate Photocopiable

1 Complete these adjectives to describe jobs.

1 In a w_ell-paid_ job you earn a lot of money.

2 You only have a t_____ job for a short time.

3 If your job is s_____ , you worry about it a lot.

4 If you have a p_____-_____ job, you don't work all of the working week.

5 A r_____ job makes you feel satisfied when you do it well.

6 In a r_____ job you have to do the same things again and again.

7 If you have a d_____ job, you find the work very boring.

8 A g_____ job is exciting because it's connected to fame or success.

9 A c_____ job is very hard work, but in an enjoyable way.

10 A d_____ job needs a lot of time and energy.

[18]

2 Fill in the gaps in the sentences with the correct form of these verbs.

| d̶o̶ have run go organise |
| be deal with work (x 2) |

1 I've _been doing_ a lot of overtime recently.

2 If you took this job, you'd have to _____ shifts.

3 I really like _____ customers.

4 John usually _____ conferences for the company and books the accommodation.

5 Doctors have to _____ unsocial hours.

6 He _____ in charge of the company since 1997.

7 I'm sure you _____ the department when Sue retires.

8 Eva _____ for another audition tomorrow.

9 When he was the managing director, he _____ a lot of responsibility.

[16]

3 Look at the picture. Complete these sentences by changing the words in **bold** into reported speech.

BILL Hi, Joe. Did I tell you? **I'm visiting** the new factory on Friday**.**

Bill said [1] _he was visiting_ the new factory on Friday.

JOE Do you have to go on Friday? **There's going to be** an important meeting that day.

Joe told [2] ....

.... an important meeting that day.

BILL I can't **visit** the factory on Thursday because of the conference.

Bill said [3] ....

the factory on Thursday because of the conference.

JOE Yes, that's true. **You won't be able to go** next week either.

Joe told [4] ....

.... next week either.

BILL Oh, dear. **I want to have** a few days off after that.

Bill said [5] ....

.... a few days off after that.

JOE Well, **Alice visited** the factory two weeks ago.

Joe told [6] ....

.... the factory two weeks ago.

BILL Did she? **She hasn't talked to me** about it. Is she here today?

Bill told [7] ....

.... about it.

JOE I think so. **She's getting** ready to go on a business trip to China.

Joe said [8] ....

.... ready to go on a business trip to China.

BILL Right. **I must go** and talk to her. See you later.

Bill said [9] ....

.... and talk to her.

[16]

4 Complete these reported questions.

1 Where's Derek going?

She asked __where Derek was going.__

2 Did you see Marian at the concert?

He wanted to know _____

_____

3 Which other countries has Fred visited?

She asked me _____

_____

4 Can you help me with the gardening?

She asked _____

_____

5 Who's taking Susan to the cinema?

He asked _____

6 How will the children get home after the party?

He wanted to know _____

_____

7 Do you have to go to London tomorrow?

She asked _____

[12]

5 Write these sentences in reported speech. Use these verbs.

> ~~agree~~ promise warn threaten refuse
> suggest offer remind admit invite

1 OK, I'll meet them at eight.

He __agreed to meet them at eight.__

2 Can I give you a lift to the station?

He _____

3 Let's go to the cinema.

Tom _____

4 I'll tell the police if you call me again.

She _____

5 Jo, don't forget to phone the bank.

He _____

6 Don't go in the park at night, Ian.

I _____

7 Sue, would you like to go to a party?

Rob _____

8 I'll definitely give the money back.

He _____

9 I won't go to bed.

His son _____

10 I stole the lady's bag.

Nigel _____

[18]

6 Fill in the gaps in the conversations with these words/phrases.

> ~~did you say~~ get all can you give sorry
> could you say talking about catch is that
> mean spelled you give

A Sorry, what [1] _did you say_ your name was again?

B Mrs Green. And I live at 59 Cutforth Street.

A Sorry, I didn't quite [2] _____ that.

B 59 Cutforth Street.

A Is that [3] _____ C–U–T–F–O–R–T–H?

A Why don't you come round on Saturday?

B Do you [4] _____ this Saturday?

A Yes, that's right. We could go to the festival together.

B Are you [5] _____ the music festival in the park?

A Jim's in hospital. He's broken his leg.

B I'm [6] _____ , this is a really bad line, [7] _____ that again, please?

A Jim's broken his leg. He's in Newport Hospital. The number's 01778 543021.

B Sorry, [8] _____ me that number again?

A Can you pick me up from the Red Lion pub in Syon Street?

B Sorry, I didn't [9] _____ of that. Could [10] _____ it to me again, please?

A The Red Lion Inn in Syon Street.

B And [11] _____ Syon with a *y*?

[10]

7 Tick the correct sentences. Change the incorrect sentences.

1 She's split up ~~for~~ *with* him.

2 I enjoy sorting out people's problems.

3 He's responsible to the finances.

4 He told me don't go there.

5 Jane asked me come to dinner.

6 My aunt's in her mid-fifties.

7 Would you mind if I left early?

8 I looked up it on the Internet.

9 Mike might watch TV at the moment.

10 That mustn't be Jim. He's in the USA.

11 Let me know when he gets back.

[10]

Name _____ Score ☐100

1 Listen to a radio interview with the actor Colin Waring. Choose the correct answers.

1 How did Colin become interested in acting?
  a) he went to see a Shakespeare play with his mother
  b) he studied plays in his English class
  c) he saw someone he knew acting in a play

2 What helped Colin most at drama school?
  a) learning how to act from some famous actors
  b) being able to see a lot of different plays
  c) working with other students on his course

3 Which play did Colin first act in professionally?
  a) *Table for Two*
  b) *Secret Lives*
  c) *The Rendezvous*

4 What does Colin like most about the theatre?
  a) the relationship with the audience
  b) being able to do the same thing every night
  c) seeing how a play changes

5 What will Colin's next job be?
  a) a new play
  b) a TV serial
  c) a detective film

☐10

2 Listen to two friends, Marie and Paul, talking about food. Are these sentences true (T) or false (F)?

1 Paul felt very bad on the second day of his health retreat. ____

2 Paul might do another retreat in the future. ____

3 Marie and Paul both like eating fruit for breakfast. ____

4 Marie thinks organic food is worth the extra cost. ____

5 Marie is a vegetarian now. ____

6 Paul prefers eating Indian food when he goes out. ____

☐12

3 Fill in the gaps with one word only.

1 I'm fed up _with_ getting up early.

2 She's really _____ computer games at the moment – she plays all the time.

3 Do you fancy _____ out for a pizza?

4 She doesn't feel _____ to eating anything. She's got a migraine and she feels sick.

5 I'd love to have a go _____ sailing.

6 I could really do _____ a holiday.

7 It's not up _____ him where they go – his wife always decides.

8 He usually hangs _____ with his friends in the park after dinner.

9 I can't be _____ to do my homework this evening. I want to watch the match on TV.

10 I'm sick _____ talking to him. He never listens to me.

11 Can you lend me £10? I'm completely _____ at the moment.

☐10

4 Fill in the gaps with the correct form of the verbs in brackets.

1 I wish he _were_ (be) more patient.

2 I wish I _____ (have) my own swimming pool.

3 I wish we _____ (go) on holiday tomorrow. I don't want to go to school.

4 My husband wishes he _____ (not have to) go back to work tomorrow.

5 I wish I _____ (can) play the piano.

6 I wish we _____ (eat) Thai food tonight, not burgers again.

7 My parents wish they _____ (not live) in such a cold country.

8 Do you sometimes wish you _____ (be) younger?

9 I wish I _____ (know) how to speak Chinese.

10 I wish I _____ (have) a horse.

☐9

face2face Intermediate Photocopiable   © Cambridge University Press 2006   Answer Key p199

5 Complete the table with verbs, nouns or adjectives.

verb	noun	adjective
attract	[1]attraction	attractive
enjoy	enjoyment	[2]
[3]	pollution	polluted
care	[4]	careful/careless
disappoint	[5]	disappointed/disappointing
entertain	entertainment	[6]
create	creation	[7]
confuse	[8]	confused/confusing
depend	dependence	[9]
[10]	employment	employed
protect	protection	[11]
reserve	[12]	reserved

| 11 |

6 Fill in the gaps with these phrases and the correct form of *get*.

> ~~home~~ lost something to eat better
> in touch with into trouble to know rid of
> fed up with excited on with

1 What time did you ...*get home*... last night?
2 You _____ if you don't take this map.
3 My son keeps _____ at school. I don't know what to do with him.
4 He's a bit unfriendly at first, but he's fine when you _____ him.
5 I left my job because I _____ it. I was so bored!
6 I'm hungry. I think I _____ .
7 My daughter always _____ when it's her birthday.
8 You _____ at English if you studied a bit harder.
9 I _____ my old computer because it didn't work any more.
10 How are you _____ your neighbours at the moment?
11 We've been trying _____ all the people we knew at school.

| 20 |

7 Put the verbs in brackets in the correct form in these third conditional sentences.

1 I ...*'d have gone*... (go) to the party last night if someone ...*had told*... (tell) me about it.
2 If I _____ (not/leave) school when I was 16, I _____ (go) to university.
3 Gabi _____ (not/miss) yesterday's meeting if she _____ (wake up) earlier.
4 Karen _____ (become) a doctor if she _____ (not/fail) her exams.
5 If you _____ (warn) me earlier, I _____ (not/say) anything.
6 If I _____ (not/have) dinner in that restaurant, I _____ (not/meet) my wife. She was a waitress there.
7 We _____ (call) you yesterday if we _____ (have) your number.

| 12 |

8 Choose the correct words.

1 I like dealing (with)/*for* customers.
2 We can only stay for a *few/little* minutes.
3 I always take an umbrella *in case/unless* it rains.
4 *Despite/Although* he was ill, he went to work.
5 Don't bother *go/going* to see that film.
6 Ian's *been/gone* to Rome. He's back on Friday.
7 I've been living here *for/since* I was young.
8 Emma threatened *to tell/telling* his parents.
9 You *mustn't/don't have to* go walking in the jungle alone. It's very dangerous.

| 8 |

9 Tick the correct sentences. Change the incorrect sentences.

1 Would you mind if I ~~sit~~ *sat* here?
2 She's on charge of the company.
3 He said me he was going to be late.
4 John told me not to call her.
5 He asked me where did I live.
6 He threatened taking me to court.
7 If I were you, I'd stay at home.
8 The museum is well worth visit.
9 The meal was much more expensive than I expected.

| 8 |

Acknowledgements

The authors would like to thank all the team at Cambridge University Press for their continuing dedication and commitment to the *face2face* project. In particular we would like to thank Sue Ullstein for her unwavering support and excellent project management, Dilys Silva for all the incredibly hard work she put in to make the Intermediate level of *face2face* what it is, Andrew Reid and Keith Sands for continuing the trend of in-house editorial excellence, and all the team at Pentacor for their superb book design. We would particularly like to thank our wonderful freelance editors, Ruth Atkinson and Diane Winkleby, for working above and beyond the call of duty and for being such a joy to work with.

Chris Redston would like to thank Gillie Cunningham for being such a generous and indefatigable co-author, Joss Whedon for all the post-deadline rewards, and most importantly Adela Pickles for her love and patience when deadlines are looming and for always being there to remind him of the true meaning of life. He would also like to thank the following teachers and directors of studies, all of whom have helped him improve his own classroom teaching over the years: Mandy Allen, Robert Kirkland, Sue Korton, Ian Parkinson, Paola Erin, Richard Ingleton, Samantha Ashton, Cecilia Ortega, Mary Parkin, Len Edwards, Tania Evesham, Colin Underwood, Nick Teale.

Gillie Cunningham would like to thank her dear co-author for continuing to be a wonderful person to work with after all this time, and for being a great pal too!

Lindsay Warwick would like to thank Anna Young for supplying the chocolate when they needed it most, the *face2face* editorial team, Chris Redston and Gillie Cunningham for their invaluable feedback and ideas, and her colleagues at Bell International for listening: finally, her parents Mal and David, her brother Leigh, and Alex, for their continued love and encouragement.

Anna Young would like to send huge thanks to Gillie Cunningham and Chris Redston for their invaluable help, advice and constant flow of ideas, and to all the CUP team, especially Sue Ullstein and Andrew Reid. A big thank you to Lindsay Warwick and her colleagues at Bell Language School, Saffron Walden, and to Mum, Dad, Tat and Na-ya for their continued love, support and encouragement.

Theresa Clementson would like to thank Dilys Silva for her patience and helpful ideas during the writing process, together with the rest of the editorial team. Special thanks go to her family, Anthony, Sam and Megan.

The authors and publishers are grateful to the following contributors:

pentacorbig: cover and text design and page layout
Hilary Luckcock: picture research

The authors and publishers are grateful to the following for their permission to reproduce copyright material:

The Council of Europe for the table on p13 from the *Common European Framework of Reference for Languages: Learning, teaching, assessment* p26 (2001) Council of Europe Modern Languages Division, Strasbourg, Cambridge University Press. Copyright of the text is held by the Council of Europe exclusively, © Council of Europe. Reprinted with permission. *The Daily Telegraph* for the adapted material on p193 'Inspector gadget: EasyFind 4-Way Key Tracker', by Rob Murray, taken from www.telegraph.co.uk, © Telegraph Group Limited, 2006.

The publishers are grateful to the following for their permission to reproduce copyright photographs:

Key: l = left, c = centre, t = top, b = bottom

Alamy/eStock Photo for p220, /©Ingram Publishing for p222, Corbis/©Steve Azzara for p133 (br) /©Tim Graham for pp133 (tc), 134 (tl), /©Toru Hanai/Reuters for p133 (tl), /©Royalty Free for p177; Empics/©Murad Sezer/PA for p 133 (cr), /©Ian West/PA for p133 (tr); Getty for pp 187, 193; Photolibrary.com for p143; Rex for pp134 (tc), 134 (tr) 134 (cr), 134 (br), 207, 213; Topfoto/©David Wimsett/Starstock/Photoshot for p204.

The publishers would like to thank the following illustrators:

Fred Blunt c/o Joking Apart; Mark Duffin; F&L Productions; Graham Kennedy; Joanne Kerr c/o New Division; NAF c/o Joking Apart; Jacquie O'Neill.